A Modern Introduction to

Indian Aesthetic Theory

A Modern Introduction to

Indian Aesthetic Theory

— The Development from Bharata to Jagannātha —

S.S. Barlingay

D.K. Printworld (P) Ltd.
New Delhi

Cataloging in Publication Data — DK

[Courtesy: D.K. Agencies (P) Ltd. <docinfo@dkagencies.com>]

Barlingay, S.S. (Surendra Sheodas), 1919-1997.

A modern introduction to Indian aesthetic theory : the development from Bharata to Jagannātha / S.S. Barlingay.

xxvi, 374 p., 23 cm.

Includes bibliographical references (p.)

Includes index.

ISBN 8124603774

1. Rasas. 2. Aesthetics, Indic. 3. Sanskrit literature — To 1500 — History and criticism. 4. Sanskrit literature — 1500-1800 — History and criticism. I. Title.

DDC 111.850 954 22

ISBN 81-246-0377-4 (Hardbound)

ISBN 81-246-0378-2 (Paperback)

First published in India in 2007

Published and printed by:

D.K. Printworld (P) Ltd.

Regd. Office: 'Sri Kunj', F-52, Bali Nagar

Ramesh Nagar Metro Station

New Delhi-110 015

Phones: (011) 2545-3975; 2546-6019; *Fax*: (011) 2546-5926

E-mail: dkprintworld@vsnl.net

Website: www.dkprintworld.com

Dedicated to

Prof. N.S. Dravid
Prof. D.P. Chattopadhyaya
Prof. P.F. Rawson

who inspired me to give my thought on linguistic form

and

to the memories of

Late M. Hiriyanna
the doyen of Indian aesthetic thought,
whose writings introduced me to our ancient thinkers

Late M.G. Deshmukh
whose theory of Bhāvagandha awakened
me from my 'dogmatic slumber'

&

Late R.J. Deshmukh
(of Deshmukh and Company)
who activised me to reduce my thought to a written form.

"We are going from one subject matter of philosophy to another, from one group of words to another group of words."

"An intelligent way of dividing up a book on philosophy would be into parts of speech, kinds of words. Where in fact you would have to distinguish far more parts of speech than an ordinary grammar does. You would talk for hours and hours on the verbs 'seeing', 'feeling', etc., verbs describing personal experience. We get a peculiar kind of confusion or confusions which come up with all these words. You would have another chapter on numerals — here there would be another kind of confusion; a chapter on 'all', 'any', 'some', etc. — another kind of confusion; a chapter on 'you', 'I', etc. — another kind; a chapter on 'beautiful', 'good', — another kind. We get into a new group of confusions; language plays up entirely new tricks".

— L. Wittgenstein

चत्वारि वाक् परिमिता पदानि तानि विदुर्ब्राह्मणा ये मनीषिणः।
गुहा त्रीणि निहिता नेङ्गयन्ति तुरीयं वाचो मनुष्या वदन्ति॥

— *ऋग्वेद* 1.164.45

नीरक्षीरविवेके हंसालस्यं कदापि तनुषे चेत्।
विश्वास्मिन्नधुनान्यः कुलव्रतं पालयिष्यति कः॥

— पं॰ जगन्नाथ, *भामिनीविलास*

सक्तुमिव तितउना पुनन्तो यत्र धीरा मनसा वाचमक्रत।
अत्रा सखायः सख्यानि जानते भद्रैषां लक्ष्मीर्निहिताधि वाचि॥

— *ऋग्वेद* 10.71.2

प्रणो देवी सरस्वती वाजेभिर्वाजिनीवती धीनामवित्र्यवतु।

— *ऋग्वेद* 6.61.4

Foreword

TRADITION holds that all enlightened activities lead to ultimate liberation and enlightenment. The study of beauty and aesthetics is one such. There is beauty in art, sculpture and poetry but most of all in the participatory fine art of drama. In drama there are three components: the playwright, the actors and the audience.

It has long been held that the operative principle is *rasa*, the flow from the author via the dramatic personae to the audience. What is the nature of this *rasa*? Is it a fluid that originates in the author's work or is it generated only in the performance itself? These have occupied many scholars in the past and various theories have been advanced. Most notable amongst them are Bharata, Bhāmaha, Abhinavagupta, and Jagannātha. Professor Barlingay's authoritative treatise surveys criticially the contributions of various authors and provides a basis for determining what is aesthetics in the Indian tradition.

Despite the advance of the social sciences, biology and the physical sciences, we continue to live in a familiar "realistic" world, and there are those who have been able to penetrate this veil and recognize a deeper reality. It is this realm in which *rasa* functions.

We do have persistent distortions of reality: we know that matter is made of molecules which themselves can be composed of smaller sub-units in perpetual motion, and that we have to use the quantum physics laws to describe it properly. Studies in psychology have made us realize that there are periods of qualitatively different clear perceptions. Despite these, we cling to the traditional world-view.

This persistence of misperception is evident in everyday phenomena. We see the sunrise and the sunset and wax lyrical about their beauty. We see our image in a mirror and, knowing how the virtual image comes about, we "perceive" the image. On a hot day we see mirages on the city roads. Our perception of heat or cold is dependent upon what was the ambience in which our skin was earlier. The clear conviction that causality is fully operative in nature is not completely in accordance with our retrospective view; what appeared as accidental is recognized as inevitable in retrospect.

Spiritual disciplines are usually prescribed for going beyond appearances. The inadequacy of our "realistic" view is recognized when we have advanced in such disciplines.

But art in general and drama in particular show us a deeper reality beyond appearance. When Ophelia wanders the fields in desperation on seeing Hamlet fully preoccupied with the murder of his father, our eyes fill with unshed tears even as we recognize it is only a play. We see that Kaṇva Maharṣi's sorrow at parting with his foster daughter Śakuntalā is incongruous with his detached world-view but we feel it when we watch the play enacted. These are the plays of *rasa* and it is an *experienced* reality.

Barlingay also deals with the repeated participation in the play; but unlike the athlete running around a track, we gain each time and "see" the play: we "see" more than we did before. So each enactment of a play is a *new* experience and not merely a repetition. Familiarity with the story and the structure of the play only improves the enjoyment of the *rasa*.

In the present book the author presents carefully the spirit of the various authorities and clearly distinguishes their view from his own critical understanding. In this way we get the various streams of Indian thought. This authoritative treatise is thus scholarly and at the same time an initiation to elicit the reader's own personal experience.

The critic is often thought of as a secondary contributor to the art. But it may be that their view is mistaken: in science a deep understanding of what has been the crystallized views of various authors is an invitation for the individual scientist's own discovery and insight. And the moment of insight is an extraordinary yet familiar state of awareness filled with awe, joy and timelessness. I believe this to be equally true of literature and drama. We are not mere onlookers but participants who function in an altered state of awareness.

I knew Professor S.S. Barlingay only for a few short years but was profoundly grateful to be able to share ideas with him. I will miss him, like so many of you; but this excellent book will be with us for the present.

E.C.G. Sudarshan

Key to Transliteration

VOWELS

अ *a*	आ *ā*	इ *i*	ई *ī*	उ *u*	ऊ *ū*
(but)	(palm)	(it)	(beet)	(put)	(pool)
ऋ *ṛ*	ए *e*	ऐ *ai*	ओ *o*	औ *au*	
(rhythm)	(play)	(air)	(toe)	(loud)	

CONSONANTS

Guttural	क *ka*	ख* *kha*	ग *ga*	घ *gha*	ङ *ṅa*
	(skate)	(blockhead)	(gate)	(ghost)	(sing)
Palatal	च *ca*	छ* *cha*	ज *ja*	झ *jha*	ञ *ña*
	(chunk)	(catch him)	(join)	(hedgehog)	(bunch)
Cerebral	ट *ṭa*	ठ* *ṭha*	ड *ḍa*	ढ* *ḍha*	ण* *ṇa*
	(start)	(anthill)	(dart)	(godhead)	(under)
Dental	त *ta*	थ *tha*	द *da*	ध* *dha*	न *na*
	(path)	(thunder)	(that)	(breathe)	(numb)
Labial	प *pa*	फ* *pha*	ब *ba*	भ *bha*	म *ma*
	(spin)	(philosophy)	(bin)	(abhor)	(much)
Semi-	य *ya*	र *ra*	ल *la*	व *va*	
vowels	(young)	(drama)	(luck)	(vile)	
Sibilants	श *śa*	ष *ṣa*	स *sa*	ह *ha*	
	(shove)	(bushel)	(so)	(hum)	
Others	क्ष *kṣa*	त्र *tra*	ज्ञ *jña*	ळ* *ḷ*	ॠ* *ṝ*
	(*kṣatriya*)	(*triśūla*)	(*jñānī*)	(*play*)	

अं (ं) *ṁ anusvāra* (nasalisation of preceding vowel) like *saṁskṛti*

अः *visarga* = *ḥ* (aspiration of preceding vowel) like (*prātaḥ*)

ऽ *Avagraha* consonant #'consonant (like:- *ime 'vasthitā*)

Anusvāra at the end of a line is presented by m (म्) and not ṁ

HINDI LETTERS (extras)

ँ = *ñ* (*candrabindu*) ं = ṅ (*anusvāra*) ड़ = *ṛa* ढ़ = *ṛha*

* No exact English equivalents for these letters.

Preface

The Basic Unity of Nāṭyaśāstra Text

IN all probability, Bharata's *Nāṭyaśāstra* is the first systematic work on drama and poetics in India. Of course, it might not be a work of a single author. It could be a compilation of works of Dṛhiṇa, Vāsuki, Bharata, etc., and Bharata himself might not have been one single person. It could be the name of a "tradition", and one could talk of Bharata as one talks of Vyāsa. Some modern scholars have made some original observations in this regard and have come to the conclusion that *Nāṭyaśāstra* has not been the work of one author. Late Narhar Kurundkar and Dadegaonkar have come to such conclusion. I appreciate the research, but for my purpose I regard the work or the compilation as one single unit, albeit with many interpolations and extrapolations. I take this view because when *Nāṭyaśāstra* was composed or compiled, it aimed at giving one cogent, coherent theory of art in general and drama in particular. That is why the compilation was made. Since who composed the work (the *Nāṭyaśāstra*) does not affect my work, I take it as one unit, of course, after due selecting and editing.

The study, which I am presenting in this monograph, is of the nature of discussion of the language and parameters employed by those who developed our tradition in music, drama, dance and poetry on the one hand, and painting, sculpture and architecture on the other. The parameters used were basically regarding the subject matter and evaluation of the art objects. In the course of time, however, the parameters used in literary arts were also employed for evaluating painting and architecture. The keywords in regard to these art forms were *rasa, saundarya* and *ānanda*. The word *rasa* was used, to begin with, for determining the status and standard of the subject matter of that art.[1] But, while describing this concept (of that particular art), foisted on *rasa* were layers of "evaluation (and satisfaction)," which follow the accomplishments of the art object. The object of art is to communicate, and for such communication two things are necessary. One is the medium and the other is the message conveyed through this medium. These two elements are evidently different, but many a time, they cannot be separated. They are like a copper wire (which is a conductor of electricity) and the electric current which flows through the wire.[2] This artistic communication is for understanding the message which one wants to convey to the other. It is *hṛdayasaṁvādī*,[3] that which is of the nature of blending two hearts, agreeable to two hearts. This communication stands for artistic beauty. All parameters of art are the parameters concerning the scale of beauty (and also communication). But, sometimes all such

1. I could have simply said "the essence of art" translating the Sanskrit word *ātman* but as the existentialists point out, one must distinguish between *existence* and *essence. Ātman* should be translated as *existence* and not *essence*.

2. During the time of Bharata, conduction of electricity was not known but the concept of *conductivity* was still expressed as can be seen in the clause "just as fire occupies the whole body of dry wood."

3. This message was the *sthāyī bhāva* in the mind of the artist. It worked as a message and took different forms and assumed different mediums. (When expressed through medium it takes the form of *artha*.).

parameters used for measuring and evaluation breakdown when the audience or spectators or readers reach a state of "silence" or speechlessness. This is the state of affairs which cannot be described at all and was, therefore, regarded as *anirvacanīya*. The highest type of *daivikī siddhi* which Bharata describes is of this type. Such a state of affairs was compared to *Brahmāsvāda*, the flavour arising from the experience of *Brahman*. Bhaṭṭanāyaka and, following him, Viśvanātha used this expression for describing the art-experience.

Dimensions of Dramatic Art

The history of the art of Indian origin shows that this theory came to light while developing the stage as performance. The stage drama has several dimensions: (1) first is the script, presented in the form of an imitation of life; (2) it requires the medium of expression or *bhāva* and acting; (3) this has to be done in a specific style; and (4) finally, it is to be evaluated in the form of the applause or otherwise from the audience. It has thus all the characteristics of any art, whether it is dance, music, painting, sculpture or architecture. Perhaps on this account, the theory of drama became a paradigm for all art-critics and the concepts in drama were employed and re-employed in different arts. They were, for example, employed in the criticism of poetry. Drama requires a continuum of time and deals with a medium. There is some media among a medium in different arts. For example, a medium in poetry and the medium of drama. The general characteristics of these media are also the characteristics of language whether they are of the nature of memory or concepts, or the material of which the art object is made. Bharata's treatise, *Nāṭyaśāstra*, discusses this. But several refinements came from time to time in understanding and developing the art theory in general. We find six types of theories developed in the course of time.

The theories of *alaṁkāra*, *rīti*, *vakrokti*, *dhvani*, *rasa* and *aucitya* can be mentioned in this context. As it appears to me, they are theories of poetry. But they can be used in all departments of arts, including music, painting, sculpture and architecture.

Different Theories of Art

Bhāmaha, who came after Bharata indicates a distinction between the ordinary language and the language of art. If language is to be understood as a medium, one could use this understanding as a tool for distinguishing the medium of art from other media of communication. Kuntaka emphasized "curvature" or *vakratā* in poetry. Curvature is an equally useful concept in architecture. It breaks the monotony and pleases the eye. When one embarks on any art project, one has before him at least two objectives. One is concerned with the body of the art itself and makes the art body living. The other is concerned with the evaluation of the art. Vāmana named these two concepts as *ātma-tattva* and *alaṁkāra-tattva* or *grāhyatā-tattva*. He also found a correlation between the two and developed what people call *rīti siddhānta*. This concept of *rīti* is also used in painting, architecture and music. This is also used in drama. *Rīti* is basically concerned with medium. But if the medium is to be effective it must be capable of conveying a certain message. It must connect the author with the audience. Abhinavagupta described this as *sarasvatī-tattva* — *sarasvatyās-tattvam kavi-sahṛdayākhyam vijayate*.

This message is also in the form of the intention of the creator or artist, and if it is properly conveyed it flashes before the audience like an explosion. This was emphasized by Ānandavardhana. Kṣemendra pointed out that the relation amongst the elements of structure, or the structure and the evaluation, must be that of fittingness or appropriateness. He called this *aucitya*. In fact, this principle seems to be employed in every work of art from music to architecture.

All these principles were employed and re-employed again and again by the masters and finally Jagannātha chiselled them properly. He discussed, for example, the relationship between the symbol, the intention of the artist and the meaning that flashes at the first or subsequent stages and finally the satisfaction of the appreciator or enjoyer.

Persons and Ideas that Influenced the Writing of the Present

I have tried to explain these different aspects in my work. I have partly differed from other interpretations given on the subject. But, I feel that with my interpretation people would be able to appreciate the art theory with greater concord, freedom and ease.

It will be informative to see how I got interested in the study of this subject. In 1948 or so Late Prof. M.G. Deshmukh in his Presidential Speech at the Annual Session of the Vidarbha Literary Association pointed out the limitations of Bharata's *rasa* theory, as was traditionally understood then. *Rasa* theory, according to Prof. Deshmukh emphasized the subjective side of poetic appreciation; he thought that a theory of poetry could not be complete unless the objective element was recognized. He was right in saying that an art process does require an objective element. He, therefore, put forward the thesis of *bhāvagandha* (emotional fragrance) which was for him the objective element. Till then, *rasa* was regarded as the subjective element of the nature of happiness or *ānanda* and taste or *svāda*. While appreciating the findings of Deshmukh, I thought he was following the traditional interpretation of *rasa*. When I read Bharata's *Nāṭyaśāstra*, I found that Bharata's concept of *rasa* and Deshmukh's concept of *bhāvagandha* were almost overlapping, although nineteenth- and twentieth-century critics gave an interpretation of *rasa* which made *rasa* of the nature of taste and happiness. Almost simultaneously, late Prof. D.K. Bedekar was involved in reinterpreting *rasa* and *bhāva*. He wrote a few articles in a local paper, *Navabhārata*. Prof. V.M. Bedekar, the then editor of *Navabhārata*, who knew that I was interested in *rasa* theory, sent the offprints to me and asked me to participate in the debate which Bedekar had started. I then wrote an article in *Navabhārata* under the title "The Nature of *Rasa*" in 1951. Later, Prof. S.D. Pendse, a great authority on *Rasa-Śāstra* and a keen student of saint-poets of Maharashtra wrote me a letter appreciating my point of view. This article is included in my book *Saundaryāce Vyākaraṇa*. I feel that my article was taken seriously by the scholars, for those who wrote after that did accept that for Bharata, *rasa* was *āsvādya* and not *āsvāda*. At that time, I was under the impression that according to Abhinavagupta, *rasa* was of the nature of *āsvāda*. Later, I found that even Abhinavagupta had not propounded his *rasa* and *āsvāda* theory in such a naïve way.

In 1958, I was in Oxford. Mr. P.F. Strawson was then working in Indian Institute at Oxford. We came to know each other and became friends. Signor Gnoli's book on *rasa* was then published. He had translated Abhinavagupta's *Abhinavabhāratī*. Gnoli was giving an idealistic interpretation of Abhinavagupta. Strawson asked me to write an article on this subject and I wrote one titled "What did Bharata mean by *Rasa*?." I do not know whether this article was published or not. But it was later published in *Indian Philosophical Quarterly* in the 1980s. I found that Dr. M.S. Kushwaha of Lucknow University included it in the book that he edited. I was happy to see that he had given me a place with scholars like Prof. Gokak and other authorities. In 1974-75 Shri R.J. Deshmukh of Deshmukh and Co., Pune, requested me to write a book on Indian aesthetics. I promised him one but somehow or the other, I have still not fulfilled my promise. But I did publish *Art and Beauty*, a book in Hindi.

The act of *abhinaya* is based on our understanding of our behaviour and the patterns it takes. Once I was discussing that if psychological concepts were to be located in Indian thought we would have to explore them in *Nāṭyaśāstra*, *Arthaśāstra*, *Caraka-Saṁhitā* and epistemological aspects dealt with by different traditions. *Yogasūtra*s also discuss the psychological concepts but they have to be supplemented by studies in other regions. M.N. Palsane asked me to deliver a few lectures on psychological concepts found in *Nāṭyaśāstra*. The chapter on *bhāva*s in this book is the result of these lectures. I should thank Palsane for allowing me to lecture on this subject in his department and make my thoughts precise. I had also occasions of discussing problems in Indian philosophy in general and my ideas on *rasa* in particular with both the senior and junior Prof. Deviprasad Chattopadhyayas. The senior Chattopadhyaya of Lokāyata fame was a good scholar disciplined in Marxist methodology and the junior D.P. is an astute thinker trained under Late Prof. Karl Popper. Discussions with them helped me to determine my position.

Prof. Dr. N.S. Dravid of Nagpur University is an authority in Nyāya. Discussions with him some thirty-five years ago introduced me to the works of Dharmakīrti and other Buddhist philosophers. Again when he came to know that I was writing a book on Indian Aesthetics, he wrote to me a letter suggesting that I should also write on *pratibhā*. His suggestions were very useful. The direction my thoughts took on Indian aesthetics was due to the inspiration I received from the works of Late M. Hiriyanna. I am indebted to all these.

I have also used and included some of my published papers in this project. I am grateful to the respective editors and publishers for permitting me to do so.

I am grateful to the Indian Council of Philosophical Research for giving me the opportunity of writing this monograph by offering me a national fellowship. I am in particular obliged to Prof. R. Balsubramanyam, Prof. Bhuvan Chandel, the then Member Secretary of ICPR, Dr. Ranjan Ghosh, the then director of research, ICPR. Dr. Bhelke, Dr. Ouse Parampil, Deepali Gadgil, Megha Mandke, Vinita Dudhat and Pushpa Mukhedkar who helped me in completing my project, I must sincerely thank. My thanks are also due to Miss K. Bhalekar who found out for me certain important references. Prof. Konnur of Jayakar Granthalaya, Dr. Manjul of Bhandarkar Research Institute, Dr. Gosvami of Sanskrit Department and Shri A.R. Hardikar, Station Director of AIR, also gave me valuable suggestions from time to time and made the necessary books available to me. I am also grateful to Mrs Tandale, and Nihal Pandey for typing out my script. Last, but not the least, I am grateful to Dr. Suneeti Dubale, Dr. Prof. Saroja Bhate, Dr. Prof. Y.S. Walimbe, Shri Bhagwat Guruji, Prof. Krishna Arjunwadkar and Prof. (Mrs.) Leela Arjunwadkar, Pfof. V.D. (Vadi) Kulkarni and Smt. Sucheta Bhide-Chaphekar, for the help they rendered me from time to time. I cannot ever forget the help extended by Prof. C.G. Dhere, Ramakant Purao, Prof. Talghatti and Shri Madhavrao Suryavanshi, the former Chairman of Maharashtra Public Service Commission, who is both a scientist and a philosopher and who happens to be a student of People's College, Nanded in the foundation of which I was instrumental.

Contents

Acknowledgement

IT gives us great pleasure in presenting one of the last works of our beloved father Late Dr Surendra S. Barlingay on Indian Aesthetics. This work was a culmination of his project as a Fellow of Indian Council of Philosophical Research. He intended to publish this in a book form in his lifetime, but that was not to be. After Dr Barlingay's demise in 1997, presenting one of his last works to the readers has been the cherished dream of our mother Mrs Sushila Barlingay, without whose continuous support and inspiration, this would not have been possible.

Publication of such a work, several years after the demise of the author, is not an easy task. But this was made possible due to the laborious efforts of our friend, Dr S. E. Bhelkey, without whose assistance this work would not have seen the light of the day. We have seen the pain he has taken towards completion of this work in spite of his indifferent health. He has not only gone through the manuscript, but has also added finishing touches to complete this work.

It was the wish of our father that this work of his was not to be edited in any way. Hence, utmost care has been taken to present this work to the readers as he had penned it.

One of us being a student of Indian Aesthetics, is aware of the dearth of such a comprehensive study on the subject. Dr Barlingay had incorporated his views on subjects like

'Indian Poetics', 'Rasavat Alaṅkāra', 'Alaṅkār Rīti', 'Vakroti' and 'Auchitya' in this work.

The present contribution, we feel, would make an interesting reading not only to the students of Indian philosophy, the students of finance, but also to a layman in general.

A few words, we feel, are needed to express our gratitude to the well-wishers of our dear father. Even after his demise, some of them continuously encouraged us to bring out his unpublished work. One of them is Dr D. P. Chatopadhyay who has supported us in this venture.

Dr Barlingay had dedicated this work, to Professor E. C. G. Sudarshan. However, after the demise of Dr Barlingay, Professor Sudershan obliged us by writing a valuable preface to this work. We are deeply grateful to him for sparing his time, in spite of his preoccupation, on our request. We are equally grateful to Shri Susheel Mittal of D.K. Printworld, Delhi for publishing this work.

Dr Krantiprabha Pande
Dr Manojha Barlingay

1

Prologue

Different Arts — Their Interrelations

IT is not my object to write a historical account of the development of the aesthetic theory in India between Bharata and Jagannātha. I am not sure whether the development which took place during this period could be regarded as a systematic aesthetic theory. Bharata wrote on *nāṭya*, Bhāmaha wrote on poetry; Vāmana, Daṇḍin, Rudrabhaṭṭa also did the same. Ānandavardhana pronounced that *dhvani* or suggestion was basic to all poetry. Abhinavagupta and his predecessors, contemporaries and successors like Bhaṭṭa Lollaṭa, Śaṅkuka, Bhaṭṭanāyaka, Bhaṭṭatauta, Mammaṭa, Viśvanātha, Kṣemendra, Mahimabhaṭṭa, Jagannātha and Appaya Dīkṣita pronounced very important theories of drama and poetry. Several important dramatists and poets like Bhāsa, Kālidāsa, Bhavabhūti, Śūdraka, Jayadeva and Jagannātha produced some beautiful dramas and poetry. Similarly, Śāraṅgadeva wrote on Hindustani music. There are also treatises on *sthāpatya* and *śilpa*. In addition, in Purāṇas like *Agni* and *Viṣṇudharmottara*, there are references to different arts and their relationships. But although literature connected with art and aesthetics is profuse, I do not know whether we can say that Indians ever developed any systematic theory. Perhaps, developing a theory of aesthetics itself might not be possible in the strict sense of the term. But these masters have definitely given us some vision and insights in regard to different problems in art and in aesthetics. In *Viṣṇudharmottara Purāṇa*, Vol. III, there is a beautiful dialogue between Vajra and Sage Mārkaṇḍeya as to "what the *citra-sūtra*" is. How can one be proficient in the art of painting? asks Vajra. Mārkaṇḍeya replies that unless one is proficient in the art of dance, one cannot be an expert in the art of painting (III.2-2.3). Then Vajra requests him to "explain the method of dance and also to talk about *citra-sūtra*." Mārkaṇḍeya replies both these arts go hand in hand, for both of them are *anukriyā*. (I am not using the word "imitation," *anukriyā* means that which arises out of action.) Mārkaṇḍeya further adds that one who does not know how to play on a musical instrument cannot be an expert in dance. Vajra then asks something about musical instruments. Mārkaṇḍeya replies that without knowing vocal music, one cannot be proficient in playing an instrument. This shows that they regarded that fine arts were related to one another and any of the arts could not be practised in isolation. This indeed is a very important insight. But nobody seems to have worked out the actual relationships among these arts. In *Nāṭyaśāstra*, there is a reference to all these arts together, and in *nāṭya* practices, they are used. In the sixth *adhyāya* of *Nāṭyaśāstra* Bharata gives the following verse:

> रसाभावाह्यभिनयाः धर्मिवृत्तिप्रवृत्तयः ।
> सिद्धिस्वरास्तथातोद्यं गानं रंगस्यसंग्रहः ॥
>
> *rasābhāvāhyabhinayāḥ dharmivṛtti-pravṛttayaḥ* ।
> *siddhisvarāstathātodyaṁ gānaṁ raṅgasyasaṁgrahaḥ* ॥

Perhaps he has left the actual co-ordination of these to the respective *sūtradhāra* of dramas.

The Parameters — Art and Beauty

When one goes to the tradition of poetics, the first name that occurs to anybody is that of Bhāmaha.[1] In his *Kāvyālaṁkāra* he says *śabdārthau sahitau kāvyam* (शब्दार्थौ सहितौ काव्यम्). Poetry requires both the words and their meanings. One cannot be segregated from the other. Most of his commentators and critics allege that this is Bhāmaha's definition of poetry and so many of them have criticized Bhāmaha. To my mind, this is one important description of the *necessary condition* of poetry.[2] It does not give sufficient conditions of poetry. In Sanskrit, *vyākhyā* does not mean definition. It means just description or explanation only. I think Bhāmaha gives a very important truth or insight regarding poetry. Perhaps Kuntaka has understood this insight. Most people think what Bhāmaha tells us is very trivial. I want to point out that what Bhāmaha says is not trivial. He is giving us some insight into the relation of the medium of art and the message of the artist. Since his topic under reference is poetry, he is talking about *śabda* and *artha*. *Śabda* and *artha* or *vācaka* and *vācya*, are like the two wings of a butterfly. They should be regarded as important in the context of poetic art. In ordinary language perhaps the intention or *vācya* may be more important, and in grammar, the words, i.e. the medium may be the subject for discussion. But in poetry, neither of these parts can be isolated or considered independently, without reference to the other.[3] When we go to Vāmana, we find one more truth about art. In fact, Bhāmaha also has talked about it, but not that specifically. Vāmana is misunderstood as a *rītivādin* or a propounder of style. But this is doing him an injustice. He also talks of the evaluative principle and calls it *alaṁkāra*.

---

1. Some say that Daṇḍin was earlier than Bhāmaha.
2. But this should not be understood in the way Jagannātha did.
3. I have tried to explain this in my section on Bhāmaha.

In very clear words, he says that what is ordinarily known as *alaṁkāra* like *upamā* or *utprekṣā* are *alaṁkāra*s in the secondary sense. The real *alaṁkāra* is beauty. *Alaṁkāra* is not embellishment or ornament primarily. It is the parameter. The word parameter also suggests the same thing. *Alaṁkāra* is the last point in the measurement or evaluation. It, therefore, means a standard, a *mānadaṇḍa*, a scale, or a parameter. What Vāmana says about poetry, may, by induction, be applied to all arts. One cannot talk of arts unless there is evaluation. Vāmana says that this evaluative concept is that of beauty. Just as Bhāmaha talks of two prongs, *śabda* and *artha*, Vāmana also talks of two scales. In one sense, both of them are evaluative although their spheres of operation are different. I have already mentioned one. The other is *rīti*. An art is known by this standard constituent. Here, Vāmana is elaborating the dictum given by Bhāmaha about *śabda*. Bhāmaha talks about *śabda*, Vāmana talks about the combination of *śabda*s. *Rīti* is concerned with it. *Viśiṣṭā padaracanā rītiḥ* (विशिष्टा पदरचना रीतिः). It is a gestalt or pattern of sounds and is therefore concerned with medium. And the evaluative character of this gestalt is given by the characteristics described by the word *viśiṣṭa*. He thus gives us the insight that we require. At least two principles of evaluation co-ordinated with each other are necessary. One is beauty which is normative and the other is the constitutive principle, *ātma-tattva*. Since any art-object has to have a body or a subject matter or medium, one cannot ignore the basic element. Vāmana calls it *ātma-tattva*. *Kāvya* thus depends on the co-ordination of *ātma-tattva* with *grāhyatā-tattva*.

I feel that although Vāmana talks of two parameters, one could even go further taking a clue from Prācīna Nyāya. In *Nyāya-Sūtra*, we get the aphorism, *jātyākṛtivyaktayastu padārthaḥ* (जात्याकृतिव्यक्तयस्तु पदार्थः). We require *jāti*, *ākṛti* and *vyakti*. Perhaps this concept could be meaningfully used in the discussion of arts.

When one talks of normative principles, the principle may not be one, but many. When one considers the social dimension of art, perhaps propriety or *aucitya* (औचित्य) assumes a very important position. Kṣemendra talks of this when he prescribes *aucitya* as the evaluative standard.

But there may be many more evaluative and constitutive parameters. Sometimes, one might not be able to comprehend the evaluative principle itself. It might be beyond one's grasp. Some of our masters like Bhaṭṭanāyaka and Viśvanātha have compared this experience with *Brahmāsvāda* which is non-comprehensible. Such a standard which is characterized by non-comprehensibility is given to us in a flash. It is beyond our capacity to analyse it.

But what about the concept like beauty, *aucitya* and *pratibhā*? Can they be analysed? Most of our masters are silent on this. They give only illustrations. It is also a flash, a *camatkṛti*. It is like the *lāvaṇya* of a woman or an *aṅganā*. *Lāvaṇyamivāṅganāsu* (लावण्यमिवांगनासु) (*Dhvanyāloka*, Chapter 4). So both the comprehensible and the non-comprehensible evaluative principles of art are given to us by intuition and are known in a flash only.

In fact, all this will lead us to a certain theory of medium. It is a theory of language. In Kāśmīra-Śaivism and grammar we get such theories of medium. Traditionally, languages are classified into four types: *parā, paśyanti, madhyamā* and *vaikharī* or ordinary language. But when *vaikharī* is applied to an art-object its main concern is its relationship with experience. Language is always a vehicle of thought. It is a model. Models are usually based on similarities. This is expressed in terms of *upamā*. But is it true that all our languages are based on similes? I have a feeling that even without any similarity, language can act as a vehicle. I think this insight is indicated by the philosophers of Kāśmīra-Śaivism. Perhaps, Jñāneśvara also gives the same insight. But I shall elaborate it in a later section.

Cultural Traditions in Art — The Parameters of Appreciation

The cultural tradition which has developed in India from the ancient times and which has come down to us to the present day, is very rich and varied. It has developed as a quantum. One can locate this tradition in music, (stage) drama and dance, on the one hand, and in poetry, drama (*rūpaka*) and other forms of literature on the other. Painting, sculpture and architecture form a third dimension or group of this tradition. The frescoes of Ajantā and the cave sculptures in Ellorā, so also the relics of Amarāvatī and Hampī and the numerous temples of south India are a testimony to the richness of this tradition. It may be pointed out that the arts on such a scale cannot develop in isolation. They must have the background of scientific development which in turn helped the development of the technology of these arts in a rich measure. In the temples of Hampī, Madurai and Thiruvananthapuram there are musical pillars which produce different musical notes or what is known in Hindi as *saragam*. This clearly indicates that our sculptors were technologically equipped with the science of selecting proper stones. Similarly the cave architecture of Ellorā which is visible in the carvings of Kailāsa shows that the artisans in those days knew engineering very well. Several works like *Kāśyapa Śilpa* and *Samarāṅgaṇa-Sūtradhāra* (काश्यप शिल्प और समरांगणसूत्रधार), attributed to king Bhoja are available till today, though many others mentioned by other authors are iost. In fact, this is not only true of architecture but is also true of the technology behind poetry, drama, dance, and music. Unfortunately, what exists today are the relics of these ancient sciences and technology which go by the name of poetics and dramaturgy.

Different theories of poetry and drama with regard to appreciation were developed in the course of time. They enriched the theory of art by emphasizing on different aspects of the composition of art. These theories developed in two ways. First, they developed the theories of appreciation of the artefact, whether the particular artefacts were beautiful or not, whether they were appropriate and useful, or otherwise. Secondly, the theories also discussed the constituent conditions and the nature of the subject matter of arts. For example, in the case of poetry they were concerned with the structure of poetic constructions, that is, with the composition of poetry, the peculiarities with which poetic composition could be structured, whether the words or sound patterns in the composition were lucid, how the rhythm of the composition was preserved and perfected and so on. It appears that all these enquiries were in regard to the parameters concerned with the constitution and appreciation or evaluation of arts.

However, in the course of time the Indian aesthetic theory was basically centred around literary arts like poetry and drama, and the concepts like *rasa* and *bhāva* assumed greater significance. Perhaps the spheres of these concepts were extended and they were used in the context of *śilpa* (शिल्प) and/or *sthāpatya* (स्थापत्य) also.

In *Vāstusūtropaniṣad* (वास्तुसूत्रोपनिषद्), for example, the concepts of *rasa* and *bhāva* are used. (They were also used in other works of *sthāpatya*.) But perhaps after CE 1215 when northern India came under the rule of Slave Dynasty, the creative activity of Indians in regard to art and architecture in the old idiom came to a standstill except in south India where the city of Vijayanagara was built. Similarly, some isolated attempts in this respect are seen in the Khajurāho temple in Central India. One can say that these architectural forms showed themselves wherever peace and prosperity, security and encouragement were available. One can also say that with the Persian, Turkish and Central Asian contact the original forms of Indian art gave way to new ones, or got synthesized with the alien forms. Thus the artists who got the royal patronage were either Persians and Central Asians or the original Indian artists and artisans who were converted to Islami faith. If these artists followed the directives of the rulers it was but natural. Thus, original Indian art and Indian artists and artisans got adapted to new paradigms. This can be seen in *masjid* and *dargāh* architecture, in the music forms like *ṭhumarī* (ठुमरी), *khyāl* (ख्याल) and *gaẓal* (ग़ज़ल) and in poetry of the form of *śer* (शेर).

In fact, weavers and carpet-makers of Varanasi today are all Muslims and they have adopted "Muslim" fashions in art. It could, of course, be that to a certain extent the taste of the rulers was influenced by the original forms. Anyway it is possible to say that the arts and crafts of India of the thirteenth century and after, were more or less a product of some kind of synthesis.

In the cultural tradition of India, with the emergence of different arts, was also developed the theory of criticism of arts. This criticism was of three kinds. First, the techniques which give us the analysis and synthesis of any work of art, were developed. Then came the development of the concepts required in different arts and artefacts of various kinds. Finally came the development of thought regarding the parameters by which we measure and evaluate arts. The arts, they thought of, were of various kinds. The first was music. When they sang Vedic hymns they sang them in a certain style with *udātta* and *anudātta* (अनुदात्त) pronunciations. They also pronounced the words as short, long, elongated (*hrasva*, ह्रस्व), (*dīrgha*, दीर्घ), and (*pluta*, प्लुत). *Svarita* (स्वरित) pronunciation was a later addition. All these gave rise to music, first, the Vedic and then the classical. The first traces of this classical music, one can find in Bharata's *Nāṭyaśāstra*. One can also find this developed in *Saṁgītaratnākara* (संगीतरत्नाकर). In poetry and music they developed *chanda* (छन्द), *rāga* (राग), etc.

Like music they developed architecture. The first significant form of architecture was connected with the creation of sacrificial altar (Vedic shapes changed, but areas remain equal). But soon it developed into the construction of buildings and city planning, etc. One can easily find varieties of these in town planning, temples and forts. Through these developments also emerged various styles. The creation of structure also proceeded in another direction, for example, in the caves of Ellorā, Ajantā and Karlā. This continued in the art of painting too. The remains of such paintings can be found in the existing caves. In Ellorā caves, for instance in Indrasabhā (इंद्रसभा), it can be seen that it was artistically painted. Unfortunately this cave painting is no more in existence today. The art of painting was preserved in a variety of ways. It is still extant in miniature, Jain and non-Jain, paintings. Some relics of Kāngrā paintings are also preserved in national museums.

The Classification of Arts

Aesthetics is the theory of art. Since there are different arts it is possible that the theory might change from art to art. Arts can be classified under *performing, literary* and *plastic* arts. But they may also be classified in a different way, on a different basis. According to philosophers of art, this difference could be gradual and shown on a certain scale. The Indian scholars put poetry and *saṅgīta* at the two ends. Under *saṅgīta* is grouped vocal and instrumental music and dance:

गीतं, वाद्यं च नृत्यं च त्रयं संगीतमुच्यते ।

gītaṁ vādyaṁ ca nṛtyaṁ ca, trayaṁ saṅgītamucyate । — *San. R.*

Under *kāvya* are included drama or *rūpaka* of ten types, lyrical poetry, epics, etc. Excluding poetry or music, several other plastic arts and crafts were included in *kalā*. Such *kalā*s formed a third group of human creations.

साहित्यसंगीतकलाविहीनः
साक्षात् पशुः पुच्छविषाणहीनः ।

sāhitya-saṅgīta-kalā-vihīnaḥ ।
sākṣāt paśuḥ pucchaviṣāṇahīnaḥ ॥ — *Su. R. Bha.* 41.30

I take *kalā* separately because any way plastic arts are not included in *sāhitya* or *saṅgīta*.

A person who does not appreciate literature (*sāhitya*), poetry, music or *kalā* (arts) is only a beast though without horns and a tail. Thus ancient and medieval Indians distinguished between three spheres of artistic creativity as the spheres of music (*saṅgīta*), literature (*kāvya*) and other arts (*kalā*). Perhaps in those days painting, sculpture and architecture were included in *kalā*s.

In Śiva's conceptual form *kalādhvan* depicts Śiva's entire limbs. Therefore *kalā* denotes finger dexterity or creation or hand-movements. In six *adhvans*, *kalādhvan* is the foremost and dominating one because all other *adhvan*s remain included and pervaded by this *kalādhvan*. It is constituted of five *kalā*s. In *aṣṭa-mūrti* form *kalā* is earth, *kalā* is *miśra-māyā* or *miśrādhvan*.

The word *kalā* must be properly understood. *Kalā* is something like the slice of a whole. It is something short of a whole. Therefore, in *kalā* we would get an incomplete picture of Life. We talk of *kalā* or a phase of the moon.

The ancient scholars did recognize that all these *kalā*s are closely related to music. In *Viṣṇudharmottara Purāṇa,* in a dialogue between Vajra and Mārkaṇḍeya, it is stated that one could not be proficient in painting unless one was acquainted with music (vocal and instrumental) and dance. They compare music and poetry to the milk flowing from the two breasts of the Goddess Sarasvatī (by drinking which people can become proficient in music and literature).[4]

In the present idiom, I shall include all creativity (except the creativity in science) under arts and try to investigate the essence of these arts. The question that arises is whether there is anything common to all the arts which could be distinctive of the arts alone. In the course of history people put their finger on the word *rasa* and pointed out that it was the necessary condition of every art. Most Indian writers wrote primarily on poetry and drama although their creativity took the *shape* of other arts like architecture, sculpture and painting. Gradually, the term *rasa* came to be commonly used for indicating the essence of all arts.

The question is what distinctive characteristics were indicated by the term *rasa,* were essential features of all the arts. I shall try to investigate this. But, before I do this, it must be pointed out that, in addition to the *rasa* theory, several other theories were enunciated for explaining the arts. For example, the theories of *alaṁkāra* (अलङ्कार), *rīti* (रीति), *vakrokti*

4. संगीतमय साहित्यम् सरस्वत्याः स्तनद्वयम्।
एकमापातमधुरमन्यदालोचनामृतम्॥

saṅgītamaya sāhityam sarasvatyāḥ stanadvayam ।
ekamāpātamadhuram anyadālocanāmṛtam ॥ — *Su. R. Bham.*

(वक्रोक्ति), *dhvani* (ध्वनि) and *aucitya* (औचित्य) were evolved in the course of time. There were also refinements made in these theories from time to time. But finally all these theories seem to have merged with the *rasa* theory which dominated the scene of art criticism. Whether this is correct, desirable or otherwise need not be discussed here. But there may be reasons for the thought taking such a turn. The *rasa* theory itself was transformed from time to time. What was the reason for the emergence of this concept of *rasa*?

Let me first ask the question what is an art, as understood in the contemporary idiom? It may be accepted that what we call art is a kind of human creativity. It is human creation arising from human experience, and the human experience is a configuration of thought, emotion, etc. This experience is not material, it is something which can be considered to be mental or belonging to memory. It was called *bhāva*s by Bharata and the writers who followed him. The most persistent of their *bhāva*s (which were mental, i.e. of the nature of *cittavṛtti* (चित्तवृत्ति)) were called *sthāyī bhāva*s. In *Nāṭyaśāstra*, *sthāyī bhāva*s are named and explained. Today, many people interpret *sthāyī bhāva*s in different ways. Many of them call them emotions. But it must be noted that basically, there are experiences which are persistent existents. Dhanika, who wrote on *Daśarūpaka* of Dhanañjaya, clearly states this in words *sthāyībhāvāḥ cittavṛtti viśeṣāḥ* (स्थायिभावः चित्तवृत्तिविशेषाः) — *citta* means mind and *cittavṛtti* means mental states. *Cittavṛtti viśeṣa*s would thus mean specific or particular mental states. In the *Yogasūtra*s also, *citta* and *cittavṛtti*s are discussed. How to reify these mental states in an order or system so that they could become the object of individual knowledge, is, according to me, the problem of art. In accomplishing this lies the creativity of man and the end-product of this is the art object. This process of reification, the medium and/or the essence or *elan vital* which flows through it, was given the name *rasa*. *Rasa* is an instrument for this transition from subjectivity to objectivity or from privacy to publicness. It was used for a medium of communication, which linked A's thought or reactions to B, C or D.

On further refinement the message passed through the medium was called *rasa*. Arriving at a medium and understanding this concept of *rasa* took a number of centuries and the concept had to pass through several stages. I shall be silent on the point whether such a transition was right or not, but it has become a historical fact. In order to know how this happened we might have to consider other theories of art and how their elements were incorporated in the "concept" of *rasa*.

In a way art is an activity of expression and communication. What is to be expressed or communicated is something that is in our mind and regarded as worth communicating or expressing. Both expression or communication would therefore require a medium which would be different from our experience which we have stored in our memory. The act of expressing itself is a vehicle of communication. Expression, therefore, would be a form given to our experience that is received and stored in our mind. Expression of something that is communicated would be a transformation of this something mental into something that has objectivity, publicness — so that it could be experienced by any other person. It could not remain private. Such a form cannot be empty. It has to be the form of some subject matter or stuff. This stuff is basically the stuff of experience. But, while expressing it, one could employ different mediums for expression. For example, it could be expressed in pure sound or sounds which could be interpreted in terms of meanings or gestures, or figures, colours, lines, and cubes, plane figures and solids. In a way, all these representations would be symbolic. But the symbols could be of different kinds — they could be concrete or abstract with different degrees and shades. On account of these differences the same experience pattern could take different forms and could be known by the name of different arts. Our mental experience is private and is not accessible to other people. When our experience takes the objective form it comes within the purview of other people. An art object is thus the objectification of something that is mental, individual and subjective. Creativity lies in this process of objectification. It is the transformation of something private into public. Without such transformation it would not become universal nor would it be measurable. It would not be uniform and of identical nature for anybody. In the course of our traditional art history this dynamism in the process was pointed out as *rasa* and its use was extended from the theory of stage drama to different arts. If we confine ourselves to the medium of drama, we will have to say that it is a mixed medium, having two prongs — one visual and the other auditory, and on the analogy of our experience and our sense-organs we could say that the mediums would be of the kind of *śabda* (शब्द), *sparśa* (स्पर्श), *rūpa* (रूप), *rasa* (रस) and *gandha* (गन्ध). But in poetry only *śabda* is required. If *śabda* is eliminated, poetry will not remain poetry. It will remain only as an idea in the poet's mind. Similar would be the case with music. Expression of the musician's mind in terms of notes is absolutely necessary for the transformation of something mental into music. So is the case with painting or sculpture. Our thought and imagination will have to be transformed to *rūpa*.

The technical words *rūpa* and *śabda* and its equivalent *vākya* are used in the history of Indian art by Abhinavagupta, Viśvanātha and Jagannātha. Vāmana also recognizes its significance and so stresses *pada-racanā* or composition of words. The process of objectification seems to be common to all arts and I have reasons to believe that to indicate this process, the term *rasa*, which was originally intended to indicate the process in the context of stage drama, was gradually applied to other arts.

This process of transformation from the subjective to the objective is significant. Unless something is made public and objective it cannot be recognized, appreciated or evaluated by others. Jagannātha expressed this by the term, *gocarīkriyamāṇa* (गोचरीक्रियमाण).

This transformation from subjective to objective is like introducing two parallel concepts — one subjective and the other objective, whose context (and also the field) is the same. Let us take the example of heat and temperature. Both these concepts are different although their context is the same. The concept of temperature would be meaningless unless there is heat. But heat is not temperature. Heat indicates quantity whereas temperature indicates quality and a different level. If one gallon of water is heated up to the boiling point the quantity of heat is definitely more than the quantity of heat contained in a quarter gallon, although the temperature of both would be the same. Heat can have a reference to volume; the temperature does not have such reference. When we are able to reduce or subject heat to additive terms we can talk of degrees of temperature. But when we say that the temperature has increased by one degree it does not mean that the heat has also increased in the same proportion. It could be the same, more or even less. Our *sthāyī bhāva*s which are mental, in a similar way, when transformed into objective medium, can be brought in the scope of a parameter and this can be called *rasa*. In fact, some other term could have been used for this.

But in the development of the history of art, *rasa* got a more important place. Since the same process is involved in the case of every art, our masters chose to use the term *rasa* for all arts.

I might point out here that the process does not end with objectification. Finally it becomes subjective. This further process from objective to subjective is again different. But in the course of time the term *rasa* was used for this process also.[5]

Time, Music and Dance: Tāla, Laya and Svara

Ancient Indian art critics thought that music (vocal and instrumental), dance and drama performance should be classified under one head. According to them these different arts are co-ordinated in a drama performance itself. *Viṣṇudharmottara Purāṇa*, as pointed out earlier, goes a step further and points out that painting, sculpture, dance and music cannot be considered in isolation and without reciprocal reference to one another. There is no doubt that although these arts are different, in some respects they overlap one another.

Let me take the case of dance and music (in some respects a musical art composition cannot be treated entirely independently). Music is based on several factors, but basically it requires three constituents. One is called *laya*,[6] the second is *tāla* (ताल) and the third is *svara* (स्वर).

Music, whether vocal or instrumental, is a temporal art, that is, when the music is being played, we move with time.

---

5. This I think is the reason for regarding *rasa* as something subjective, of the nature of *ānanda*.

6. *Laya* is a masculine word though usually employed in the feminine gender by the artists and critics today.

We are governed by succession. This may give an impression that time is moving. But in the context of music time is in the background. If we regard the time as a flow, even then, in the context of sound series, time would have to be regarded as relatively constant and of the nature of background. In fact, there can be three series imposed one over the other in succession. First is the time series; second on this is imposed the sound series; and, sometimes, third on this is further imposed the language series, as is seen in lyrical poetry or drama. This third series is not always necessary. Again in the context of music, when we are talking of time, we are talking of time of one co-ordinate system. The theory of relativity is not likely to operate here. We are only concerned with time as understood by Newton, Kant, etc. We have to take time in the sense of absolute time and regard it as a container, or a river-bed in which sound patterns (or sound-and-silence patterns) move. This *time-bed* is absolutely important for music. But although it is taken for granted that time is a container or a river-bed, it is necessary to know that time does not behave in the way space behaves. In space one can come back to the point from which one starts but in time it is never possible. Although one may use the spatial language off and on, time is not reversible. For example, in Hindustani music when one uses the word *sama* or *samā*, one is supposed to come back to the original point, but one does not come back to the same physical time point. One could be the same point of the sound pattern indeed. But we have moved from one point of time to another point of time already.

Although we take time as a background or a support, time has length, continuity and one can divide this continuity in some occurrent points. The distance between two such adjacent occurrent points can be posited as having a uniform temporal distance, for unless the concept of uniform distance is applied it would never be possible to measure anything. We always require some uniformity when we talk of measurement, parameter and objectivity. Kāśmīra-Śaivism propounds that the universe is continuously throbbing or having *spanda*. (They say, that all evolution is due to this throbbing.) In fact, such throbbing is perceptible in our heart beats *lub, dub* and in pulse rate which can be measured. When one talks of music, one talks of this throbbing of the temporal background and divide it into equal parts. Unless we divide time and measure in terms of equal parts the concepts of *tāla* could not be used. Music moves on this background. It may move quickly or slowly. It is the sound which moves but perhaps by transferred epithet we say that the *laya* is slow or fast. Sometimes it is called *druta*, or *vilambita* (विलम्बित). For the fast *laya* the word *druta* and for slow *laya* the word *vilambita* are used. *Vilambita* means delayed. On this background of time, the sound moves. It can have different pitches and timbres, etc. It can be pronounced in different ways and so on. The musicians classify this sound in *śruti* (श्रुति). A sound pattern can be measured by such measures as *hrasva* and *dīrgha* and *pluta* or in music by *mātrā*s. A sound may be simple or compound but we are now able to measure it in terms of *mātrā*s. The counting of *mātrā*s and the movement of sound give rise to *tāla*. With the help of *tāla* and *laya* musical notes can be measured and different patterns of *tāla* like *ekatāla* (एकताल), *tritāla* (त्रिताल), *jhapatāla* (झपताल), etc. can be designed. The actual temporal distance of each *mātrā* can also be reduced according to the skill of the musician.

It has to be pointed out here that the word *laya* is many a time metaphorically used and in that case it conveys something more than the concept of *laya* in music. For example, one can talk of *laya* in poetry and so on. Mardhekar, a great Marathi poet and critic, talks of *saṁvāda, virodha* and *samatola laya*. In fact, these are different patterns or designs which can be used in the sense of a whole. Let me explain the peculiarities of the concept of *laya*.

Although the concept of *laya* is understood and used by musicians and their critics, they do not seem to have defined or analysed the concept. First, in all arts, which are temporal, the concept of *laya* is presupposed. *Laya* is a kind of temporal continuum, which also assumes the possibility of equal division.

But time should "flow" evenly, even in the absence of anything flowing through it.[7] *Laya* as used in music requires a correlate in the form of *sound-gestalt* superimposed on the time series. (It is of course possible that this series is only of "silent" sounds.) Many times people describe *laya* as rhythm. I feel that this would not describe the concept of *laya*. In its metaphorical use, *laya* not only gives the "starting" point of time of the musical composition, it also tells us how it flows. It is also a metaphorical use of "flow."

It also suggests as to where the *laya* would be complete and form a whole. It certainly presupposes a smooth flow of sound superimposed on the time series. Thus with *laya* one also cognizes (1) time series, (2) sound/or a sound-continuum which vanishes at one point and is produced successively, (3) a whole of sound and time, and (4) which can be measured with regular time intervals through beats (*tāla*). Since time is "flowing" smoothly and evenly it could be broken into equal bits (with a pause after each bit). These time bits are at the base of *tāla*. They are grouped together so as to make a design, a design or musical beats. And although the sound can go up and down, that is, although it can be composed of two or

---

7. As a matter of fact if it flows it flows from the future to the past.

more beats, they give us a certain gestalt. This is of course not the gestalt of pure time but it can be measured in terms of the bits of Time.[8] In *nṛtta* (नृत्त) or pure dance, the sounds superimposed on the time series may not always be present, although they are not always absent. The end of *tāla* in dance is, for example, marked by certain sounds, particularly of the foot (feet) but in dance the time flow is imagined and the sound flow is also presupposed and determined in some silent manner. In addition to time flow and *tāla* what is further presumed is the concept of "balance," contrast and similarity. Dance is the bodily action of an individual or a group of individuals. Our body consists of several limbs which are joined together. They can be moved in different directions. A design of these patterns is the material used for dance. The science of Indian dance states (it must be presupposed in folk dances also) that our body has to be considered as composed of different parts. The main part is from the shoulders to the hips (over this is the head). Now this is called *aṅga* (अंग). It is three-dimensional, that is, it has sides. It is on this account that we get profiles and poses. These profiles are called *pratyaṅga*s (प्रत्यंग).

In addition, there are legs, hands, feet, paws, and fingers. All these can be moved and bent in some rhythmic manner. The basic concepts of dance are carried out with the help of these *upāṅga*s and certain dynamic designs can be arranged. Since they are action-based, certain movement is also implied and effected. Perhaps the underlying concept is that, whatever the posture the dancer takes, it is pleasing to the eyes, and is beautiful. All these postures and steps are, of course, rhythmic and are based on *tāla*. The dancers and the choreographers

8. "Beat" is a technical term in music, but it goes without saying it is related to "bit" which shows a *division* of time.

claim this. In fact, all this is a manifestation of the natural law of certain uniformity and design. The regularity and the rhythm that the artist tries to bring in his art is also seen in the natural behaviour of the flowing of wind and the movement of leaves and branches of trees, fluttering of the wings of birds, butterflies and other insects and the beats of heart.

As in music, the concept of *laya* is also used in poetry, dialogue and speech. Although *laya* is, in the first instance, an even flow of time, on it can be superimposed anything which flows. *Laya* thus could be basically used as a measurement of time in the context of arts. A measure has to be uniform and this is supplied by the *laya* concept. This evenness is suggested by the pulse-rate. Kāśmīra-Śaivism, as pointed out earlier, introduces the concept of *spanda* which means throbbing and perhaps suggests that there is a cosmic throbbing at the back of the dynamism in the universe. But the throbbing or *spanda* may also suggest the division of time. This division, which is potentially present, is suggested to us by *tāla*. If an analogy is to be given, one may take automobile cylinders which give us perpendicular movements. But when the cylinders move in a rhythmic way and lead to cylindrical motion, that motion is smooth. *Tāla* or rhythmic movement gives us this division of smooth movement of certain designs of specific parts, but the *laya* does not indicate any real or actual break. It gives us smoothness. The break is man's conception of time and is used for measurement. In dance also the same thing occurs. At times it is in fact governed by *tāla* and *laya*, but the *laya* part is only silently present. It is something like this. I have earlier said that on the time series is superimposed a sound series. But just as we can sing a song in our mind or think something without making it loud, similarly, although, in *laya*, some other series is superimposed on the time series, the other series can be felt even silently.

I may refer here to another paradox connected with infinite divisibility of space. Pure space is never divided, it is only the thing in the space which can be divided. But we do say that space is infinitely divisible. In the same manner the other series which is imposed on the time series is ignored and we begin to think that pure time-flow is the *laya*. As a matter of fact I am not sure whether we can really use expressions like the *flow of time*. Perhaps time does not flow, it is something occupying time or its cross-section which flows. This is *laya*.

I may repeat that in dance this *laya* and *tāla* are used to make some dynamic designs and movements which are based on the body and which can be moulded in several ways. It is perhaps presupposed that every such moulding is pleasing to the eyes and is beautiful. It is assumed that dance is beautiful. It is *hṛdaya saṁvādi*.

The language of dance is also the medium which results in certain ripples of meanings. Beauty, pleasure or happiness could be pointers to these ripples. Perhaps dance provides the natural signs or medium as dance movements are primarily concerned with our moods.

In the same fashion we can talk of other arts like sculpture, painting and architecture. Dance is dynamic, while sculpture is static. But although static, it gives us the feeling that it is animated, that it is dynamic. This is on account of the fact that it suggests that it is only a cross-section of the whole, something which contributes towards the whole. This is more clearly seen in painting. If trees are painted and if they are bent in a certain direction, they give a feeling that they are moving on account of the wind. In this way one can say that all arts provide a certain medium, which to the observer, appears as yielding some meaning which is basically the intention of the artist.

What is the difference between a stage drama and a dance performance? In Bharata's time the *nṛtya* (नृत्य) and *naṭ* (नट) stood for the same act. Both mean acting and both are performance-oriented. These performances are based on certain intentions of the creative artist, poet or producer, and even a dance presents a certain theme. Bharata in his *Nāṭyaśāstra* gives a *saṁgraha* of *nāṭya*. He says,

रसाभावाह्यभिनयाः धर्मिवृत्तिप्रवृत्तयः
सिद्धि स्वरास्तथातोद्यं गानं रंगश्च संग्रहः ॥

rasābhāvāhyabhinayāḥ dharmivṛttipravṛttayaḥ ।
siddhisvarāstathātodyaṁ gānaṁ raṅgaśca saṁgrahaḥ ॥

Of these *rasa, bhāva, abhinaya* (in fact, everything including *ātodya*), *abhinaya* is common to both *nāṭya* and *nṛtya*; for the performance of both depend on *abhinaya*. Barring *mudrā*s in *nṛtya*, the technique of *nṛtya*, however, is concerned with the natural signs, which can be regarded as *abhinaya*. This *abhinaya* is described as of four kinds — *vāk, aṅga, sattva* and *āhārya*. *Āhārya* is concerned with the stagecraft (setting, lighting, etc.). Dance performance basically depends on *aṅga abhinaya* whereas *nāṭya* is based on all the four. Of course in a usual drama, *aṅga abhinaya* is not as minute and fine as is seen in a dance performance. This lacuna is compensated by *vāgabhinaya* which consists mainly of dialogues, etc. The theories of drama are also more developed. They can be social also. The story in dance is usually not as developed; for, in sign-language we cannot express more developed ideas. At any rate this language will require a meta-language to explain the ideas to common men. *Sattva abhinaya* requires some excellence of acting and may or may not be present either in drama or dance. So, basically, so far as techniques are concerned both of them are *abhinaya*-based and both of them are governed by some definite intentions. Drama can be easily followed by the spectators.

To follow dance performance may require some special training to the spectators. At present in India a few styles are known. They are Bharatanāṭyam, Kathak, Maṇipuri, Oḍissī and Kathakalī. None of these is very ancient and not more than 300 to 400 years old. However all these follow certain norms laid down in Bharata's *Nāṭyaśāstra*. As stated above these norms are connected with (the flow of) time and the dynamic particular gestalts. Besides *Nāṭyaśāstra* there are some other books like *Nāṭya-darpaṇa* on theory and practice of staging a drama. But *Nāṭyaśāstra* gives a number of varieties, if not all, and they are sufficient to give us the understanding of the nature of dance.

Besides these varieties like Bharatanāṭyam, etc. there are also folk-dances, and aboriginal dances. All of them follow the basic arrangements of limbs and their movements. Drama requires a certain theme. These themes are classified by Bharata, and later by Dhanañjaya, into ten varieties which are called *rūpaka*s. Each of them is basically concerned with *vāgabhinaya*, though other varieties of *abhinaya*s are not eliminated. It must be understood that by *abhinaya* is not meant what is understood by *abhinaya* today. *Abhinaya* means encoding something that is mental into something which is facial or bodily. No message can be transmitted between one individual and another or from the dramatist to the actors and then to the spectators unless it is encoded in bodily and sound signs. So by extension of meaning, *abhinaya* means that which carries the message from "what is in the mind of . . . to the face or movement of . . ." carrying it to the spectator. The current meaning of *abhinaya* is thus merely the extension of its earlier meaning.

Perception of Time and Space in Art

In the last section it was pointed out that music and poetry are related to time. In fact, all arts are related to time. For, time is the base of all experience.[9] In the same way, painting, sculpture and architecture are related to space although their relation with time cannot be ignored. In addition to time, music also requires sound or *nāda* and *laya* or flow of time. Similarly, poetry not only uses sound but also makes use of language, which is a kind of articulate manifestation of sound or *nāda*. For explaining the nature of language the concept of *sphoṭa* or explosion of sound (into meaning) is made use of by the Indian metaphysicians. Particularly Kāśmīra Śaiva school uses the words *spanda* and *sphūrti* while explaining its theories of creation. Thus, in the context of art, the words *laya*, *pratibhā*, *sphūrti*, *spanda*, etc. are used. If art is accepted as a kind of creation, which certainly it is, then the concept of *spanda* and *sphūrti* should, in some sense, be related to *laya* and *pratibhā*. It will therefore be desirable to examine and analyse concepts like *kāla* (काल), *nāda* (नाद), *śabda* (शब्द), *kāvya* (काव्य) and *rasa* (रस) on the one hand and *sphūrti* (स्फूर्ति), *laya* (लय), *pratibhā* (प्रतिभा), *sphoṭa* (स्फोट) and *spanda* (स्पंद) on the other. In the course of my monograph and even in the present section, I shall try to analyse them.

Any creation first disturbs the original state, and then alone comes something new. A creation is the product of disturbance, whether it is material or mental. Sometimes, it presupposes a certain kind of chain or succession. Our concept of time is connected with succession. That is why we talk of past, present and future or "earlier than" and "later than" or in Mctagart's terminology, A series and B series. Our philosophical theory of Advaita or Sāṁkhya also talks of the reality that is constant (*Brahman*) and the reality that is continuously changing or moving. Etymologically or in

9. *Sarvādhāraḥ kālaḥ*, सर्वाधारः कालः.

practice, *jagat* (जगत्) means this. Sāṁkhya also talks of *prakṛti* the existence of which is constant, but which, on account of some indirect intervention (*chāyā*, छाया) or *cit-chāyā* of *puruṣa* takes different forms, *vikṛti* (विकृति) like *buddhi*, *pañcatanmātra* and *pañcamahābhūta* on the one hand and *manas* (मनस), *ahaṁkāra* (अहंकार), *pañcajñānendriyas* (पंचज्ञानेन्द्रिय) and *pañcakarmendriyas* (पंचकर्मेन्द्रिय) on the other hand. What happens when from the basic undisturbed stage one arrives at something which has an altogether different form, a form which is continuously changing? I think something like the laws of inertia and force operate here. The law of inertia says that if something is in a moving state, other conditions remaining the same, it would move constantly. On the other hand, if something is at rest, at a certain place, at a certain moment of time, it would always remain so, unless by some external force its position is disturbed and changed. The biological world is marked by constant and continuous change. This change is obvious both at the level of organization, as also at the level of thinking in the anthropocentric world. A living organism is characterized by certain kinds of vibration or throbbing. Even our heart beats are constant vibrations. We have already seen that if something is to change from one state to another then vibrations are necessary. Without such vibrations a transition from one state to another would not be possible. It means that everything, whether physical or mental, is characterized by a power or ability and can be regarded as "two in one." If by some impetus or force, it starts moving then its basic ability to be stable becomes inoperative. On the other hand, if it is stationary, then its basic ability to change or move becomes inoperative.

In fact, this dual capacity is at the back of the notions like inertia, used in physics. But this appears to be operative in every sphere of experience and is expressed by concepts like being and becoming. For continuance or occurrence, both these are necessary. Even in the case of language, this is observed. A sound changes into language and acquires meaning only after a certain explosion of sounds or *sphoṭa*. *Spanda* and *sphoṭa* are so related. So is the case with *sphūrti* and *pratibhā*. *Pratibhā* is described as *navanavonmeṣaśālinī*, i.e. at each state it is characterized by new *unmeṣas*, new flashes, new manifestations, new vibrations. Rājaśekhara says that this *pratibhā* is of two types, and names them as *kārayitrī pratibhā* and *bhāvayitrī pratibhā*. This theory of Rājaśekhara has been accepted by all later writers, particularly, Hemacandra, Mammaṭa and Jagannātha. Although *pratibhā* is classified under two types, *bhāvayitrī* and *kārayitrī*, by Rājaśekhara and his successors, both the elements — *bhāvayitva* and *kārayitva* — are present in each type in a certain proportion. Of course, one element would dominate in one and the other would dominate in the other. Jñāneśvara also talks of *sphūrti*, and in today's Indian language *sphūrti* and *pratibhā* are used more or less as synonyms. Both of them presuppose spontaneity and flash. It means that all these words are "power words" and without the operation of this power, one would not be able to make a transition from one state of mind to another; and in the case of arts like music or poetry there would not be a transition just from A to B, C, D, or E. This is indicated by the words like *sphūrti*, *pratibhā*, *laya* and *spanda*.

In the previous section I have discussed *laya*. *Laya* is a division of time into equal parts. How does this division of time take place? And why are they regarded as of equal length? I have discussed these earlier. But I shall now discuss some other dimensions of the same concept. It is necessary to know that if there were just time and nothing else, a transition would not be known. The knowledge and the understanding of coming into existence of one moment and vanishing of another is made possible because in addition to time, there is also a knower or a mind, and time is constantly contrasted by this mind against itself. That the mind is "contrasted" means that it is measured. Our mind is the parameter by which it is measured. Due to this parameter the knower is able to see the "movement" of time. But the "whole" time is never perceptible to him. He only senses some length of time, just as when one perceives space, one doesn't perceive the whole space nor just a point, but a point having some length. Man's perception of space and time is of elongated space and time.

Similarly, his perception of sound is that of elongated sound or rhythm. On account of his perception of elongatedness he is able to conceive length and change. He not only sees the beginning of the "time-cross-section," he is also able to see the end or vanishing of this cross-section. *Laya* literally means vanishing. But it is also a beginning of new creation (of understanding of time). It is possible that this concept of time can be measured differently by different people. But unless we talk of the same spread of time, it would not be possible for two people to talk about it. Objectivity means having the same parameter of measurment for all. This parameter of time is at the back of the concept of *laya*. I have talked of measurement of time on the background of mind. But this also would be a very rare case of measurement. Perhaps without some other thing superimposed on time, it would not be possible to measure time in arts. The "time factor" would not be located at all, for time is merely a form constructed out of the same subject matter, and the subject matter is superimposed on it. The matter and form can be regarded as different but they are still inseparable. We get the knowledge of *laya* in music on account of the sound series superimposed on the time series. But this is not the whole story. We not only utter sounds, we can imagine sounds. A man can sing a song silently, i.e. he can make a mental division of time without it being perceived by any other person. That is perhaps the reason why our masters have made a classification of *nāda* into *āhata* and *anāhata* (अनाहत). But the superimposition does not end here. In the case of music, *nāda* (नाद) is changed into *svara* and in the case of language the *svara* is changed into meaningful words. In the case of poetry the words and their meanings are changed into a flow and if the flow is significant it further assumes the form of transcendental vision. Jñāneśvara, a great saint-poet of Maharashtra brings out these steps in the following verse:

वाचे बरवे कवित्व, कवित्वी रसिकत्व।
रसिकत्वीं परतत्त्व स्पर्शु जैसा॥

vāce barave kavitva, kavitvī rasikatva ।
rasikatvīṁ paratattva sparśū jaisā ॥

On account of this equal division of time, we get the concept of *tāla* and on account of the elongation of time we know where the *laya* begins and ends.

Milestones in the History of Dramaturgy and Poetics

The first known and extant work on dramaturgy in Indian tradition is *Nāṭyaśāstra* attributed to Bharata or Bharatamuni. But Maheśvara in his *Kāvyaprakāśādarśa* and Vidyābhūṣaṇa in his *Sāhitya-Kaumudī* say that Bharata summarized *Vahnipurāṇa* and formulated the *kārikā*s of *Nāṭyaśāstra*. Bharatamuni learnt the techniques of *nāṭya* from Pitāmaha Maheśvara. According to another tradition some techniques and theory of stage drama first came from Vāsuki. Vāsuki was a *nāga* which was the name of people belonging to a certain race. It appears that in ancient India, Nāgas were very dominant. In fact, the *Mahābhārata* story in a way, is a story of the defeat of Nāgas. It was by defeating Nāgas that Indraprastha was established on the site of Khāṇḍavaprastha and similarly Hastināpura too was earlier an abode of Nāgas. Even Patañjali (पतञ्जलि) was supposed to be an incarnation of Śeṣa (शेष), who was a Nāga (नाग). It is possible that the Nāgas had developed several cultural traits and might have known teachniques of theatre and drama. But today, the first of known text on dramatic art comes from Bharata.

The tradition of poetics has come down to us from Bhāmaha and Daṇḍin.[10] But Mahāmahopādhyāya Kane refers to *Hṛdayaṅgama* a commentary on *Kāvyādarśa* and informs us that Kāśyapa (काश्यप) and Vararuci (वररुचि) had composed works on poetics before *Kāvyādarśa*. Vararuci was also supposed to be the *avatāra* (अवतार) of Śeṣa (*History of Sanskrit Poetics*, p. 3).

Śrī Śāradātanaya, the author of *Bhāva Prakāśana* says that Nandīkeśvara taught *nāṭya* to Bharata. Several treatises on art are attributed to Kāśyapa. The ancestry of *nāga* is also traced to him. It means that even in the ancient times the concepts of arts and art criticisms were discussed in India.

But today Bharata is the first known author on dramaturgy and so is Bhāmaha on poetics. Perhaps even *Nāṭyaśāstra* might be a compilation of several authors. In *Nāṭyaśāstra*, the techniques of stage-craft are discussed. But in addition are also discussed the different forms of drama, literary criticism and music. Bhāmaha discusses, though not in a systematic manner, some important aspects of poetry. Another important author was Daṇḍin of *Kāvyādarśa*. He was also a very well-

---

10. In *Nāṭyaśāstra* also there are discussions about the theory of poetry under *vāgabhinaya* (vide chapter 2 of this treatise).

known poet. Vāmana's contribution to poetics is significant. Bhāmaha, Daṇḍin and Vāmana talk of *alaṁkāra*; they also talk of *rīti*. Perhaps all important concepts of literature and theatre, including the evaluative concepts can be traced to *Nāṭyaśāstra*. The theories of literature and drama are also discussed in *Agni Purāṇa* and *Viṣṇudharmaottara Purāṇa*. Udbhaṭa, Rudrabhaṭṭa and Rājaśekhara are also important names to be recorded in the theory of poetics. The commentators on all these authors were also very important scholars. The names of Pratihārendurāja and Jayaratha may be mentioned in this connection. Vāmana indeed is a very important author of poetics. It is he who for the first time talks of poetic parameters explicitly, and also distinguishes between parameters of evaluation and constitutive parameters. Another milestone in poetics was achieved by Ānandavardhana.

Abhinavagupta, an important philosopher of Kashmir Pratyabhijñā school wrote a commentary, *Locana*, on *Dhvanyāloka*. He also wrote a commentary on *Nāṭyaśāstra*, called *Abhinavabhāratī*. Unification of *rasa* theory and *dhvani* theory is attributed to Abhinavagupta. Abhinavagupta mentions Śrī Lollaṭa, Śaṅkuka, Bhaṭṭanāyaka and his own *guru* Bhaṭṭatauta. Bhaṭṭanāyaka is also mentioned by several other authors. But his work *Hṛdayadarpaṇa* (or *Sahṛdayadarpaṇa*) is still not found. The theories of Bhaṭṭanāyaka are fascinating but they are available only in extracts. *Kāvyamīmāṁsā* of Rājaśekhara is another important work. The oral tradition says that he tried to explain the *nirmiti prakriyā* or creativity process of poetry. But this particular part of his work is lost. Ānandavardhana is another milestone in the development of the theory of poetry. But although *dhvani* theory got an approval of the majority of paṇḍits, it was not without opposition. Mahimabhaṭṭa was the main opponent of this theory. A mention must be made of

Kuntaka who gave us a theory of *vakrokti*. It was mentioned as one of the embellishments of poetry by authors starting from Bhāmaha. But Kuntaka gave it a central place in his theory. Another Kashmiri paṇḍit, Kṣemendra, has also to be mentionend in this connection. He is well-known for his *aucitya* theory of poetics. Dhanañjaya, the author of *Daśarūpaka*, and his commentator Dhanika also contributed to the theory of drama. King Bhoja is known for his works *Śṛṅgāraprakāśa* and *Samarāṅgaṇasūtradhāra*, a treatise on architecture. Some books on *Śilpaśāstra* attributed to Kāśyapa and an Upaniṣad called *Vāstusūtropaniṣad* (वास्तुसूत्रोपनिषद्) (of *Atharvaveda*), attributed to sage Pippalāda are also found. In Jain tradition Hemacandra, a great scholar wrote several treatises on poetics. The other important authors are Mammaṭa (whose *Kāvyaprakāśa* is a classic), Viśvanātha (the author of *Sāhityadarpaṇa*), Appaya Dīkṣita (the author of *Citramīmāṁsā* and *Kuvalayānanda*), Jagannātha Paṇḍit and Jayadeo (the author of *Candrāloka*). This tradition of philosophers of art and poetry is highly elaborate (see Appendix 2). But, for the present a brief information presented here is enough for an understanding of the theories of literature and art and the way they developed.

2

Psychology of Bhāvas

Bhāvas: Meaning and Types

For the Indian theorists of art stage drama was the paradigm. The central notion in the staging of drama was that of *rasa*. The basic elements in the phenomenon of *rasa* were *bhāvas*. Bharata explained these *rasas* in terms of *bhāvas* which included *sthāyī bhāva, vibhāva, anubhāva, vyabhicārī bhāva* and *sāttvika bhāvas*. They required some organization either in the form of *svabhāva* or *vibhāva*. *Bhāvas* are common both to real life and the artistic process. Bharata explains these different *bhāvas* in the seventh chapter of *Nāṭyaśāstra*. Bharata raises the question, whether that which happens is *bhāva* or that which causes the manifestation of experience (*bhāvayati*, भावयति) is *bhāva*. He answers this question by saying that *bhāva* is that which causes the manifestation, which makes something (that which is in the mind of the poet) explicit. The root *bhu* (√ भू) is used in the sense of *kṛ* (√ कृ). Hence *bhāvita* (भावित), *vāsita* (वासित) and *kṛta* (कृत) — are all synonymous. He then, says further that even in the ordinary usage, *bhāvita* is that which is caused and what we call realities such as "happened" (*bhāvitam*, भावितम्) is actually caused by *gandha, rasa*,[1] etc. Therefore everything is caused. In this explanation, however, there is an important commitment. When he asks the question, whether what

1. *NŚ* 7 Intro.

happens is *bhāva*, or that which is caused is *bhāva*; he admits that in some sense, *bhāva*s are what exist whether they exist on their own or are caused. The natural *bhāva*s are merely the states of affairs. Anything that is, is a *bhāva*. And, therefore, in the theory of drama, where we have to reproduce these *bhāva*s, we can say that *bhāva*s are caused. Nevertheless, what are caused also "are" or exist.

In fact, he himself clarifies this in the verse:

कवेरंतर्गतं भावं भावयन् भावमुच्यते ।

kaverantargataṁ bhāvaṁ bhāvayan bhāvamucyate ।

— *NŚ* 7.2

Here, the word *bhāva* occurs thrice, twice as a noun and once as a verb. It means that *bhāva* is the *manifestation* of something (*bhāva*) *in the poet's mind*. Here, the first *bhāva* is some internal experience of the poet and therefore it is something which actually exists in the poet's mind (although in its own turn, it might have been caused by something else). Bharata uses the word *bhāva* in one more context — when he talks of *hāva* (हाव), *bhāva* (भाव) and *helā* (हेला). Under the *bhāvas*, he considers *vibhāva*s (विभाव) (for in some sense *vibhāva*s are also caused and are kinds of *bhāvas*). We shall deal with *vibhāva* later on. But, the *bhāvas*, which he describes here, are *sthāyī*, *sañcārī* and *anubhāva*. I want to point out that in the world of drama, these are existent in some form. Bharata enumerates them as 49.

एकोनपंचाशदिमे यथावद् भावास्त्र्यवस्था ह्युदिता मया वः ।

ekonapañcāśadime yathāvad bhāvāstryavasthā hyuditā mayā vaḥ ।

— *NŚ* 7.107

STHĀYĪ BHĀVAS

Out of these 49, 8 are *sthāyī bhāvas*. Another eight are *sāttvika* *bhāva*s and thirty-three are *vyabhicārī bhāvas*. The *sthāyī bhāva*s are:

1. Rati (रति) (pleasure)
2. *Hāsya* (हास्य) (laughter)
3. *Śoka* (शोक) (grief)
4. *Krodha* (क्रोध) (anger)
5. *Utsāha* (उत्साह) (enthusiasm)
6. *Bhaya* (भय) (fear)
7. *Jugupsā* (जुगुप्सा) (aversion)
8. *Vismaya* (विस्मय) (wonder)

VYABHICĀRI BHĀVAS

These days, it is a commonplace to regard *bhāva*s as feelings/emotions/emotional moods/sentiments. But, it is none of these. They are merely the states of our atomic behavioural patterns. The *vyābhicāri bhāva*s are as follows:

1. *Nirveda* (निर्वेद) (depression or complete indifference to worldly things)
2. *Glāni* (ग्लानि) (exhaustion or fatigue)
3. *Śaṅkā* (शंका) (doubt, hesitation, supicion)
4. *Asūyā* (असूया) (envy, jealousy, anger, indignation)
5. *Mada* (मद) (intoxication, madness, exhilaration, the inflammation of passion, infatuation)
6. *Śrama* (श्रम) (toil, labour, exertion)
7. *Ālasya* (आलस्य) (idleness, laziness, sloth)
8. *Dainya* (दैन्य) (poverty or miserable stage, also affection, dejection, feebleness)
9. *Cintā* (चिन्ता) (anxiety, sorrowful thought)

10. *Moha* (मोह) (loss of consciousness, fainting, swoon, delusion, confusion, folly, infatuation, astonishment)
11. *Smṛti* (स्मृति) (remembrance, recollection, memory)
12. *Dhṛti* (धृति) (steadiness, constancy, fortitude, resolution, courage)
13. *Vriḍā* (व्रीड़ा) (shame, modesty, bashfulness)
14. *Capalatā* (चपलता) (quickness)
15. *Harṣa* (हर्ष) (joy, delight, pleasure, satisfaction)
16. *Āvega* (आवेग) (uneasiness, excitement, agitation)
17. *Jaḍatā* (जड़ता) (dullness, lethargy)
18. *Garva* (गर्व) (pride, arrogance)
19. *Viṣāda* (विषाद) (dejection, sadness, depression of spirits, despair, languor)
20. *Autsukya* (औत्सुक्य) (anxiety, eagerness, ardent desire, zeal, curiosity)
21. *Nidrā* (निद्रा) (sleep)
22. *Apasmāra* (अपस्मार) (forgetfulness, epilepsy)
23. *Supta* (सुप्त) (sound sleep)
24. *Vibodha* (विबोध) (awakening, becoming conscious)
25. *Amarṣa* (अमर्ष) (non-endurance, intolerance, impatience)
26. *Mati* (मति) (intellect, understanding and judgement)
27. *Vyādhi* (व्याधि) (sickness, ailment)
28. *Unmāda* (उन्माद) (intense passion, madness)
29. *Maraṇa* (मरण) (death)
30. *Trāsa* (त्रास) (frightening)
31. *Vitarka* (वितर्क) (argument, reasoning, guess)
32. *Avahita* (अवहित) (dissimulation, concealment of interest or internal feeling) and

33. *Ugratā* (उग्रता) (fierceness, cruelty, ferociousness, violence)

These are all elements or atomic states or behaviours which are to be staged in a dramatic performance. But they (all of them) do not fall under the class of feelings.

SĀTTVIKA BHĀVAS

In addition to the *sañcārī bhāva*s there are eight *sāttvika bhāva*s. They are:

(1) *Stambha* (स्तम्भ)

(2) *Sveda* (स्वेद)

(3) *Romāñca* (रोमांच)

(4) *Svarabhaṅga* (स्वरभंग)

(5) *Vepathu* (वेपथु)

(6) *Vaivarṇya* (वैवर्ण्य)

(7) *Aśru* (अश्रु)

(8) *Pralaya* (प्रलय)

I feel that these eight *sāttvika bhāva*s are either organic sensations or they come very near to organic sensations. *Sāttvika* literally means that which exists, i.e. belonging to the real world. Even in our ordinary life we experience these *sāttvika bhāva*s and they are manifested in everyone of us in certain given circumstances. In the staging of drama, they need not be naturally produced, i.e. produced by virtue of the skill of the actor. They can be artificially made to appear and the spectators may feel that they were naturally produced by the actors. Without actually enacting them the director could produce the intended effect by virtue of his originality and ingenuity. But they can be naturally produced also, if the actor is talented enough. I shall begin by explaining these *sāttvika bhāva*s first.

1. *Stambha* literally means fixedness, stiffness, numbness, stupefaction. It points to a certain state of mind and if an actor is a good one he can produce this state on his own.
2. *Sveda* literally means perspiration or sweat. This is naturally produced in man on account of the humidity but if one is excited, then also he perspires. A heart patient can also show these signs in some kind of heart-attack. A good actor can produce this on his own.
3. Third is *romāñca*. It literally means the erect standing of the hair on the body, perhaps on account of some glandular secretion like adrenaline. This bodily state can be experienced. This state is also created in excitement, anger, love and so on.
4. The fourth such sensation is called *svarabhaṅga*. In certain emotional state of mind we are not able to speak out our ideas except in broken articulation. Our utterances get thwarted intermittently. A drunken person, a man who is afraid, one who is under the spell of passion, experiences this state of mind. But with excellent acting this can be stimulated.
5. A state very similar to *sveda*, *romāñca* and *svarabhaṅga* is also experienced in *vepathu*, when a person loses his nerve control, slightly trembles, has a tremor or shows signs of sweating. A good actor can exhibit this on his own through acting.
6. The sixth state is that of *vaivarṇya*. It occurs when a man loses his consciousness. He becomes pale, the colour of his body changes, his complexion changes. These are the symptoms when a person either becomes unconscious or is on the way to become unconscious.

7. The seventh is *aśru*. *Aśru* means tears. When one is subjected to certain emotional excitement such as happiness, grief or sympathy, one is in tears. Sometimes, while reading a novel or viewing a scene or when one comes across a real scene of grief tears naturally flow out of one's eyes. In drama, such a thing can be directly enacted. If the actor does it on his own, then it comes under *sāttvika bhāva*.

8. The last such sensation is called *pralaya*. It is a complete nervous breakdown and one may experience this in our actual life too. If an actor shows this by his own skill, then it comes under enacted *sāttvika bhāva*.

Although Bharata has classified this under eight varieties, actually the classification may overlap.

Bharata also talks of *anubhāvas*. They are physiological symptoms accompanying certain inner states of mind. The *sañcārī bhāvas* or the *sthāyī bhāvas* are known to others through these *anubhāvas* only. They are called *anubhāvas* because they follow the *bhāvas*.

The *bhāvas*, *anubhāvas*, *sañcārī bhāvas* and *sāttvika bhāvas* combine themselves in a unique way and lead to behavioural patterns.

Let me now see what the *sthāyī bhāvas* and *vibhāvas* are. In *Naṭyaśāstra*, the following sentence is found:

एवं एते स्थायिनो भावाः रससंज्ञाः प्रत्यगन्तव्याः ।

evaṁ ete sthāyīno bhāvāḥ rasasaṁjñāḥ pratyagantavyāḥ ।

— *NŚ* 7.after 27

This shows that even Bharata had recognized that *rasa* and *sthāyī bhāvas* were modifications or states of identical experience or entity. And, in one sense, there is really no difference in *sthāyī bhāva* and *rasa* except that:

(1) *sthāyī bhāva* can occur in real life experience, whereas *rasas* are artificially made[2] to occur in the world of drama or art.

(2) *rasas* occur on account of the decoding of the poet's mental states or in another sense encoding of the poet's mental states into some form which occupies the stage, i.e. the artists and their movements.

Of the 49 *bhāvas*, the most important of course are *sthāyī bhāvas*. Bharata says:

बह्वनां समवेतानां रुपं यस्य भवेद् बहुः।
स मन्तव्यो रसः स्थायी [शेषाः संचारिणोमताः] ॥

bahūnāṁ samavetānāṁ rūpaṁ yasya bhaved bahuḥ ।
sa mantavyoḥ rasāḥ sthāyī (śeṣāḥ sañcārīṇomatāḥ) ॥ — *NŚ* 7.120

These *sthāyī bhāvas* are mental, i.e. they are mental states. Dhanika, the commentator of Dhanañjaya's *Daśarūpaka* clearly says that *sthāyī bhāvas* are *cittavṛttiviśeṣāḥ*. As a matter of fact, our experience is finally reduced to *sthāyī bhāvas* and one's personality ultimately comprises of the *sthāyī bhāvas*. Whether it be art-communication or the actual communication it is the experience contained by the *sthāyī bhāvas* which is carried from one individual to another and in this transition, *sthāyī bhāvas* take the form of bodily or facial experience or expressed through some medium, e.g. through bodily movements of feelings or sentiments, etc. These *sthāyī bhāvas* are common to an ordinary man as also to an actor. In an ordinary man, these occur naturally. In an actor they are expressed as in the form of imitation of the emotions or other form of experience of some other person.

---

2. If one analyses our experience of communication from one man to another, into medium and message, then one can talk of *rasa*, in actual life also. But, usually, we do not do so. Perhaps, this can be done in a psychology laboratory.

In this transformation, the *sthāyī bhāva*s become objective and take the form of *vyabhicārī bhāvas, anubhāva*s and *sāttvika bhāvas*.

STHĀYĪ BHĀVAS AND RASA

Bharata raises the question that if some of the 49 *bhāva*s of the form of *anubhāva, vyabhicārī bhāva* and also *vibhāva*s participate in the process, then how do we say that only *sthāyī bhāva*s take the form of *rasa*s? Perhaps, in the days of Bharata, what we now call (in communication), decoding and encoding were not known, and, therefore, he had to explain it in some different language. What is experienced, are actually the *vibhāva*s, *anubhāva*s and *vyabhicārī bhāva*s. But, what are conveyed are *sthāyī bhāva*s. These other *bhāva*s are only secondary expressions which point to *sthāyī bhāva*s. Bharata says, just as a king when surrounded by his courtiers alone is known as a king, similarly, the *sthāyī bhāvas*, although in the company of *vibhāva, anubhāva* and *vyabhicārī bhāva*, alone, are known as *rasa*s.

According to Bharata the *sthāyī bhāva*s are eight, i.e. corresponding to each *rasa*, there is one *sthāyī bhāva*, or corresponding to one *sthāyī bhāva* there is one *rasa*. Thus *rati* which is a *sthāyī bhāva* goes with *śṛṅgāra*. *Rati* means pleasure, delight, satisfaction, joy, fondness for, devotion or attachment to. Corresponding to *hāsya*, there is the *sthāyī bhāva* called *hāsa* which again means laughter, smile, joy, merriment. Corresponding to *karuṇa* there is *sthāyī bhāva śoka*, which means sorrow, grief, distress, affliction, lamentation or anguish. Then, comes *krodha* which is wrath, anger, etc. Then comes *utsāha*, which is at the back of *vīra*. Similarly, *bhaya* or fear which also stands for alarm, dread, apprehension, fright, terror, risk, hazard, etc. is what leads to *bhayānaka rasa*. *Jugupsā* which means keeping something secret, censure, reproach, dislike, aversion or disgust, gives rise to *bībhatsa rasa*. *Vismaya* or wonder, surprise, astonishment, amazement or pride is at the back of the *rasa* known as *adbhuta*. In addition to these eight, people have added *nirveda* which is complete indifference to worldly objects. This is a psychological state giving rise to *rasa* known as *śānta*. But there can be some additional patterns of mental states giving rise to different *rasa*, such as *bhakti*, *prakṣobha*, *vidroha* and the like.

STHĀYĪ BHĀVAS AND MENTAL STATES

It is necessary to point out here that the mental states need not be pure states having one *sthāyī bhāva*. They can consist of more states (than one) as I have pointed out elsewhere. What is known as *kavi-antargata-bhāva* is a gestalt of one such complex. Sometimes, the artist has to select only a part of this complex and present it in the form of an art object. We have, for example, pointed out that when Vālmīki cursed the hunter (in the form of a verse) *mā niṣāda pratiṣṭhaṁ tvam* (मा निषाद प्रतिष्ठां त्वम्) etc. and composed *Rāmāyaṇa*, what was objectified in the art object was not all of his experience nor all his feelings. Although his feelings gave rise to the poem, it was only the select part of Vālmīki's experience which took the objective form of a poem.

One more thing has to be clarified. *Sthāyī bhāva*s literally mean those mental existents which endure in time. They can be complex states but they need not always be of the nature of emotions. Although emotions play a very important role in our life, our life activities do not consist of emotions alone, and for Bharata and his followers *sthāyī bhāva*s represented a much wider canvas than can be depicted by emotions. But, perhaps, when poetry became dominantly emotional, the emotions did not merely remain emotions qua emotions. At some stage, they developed into sentiments. Since in this process of art-communication, the *sthāyī bhāva*s developed into *rasa*s, people began to think that *rasa*s also are mental and therefore, they stand for taste or sentiments or even happiness; but Bharata does not seem to have any of these things in his mind. *Rasa,* for Bharata and his followers, was connected with the process of making this experience public. Otherwise in his sixth chapter of *Nāṭyaśāstra* he would not have asked the question, *kāthām āsvādyate rasāḥ.*

In the context of drama, *sthāyī bhāva* thus should strictly mean that persistent meaning or sense or poet's idea arising from poet's experience and which continues to associate with the stage. It is necessary to remember that, in drama too, as in ordinary language there are symbolic expressions and there are meanings of these symbolic expressions. If the two do not go together, the whole gamut of drama would be meaningless. It is really strange that most writers have completely ignored the fact that Bharata persistently uses the expressions *artha* and *saṁjñā* and adds that *sthāyī bhāva*s are *rasasaṁjñā,* i.e. those (meanings) of which the symbols are *rasa* (*Nāṭyaśāstra,* p. 112 — Nirṇaya-Sāgar edition). Similarly, he stated that in the dramatic process no "sense" or meaning could be had without *rasa.*

न हि रसादृते कश्चिदपि अर्थः प्रवर्तते।

na hi rasādṛte kaścidapi arthaḥ pravartate ।

He again repeats the word *artha,* in describing *sthāyī bhāva* in the *Kārikā.*

योऽर्थो हृदयसंवादी तस्य भावो रसोद्भवः।

yo 'rtho hṛdayasaṁvādī tasya bhāvo rasodbhavaḥ ।

— *NŚ* 7.7

If this fact is taken into account then alone the meaning of verse 39 in chapter 6 of *Nāṭyaśāstra* would be clear that the meanings or *bhāva*s (for appreciator) emerge from *rasa*s. It is unfortunate that almost every writer of Indian rhetoric thought that *sthāyī bhāva*s stand for certain "emotional states" or sentiments. It is certainly a mental state, a *citta vṛttiviśeṣaḥ* as Dhanika has clearly stated. It must not be forgotten that Bharata is only describing the process of stage communication, though this process presupposes the mental states which influence the stage process. And this is certainly the reaction to experience. In such a process, poetry is taken for granted and translated in stage language. It is absolutely necessary to bear in mind that Bharata gives the list or *saṁgraha* of elements which are connected with the stage. Every symbol or art object has a meaning, but on the stage, different "art" objects present a continuum of meaning. It is this meaning-continuum which gives a homogeneous meaning to drama, which is *sthāyī bhāva* and which, in its turn, is a persistent mental state of the author. Just, as in ordinary language, a sentence meaning is different from the meaning of words, so in dramatic language a totality of art objects leads to a sort of collective sense which is *sthāyī bhāva*, or *kāvyārtha*. In being of the nature of cognition or meaning, it is related with stage symbols on the one hand and with the spectator on the other. Bharata is aware of this (Ref. *NŚ* 27/87).

It is this which makes it *hṛdayasaṁvādī*. That the *sthāyī bhāva* as referred to in drama is something connected with the stage will be clear from the verses 52 and the following in chapter 8 of the *Nāṭyaśāstra*.

STHĀYĪ BHĀVAS AND ARTHA

There is absolutely no doubt that Bharata uses the terms *sthāyī bhāva* and *kāvyārtha* as identical. If we look at passage 1 in Chapter

6 he writes: *vāgaṅga sattvopetān sthāyibhāvān* (वागंग सत्त्वोपेतान् स्थायिभावान्), i.e. *sthāyī bhāvas* which take the form of *vāgaṅgasattva abhinaya* on the stage. In chapter seven, he writes:

वागंग सत्त्वोपेतं काव्यार्थम् ।
vāgaṅga-sattvopetānkāvyārthām । — *NŚ* 7 intro.

that it is the *kāvyārtha* which has taken the form of *vāgaṅga sattva abhinaya*. The loose use of the two words *kāvyārtha* and *sthāyī bhāva* is unfortunate; for, they have different significance in different arts. Nevertheless, this loose use of the two words gives a clue to the understanding of the notion of *sthāyī bhāva*. *Sthāyī bhāvas*, essentially being "meanings" cannot be one in poetry and another in staged drama. If the essential identity of *sthāyī bhāva* and *kāvyārtha* is taken into account, some of the apparent contradictions in Bharata's writings are removed. The staged drama is essentially a translation of a "form of literature" into a "form of presentation." This is the translation of poetic meaning in stage symbols. The stage symbols again yield a meaning which is equivalent to poetic meaning. *Sthāyī bhāvas*, considered as meaning, then, are both prior and posterior to stage symbol or as I understand by it, *rasa*. Thus, *in the process of the creation* of dramatic art, *sthāyī bhāva* (*kāvyārtha*) leads to *rasa*, and *in the process of appreciation* and understanding of staged drama, *rasa* leads to *sthāyī bhāva*. When the *sthāyī bhāvas* or *kāvyārthas* take the form of different *bhāvas*, they become *rasa*.

Nānābhāvopagatā api sthāyino bhāvāḥ rasatvam āpnuvanti (नानाभावोपगता अपि स्थायिनो भावाः रसत्वम् आप्नुवन्ति) (*NŚ* 6) and it is these *sthāyī bhāvas* which exist in *vāgaṅga sattva abhinaya*, that the spectators enjoy (*vāgaṅga sattvopetān sthāyibhāvān āsvādayanti sumanasaḥ prekṣakāḥ*) (*NŚ* 6).

Vibhāvas

In the seventh chapter of *Nāṭyaśāstra* Bharata also describes *vibhāva, anubhāva, sthāyī bhāva, sañcārī bhāva* and *sāttvika bhāvas*. (Out of these we have already discussed *sañcārī* or *vyābhicārī bhāva, sthāyī* and *sāttvika bhāvas*). We shall here discuss *vibhāvas* and *anubhāvas*. He asks the question, what is *vibhāva* and he answers, *vibhāva* is the object of *vijñāna*. He explains this further by using the words *kāraṇa, nimitta* and *hetu* (कारण, निमित्त, हेतु).

विभावो नाम विज्ञानार्थः।
विभावः कारणं निमित्तं हेतुः इति पर्यायः॥
विभाव्यन्ते अनेन वागंगसत्त्वाभिनयः इति विभावः।
यथा विभावितं विज्ञातम् इति अनर्थान्तरम्॥

vibhāvo nāma vijñānārthaḥ ।
vibhāvaḥ kāraṇaṁ, nimittaṁ, hetuḥ iti paryāyaḥ ॥
vibhāvyante anena vāgaṅgasattvābhinayaḥ iti vibhāvaḥ ।
yathā vibhāvitaṁ vijñātam iti anarthāntaram ॥

— *NŚ* 7.after 3

Here, the word *vibhāva* is used in the sense of the cause of manifestation. At other places he says, *ātmābhinayanaṁ bhāvaḥ, vibhāvaḥ paradarśanam* (आत्माभिनयनं भावः विभावः परदर्शनम्) [*NŚ* 25.40].

TYPES OF VIBHĀVAS

In these two passages, there appears to be some discrepancy. *Vibhāva* is a technical term used in the context of drama, and usually the *vibhāvas* are of two types. They are classified as *uddīpana vibhāva* and *ālambana vibhāva*. *Ālambana vibhāvas* are those on which the drama basically depends. *Uddīpana vibhāvas* are those which help the successful performance of the dramatic scenes or acts. For example, the actors in the drama are *ālambana vibhāvas*. Bharata says that *vibhāvas* and *anubhāvas* are *lokaprasiddha* and so he would not define them.

तत्र विभावानुभावौ लोकप्रसिद्धौ।
लोकस्वभावानुगतत्वाच्च तयोर्लक्षणं न उच्यते।

tatra vibhāvānubhāvau lokaprasiddhau ।
lokasvabhāvānugatatvācca tayorlakṣaṇam na uccyate ।
NŚ 7.after 5

भवति च अत्र श्लोकः।
लोकस्वभावसंसिद्धाः लोकयात्रानुगामिनः।
अनुभावा विभावाश्च ज्ञेयास्त्वभिनये बुधैः।

bhavati ca atra ślokaḥ ।
lokasvabhāva saṁsiddhāḥ lokayātrānugāminaḥ ।
anubhāvāvibhāvāśca jñeyāstvabhinaye budhaiḥ ॥ — *NŚ* 7.6

But at other places he contrasts *vibhāva* with *svabhāva*.

स्वभावो लोकधर्मी तु विभावो नाट्यमेव हि।

svabhāvo lokadharmī tu vibhāvo nāṭyameva hi ।
NŚ 21.193

He also brings in the concept of *pātra* which literally means a pot. If we take *vibhāva* as a pot then it would mean the actor devoid of his original *bhāvas*. If we mean by it as one having special *bhāvas* then it would mean that the actor has only suppressed or concealed his *bhāvas* for exhibiting the *bhāvas* of some other persons.

It will be interesting to see how Bharata proceeds further. *Vibhāva* is infact the *karaṇa* (instrument) or the substratum which supports the imitation. That it is "substratum" and the instrument may not be clear from Bharata's words, for he does not use the word *karaṇa* but only uses *nimitta*, *hetu* and *kāraṇa*. *Vibhāvāḥ kāraṇam nimittam hetuḥ iti paryāyāḥ* (विभावः कारणं निमित्तं हेतुः इति पर्यायाः) (*NŚ* 7.after 3). But in the next sentence, this becomes clear, for he makes use of the *instrumental* case while explaining the meaning of *vibhāva*. And the instrumental case is used in the sense of *karaṇa* (*vibhāvyante anena,* विभाव्यन्ते अनेन) *NŚ* 7.after 3. Perhaps the Nyāya classification of *nimitta kāraṇa* into *karaṇa* and the rest did not exist when Bharata wrote his treatise. It is interesting to note that Bharata thinks that *vibhāva*s produce, i.e. in a sense lead to, *sthāyī bhāva*s. He always uses the word *samutpadyate* (समुत्पद्यते) when he wants to state that a certain *sthāyī bhāva* is produced by a certain *vibhāva*. *Vibhāva*s are to be understood as substrata only so far as they refer to living beings. In so far as they refer to the environment, they are only instruments. But, *ālambana vibhāva* as well as *uddīpana vibhāva* can be regarded as instruments. (It is an instrument if imitation is considered in active aspect, substratum if considered in the passive aspect.)

The concept of *vibhāva* is very complicated and difficult to grasp. So, its significance should be carefully studied. It is not only the "actor" and the environment that are *vibhāva*s, but also relations between several actors on the one hand and the actors and the environment on the other that are *vibhāva*s. Thus, a separation of the beloved person is a *vibhāva*. It is a sort of a fulcrum which may hold actors, environments and their bodily exhibitions together. It is necessary to understand that the concept of "separation" cannot be regarded as a *bhāva*. *Bhāva* is a physical or mental state of an individual. Thus, happiness or pain, the smile (not the bodily symptoms of smile, which are *anubhāva*s) or weeping, the state of swoon or the state of death — all these can be regarded as *bhāva*s or *vyabhicārī bhāva*s, but "the separation . . ." cannot be so regarded.

Anubhāvas

The *anubhāva*s, however, are not causes. They are bodily reactions by which *vibhāva*s and the *bhāva*s are understood or recognized. When somebody weeps or laughs, the physical counterpart of what is called the state of weeping or laughing, is understood in its passive or objective aspect. It is *anubhāva*. This, as a matter of routine, exists in a natural stage and is artificially created in imitation, pretending or drama. That is why Bharata calls it : *lokayātrānugāmin* (लोकयात्रानुगामिन्). It is necessary to realize that there is hardly any difference between *anubhāva* and *abhinaya* understood as effects. It is, however, the *abhineyatva* which distinguishes the one from the other. It is the potential ability which acts as incentive and produces certain bodily symptoms or states known as *anubhāva*s.

3

Theories of Poetry

The Basic Parameters of Literature

In my scheme of investigation I should deal with all arts and their parameters. But, I shall begin not with arts but with literature. I have a justification for it. In the first place, literature itself is a kind of an art. Although there are differences between literature and other arts, both plastic and performing, there are a good many similarities between them. Moreover, the basic concepts, which are developed in the Indian tradition, are more in regard to literature than in regard to other arts. I am aware that in ancient India not only literature but music, painting, sculpture and architecture did develop and there are volumes which discuss "music" and "architecture," *saṅgīta* (संगीत) and *sthāpatya* (स्थापत्य). But, whereas the critics of literature discussed the constituent and evaluative standards in regard to literature, they did not discuss the evaluative or value standards of either music or painting or architecture directly. The reason, perhaps, is that, in arts other than literature, the evaluative standards cannot be clearly discerned. Therefore, I should better take into consideration the basic parameters of literature, for they would not only apply to literature but also to other arts.

Our literary tradition began from the Vedic times and continues even today. Our tradition of literary criticism also has its roots in ancient times and has progressed without any break. In this second tradition, namely the tradition of criticism, there are a few primary stages or turning points which take our thought from one level to another. At times, such a theory of criticism develops in several directions, simultaneously. I shall try to discuss some of these milestones in regard to literary theory. A word of caution may be necessary. In the course of time not only the meanings of the words changed but also the meanings of concepts behind words changed. Therefore, many times we cannot make out what our ancient thinkers had to say. It will be my effort to get at their intention and theories behind what they say.

Nāṭya or Drama

Sage Bharata is regarded as the pioneer of all literary theories. A treatise on dramaturgy called *Nāṭyaśāstra* (नाट्यशास्त्र) is attributed to him. It is on the performing techniques of drama. In the ancient tradition the term *nāṭya* stood not only for drama but for dance also. There is positively a difference between a drama text and a drama that we perform in a theatre. Another important point is that we do not know whether Bharata is a single individual or a name of our dramatic tradition. In case the name Bharata indicates a tradition there would be many Bharatas and what we call *Nāṭyaśāstra* today, could be a compilation of the then current drama practices.[1]

Rūpaka

In the ancient past the text that is used for theatrical performance was called *rūpaka* and not *nāṭaka*. Bharata himself talks of ten types of *rūpaka*s. Dhanañjaya also discusses them

---

1. Perhaps there was one more drama tradition which goes in the name of Vāsuki. A large part of it is however extinct.

in his treatise, *Daśarūpaka*. In fact, Bharata's theory is confined to Dramaturgy only. But, it was gradually applied to all forms of literature and Bharata was regarded as the pioneer not only of the techniques of drama but also of poetics in general.

Contents of Nāṭyaśāstra

The concepts which Bharata has discussed in his treatise are primarily *rasa* (रस), *bhāva* (भाव) and *abhinaya* (अभिनय). By *abhinaya*, he meant acting, in the context of performing drama. He also uses the concepts, *dharmi* (धर्मि), *vṛtti* (वृत्ति) and *pravṛtti* (प्रवृत्ति). Again, he talks of music and instruments (*vādya*, वाद्य). The concept of *saṅgīta* has been described in our tradition as consisting of vocal and instrumental music and dance: *gītaṁ vādyaṁ ca nṛtyaṁ ca trayaṁ saṅgītam ucyate* (गीतं वाद्यं च नृत्यं च त्रयं संगीतम् उच्यते) (*SR*). He also talks of two types of *siddhi* (सिद्धि), the fulfilment of which is regarded as the ultimate objective of drama.

ABHINAYA AND POETRY

Bharata classifies *abhinaya* under four heads, *vāk* (वाक्), *sattva* (सत्त्व), *aṅga* (अंग) and *āhārya* (आहार्य). *Vāgabhinaya* (वागभिनय) is concerned with speech and dialogues. It is in this context that Bharata talks of poetry and its different embellishments. In course of time this original thought of Bharata got slightly brushed aside and the concepts of *rasa* and *bhāva* became more significant and were also used in the context of poetry. Today, when people think of the concepts of poetry and poetic criticism, it is *rasa* and *bhāva*, which are in their mind. Perhaps, this change came over at the time of Rudrabhaṭṭa.[2] Poetry is classified under two types :

(1) That which is heard (*śravya*)

(2) That which is seen (*dṛśya*)

2. Rudrabhaṭṭa is different from Rudraṭa.

DANCE AND DRAMA

Dance and drama come under the second head. These two performing arts have been evolved by men in the earlier stage of civilization. Audible poetry could be a later development. This transition is very important for tracing the development of the *rasa* theory. I do not find that the concept of *rasa* was applied in the context other than drama in earlier times. In staging a drama two processes are involved: first the actual process of production. This may be called the process of creation or *nirmiti prakriyā*. The second process is the actual performance on the stage before the audience, the resultant of the creative process. This is known as the process of appreciation or *āsvāda prakriyā*. These two processes are experienced in the case of visual arts — dance and drama. But in the case of poetry, the first process, the process of creation is hidden though it exists. The only thing that we can say is that poetry is the outcome of imagination and creativity of the poet. With the introduction of Freudian psychology and discovery of the unconscious and subconscious mind, today we might be able to explain the process of creation. But, nothing of this kind was possible in the ancient past. So, whereas one could evaluate the proper poetry one could not say anything about the creative process of poetry which was inspired and brought to form by a poet. In the case of stage drama on the other hand one has to translate the text of the drama into the stage language, and therefore the technique of staging takes the form of creative process and assumes importance. In the case of some performing arts at least, like drama, one could even say that it is born thrice. Initially, when it is created by the one who composes the text; the second time, when it is visualized by the director or *sūtradhāra* and, the third time, when it is actually performed by the actors. The director conceives the performance and the actors give it a visual form which is watched and appreciated by the audience. In the case of poetry, the happenings in the poet's mind can only be inferred. But, they are private. The poetry is known as poetry when it is made public and is presented to us in the actual (sound or sign) form. The poet's creativity consists in encoding of his experiences. But, the stage between experiencing and the encoding is kept away from us. We are in the dark about what happens in the poet's mind. When we read the poem that is produced, we are primarily concerned with the meaning of the composition, and we only *infer* about the intention of the poet. When I say "meaning of the composition" I am aware that it is not merely the meaning in terms of our conventional language, we are certainly concerned with the meaning and/or sound patterns which form a whole. But the poet's intentions always remain in the background and are hidden. The staging of a drama on the other hand is an open process. The stage director has to use the talents of the actors and the stage apparatus in order to make the scenes *animated,* i.e. the director has first to decode what is encoded by the play-wright in a language or script and encode it again in a language of drama. In decoding, he is in fact decoding the mind of the writer and in encoding again he is translating the writer's language into a drama language. Thus, in the case of stage drama the process of creation and process of tasting-cum-evaluating can be separated from the process of creating. This does not happen in pure audible poetry.

The Main Authors and their Theories

While discussing the development of poetic theory, I shall have to discuss along with Bharata, Bhāmaha and Vāmana, Ānandavardhana and Bhaṭṭanāyaka. I would not mention other writers because although their contribution to the poetic theory is substantial, I wonder whether it is significant philosophically. It is rather a development of details. They did not propound any thesis which brought about some revolutionary change in our attitude to look at the poetic theory. The theories which these and other masters propounded can be grouped mainly as *rīti, alaṁkāra, vakrokti, rasa, dhvani* and *aucitya*. It may be pointed out that most of these theories were not exclusive or independent. There was quite a lot of criss-crossing and many a time a philosopher did hold and accept more than one aspect from one theory and some other aspects from the other. Thus, most philosophers of poetry seem to hold *alaṁkāra* and *rīti, rasa* and *aucitya, rasa* and *dhvani* or *alaṁkāra* and *vakrokti* together. Similarly, the theory of *aucitya* seems consistently to be held along with any or all of these concepts. But, as each of these six concepts had something specific to say, although their domain overlapped many a time, I prefer to treat them separately at least for some time.

Drama vs. Literature

Bharata has been regarded as the first systematic writer on poetics and this belief is confirmed and reconfirmed ever since the *rasa*-theory of poetics, particularly formulated by Abhinavagupta, has come to stay. There is no doubt that Bharata is the first known writer on poetics, but I think that it is not for the reasons held by the protagonists of *rasa*-theory of poetics. Bharata's *rasa* theory was essentially a theory in dramaturgy and whether it was *rasa* or *bhāva* or *vṛtti* or *pravṛtti*, Bharata's theory was primarily concerned with stage drama, and, therefore, with acting and what took place on the stage. However, while one enumerates and analyses the elements in drama and develops a theory about it, one incidentally develops a theory of poetics also both directly and indirectly.

This has also happened in the case of Bharata, directly because in the variety of *abhinayas*, *vācika abhinaya* occupies a significant place and requires a certain text which has to fulfil the criterion (*mānadaṇḍa*) of literature. Bharata himself has very clearly stated in the fourteenth chapter that the *abhinaya* which takes the form of language is an important feature of acting. It is the body of stage drama *nāṭyasyeyaṁ tanuḥ smṛtā* (नाट्यस्येयं तनुः स्मृता) (*NŚ* 14.2). He further says that both *aṅga* and *nepathya* are useful only in so far as they enrich the meaning of sentences — *aṅganepathyatattvāni vākyārthaṁ vyañjayanti* (अंगनेपथ्यतत्त्वानि वाक्यार्थं व्यंजयन्ति) (*NŚ* 14.2).

Bharata's Mode of Theorization

It is also my feeling that concepts like *rasa*, *vṛtti* and *pravṛtti* help building a literary theory; because, they represent a certain form, picturesque or visual in the form of *rasa* and stylistic in the form of *vṛtti* and *pravṛtti*. However, Bharata gives the theory of literature directly under the *vāg-abhinaya*. I shall omit certain parts of his discussions under *vāg-abhinaya* (which are unimportant in this context) and deal only with those parts which are directly concerned with literature proper. For example, in giving the theory about literature he deals with grammar too. He talks of vowels and consonants and how they are combined into words and sentences. He also talks of nouns and the forms they take through cases and also talks of indeclinables *avyaya* and *kāraka*s (अव्यय, कारक). At some point, he also talks of metres, *chanda*s (छन्द) which in a way are important for the development of poetry. He also gives the definitions of metres and enumerates several of them like *mālinī* (मालिनी), *vaṅśastha* (वंशस्थ), *rathoddhatā* (रथोद्धता), *krauñcapada* (क्रौंचपद), *āryā* (आर्या), etc. He lays down that the poetic structure should be composed in such metres. No such discussions have any direct bearing upon literature proper.

But, in the sixteenth *adhyāya* he talks of the embellishments and meaning of poetry. He also talks of *kāvya-guṇa* (काव्य-गुण) and *kāvya-doṣa* (काव्य-दोष).

Bharata's Context : Stage Drama

Let me in the beginning itself point out that the literary composition he talks of is only in the context of stage drama in so far as it supplies the material for stage. For, as Bharata has very clearly said, the literary composition is, in fact, the main body of stage drama. It is this body which is to be given a form suitable for the stage. Of course, the literary composition may be in the form of prose or poetry. And so one has to consider naturally both the essential and aesthetic elements in prose and poetry. It must be noted that it is in these forms that we get the patterns of sounds and patterns of meanings. The greater the harmony between these two patterns, the greater excellence a literary composition attains. But, although, sounds act as symbols for the meanings, it is not necessary that with every embellishment connected with sound there should necessarily be a similar embellishment in the meaning pattern. In other words, there need not be any isomorphism between the sound patterns and meaning patterns. But, it must also be realized that the excellence of the literary artist depends on the extent to which he is able to harmonize this correlation also. One can then say that isomorphism between the sound-patterns and the meaning-patterns is one of the objectives of literary art. What is true of literary arts is also true in equal measure of all arts. Only in the case of these arts, instead of sound-patterns and meaning-patterns, we will have to substitute the concept of medium and artist's intention. But, the harmony or the isomorphism between the sound symbols and their meaning is only contingent. This can well be seen by referring to either the music of the sound-patterns or the metre of the sound-patterns and to such embellishments and *anuprāsa* (अनुप्रास)and *yamaka* (यमक). In Jaideva's poetry for example, the softness of the use of sounds can be experienced in *virahati haririha sarasavasante* (विहरति हरिरिह सरसवसन्ते) (GG). Every *svara* here is *komala*. Even in the grammatical language we have to say that it is only a soft consonant. But, the softness of sound or consonant has nothing to do with the meaning. Similarly, in Jagannātha's composition in *Aśvadhāti* you can notice a rhythm, a music. But it does not seem to have any correlation with the beauty or the sublimity of meaning. A composition of sounds may itself look very beautiful and one may perhaps want it for its own sake. Appaya Dīkṣita's composition *naivaṁ sudhāṁśuḥ kiṁ tarhi vyomagaṅgā saroruham* (नैवं सुधांशुः किं तर्हि व्योमगंगा सरोरुहम्) (*KN*) for example demonstrates the *āroha* (आरोह) and *avaroha* (अवरोह) corresponding to the ripples in the water. But, the emerging meaning-patterns are not dependent on such word-patterns. We can, therefore, distinguish meaning-patterns in art activities and corresponding sound-patterns which are media for the meanings. Perhaps, a literary composer has to make use of these different patterns with a view to fusing them ultimately into the pattern of meaning. This concept of fusion is intensely aimed at when the patterns of acting (*āṅgika* and *sāttvika abhinaya*) are fused with *vācika abhinaya* in one whole. Since the embellishments of sounds are not the necessary elements in poetic composition, I shall leave them for the time being and shall return to them when I discuss poetic qualities of *guṇa*s.

Rūpakas

The text which is to be exhibited on stage is naturally a text for the visual art, or what Bharata calls the *rūpaka*s. The text which is *itivṛtti* (इतिवृत्ति) thus takes the form of *rūpaka*. It is a literary form which is suitable for stage exhibition. Bharata classifies these *rūpaka*s into ten varieties. The most evolved form of these is *nāṭaka*. The other forms are *bhāva* (भाव), *samaya kāla* (समय काल), *tithi* (तिथि), *prahasana* (प्रहसन), *ḍima* (डिम), *ihāmṛga* (इहामृग), *prakaraṇa* (प्रकरण), *aṅka* (अंक) and *nyāyoga* (न्यायोग). Of these, I have a feeling that *nāṭaka* corresponds to the Greek-tragedy. On account of the Shakespearean form of tragedy given by A.C. Bradley the original form of tragedy is lost sight of by us. But in the original Greek form it was not necessary that tragedy would have an unhappy ending such as death. Those dramas which exhibit man's helplessness against the supernatural and point out that the prosperity or adversity of man was totally dependent on the supernatural forces or destiny were classed under tragedy. Some of the old Greek tragedies like *Electra* conform to this hypothesis and it is also accepted by the litterateurs and literary critics of Europe. On this basis, if we examine some of our important *nāṭaka*s, for example, *Abhijñānaśākuntalam*, *Uttararāmacarita*, *Mṛcchakaṭika*, etc. we find that they are tragedies, because the whole development of dramas is steered by the will of the supernatural. For example, in *Abhijñānaśākuntalam* although Duṣyanta and Śakuntalā were in love with each other the love was affected by the memory pattern. The tragedy occurs in the first instance because whereas Śakuntalā retains her memory intact, Duṣyanta loses his memory on account of the curse from Durvāsā and because Śakuntalā is not able to present as an evidence of her marriage, the royal ring that Duṣyanta had presented her. The second part of the tragedy begins when the fisherman finds the ring and presents it to the king. The king then regains his lost memory. So whether there is a final union of Śakuntalā and Duṣyanta, the whole play is developed around the concept of helplessness of man, although he may be born of royal family. In the light of this, it will be interesting to see the particular aspect in definition of *nāṭaka* given by Bharata, He says,

प्रख्यातवस्तुविषये प्रख्यातोदात्तनायकं चैव ।
राजर्षिवंशचरितं तथैव दिव्याश्रयोपेतम् ॥

prakhyātavastuviṣaye prakhyātodāttanāyakaṁ caiva ।
rajarṣivaṁśa-caritaṁ tathaiva divyāśrayopetam ॥ — *NŚ* 18.10

The words, *tathaiva divyāśrayopetam* deserve to be specially understood. Similarly, in another stanza Bharata writes:

नृपतीनां यच्चरितं नानारसभावसम्भृतं बहुधा ।
सुखदुःखोत्पत्तिकृतं भवति हि तन्नाटकं नाम ॥

nṛpatīnāṁ yaccaritaṁ nānārasabhāvasambhṛtaṁ bahudhā ।
sukhaduḥkkhotpatti-kṛtaṁ bhavati hi tannāṭakaṁ nāma ॥
— *NŚ* 18-12

So, evidently, the *nāṭaka* may give rise either to happiness (*sukha*) or to misery (*duḥkha*). Today, in Indian languages in general and in Marathi in particular, the word *nāṭaka* has become a synonym of the word *rūpaka* and we have forgotten the import of *nāṭaka* of Bharata's concept.

Beautiful in the Text

When Bharata deals with the text or the *pāṭhya* of the *rūpaka*s he naturally deals with the qualities (the embellishments) that make the text beautiful. He, thus, calls his 16th chapter as *alaṁkāra lakṣaṇa* (अलंकार लक्षण) and says that just as full bloomed lotuses, when they are interspersed with swans, appear beautiful, similarly, poetic compositions when they are beautified with soft, generous, sweet words, appear beautiful. He, thus, explains the embellishments of language which make the poetry beautiful. *Hetu* (हेतु), *saṁśaya* (संशय), *dṛṣṭānta* (दृष्टान्त) and *śobhā* (शोभा) are such embellishments (*NŚ* 16.1, 122). He talks of 36 varieties of *kāvya vibhūṣaṇa* or embellishments, *ṣaṭtriṁśat* (*NŚ* 15.172) and again *ṣaṭtriṁśattu uddeṣyanidarśanāni* (षटत्रिंशत्तु उद्देश्यनिदर्शनानि) (*NŚ* 16.42); of these he discusses four basic *alaṁkāras* (अलंकार), *upamā* (उपमा), *dīpaka* (दीपक), *rūpaka* (रूपक) and *yamaka* (यमक):

> उपमा दीपकं चैव रूपकं यमकं तथा।
> काव्यस्यैते ह्यलंकाराश्चत्वारः परिकीर्तिताः।
>
> *upamā dīpakaṁ caiva rūpakaṁ yamakam tathā* ।
> *kāvyasyaite hyalaṁkārāścatvārah parikīrtitāḥ* ॥ *NŚ* 16.43

After discussing *alaṁkāras* he discusses the *kāvya doṣas* or demerits of poetry. He enumerates them as ten. This may be arbitrary:

> गूढार्थमर्थान्तरम् अर्थहीनं भिन्नार्थमेकार्थमभिप्लुतार्थम्।
> न्यायादपेतं विषमं विसन्धि शब्दच्युतं वै दश काव्यदोषाः॥
>
> *gūḍhārthamarthāntaram arthahīnaṁ bhinnārthamekārthamabhi-plutārtham* ।
> *nyāyādapetaṁ viṣamaṁ visandhi śabdacyutaṁ vai daśa kāvyadoṣāḥ* ॥ *NŚ* 16.89

That is, if the meaning of poetic composition is unintelligible or mystifying, if it means something else, if it is meaningless, if it means different things, if it is *ekārtha* (synoymous) similarly, if it is *abhipluta* (translation) *artha*, if it is without any basis, if it has a faulty metre, if it has a word which is unfitting to the diction, if a word which ought to be used is not used — all these are regarded as demerits of a poetic composition. Similarly, he describes ten merits of poetry. They are *śleṣa* (श्लेष), *prasāda* (प्रसाद), *samatā* (समता), *samādhl* (समाधि), *mādhurya* (माधुर्य), *aujas* (ओजस), *padasaukumārya* (पदसौकुमार्य), *arthavyakti* (अर्थव्यक्ति), *udāratā* (उदारता) and *kānti* (कान्ति) (*NŚ* 16.97). Since all these are discussed later by Vāmana and others, I need not discuss them here. I would only like to point out, however, that in some context, whatever is demerit may become a merit of a poetic composition in some other context. For example, between *śleṣa* and *bhinnārtha*, there does not appear to be a qualitative difference but one becomes merit and the other becomes demerit.

I would, specifically, point to one important reference, viz. *śobhā* (*NŚ* 16.8). I feel this has the germs of *dhvani* theory in it. I may, of course, agree that accredited *alaṁkārin*s also discuss the concept of *śobhā*. Bharata explains *śobhā* as follows: where the known and accepted meaning leads to the meanings which are not directly indicated and where the unindicated meaning is something unusual and beautiful it is called *śobhā*. He also discusses the other things such as *bhūṣaṇa* (भूषण), *akṣara* (अक्षर), *saṁghāta* (संघात), *udāharaṇa* (उदाहरण), *hetu* (हेतु), *saṁśaya* (संशय), *dṛṣṭānta* (दृष्टान्त) and *prāptābhiprāya* (प्राप्ताभिप्राय). Since all these are discussed by later *alaṁkārins*, I have only mentioned them. I do not exclude the possibility that some of them might have been interpolations, but one thing remains certain that the *Nāṭyaśāstra* discusses the things which are to be discussed with reference to the text of a poetic composition.

Alaṁkāra : A Parameter of Poetry

Alaṁkāra theory is perhaps the earliest theory of poetics and was advocated by most of the rhetoricians like Bhāmaha, Daṇḍin, etc. In fact, as we have seen in the previous section, Bharata also referred to *alaṁkāra* while considering the *pāṭhya* or *itivṛtta* and *vācika abhinaya*. But, Bhāmaha is, perhaps, the first well-known exponent of the *alaṁkāra* theory. Daṇḍin, Vāmana and several others including the Jain authors like Rāmacandra, Guṇacandra and Hemacandra also wrote on *alaṁkāra*. But, it was Vāmana who took a distinctive leap and pointed out that *alaṁkāra*, in its primary sense meant a parameter. His theory was, therefore, the theory of poetic parameter. He distinguished between *guṇa*s and *alaṁkāras*. He pointed out that *alaṁkāra*, as we ordinarily understand, is its secondary sense. According to him, *guṇa*s are a necessary condition of poetry. But, *alaṁkāra*s in the secondary sense are not necessary, although they give additional splendour to poetry. Bhāmaha was the predecessor of Vāmana. He compared poetry to the face of a beautiful woman and said that although a woman may be beautiful, without *alaṁkāra*s (ornaments) her beauty is not appreciated.

Another name in this context is that of Daṇḍin. According to some schools he flourished even earlier than Bhāmaha. In this book, *Kāvyādarśa*, he says,

काव्यशोभाकरान् धर्मानलंकारान् प्रचक्ष्यते ।

kāvyaśobhākarān dharmānalaṁkārān pracakṣyate ।

According to Bhāmaha, whereas *śabda* and *artha* are necessary conditions, *alaṁkāra*s act as the sufficient conditions for poetry. When we use *alaṁkāra*s, we are not describing the situation in a straightforward way, we are saying something in a roundabout way. We are also adding something original to the situation, we are describing it in an exaggerated manner. *Alaṁkāra* according to him is both *atiśayokti* (अतिशयोक्ति) and *vakrokti* (वक्रोक्ति). Vāmana who came after Bhāmaha distinguished between *kāvya-guṇa* (काव्य-गुण) and *alaṁkāra* (अलंकार). According to him, poetry or *kāvya* cannot be thought of in the absence of *guṇa*s. He explains this in the aphorism *pūrve* [*guṇāh*] *nityāḥ* (पूर्वे [गुणाः] नित्याः). He describes *alaṁkāra*s as,

तद् [काव्यशोभायाः] अतिशयहेतवस्तत्त्वलंकाराः ।

tad [*kāvyaśobhāyāḥ*] *atiśayahetavastattvalaṁkārāḥ* ।

On account of this difference in point of view, Vāmana does not think that *alaṁkāra*, in the sense of embellishment, is necessary for poetry. He says: *yuvateriva rūpabhaṅgaṁ kāvyaṁ svādate śuddhaguṇaṁ tadapyatīva* (युवतेरिव रूपभंगं काव्यं स्वादते शुद्धगुणं तदप्यतीव).

Vāmana, however, uses the term *alaṁkāra* in two different senses. In the most important sense, he regards *alaṁkāra* as an evaluative parameter of poetry.

काव्यं ग्राह्यमलंकारात्।
काव्यं खलु ग्राह्यम् उपदेयं भवति अलंकारात्॥
काव्यशब्दोऽयं गुणालंकार-संस्कृतयोः शब्दार्थयो वर्तते।
भक्त्या तु शब्दार्थमात्र वचनो अत्र गृह्यते॥

kāvyaṁ grāhyamalaṁkārāt ।
kāvyaṁ khalu grāhyam upadeyaṁ bhavati alaṁkārāt ॥
kāvyaśabdo 'yaṁ guṇālaṁkāra-saṁskṛtayoḥ śabdārthayo vartate ।
bhaktyā tu śabdārthamātra vacano atra gṛhyate ॥

Bhaktyā means in the secondary sense. According to him the real *alaṁkāra* is beauty or *saundarya* — *alamkṛtiralaṁkāraḥ* (अलंकृतिरलंकारः).

The word *alaṁkāra* in secondary sense is also used for denoting or describing simile, metaphor, etc. Unlike his predecessor and other successors, Vāmana is quite definite about his poetic concepts. He doesn't regard that simile, metaphor, etc. are necessary conditions for poetry. Vāmana's view doesn't seem to be followed, *in toto*, by his successors. But, what he suggested was carried out by them by saying that *rasa* is the soul of poetry and here they use the word *rasa* for conveying the aesthetic sense. I have, elsewhere, pointed out that poetry requires to be judged by several parameters, some of them are for judging the constituents of poetry and the others are evaluative. Beauty, for Vāmana, is an evaluative parameter. (But he does not disregard the secondary use of the word *alaṁkāra*.) In this sense too, in order to explain our thought in ordinary language, we are many a time required to use some models which are moulds in which language and/ or its meaning are expressed. In fact, the *alaṁkāra*s are based on the similarity between *upameya* and *upamāna*. Those critics who came after Vāmana have made use of the concept of *alaṁkāras*, but have at the same time given them a secondary status. They classified the *alaṁkāra*s under *citrakāvya* which is given a very insignificant place by rhetoricians. Nevertheless whenever we want to communicate our thoughts to others we have to make use of such models, and so, whether in ordinary language or in poetry, the use of *alaṁkāra*s cannot be avoided. There is not a single poet who doesn't use *alaṁkāra*s and not a single rhetorician who regarded them as trivial. *Alaṁkāra*s represent the basic mode of our language.

Let me explore now what rhetoricians like Bhāmaha, of post-Bharata period, have said about poetry. I shall discuss in this section the views of Bhāmaha and Vāmana. Both have given their works the same title that is *Kāvyālaṁkāra*. Since Vāmana has also written a commentary on his own book, the two together are called *Kāvyālaṁkārasūtravṛtti* (काव्यालंकारसूत्रवृत्ति). Bhāmaha in his *Kāvyālaṁkāra* says,

śabdārthau sahitau kāvyam (शब्दार्थौ सहितो काव्यम्)

It is thought that this was Bhāmaha's definition of poetry. But this is not so. Bhāmaha never said that he was giving a definition of poetry. However, in these words Bhāmaha is giving us a necessary condition of *kāvya* or poetry.[3] There may be other necessary conditions also and certainly sufficient conditions too will have to be discussed. But there is no doubt that this aphorism gives us an important necessary condition

3. *Vyākhyā* in Sanskrit means an explanation or description and not definition. The word for definition is *lakṣaṇa*.

of poetry. What Bhāmaha says about poetry in this aphorism does not just mean that there are just words and meanings in poetry, for any language does consist of words and meanings. Even when men talk to one another (or have a vocal communication with somebody) the words or sound-patterns cannot be ignored. But, finally, the sound patterns recede into the background — and the meaning patterns come to the forefront. This is always the case in our ordinary use of language. Many a time, we also talk of art — the language of arts. But, this is merely a metaphorical way of referring to the medium of arts. Language is a medium of expression and communication and what we call the language of arts is a medium of expression as well as of communication. But, in language of arts, the medium cannot be ignored. It is as important as the content that is expressed through it. In fact, Jagannātha [*RG*] says that the medium is more important than the meaning. The words, of course, should be meaningful and beautiful. But the *śabda* and *artha* still retain their independent status. Otherwise, they together would be understood as a *paryāpti* relation which would be incorrect. Take the case of a portrait. When the portrait is sketched, the intention behind it is that it should be a portrait of someone, some particular person, whom we know directly or through description, and certainly, the success of portrait painting lies in the actual resemblance between the painting and the person who is the object of that painting. Recognition of the person who is painted on the canvas is very important and vital. But, in this kind of painting, there is equal emphasis on the medium itself. It cannot be just symbolized. If there is no one-to-one correspondence between the two, it would no more be a portrait. Even in cartoons, the resemblance with the original is still maintained although the painter is caricaturing. The importance or significance of medium increases, when we proceed from portrait painting to landscape and other kinds of art objects in painting. In such art objects, the meaningfulness of the object is retained, but, there would not be one-to-one correspondence or for that matter any correspondence at all, for it would be actualizing something which is ideal and imaginary; and the correspondence is with the ideal. In fact, the medium becomes still more significant when we proceed to sculpture. It is the medium which gives us the beauty in such art objects. As the artist involves himself in painting or in sculpture, the artist's original intention may undergo a change and his art may proceed not by the artists' original intention but by the acquired interest. (Sometimes, it is termed as "Intent of the Art Object.") This is the difference, according to me, between the art language, and the ordinary language and so although we talk of art language it is not a language in the ordinary sense of the term.

Let me also explain the role of medium and that of meaning in a different context also. Grammar for example is about the language. But, the use of language in grammar is different from the use of that in ordinary language. When, for instance, we say that "such and such an affix is added to the word" it is added to the word itself and not to its meaning. If we say that the affix *ḍhak* (which means *eya*) is added to *agni*, it means it is added to the word, *agni*. It is not added to any other word which stands for *agni* only. For example, it is not added to the word "fire." Pāṇini, in order to explain this gives the aphorism, *svaṁ rūpaṁ śabdasya aśabda saṁjñā* (स्वं रूपं शब्दस्य अशब्द संज्ञा). He thereby means that the word or sound pattern is its own *rūpa* or form and this original form is important in grammar. But, it is not important in day-to-day language, for in day-to-day language we do not get the *svarūpa* or *śabda*; but, merely, the *saṁjñā* or meaning of *śabda*. As against these two uses we should also posit the third use. In art, not only the *svarūpa* or the *saṁjñā* alone is significant, but, the combination of the two (in varying degrees) is also significant. In language *śabda* (symbol) and *artha* (meaning and/or the bearer) are the two prongs which are usually expressed by *vācya* and *vācaka*. In art (poetry), both the *vācaka* and *vācya* are important. To express this, Bhāmaha uses the dual of *śabda* and *artha*. Bhāmaha's intention can be brought about only by using a dual number and not by anything else. Of course, the significance of the medium and intention signified by the medium will vary from art to art. But in any art, the importance of medium cannot be ignored. That is why it is said that a particular word from the poet's composition cannot be altered arbitrarily. We cannot replace it in an appropriate manner. If someone is a good poet then the word that he uses alone must fit properly in the composition and nothing else. This significance of the medium is emphasized by Bhāmaha when he talked of poetry and used the aphorism,

śabdārthau sahitau kāvyam (शब्दार्थौ सहितौ काव्यम्) ।

Rasavat Alaṁkāra : Its Introduction and Elimination

Rasavat alaṁkāra has played a historical role in the transition from stage drama to poetry. If we see the history of *rasavat alaṁkāra*, this transition from the stage drama to poetry will reveal itself. Bhāmaha, Daṇḍin and Rudraṭa list this in their scheme of *alaṁkāras*. In Bhāmaha's *Kāvyālaṁkāra* (3.6), this first stage of *rasavat* was clearly depicted, when he said,

रसवद् दर्शितः स्पष्टं शृंगारादि रसस्तथा ।

rasavad darśitaḥ spaṣṭaṁ śṛṅgārādi rasastathā ।

Vāmana does not mention it, but instead, mentions *rasa* under *kānti*, a quality of poetry (*dīptarasattvam kāntiḥ*, दीप्तरसत्वम् कान्तिः). Mammaṭa, on the other hand, omits *rasavat* from his scheme altogether. Thus, with different approaches of rhetoricians, *rasavat* became either basic or superficial. There is a hidden relationship between *rasavat* and *rasa*. *Rasavat* was understood in one of the two ways in the course of history. The concept of *rasa* was originally a concept in stage drama which was to give a visual picture or scheme. In recitable poetry when a similar visual effect was produced even without the advantage of a stage, it was regarded as an instance of *rasavat* that which is like *rasa* (*vat* means "like"). But when *rasa* was accepted as the basic concept of poetry and arts, by *rasavat* was meant that which had *rasa* (power of producing image) in it (*rasa* + *vat* (*matup*)). Kālidāsa's description of the running of a deer:

> **वियति बहुत्तरं स्तोकमुर्व्यां प्रयाति (अथवा)**
> **संचारिणी दीपशिखेव रात्रौ**
>
> *viyati bahuttaraṁ stokamurvyāṁ prayāti Śākuntalam* or
> *sañcārīṇī dīpaśikheva ratrau* । — *Raghuvaṁśa*

creates such an effect. *Rasavat*, therefore, referred to that poetry which had *rasa* or picturesqueness in it (even in the absence of a stage). Thus a particular gestalt of word and meaning resulted in what is known as *rasavat alaṁkāra*. At a later stage, when the concept of *rasa* was introduced in poetry, for some time *rasavat* was still used. But then it indicated a mixture of one *rasa* in another. Later when *rasa* was identified with savour and *ānanda rasavat alaṁkāra* became superfluous and finally was dropped from the scheme of *alaṁkāras*. In the post-Abhinavagupta period, this influence was on the wane. *Rasa* was identified first with *āsvāda* and then with *ānanda*. In this process, *rasa* as *āsvāda* and *ānanda* became the sole objective of all poetry whether auditory or visual and perhaps on this account, *rasavat* must have been dropped by Mammaṭa and those who came after Mammaṭa, from their scheme of figures of speech. For there was no additional necessity of *rasavat* after *rasa* was freely employed in the distinction of poetic art. The unification of *rasa* theory with *dhvani* at the hands of Ānandavardhana and Abhinavagupta also must have played its role in this regard. Ānandavardhana's classification of *dhvani* into three types — *vastu-dhvani, alaṁkāra-dhvani* and *rasa-dhvani* must have wielded its influence in this modification and in the exit of *rasavat alaṁkāra*. What is *rasa-dhvani*? In all probability *rasa-dhvani* was that suggested meaning where the images of the incident came before the mind's eye. But later this concept also got modified. Anyway, the *rasavat* was dropped from the scheme of *alaṁkāra*s but got a place in the theory of *dhvani* or suggestion.

Rīti and Similar Concepts

Vāmana who came after Bhāmaha talks of *rīti* explicitly: *viśiṣṭa padaracanā rītiḥ* (विशिष्टपदरचना रीतिः). But, this was in the mind of Bhāmaha also when he described poetry as *śabdārthau sahitau* (शब्दार्थौ सहितौ).

Among the six theories mentioned earlier, *rīti* occupies an important place. As a matter of fact, *rīti* is integral to every art. Since any act is concerned with the subject matter, using the subject matter and the symbols required by the subject-matter become an important feature of art, nay an art is known by the symbols; for, it is the symbols which are the constituents of the medium. Thus, whether it is poetry or drama or painting or music, *rīti* becomes an important feature of art. In fact, it is merely the extended use or the extension of the concept of *śabda*. It is concerned with how the art is presented. Bharata, who was a theorist of dramaturgy, does not use the word *rīti*. He uses the word *vṛtti* (वृत्ति) in the case of stage drama.[4] But his use of *vṛtti* is slightly different from that of *rīti*. In music

4. His use of *vṛtti* is slightly different from that of *rīti*.

also the style is significant and a musician is known as an exponent of a style. For example, a certain school (*gharānā*, घराना) of music is known as Kiranā Gharānā, Gwalior Gharānā, Jodhpur Gharānā, etc. But *gharānā* style is not *rīti*. Perhaps the combination of sounds will constitute the *rīti* part in music. I am not sure whether the words "school" or "gharānā" can be brought under *vṛtti*. In *Nāṭyaśāstra*, there is also another word which is employed to convey a specific style; Bharata calls it *pravṛtti* and not *vṛtti*. *Vṛtti* seems to be more general than *pravṛtti* and so I feel that *vṛtti* can be compared, not be *gharānā*s but to the specific form of music as for example, *dhrupada*, or *khyāla* or *ṭhumrī*, etc. In dance also the several styles known to us today, like Bharatanāṭyam or Katthaka, or Maṇipuri, Oḍissī, etc., give us the different styles though the basic elements of all these different forms are the same. Similar is the case with painting. It can be classical, biblical[5] or it can, for example, be modern. But, under these general styles there may be a special style of each painter, for example, Vermeer's style is quite different from Rambrandt's and the paintings of Picasso are again in a different style from both these. But, the elements of these general styles and special styles may be inseparable and any individual style might be a combination of both. Bharata also recognized this and agreed that *vṛtti* and *pravṛtti* go together. Bharata recognized four such *vṛtti*s — *bhāratī* (भारती), *ārabhaṭī* (आरभटी), *sātvatī* (सात्वती) and *kaiśikī* (कैशिकी). The rhetoricians of poetry talk of *rīti* and Vāmana recognizes three such *rīti*s — *vaidarbhī* (वैदर्भी), *pāñcālī* (पांचाली) and *gauḍī* (गौड़ी). Other writers, who came after Vāmana have sometimes recognized five. But, whether they are three or five or more is a matter of details and it does not affect the theory as such.

5. Many times these are also called styles of painting.

As stated earlier, *vṛtti* or *rīti* is concerned with the material constituents of each art, and, therefore, it gives us a parameter about its constituents regarding art. Vāmana says that *rīti* is the soul or the prime constituent of art — *rītirātmā kāvyasya* (रीतिरात्मा काव्यस्य).

The very existence of art depends on *rīti*s. (I am not using the word essence for the word *ātman* because due to the ambiguous use of the word *ātman* the constituent and evaluation parameters can be mixed up.) Vāmana defines *rīti* as a specific arrangement of gestalt of words, *viśiṣṭapadaracanā rītiḥ* (विशिष्टपदरचना रीतिः). What is this specific (*viśiṣṭa*) arrangement of words? Vāmana answers that *viśeṣa* is that in which specific characteristics or *guṇa*s are embodied, *viśeṣo guṇātmā* (विशेषो गुणात्मा). He defines *guṇa* and *doṣa* and enumerates ten kinds of *guṇa*s and distinguishes them from the *doṣa*s or blemishes. He regards *vaidarbhī* style as the best because it consists of all *guṇa*s. In fact, according to him, that which constitutes all *guṇa*s is *vaidarbhī*. This last step may not be quite correct and in experience we need not have only the good qualities to make the whole beautiful or valuable. Perhaps, an organic whole consisting of some good, some bad and some indifferent qualities may be better than a whole which consists of only the good qualities; for, what is important in a whole is not just a combination of parts, but, a co-ordination, a fusion, or blending of parts. It is coherence of different parts or elements which is more important. It may also be pointed out that the names *vaidarbhī*, *pāñcālī* and *gauḍī*, although derived from the specific regions, might not be indicative of the fact that in these regions everyone followed a particular style or *rīti*. It may also be pointed out that although according to Vāmana *vaidarbhī* style was the best, Vāmana did not belong to Vidarbha. It may be further pointed out that some of the instances which Vāmana gives of poetry in *vaidarbhī* style are not the instances of the best and the most lucid poetry. But it has to be recognized that Vāmana was trying to relate the constituent conditions of poetry to the evaluative ones and it may be further pointed out that without the constituent conditions one cannot really talk of poetry at all. In the absence of constituents there cannot be any artefact and so there cannot be any art also. (For details of Vāmana's theory, see Appendix 2.)

Vakrokti

Of the six kinds of theories propounded in India, theories of *vakrokti* and *aucitya* operated at two levels. They are concerned with the structure of arts and also with appreciation and evaluation of arts. Of course, the concepts governing the theories operated in the field of poetry. But they could be usefully employed in the field of any art. It is so because, although it is not stated explicitly, the concepts of *vakrokti* and *aucitya* were actually concerned with the parameters of art, both constitutive and evaluative. The propounders of the theories of *vakrokti* and *aucitya* give examples of both these cases. This is so because the concepts of *vakrokti* and *aucitya* are elastic.

Sometimes, of course, the parameter belonging to and governing one type is regarded as belonging to and governing the other type. This has in particular happened in the case of *rīti, dhvani* and *rasa*. It has not happened in the case of *vakrokti* and *aucitya*. But being flexible, they could be properly applied to both the types. This point would be clear in the course of further discussion. In the case of *rasa*, I feel that the concept was operative originally in the context of the staging of drama, but for good or bad reason it was used beyond its original limit and was applied to explain both the structural and evaluational context. In particular, it happened when the word *ātman* was used in connection with these parameters. The writers on poetics have, for example, used the expressions like:

1. रीतिरात्मा काव्यस्य [काव्यलंकारसूत्रवृत्ति; वामनकृत] *rītirātmā kāvyasya* (*Kāvyālaṁkāra Sūtravṛtti*; by Vāmana)
2. काव्यस्यात्मा ध्वनिरिति . . . [ध्वन्यालोक] *kāvyasyātmā dhvaniriti* . . . . (*Dhvanyāloka*)
3. वाक्यं रसात्मकं काव्यम् [साहित्य दर्पण]; *vākyaṁ rasātmakaṁ kāvyam* (*Sāhitya Darpaṇa*) and
4. वक्रोक्ति जीवितम् *vakrokti jīvitam*.[6]

According to this theory, *vakrokti* is the differentia or core of all poetry.[7] In fact, we should, rather, say that poetry comes into existence on account of *vakratā* or curved or indirect expression. This theory is propounded by Kuntaka (sometimes called Kuntala also). But the word *vakrokti* was first used by Bhāmaha and Daṇḍin and other *alaṁkārins*. Bhāmaha has used the word *vakrokti* as against *svabhāvokti* and in the list of *alaṁkāras* given by the *alaṁkārins*, both *svabhāvokti* and *vakrokti* find a place.

In discussing *vakrokti* Bhāmaha makes an important statement. He says that *vakrokti* is *atiśayokti* or exaggeration. Some writers say that *atiśayokti* is an independent *alaṁkāra*.

---

6. In fact, if *jīvita* is taken as another name for *ātman* then *vakrokti jīvitam* would mean that *vakrokti* is the *ātman* of *kāvya*. Thus, *vakrokti jīvitam* is a thesis which says that *vakrokti* is the core of *kāvya*. It is translated as the essence of poetry. But the better translation would be that it is the very existence of *kāvya*. I should make it clear that in Christian theology too two such words are used in a similar way. They are "existence" and "essence." They mean two different things. But sometimes one is used in the sense of the other and vice versa.

7. *Kāvyālaṁkāra* of Bhāmaha, Tṛtīya Pariccheda 81, 84, 85, 86 and 93.

What is important is that *atiśayokti* is not only important in the context of *vakrokti*, it is equally significant in the case of all *alaṁkāras*, for, it is the *atiśayatva* (exaggeration part) which gives us the parameter of arts, and in some sense even when we talk of *svabhāvokti* it is not just a simple description, it is a hyperbolic description. In *Śākuntalam*, when Duṣyanta enters the *āśrama* of Kaṇva, he comes across a deer, and Kālidāsa describes the movement of the deer:

ग्रीवाभंगाभिरामं मुहुरनुपतति स्यन्दने बद्धदृष्टिः
पश्चादर्धेन प्रविष्टः शरपतनभयाद् भूयसा पूर्वकायम्।
दर्भैरर्धावलीढैः श्रमविवृतमुखभ्रंशिभिः कीर्णवर्त्मा
पश्योदग्रप्लुतत्त्वाद्वियति बहुतरं स्तोकमुर्व्यां प्रयाति॥

grīvābhaṅgābhirāmaṁ muhuranupatati syandane baddhadṛṣṭiḥ ।
paścādardhena praviṣṭaḥ śarapatanabhayād bhūyasā pūrvakāyam ।
darbhairardhāvalīdhaiḥ śramavivṛtamukhabhranśibhiḥ kīrṇa-vartmā ।
paśyodagraplutattvādviyati bahutaraṁ stokamūrvyāṁ prayāti ॥

We usually say that this is the natural description of the movement of the deer. But the fact is that although it looks like a realistic description, its beauty comes from exaggeration. Bhāmaha says that this exaggeration is also the crux of *vakrokti*, although *vakrokti* is to be distinguished from other kinds of exaggeration. In fact, one could ask here a question as to what is the difference between a parameter and its instances. To me, the parameter gives us the last limit of the characteristic, which it holds in common with its instances. Ordinarily, a parameter and its instances have a common characteristic which can be used for measuring the instances (coming under the same parameter); so although Bhāmaha did not accept a special theory of *vakrokti* in distinguishing *vakrokti* from *svabhāvokti* and in saying that *atiśayokti* is its differentia, he states a very important truth about parameters.

Kuntaka makes use of this information. He also makes use of the other statement of Bhāmaha that in poetry or art, *śabda*, i.e. (medium) and *artha* (intention) go inseparably together. *Śabda* and *artha*, *vācya* and *vācaka* are like *yugala* or a couple. So, *vakrokti* can be both in regard to *vācaka* and *vācya* and therefore, *vakrokti* introduces a standard or a parameter, which is concerned with the subject matter as also with its evaluation.

Aucitya : A Constitutive and Evaluative Parameter of Beauty

Aucitya means propriety or appropriateness. It is another parameter which Kṣemendra and his followers suggest for measuring the merits of literary arts. By extending the meaning of the term it may be used for plastic and other fine arts.

Earlier, I have pointed out that there should be two kinds of parameters — one concerned with the constitution of the body of the art and the other concerned with its evaluation. *Aucitya*, like *vakrokti*, may be used in both these spheres. Just as in grammar one talks of syntax and also semantics; similarly, in the sphere of art one may have to deal with *aucitya* in composition, and *aucitya* in the context of its evaluation. Both these kinds of *aucitya* will be meaningful in any particular context. When, for example, we consider a sentence, we are concerned with *ākāṅkṣā*, with the use of words, i.e. which words should follow which. If we have to say Rāma has killed Rāvaṇa, then the order should be:

1. 'Rāma' [followed by]
2. 'Has killed' [and then]
3. 'Rāvaṇa.' If this order is changed and Rāvaṇa is put first and Rāma last, the meaning of the sentence (in English) will be entirely different.

By *aucitya,* if we mean appropriateness or propriety, then the appropriateness of the composition will be concerned with the syntax. This is what is in Sanskrit called *ākāṅkṣā* and it is significant in the context of the body of the sentence. In the social sphere on the other hand, the propriety will depend on the customs and culture of the society and the social relations among individuals. When we are evaluating the artistic character of a certain artefact or a composition, *aucitya* will be concerned with beauty. Thus, *aucitya* will be both a parameter for judging the art as also for designing the art in a particular way. Propriety will thus differ from situation to situation. How will this propriety be determined? Kṣemendra says, that which coheres with the other part is *ucita,* i.e. the two parts of a situation must make a coherent whole *ucitaṁ prāhurācāryāḥ sadṛśaṁ kila yasya yat* (उचितं प्राहुराचार्याः सदृशं किल यस्य यत्). Although the word *sadṛśa* is generally used for pointing out the similarity, here it does not point out similarity. On the other hand it points out the uniqueness and fittingness. It is not a simile. It cannot be defined and has to be treated as unique. The propriety will be determined thus by context and it would be of two types:

1. Constituent propriety, and the other
2. Evaluative propriety.

Kṣemendra lays great emphasis on *aucitya*; but the word has also been used by Kuntaka and Ānandavardhana.

Dhvani

In ancient and medieval India, not only several arts flourished but the theories of these arts and their criticism were also advocated by scholars from time to time. Of these, the theories of *rasa* and *dhvani* were most prominent. In fact, Abhinavagupta, the famous philosopher of Kāśmīra-Śaivism and Pratyabhijñā school, wrote commentaries on Bharata's *Naṭyaśāstra* as also on Ānandavardhana's *Dhvanyāloka*. In these commentaries, he advocated a unified *rasa* theory. Since then, *rasa* and *dhvani* were regarded as indentical terms, although Abhinavagupta did not mean any such identification. He only thought that the two theories supplemented each other and that *rasa* and *dhvani* represented two important aspects of the theory of art. He said, *rasāḥ dhvaniḥ eva*. This was interpreted as identification of *rasa* and *dhvani*. But the fact is that *eva* in the above quotation does not stand for the concept of identification. It only suggests that *rasa* and *dhvani* have to be taken together, that they are two inseparable aspects of the whole, just as *śabda* and *artha* are two inseparable aspects of audible poetry; that the theory of *rasa* or that of *dhvani* would be incomplete, unless supplemented by the other. I have elsewhere[8] said that for Bharata, the word *rasa* was *āsvādya*, i.e. it operated in the sphere of things and symbols. On the other hand the locus of *dhvani* was determined by the concept of meaning. Just as in ordinary langauge *vācaka* and *vācya* go togehter though they are different, similarly in any meaningful art, the *rasa* and *dhvani* stand as a *yugala* or *yugma*. It is like a pair or a couple. In fact, I have stated elsewhere[9] that they are like two wings of a butterfly. One is not the other. Somehow later Indian writers and thinkers have mixed up all these

8. *Vide* Chapters IV, V, VI, VII, VIII and IX.

9. Like Bharata, Abhinavagupta too has made a distinction between *āsvāda* and *āsvādya*, in the same way as we make between *viṣayī* and *viṣaya*, which stand for knowledge and its object respectively. It may be that the object of knowledge itself may be in the sphere of knowledge, when, for example, we go from consciousness to self-consciousness, and say that "I know that I know" "that I know" as much belongs to the sphere of knowledge as my knowing. But, they are still different.

concepts. They forgot that the status of *rasa* and *dhvani* was like the *symbol and its meaning*. One is different from the other and still supplements the other.[10] Abhinavagupta wanted to make a distinction between symbol and its meaning or symbolic presentation and its meaning and, therefore, said, "the symbol of the meaning and the meaning of the symbol have to be taken together." But, the theories about symbols would evidently be different from those of the meanings of symbols. *Dhvani* theory is, therefore, different from the *rasa* theory. *Dhvani* theory is a theory of meaning, and therefore it will be necessary to bring out a few points about *dhvani* theory here. Before I actually proceed further, I may point out that it is a theory about literature and it cannot apply directly to other arts although every art would be conveying some suggested meaning and that the meaning of art is determined by the intention which the symbol conveys.

Types of Meaning

Some of the Naiyāyikas who preceded Ānandavardhana thought that every word had two sets of meanings. One was its direct meaning which was determined by *vācya-vācaka bhāva* and the other was *lakṣyārtha* or implied meaning. Ānandavardhana thought that in addition to these two meanings there was a third meaning also and that was a suggested meaning. It was dependent on the direct meaning and was still far remote from it. *Gaṅgāyām ghoṣaḥ* (गंगायाम् घोषः) is given as an instance of suggested meaning. *Ghoṣa* means a crowd. Literally, the phrase means the crowd in Ganges. But, the suggested meaning is not that the crowd is *in* the water of the Ganges, but *on* the bank of the Ganges. But, if we look at the word Ganges in its cultural background, we come to know

10. Op. cit.

that the Ganges is a *sacred* river. And, we further know that the crowd gathers on the bank of the Ganges on account of the belief that the holy river would clean the visitors of their sins. It is due to such faith of sensibility that the visitors come to the bank of the Ganges. Ānandavardhana says that such tertiary meaning immediately gives a new dimension to the poetic feelings which is the essence of poetry. He suggests that such meaning suddenly flashes and the new dimension is accomplished. Perhaps, he classifies the implied meaning and suggested meaning together and calls the compounded meaning as *pratīyamāna artha* (प्रतीयमान अर्थ), as against the direct meaning.

What is *pratīyamāna artha*? Is the *pratīyamān artha*, altogether of a different type from the direct meaning or *vācyārtha*? The grammarians who flourished before Ānandavardhana propounded that even the *vācya* meaning was of the nature of explosion, but since the *vācya* meaning was socially accepted, its novelty got thwarted and was not paid heed to. However, this is not the case with the suggested meaning; for, it is not a common meaning, and might not be grasped by everyone. Nevertheless, in every case the meaning is a kind of an explosion and is known instantaneously and intuitively.

Sphoṭavāda: Abhihitānvayavāda and Anvitābhidhānavāda

The grammarians like Sphoṭāyana, Pāṇini, Patañjali, Bhartṛhari accepted this *sphoṭa* theory. The latter grammarians also accepted this theory. But since this theory was subjected to criticism and modification at the hands of Pūrvamīmāṁsakas and Naiyāyikas, it took the form of *abhihitānvayavāda* and *anvitābhidhānavāda*. Both these theories are modifications of *sphoṭa* theory of meaning. But the model that is used here is that of *succession of utterances* (which is called a sentence). When we utter certain sounds, we get certain sounds as also their meanings. When do we get the meaning part? Is the meaning successively added as the sounds are uttered? Is there a symbiosis of meanings? Or is the meaning conveyed to us at the last step of utterance? The two theories are based on these two views and their model is audio-model. (The video model would be different and if only one video snap is taken the flash would be simultaneous and not successive.) But instead of audio-model where we get something gradually and in succession if we have a video model as a paradigm, then it would be governed not by successive steps but instantaneously, where the whole thing would come in one span of attention and would be known together and simultaneously. When we talk of words and their meanings, we talk of things one after another. We also hear them one after another. But all our experience need not always be of that kind, and, perhaps, succession is unimportant and the meaning of a sentence could be governed by the *total sentence* in one flash. Perhaps the part of this "sudden explosion" is forgotten by us on account of the familiarity that we have with language and its constituent words. That is why it is forgotten that even in ordinary language and experience *the language and experience* comes to us in a flash. Although Ānandavardhana classifies the language and its meaning in two groups *vācya* and *pratīyamāna* and although it is necessary to make this classification, it is equally important to realize that meanings in both these groups are based on *pratīyamānatā* (प्रतीयमानता) alone.

Ānandavardhana's View

It appears to me that Ānandavardhana has said something very basic, when he describes that the suggested meaning is a flash. What Ānandavardhana says is an extension of what the grammarians had said. Bhartṛhari, in his *Vākyapadīya*, has said this and I would like to repeat it: "what we call meaning need not be one and single. There could be successive meanings like the ripples produced on the surface of water." The theory of *dīrgha abhidhā* says something like this. But I shall deal with it in the chapter on Observations and Remarks. It may be pointed out that the critics of Ānandavardhana like Mahimabhaṭṭa denied the *dhvani* theory and upheld *abhidhā* theory with certain modifications. He says that *abhidhā* is of two types. One is what we get directly and the other is what we get through inference. The first knowledge of symbols leads to some meanings, and the symbol and the first meaning lead to the second meaning and in this way we get different meanings gradually.

This theory has one very important significance. It says that meaning is a kind of a relation, that it is a diadic relation and the symbol and its meanings are the two relata. I, however, feel that it is a triadic relation, which tends to become diadic and again tends to become triadic. The first term of the relation lapses and gradually a fourth term or relatum comes into existence instead. It is this process which paves the way for the different meanings. It also makes communication possible between the author and the reader, the artist and the appreciator of art, of the speaker and the audience. But, in order to explain this relation and the concept of communication underlying, we would have to ask the question about symbol and its interpretation in terms of meaning.

Symbol and its Interpretation

What is a symbol? To me it appears that it is a kind of a sign introduced by the speaker, the artist or the author, to explain what is in his mind. Meaning, on the other hand, is explication of what is in the mind of the speaker. It is his intention. But, symbolizing the intention means objectifying the intention. It then no longer remains his intention (The process of *sādhāraṇīkaraṇa* (साधारणीकरण) is operating here also.) It can be shared by all those who understand what the sign or symbol stands for. Philosophers these days talk of *use* instead of *meaning*. But what is "use"? It is the way the symbol is used and understood by the people who *use* it. It relates the intention of the author to all those who play this game of communication. But once this subjective intention is objectified and made available to all those in the context, it is made public. The significance of the speaker or the author or the artist vanishes and what remains are the symbols and how the symbols are understood by the persons around. It is of course possible that in this game, as soon as the author whose intention under reference is dropped, the message of the author might not be transmitted to those who are at the other end. Nevertheless on account of the objectification of the symbol, something is bound to be communicated to others, although in all likelihood the intention of the author and that which is understood by the others would be overlapping. This means that while one relatum of the relation vanishes, the other relata are created. If the terms of the relations are A, B and C, then while A is disappearing another relatum D (which means D_1, D_2, D_3, etc.) can come into existence and influence the context. Thus a new pattern of triadic relation gets formed. But, this third set of terms might not immediately come into existence and there may be merely the symbol, and its possible understanding by only a potential hearer, who may not be actually existing at that moment. During such a stage, we can say that the original triadic relation has shrunk into a diadic relation. It is, also, necessary to understand the nature of this diadic relation. There is a difference between a discharged battery and a charged one; the symbol which gives rise to some meaning behaves like a charged battery and anyone who comes in contact with the symbol gets a flash (of understanding) like an electric flash or shock. It means that even in the absence of a person who comes in contact with the symbol the symbol has attained the power or potentiality to release some "power" or "light." This makes the relation diadic. This is the kind of meaning which we try to find in a lexicon. This meaning is like a flash. Our grammarians and rhetoricians regarded it as *pratīyamāna,* and whether it is the direct meaning or the implied or suggested meaning, the *pratīti* or cognition of it seems to be the property of the symbols which are not nonsensical.

4

Various Senses of the Word Rasa

Rasa Theory — Historical Survey

In the growth of Indian civilization, the word *rasa* with several concepts foisted on it from time to time has played a very pivotal role. It is used in the Vedic literature, in the different orthodox and heterodox philosophical systems, in Āyurveda, the science of medicine developed in India, and in *Nāṭyaśāstra* and other works of dramaturgy and poetics. Today, what is commonly known as *rasa* theory is associated with the concept as it is used in the development of poetics. Literally, the word *rasa* stands for liquid or that which flows. But it was also used for indicating different things — mercury, a chemical in general, and "essence" or the vital principle. Due to metaphorical and suggested meanings it was also used for self, bliss and pure joy. Professor Hiriyanna thinks that the word *rasa* primarily means "taste" a "savour"[1] such as sweetness; and by metaphorical extension, it is now applied to the type of experience referred to above (i.e. aesthetic experience of happiness).[2] While agreeing with Hiriyanna that the aesthetic use is metaphorical, I think what he calls the primary use is also acquired or metaphorical.

---

1. M. Hiriyanna, *Art Experience*, p. 38, Kāvyalaya Publisher, Mysore, 1954.
2. The brackets in the above quotation are mine.

Rasa in Vedas and Upaniṣads

In the Vedas, *Ṛg* (ऋग्) and *Atharva* (अथर्व), there are several hymns in praise of *rasa*. In *Atharvaveda kapittha* (कपित्थ) or wood-apple is regarded as a counterpart of the moon on this earth. The moon was recognized as the Lord of all medicines. *Kapittha* was also identified with *rasa*. In the hymns, it is pointed out that *kapittha* cures several diseases. The word, *rasa* is also used in Upaniṣads. *Taittirīya Upaniṣad* states that having obtained *rasa* one is able to attain happiness or bliss: *raso vai saḥ rasam hi eva ayaṁ labhdhvā ānando bhavati* (रसो वै सः रसम् हि एव अयं लब्ध्वा आनन्दो भवति). In *Bhagavad-Gītā rasa* has been referred to as liking for sense objects (2.59).[3]

Rasa in Āyurveda

In Āyurveda, *rasa* is regarded as one of the seven basic elemetns or *dhātu*s (धातु) in the (human) body. Āyurveda uses it in the sense of mercury or *pārada* (पारद). This must have happened when the medical researchers found out that mercury played an important role in (Āyurvedic) medical therapy. Thus, a medicine *makaradhvaja* (मकरध्वज) was prepared by researchers of Āyurveda by using mercury (*pārada*, पारद) as its base. The medicines were classified into *kāṣṭhauṣadhi* (काष्ठौषधि) medicines prepared from vegetable world and *rasāyana* (रसायन) medicines prepared from other chemical and organic substances.

Rasa in Different Philosophical Systems

The different philosophical systems including that of Cārvāka make use of the word *rasa*. In the Sāṁkhya system, while stating the development of the cosmos, or while giving the analysis of experience, it is, for example, stated that *prakṛti* gives rise to *tanmātra*s through *mahat* and *ahaṁkāra*. *Tanmātra* literally

3. I believe this to be the secondary use.

means "that itself." Thus *tanmātra* may stand for the *prakṛti* itself. Since the *tanmātra*s are five and are known by five sense-organs, each *tanmātra* could be taken as that particular pure aspect of *prakṛti* known by each particular sense-organ. Sāṁkhya lists five such *tanmātra*s: *śabda, sparśa, rūpa, rasa* and *gandha.*[4] All macro things in the world are compounds of these five. They are *ākāśa* (आकाश), *vāyu* (वायु), *tejas* (तेजस्), *ap* (अप्) and *pṛthvī* (पृथ्वी). They are called *mahābhūta*s (महाभूत). Some scholars regard them as sense data and think that what is a part of knowing or epistemological process is somehow or the other regarded as ontological. Others regard these *tanmātra*s as things-in-themselves. But the *tanmātra*s themselves are never perceived. What is perceived is a *mahābhūta*. According to Vedānta each *mahābhūta* is an amalgamation of all the *tanmātra*s having a certain ratio to one another. *Rasa*, for example, gives rise to water which will contain a major quantity of *rasa* but will also contain *śabda, sparśa, rūpa* and *gandha*. The process by which the *tanmātra*s are transformed into *mahābhūta* is called the process of *pañcīkaraṇa.*[5] *Rasa* and the other *tanmātra* words, *śabda, sparśa, rūpa* and *gandha* are also used in Nyāya-Vaiśeṣika systems where they stand for certain qualities.

Rasa in Nāṭyaśāstra

The word *rasa* was borrowed, as is stated, by Bharata, from *Atharvaveda* for explaining the theory of stage-drama. He states this in the seventeenth verse of the first chapter of *Nāṭyaśāstra*: *rasān atharvaṇād api* (रसान् अथर्वणाद् अपि). Rhetoricians belonging to the school of *alaṁkāra* (poetic embellishments) like Bhāmaha, Daṇḍin and Vāmana use it for explaining the nature of poetry. The word *rasa* is also used in the sense of sound or noise as

4. Since these *tanmātra*s are known by sense-organs they are sometimes identified with sense data.

5. Some Upaniṣads talk of *trivṛtkaraṇa* process.

also for taste. Its etymology is traced to the root, *ras* + (*ghañ*) which stands for making noise or sounds. Thus, when the theory of *dhvani* (which literally means sounds but which also stands for *vyañjana* or suggested meaning) was introduced in Indian poetics by Ānandavardhana, the scholars like Abhinavagupta tried to synthesize the theory of *rasa* with that of *dhvani* and pointed out that the theories of *rasa* and *dhvani* have to go together, that etymologically *rasa* and *dhvani* are not different, that they are the two prongs of the same thing (like *śabda* and *artha*).

Bharata uses the word *rasa*, for explaining the nature of drama as a performing art. He had before him the poet or the dramatist who is the author of the script of drama. This script is used by the director, the *sūtradhāra*, for translating into stage language what was earlier in ordinary language. This he does with the help of the actors, the stage equipment or other accessories, the theatre and the spectators. Bharata thinks that a stage-drama was a kind of a temporal-continuum which has a beginning in the dramatist's experience as thought-feeling-continuum and which ends with the experience and appreciation by the spectators. The stage along with the actors and the (actual) performance, collectively stands for a medium or rather a conductor, through which a current or that which is in the dramatist's mind or the dramatist's intention passes, and is communicated to the spectator.[6] The spectators who have the role as appreciators are to be regarded as *pramāṇa* or the parameters for the success or failure of the drama: *Tasmāt lokaḥ pramāṇam hi* (तस्मात् लोकः प्रमाणम् हि). That which is in the poet's mind in the form of experience is called *kavi antargata bhāva* (कवि अन्तर्गत भाव), and what the poet tries to convey is called *sthāyī*

6. This may be truthfully communicated or may be communicated in an exaggerated or distorted form.

bhāva. (It may also be called *kāvyārtha* (काव्यार्थ) or the intended meaning or the meaning to be conveyed.) Such intended meanings are, according to Bharata, of eight types.[7] These meanings or intentions which are, in some sense, of the nature of thought and feeling are transformed into some objective form or a continuum of such objective form by the director, with the help of actors and other stage equipment. These are called *vibhāva*s and are classified under *ālambana* (आलम्बन) and *uddīpana vibhāva*s (उद्दीपन विभाव) respectively. The actors belong to the class of *ālambamavibhāva*s (आलम्बनविभाव). The actors convey this message by simulating the outward expressions, physical and organic sensations and bodily movements, which are appropriate to the occasion in order to bring about the effect.

This whole presentation or performance is again transformed into meaning (with relevant emotional tone) when it reaches the spectators and is understood by them with empathy and sympathy. The action of the actors is of two kinds. (1) If it is triggered intelligently through his own ability then it is called acting. For example, the tears in the eyes of the actor when required as a part of the performance, are produced by the actor himself on account of his own ability. (2) If the tears in the eyes are produced with glycerin or some other chemicals, it will not be acting although it would be taken as a part of the actor's action. The gestalt of the stage-presentation is understood by the spectators almost in the same way as we understand the sound signs in our ordinary language, not as signs but as the meanings of the signs. Bharata says that the *kavi-antargata-bhāva*[8] is transformed into a gestalt of *vibhāva*, *anubhāva* and *vyabhicārī-bhāva* and that in turn is again transformed into the spectator's *sthāyī bhāva*. Bharata

7. *NŚ* 25.129.

8. *NŚ* 7.2.

says that these *bhāvas* are forty-nine and they are seen in three different sets (*trayāvasthā*), once with the poet (the artist) then with the stage and again with spectators. One of these *bhāvas* becomes central to the theme and becomes the continuant or *sthāyī bhāva*. In a sense it continues through the art (or art continuum if the art is temporal), though it undergoes several transformations in this process. As Jagannātha points out it can become *gocarīkriyamāṇa* (गोचरीक्रियमाण). That is, the original subjective state is made objective or public.

The second stage of this *performance gestalt* is the objectified form on the stage. This is what is *āsvādya*, i.e. that which is to be tasted or appreciated. I think that for Bharata this was *rasa*, the objectified form of the poet's intention which can be tasted and appreciated by the spectators.[9] This comes into existence due to the combination of the *kāraṇa sāmagrī*, i.e. *vibhāva*, *anubhāva* and *vyabhicārī bhāva*.

Thus, that which is in the poet's mind and which takes the form of (dramatic) poetry with sound signs becomes possible when this (audible form) takes the concrete audio-visual form as in our actual experience. The poet's experience in audio-visual form is, thus, captured by the spectator in the form of meaning of the drama or *rūpaka* which is only a species of poetry. In other words the *rasa* is tasted or appreciated by the spectators. The appreciation is accompanied by a feeling of pleasure (etc.) *nānābhāvābhinaya-vyañjitān vāgaṅga-sattvopetān sthāyibhāvān āsvādayanti sumanasaḥ prekṣakāḥ, harṣādīn ca adhigacchanti* (नानाभावाभिनयव्यंजितान् वागंग सत्त्वोपेतान् स्थायिभावान् आस्वादयन्ति सुमनसः प्रेक्षकाः हर्षादीन् च अधिगच्छन्ति, *NŚ* 7.before 33). The spectators having a good sensitive mind taste (appreciate) the *sthāyī bhāvas*

9. *Śṛṅgāra, vīra, karuṇa, hāsya, adbhuta, bhayānaka, bībhatsa* and *raudra*. Abhinava adds *śānta* to it. Later writers have also added *bhakti, prakṣobha*, etc. to the list. Perhaps *vidroha* may be added to it now by commentators of *Dalit Sāhitya*.

which have now taken the form of different *bhāvas* through speech or dialogue, and different bodily gestures and actions presented through different manifestations, expressions or *bhāvas* (like *vibhāva, anubhāva* and *vyabhicārī*) and which result in the emotive overtones of pleasure, etc. (By *harṣādin ca*, Bharata perhaps means pain or unhappiness.) But, this process simply does not stop there.

The Purpose of Drama : Siddhis

Bharata here points to the purpose of stage drama. He says that a drama is staged for evoking certain reactions of fulfilment or *siddhi* in the minds of the spectators: *yasmāt prayogaḥ sarvo 'yaṁ siddhyarthaḥ sampradarśitaḥ* (यस्मात् प्रयोगः सर्वोऽयं सिद्ध्यर्थः सम्प्रदर्शितः, *NŚ* 27.1). Bharata says that the *siddhi* is of two types, *mānuṣī* and *daivikī*. *Mānuṣī siddhi* is concerned with ordinary reactions which the spectators exhibit as per their likes and dislikes. But the *daivikī siddhi* is of two varieties, (1) where there is emotional exuberance and overflow of feelings and (2) where the spectator is in a state of calm, is completely silent, absorbed in himself and not showing any sign of exasperation or agitation.[10] This is the completeness of *raṅga* or presentation of drama; *siddhi* is the complete fulfilment (both of the spectator and of the drama itself). *Siddhi* is thus the objective of drama (or art in general). Bharata mentions different elements in drama. He says:

रसा भावाह्यभिनया धर्मिवृत्तिप्रवृत्तयः।
सिद्धिः स्वरास्तथातोद्यं गानं रंगश्च संग्रहः॥

rasā bhāvāhyabhinayā dharmivṛttipravṛttayaḥ ।
siddhiḥ svarāstathātodyaṁ gānaṁ raṅgaśca saṁgrahaḥ ॥ *NŚ* 6.10

Rasa, bhāva, abhinaya, dharmi, vṛtti, pravṛtti, siddhi, svara, ātodya and vocal music are the elements of *Raṅga.*

10. In other words, the spectator is led to the pensive state.

But of these what are immediately relevant for the theory of drama are *rasa*, *sthāyī bhāva*, and *siddhi*. As pointed out earlier, *siddhi* is concerned with the satisfaction of the spectators which is also the satisfaction or the fulfilment of the artist or poet who is the creator of art. But, this fulfilment is attained through the successive transformations of the message which the artists aim at transmitting successfully; and, whether this transmission is successful or not, is measured by the applause or reaction of the spectators. Kālidāsa wrote in *Mālavikāgnimitra*:

आपरितोषात् विबुधां न साधु मन्ये प्रयोगविज्ञानम् ।

āparitoṣāt vibudhāṁ na sādhu manye prayoga-vijñānam ।

The staged drama cannot be regarded as *good* unless the learned (spectators) are pleased with the presentation.

The Process of Art-Creation

I would like to analyse this complex process of art-creation using an illustration, namely the Krauñcavadha episode, which initiated Vālmīki's *Rāmāyaṇa*. While a couple of *krauñca* birds is engaged in love-making and mating, a hunter with his arrow shoots the male of the couple. This situation should arouse different kinds of reactions in (1) the male *krauñca*, (2) the female *krauñca*, (3) the hunter and (4) the poet Vālmīki. Although the feelings of both the male and the female *krauñca* would be different — they should indeed be that of grief and distress — the feeling of the hunter would be that of happiness (for he has achieved his target). But the feeling of Vālmīki would be much more complex. It would be that of compassion. His sadness would be different from the sadness of the she-*krauñca* and the hurt *krauñca* male. It would be a reaction to the grief of the birds, but it would also be arising out of the cruel act of the hunter. This reaction could have taken the form of action in challenging the hunter, but it is manifested at the hands of the poet, in the form of poetry. The state of mind which leads the poet to transform it in *some objective* form, is *kavi-antargata-bhāva.*[11] But, while giving it the objective form the poet does not transform the whole of his experience (personal subjective feelings) although he expects that the objective form when experienced by the spectators or the readers would be able to evoke a similar kind of feeling as the poet had, when he went through the experience himself. (We need not go into how successfully this is carried out.) He, therefore, transmits, so to say, the plasma of his experience in some kind of language — poetic language in the case of poetry. If it is a stage-drama, this language again undergoes a transformation and is reduced to a contiuum of *vibhāva, anubhāva, vyabhicārī bhāva,* with different kinds of acting or *abhinaya* fused with it. This presentation is only some kind of symbolic representation. But, what the spectator understands by this is not just the symbolic representation, but the meaning of that symbolic representation (along with the symbolic representation itself). In the case of any art form, it is not just the meaning segregated from the symbolic form as in ordinary language, it is meaning along with the symbolic form. The pure symbolic form may differ from ordinary language to art language and from one art to another art. In the case of *poetry* it would assume the form of *śabda* or word; in the case of painting or sculpture it would be *rūpa;* in the case of dance and drama, it would be *rasa,* where *śabda* and *rūpa* are amalgamated into one. The meaning-part which is represented in symbolic form is *sthāyī bhāva* (as transformed in this process).[12] It is the continuum of the continuing, basic and

11. *Kaverantargatam bhāvam* (NŚ 7.2).

12. In fact, the *sthāyī bhāva* can grow from complexity to complexity. Thus, the *sthāyī bhāva* of the poet would be more complex than the *sthāyī bhāva* of the *krauñca* assuming of course that the *krauñca* has *sthāyī bhāva* and self-consciousness.

sufficient "thought and/or feelings." Such *sthāyī bhāvas* are latently present in the symbolic form of any kind or medium, and must be present, *ipso facto*, in the mind of the artist in the form of intentions.[13] These *sthāyī bhāvas* are again aroused in the mind of the spectator when the artists' intentions are communicated to him. These *sthāyīs* are, therefore, *trayāvasthā*[14] i.e. having three kinds of transformations, whether they are represented in symbolic forms or are the inmates of the artist's and spectator's mind. When they assume the symbolic forms they are called *rasa*[15] (in the case of drama) or *śabda* (in the case of poetry) or *rūpa* (in the case of painting or sculpture). But whether in the symbolic form or in the form of meaning or intention of the artist, it is the transformation of the same stuff, namely, the experience of the artist. Bharata mentions this clearly when he says: *evam rasāśca, bhāvāśca, tryavasthā nāṭake smṛtāḥ* (एवं रसाश्च भावाश्च त्र्यवस्था नाटके स्मृताः, *NŚ* 7.130). But, there is something more in this process. The spectator does not merely stop at understanding the meaning of the symbolic form. If the representation is proper it may arouse in him a state which the poet or the artist had not reduced to a symbolic form. Like the poet or artist, the spectator also will be charged with some emotion. He would be happy or sad (*harṣādīn ca adhigacchanti* (हर्षादीन च अधिगच्छन्ति) (*NŚ* 6.before 33).

Bharata thinks that this representation is of eight kinds (*aṣṭau nāṭyarasāḥ smṛtāḥ*, अष्टौ नाट्यरसाः स्मृताः) and corresponding *sthāyī bhāvas* are also of eight types, although the emotional charge will be only of two types, either of happiness or of sadness. But, the process of arousing a reaction does not stop

---

13. Whether these intensions are successfully transmitted or transmitted in some deviated form.
14. *Evam rasāśca bhāvāśca trayāvasthā nāṭake smṛtāḥ* (*NŚ* 7.130).
15. Later this concept was further and further extended.

here. The spectator knows that it is only an art and not a reality. So although the basic emotional reaction is of happiness and of sadness, ultimately it leads to enjoyment only. This is described by Bharata as *daivikī siddhi*. He says, one who knows that *rasas* and *bhāvas* are transformed into three stages and knows them in their right perspective, attains the best of the *siddhis* — *ya evametān jānāti sa gacchet siddhimuttamām* (य एवमेतान् जानाति स गच्छेत सिद्धिमुत्तमाम्). And this *siddhi* is explained by Bharata as a state where the spectator is silent, without any kind of mild or violent reaction, etc. (*supra* 7.after 5).

The concept of *rasa* is central to Bharata's theory of drama. It stands for the (dramatic) continuum[16] which the dramatist, the director and the actors create and which is appreciated by the spectators. But as a matter of fact the appreciation actually begins with the poet. The stage director and the actors in addition to being the creators of stage-drama, have also some kind of a role in the process of appreciation, for without the prior appreciation of the poetry it would not be possible to translate the poetry into the stage-medium. Bharata in *Nāṭyaśāstra* mentions two processes relevant to stage-drama: the process of creation and the process of appreciation; *rasa* should arise at the end of the first process and the second process should begin with the tasting of *rasa*. *Rasa* is the object of both these processes[17] and is manifested in the form of *nāṭya*.

16. Perhaps the total stage medium cannot be separated from this continuum, although like an electric current which can be distinguished from its conductor, the essence or *rasa* could be distinguished.

17. When the concept of *rasa* was used in the context of (audio) poetry, this concept of *rasa* was the object of the creative process of appreciation, but since there was no visible creative process in poetry, finally *rasa* became the end object in the process of appreciation.

Rasa was thus associated with some kind of audio-visual image — *dṛśya-śravya kāvya*.

Rasa for Alaṁkārins

The word *rasa* was taken by *alaṁkārins* from Bharata. It was used by Bhāmaha, Udbhaṭa, Vāmana, Daṇḍin, Rudraṭa, Rudrabhaṭṭa and others, for explaining auditory poetry which has significant visual overtones and which takes the form of visual images even in the absence of a stage. In order to explain this phenomenon sometimes they added the term *vat* to it. Thus *rasavat* (*rasa* + *vat*) was recognized by them as one of the *alaṁkāras* in poetry. The *alaṁkārins* thought that it was due to the presence of the *alaṁkāra* called *rasavat* that we have the feel of seeing a picture while reading or hearing. The word *rasavat* was used in two ways: (1) that *which possessed rasa* and (2) that *which was like rasa*. Vāmana while explaining the poetic characteristic called *kānti* says, *dīptarasattvaṁ kāntiḥ* (दीप्तरसत्वं कान्तिः).[18] Glowing *rasa* is *kānti*. In the course of time the theory of *rasa* was used more and more in the context of poetry, perhaps, because poetry became more popular than the stage. The appreciation of poetry was also expressed in terms of *rasa*. From Rudrabhaṭṭa to Mammaṭa and Viśvanātha through Ānandavardhana, Bhaṭṭanāyaka, Bhaṭṭatauta and Abhinavagupta one can locate this transition.

Transformation in the Meaning of Rasa

In this transition the theory also assumed a new form. *Rasa* stood for taste, happiness and (some kind of artistic) bliss. Viśvanātha mentions that *rasa* is *Brahmāsvādasahodara* (ब्रह्मास्वादसहोदर), i.e. *rasa* is like a sibling of the experience (or taste) of *Brahman*. The original theory of Bharata went into

18. *Kāvyālaṅkārasūtravṛtti*, by Vāmana.

oblivion till D.K. Bedekar, Barlingay and Kangle pointed out that originally *rasa* stood for *āsvādya* and not for *āsvāda*. It is important to point out that some ancient Sanskrit scholars actually mention this transition. Rudrabhaṭṭa, for example, says that *rasa* which was originally used by Bharata in the context of *nāṭya*, he would now use in the context of poetry,

> प्रायो नाट्यं प्रति प्रोक्ता भरताद्यैः रसस्थितिः ।।
> यथामति यथाप्येषा काव्यं प्रति निगद्यते ।।
>
> *prāyo nāṭyaṁ prati proktā, bharatādyaiḥ rasasthitiḥ* ।
> *yathāmati yathāpyeṣā kāvyaṁ prati nigadyate* ।।[19]

Focus on Appreciation

When the concept of *rasa* was used in the context of poetry in general (and not only in the context of performing arts like stage-drama) the process of production of *rasa* became more and more insignificant and the process of appreciation assumed greater importance. This new approach to *rasa* theory also marked an important development. Earlier, nobody had paid attention to the nature and status of poetry although they had suggested that it was an outcome, or expression of a poet's experience. Bharata had distinguished between taste or *āsvāda* and that which is tasted (experience) or *āsvādya*. Abhinavagupta retained this distinction but pointed out that the world of art was different from reality and was on another plane in the strict sense of the term, that is, the world of art was of the nature of taste only, that it was like *alātacakra* and that while dealing with art one had to follow the *vijñānavāda* theory, *vijñānavādā-valaṁbanāt*[20] (*NŚ* with *Abhinavabhāratī*, BOS). Let us have a look at the development of the theory from Bharata

---

19. *Śṛṅgāra-Tilaka* (1/5).
20. Bharata had this in mind. For example, in the second chapter of *Nāṭyaśāstra* he says, →

to Abhinavagupta. Perhaps in this development three different currents merged into one. On the one hand there were *alaṁkarins* like Bhāmaha, Vāmana, Daṇḍin, Rudraṭa and Rudrabhaṭṭa who were trying to apply the theory of *rasa*, either through *rasavat alaṁkāra* (रसवत् अलंकार) or through a poetic quality called *kānti* (which manifested through *rasa*). On the other hand there were scholars of poetry who were developing the concepts of *dhvani* (ध्वनि), *vakrokti* (वक्रोक्ति) (and *aucitya,* औचित्य). In addition, there was the third school, to which scholars, who interpreted Bharata's *Nāṭyaśāstra* belonged, scholars like Bhaṭṭa Lollaṭa, Śaṅkuka, Bhaṭṭanāyaka and Bhaṭṭatauta. Abhinavagupta, while criticizing his predecessors incorporated their views which were consistent with his and brought forth a new theory which came to be known as *Rasa-Dhvani Siddhānta* (रस-ध्वनि सिद्धान्त).

Views of Lollaṭa, Śaṅkuka and Bhaṭṭatauta

Bhaṭṭa Lollaṭa while accepting Bharata's theory about the emergence of *rasa*, interpreted the aphorism, *nahi rasādṛte kaścidapi arthaḥ pravartate* (नहि रसादृते कश्चिपदि अर्थः प्रवतते, *NŚ* 6.after 32) in his own way. He asked the question: the union of *vibhāva, anubhāva* and *vyabhicārīs with what?*[21] and replied that it was the *union* with *sthāyī bhāva* in the poet's mind (and not the transformation of *sthāyī bhāva*). This was a blow to the view that on account of a poet's/director's strength of *imagination,*

→ देवानां मानसी सृष्टिगृहेषूपवनेषु च। यथाभावाभिनिर्वर्त्याः सर्वे भावास्तु मानुषाः ॥

devanām mānasī sṛṣṭrgṛheṣūpavaneṣu ca ।
yathā bhāvabhinirvartyāḥ sarve bhāvāstu mānuṣāḥ ॥ (*NŚ* 2.5, 27-28).

This again is repeated in 27th and 28th verse in the same Chapter.

21. Bharata wanted to say that the main continuum in the poet's mind is objectively expressed in the form of *vibhāva*, etc. and again understood by the spectators in the form of meaning or *kāvyārtha*.

the *sthāyī* takes the objective form — *rasa*, through the combination of *vibhāva*, *anubhāva* and *vyabhicārī*. What kind or relation did Lollaṭa envisage, between *sthāyī* and *vibhāva*, *anubhāva* and *vyabhicārī*? Perhaps he did not want to say anything different from what Bharata had said. But, Lollaṭa's theory, in the hands of his traditional interpreters, gave more importance to *sthāyī* as *kāvyārtha* and the objective element (the medium, etc.) in stage drama was ignored. It helped the theory to assume that the status of *rasa* was of the nature of taste which indeed was true. But it was still necessary to maintain the distinction between the taste and the object of taste. Abhinavagupta (and perhaps Bhaṭṭanāyaka) in his commentary maintains this distinction. He says actors as such are just like pots or *pātra*, and then argues, a *pot* which is filled with liquor does not itself have the feel of the liquor's taste: *pātre na madyāsvādaḥ* (पात्रे न मद्यास्वादः).[22] But in the post-Abhinavagupta period the distinction gradually disappeared. Śaṅkuka who came after Lollaṭa (and before Abhinavagupta) objects to the argument of Lollaṭa and says *rasa* is merely the imitation (*anukaraṇa*, अनुकरण)[23] of *sthāyī*. The real *sthāyī* is not in the mind of the actor but in the mind of that person whom the actor is imitating. But if the imitation is to become *exact* it would go against the spirit of *drama* that is staged. Drama is not a photocopy of a real objective situation. Bhaṭṭanāyaka, therefore, brings in the concept of *sādhāraṇīkaraṇa*. The (real) person and the (real) event which he brings about in real life are particulars, but when they are presented in drama, poetry or art their particularity is erased. Bharata himself recognizes this and says, *sāmānaya-guṇa-yogena* (सामान्यगुणयोगेन). What the

22. *NŚ* BOL, p. 291.

23. Here *anukaraṇa* is to be understood as that which comes after *karaṇa* just as *anubhāva* is that which comes after *bhāva*.

spectator feels is the experience, bereft of any particularity attached to it. Bhaṭṭatauta while commenting on Śaṅkuka, says that an actor does not *imitate* the *sthāyī* of the person whose role he performs. He understands his thought and then acts on his own.[24] The whole process on the stage is that of simulation.

Abhinavagupta's View

Abhinavagupta incorporated all these arguments in his theory and drew some important conclusions.

1. Drama, poetry or any art in general is not a piece of reality. It is a creation of the human mind. In this context we have to follow the *idealistic*[25] model, *vijñānavādāvalaṁbanāt*.[26] Since it is a human creation it belongs to an order other than the first. It is not *laukika*. It is *alaukika*.
2. In this world, of course, we would distinguish between the object of taste (*āsvādya*) and the taste of *āsvāda*. *Rasa* may be the *object* of taste and still it belongs to the category of taste only. This should be understood on the model of *pratyabhijñā* where both the *viṣaya* and *viṣayī* are of nature of *jñāna* only.
3. Since poetry (or drama) is *alaukika*, even if it is concerned with *duḥkha* it belongs to the world of enjoyment and so it would result in some kind of pleasure or happiness which the spectators experience after experiencing earlier sadness expressed in poetry

---

24. According to Bhaṭṭatauta, the actor is not doing the act of initiation (*anukaraṇa*). What he does is due to *anuvyavasāya*.
25. Perhaps Bharata has something similar in his mind when he says: *devānām mānasi sṛṣṭiḥ*.
26. *Abhivanabhāratī* (BOS).

or drama.

Bhaṭṭanāyaka's View

Bhaṭṭanāyaka who was the elder contemporary of Abhinavagupta, had perhaps some important thesis on this point. But his work is lost and all that we now have are a few fragments which Abhinavagupta and a few others have quoted. Bhaṭṭanāyaka makes a distinction between the use of *rasa* in singular and use of *rasa* in plural. When he is commenting on *nahi rasādṛte kaścidapi arthaḥ pravartate* (नहि रसादृते कश्चिपदि अर्थः प्रवर्तते), he says that here the word *rasa* is used in singular and so is *mahārasa*.[27] Perhaps he is suggesting that this *mahārasa* is a parameter, a standard or scale by which the *rasa*s (and poetry) are to be measured or evaluated. The different *rasa*s are only the illustrations of the *mahārasa*. As regards the *mahārasa* he says, *na pratīyate, na utpadyate, na abhivyañjate . . . apitu abhyupagamyate* (*eva*) (न प्रतीयते, न उत्पद्यते, न अभिव्यंजते . . . अपितु अभ्युपगम्यते (इव)).[28] It is not cognized, it is not created, it is not experienced. It is only to be taken as a hypothesis. It is *parā-brahmāsvāda saṁvid* (परा ब्रह्मास्वाद संविद्) . It is somehow felt (through *bhāvanā*). *Bhāvanā* is a technical term in Pūrva-Mīmāṁsā. Therefore, scholars think that Bhaṭṭanāyaka could have belonged to the school of Mīmāṁsā, and that he was explaining the theory of *nāṭya* and poetry on the basis of Pūrva-Mīmāṁsā. Bhaṭṭanāyaka could have belonged to the school of Mīmāṁsā, but from the way he is explaining the theory it does not follow that he belonged to Mīmāṁsā school (at least in this context). A Mīmāṁsaka would certainly not talk of *parā-brahmāsvādasaṁvid*. But in the absence of any material available now on this subject by Bhaṭṭanāyaka, it is better not to comment further on his thesis. What Bhaṭṭanāyaka was pointing at was that *taste-model*

27. The word *mahārasa* is also used in Bharata's *Nāṭyaśāstra* (19.119).

28. *NŚ* (BOL), pp. 276-77.

is different from the *knowledge-model* and the *bhogīkaraṇa* process should not be understood on the lines of the knowledge process.

In the next chapter, I shall explain in greater detail how Bharata understood the concept of *rasa* and how it was differently intepreted by those who followed him.

5

Bharata's Rasa Theory

Rasa Theory: Bharata and Abhinavagupta

In the last chapter, I have taken the survey of how the word *rasa* was used from the Vedic times till the present day. The recent and contemporary scholars of poetics, however, forget that *rasa* theory was interpreted progressively in the course of time. They think that *rasa* was beatitude, happiness and lysis.* Abhinavagupta's interpretation of Bharata's *rasa* theory, as understood by these scholars, is also regarded as the authentic view of Bharata. This view is well reflected in R. Gnoli's work: *Aesthetic Experience According to Abhinavagupta* (1st edition). He writes, "In this way Bhaṭṭanāyaka and Abhinavagupta rescued the idea of *rasa* from the primitive and too concrete form which it had been given by Bhaṭṭa Lollaṭa and Śaṅkuka. *Rasa* is not a thing in itself, formed previous to the act of consciousness by which it is perceived, but the consciousness itself (and therefore, the perception) which, freed from external interference and from all practical desires, becomes *rasa* or aesthetic consciousness. The subject, when immersed in this state, finds in it the fulfilment of all his desires: in this sense, therefore, *rasa* is pleasure, beatitude, rest, lysis!" The remark is based on the present Indian tradition

* In the original Greek sense, loosening. The English sense denotes disintegration.

and perhaps correctly describes one particular aspect of aesthetic consciousness. But, did Bharata mean by *rasa* this particular experience, or, was the theory fathered on him by his modern followers? It is claimed that it is Abhinavagupta's interpretation of Bharata. It is not my object to criticise Abhinavagupta's theory of aesthetic consciousness for I believe that it correctly depicts one aspect of aesthetic experience. It is my object, however, to show that there are reasons for believing that by *rasa* Bharata meant something different which is in fact an essential element in his whole theory of dramatic art or *nāṭya*. In the following pages an attempt is made to disentangle this extremely important theory of artistic creatism which Bharata seems actually to have held, from the theories of later ages.

Nāṭya and Nāṭaka

I shall begin by asking a question about the meaning of the word *nāṭya*. The word *nāṭya* should be distinguished from the word *nāṭaka*, though it is not often done. Both these words are derived from the word *naṭ*, but on account of the different terminations added to *naṭ*, the words stand for two entirely different concepts. The word *nāṭya* is formed by adding *ṣañ* to *naṭ* and means the action or performance of the actor. *Nāṭya* is, thus, concerned with the staging of a drama (or *nāṭaka*). Bharata himself defines *nāṭya* as the imitation of that which takes place in the real world.

नानाभावोपसंपन्नं नानावस्थान्तरात्मकम् ।
लोकावृत्तानुकरणं नाट्यमेतन्मया कृतम् ॥

nānābhāvopasampannaṁ nānāvasthāntarātmakam ।
lokavṛttānukaraṇaṁ nāṭyametanmayā kṛtam ॥ — *NŚ* 1.112

The word *nāṭaka*, on the other hand, is formed by adding *aka* (*ṇvul*) to the word *naṭa*, which again is formed by adding *ac* to the root *naṭ* and is to be classed under the genus "poetry," e.g. in *kāvyeṣu nāṭakam ramyam*. It can very well be seen that though of course *nāṭya* and *nāṭaka* are closely related to each other, *nāṭaka* is connected more with the content or story aspect, e.g. in

> नृपतीनां यच्चरितं नानारसभावसंभृतं बहुधा ।
> सुखदुःखोत्पत्तिकृतं भवति हि तन्नाटकं नाम ॥
>
> *nṛpatīnāṁ yaccaritaṁ nānārasabhāva-saṁbhṛtaṁ bahudhā* ।
> *sukhaduḥkhotpattikṛtaṁ bhavatihi tannāṭakaṁ nāma* ॥

and *nāṭya* with the manifestation of the story on the stage. It should be borne in mind that when a *nāṭaka* is not staged it still remains a *nāṭaka* even if it has been reduced to spoken or written symbols. But it cannot be a *nāṭya* unless it is staged.

Stage Medium: An Aspect of Nāṭya

This stage medium, then, is an important aspect of *nāṭya*. It is a medium in which the poet's or rather artist's mental states become, so to speak, objectified. In *nāṭaka*, they become objectified in a different way, that is, in written letters or spoken sounds. In Sanskrit, this medium is called *śabda*, sound. Let me call the written or spoken symbols, the language of poetry or *nāṭaka* and the stage medium, the language of *nāṭya*. All the constituents of stage performances will thus from the language of *nāṭya*. It may be objected, and perhaps rightly, that at the time of Bharata this was not the conception of *nāṭaka*. But at any rate this was the conception of poetry or *kāvya*, and the language or medium of *kāvya* was *śabda*. What is relevant for my purpose is to show that just as *śabda* is a medium for poetry, it is not a medium for *nāṭya* if it is isolated from the other constituents. Bharata was interested in giving us a system of rules about *nāṭya*. He wanted to show us how to transform the content that was in a poet's mind into the stage language.

It was this language — or at least a part of it — that, I hold, was called *rasa* by Bharata.

The Sāṁkhya Theory

In almost all the systems of Indian philosophy, the words *śabda, sparśa, rūpa, rasa* and *gandha* occur, in the Vedas and Upaniṣads too. But, I think, the earlier technical use of these words can be found in the Sāṁkhya system. Unfortunately, almost all the literature on Sāṁkhya is lost and the only commentaries on the *Kārikā* of Īśvarakr̥ṣṇa (ईश्वरकृष्ण सांख्य-कारिका) that exist are written from the Vedāntic point of view. In spite of these difficulties, it is possible to discuss the place of the concepts of *śabda*, etc. in Sāṁkhya. I have, of course, to base my view on the scanty material that is available to me in the *Kārikā* of Īśvarakr̥ṣṇa, with the commentaries thereon by Gauḍapāda and Vācaspati Miśra and Yuktidīpikā (with an anonymous commentary on it) by Vijñāna Bhikṣu, and exposition of Sāṁkhya in other systems such as Buddhism and Vedānta. From the information that is available, it can be safely asserted that for Sāṁkhya, *śabda, sparśa, rūpa, rasa* and *gandha* are *tanmātra*s, and that *tanmātra* is a word that is indigenous to Sāṁkhya system. *Tanmātra* means "that itself," *tadeva iti tanmātram* (तदेव इति तन्मात्रम्). The concept is something like Kant's concept of the thing-in-itself. The world as it is known to us is a product of the mind and the *tanmātra*s together (not the product of mind alone). This world, therefore, consists of five gross elements or *pañca mahābhūta*s. *Mahābhūta*s are thus the knowable or epistemic objects, and *tanmātra*s are the ontological objects which reach us as *mahābhūta*s. It is in this sense, then, that we can say that *mahābhūta*s are born out of *tanmātra*s. But, the language of Sāṁkhya should not be literally understood. It is on account of the difficulty of expressing the thought that Sāṁkhya has to use such a language. The *tanmātra*s cannot be known by us, their existence is postulated in order to distinguish veridical knowledge from something false of knowledge process would consist of three elements: (1) the knower or the subject, (2) the thing in itself that is known, and (3) the thing as it is known to the subject. Whenever a knower comes in contact with a *tanmātra*, what he knows is a *mahābhūta*. *Tanmātra* is thus logically prior to *mahābhūta* and serves in the realm of Sāṁkhya ontology as an intermediary between the knower and *mahābhūta*. It is necessary to remember that neither the *tanmātra*s nor the *mahābhūta*s are psychological in nature, though they are usually so thought. *Mahābhūta*s are sensible objects and since the sense-organs are five, at least, in the Sāṁkhya conception of the term *mahābhūta*s are divided into five classes. Naturally, the nucleus (or the physical things) on which our sense-organs act are also regarded as five. The idea is that each sense-organ has a separate object for acting on. Of course, one could as well think that the object of five organs is one. But, the prejudice that each sense-organ has a separate object does not seem to be uncommon, as can be seen from the sense-datum theory. *Tanmātra*s, however, should not be confused with sense-data. For, as per Sāṁkhya, the physical objects and the *tanmātra*s are not different. The five *tanmātra*s are named after five senses because (1) no other convenient names are available, and (2) they are connected in a sense, with the sense-organs.

Rasanirmiti and Rasāsvāda Prakriyās

In some broad sense at least, a work of art is a thing, an entity. On one side, it is connected with its creator, the artist; and on the other side, it is connected with the appreciator. Art, thus, may be called a process, with three distinct stages involved in it. This may roughly be represented as (1) the states of artist's mind, (2) the objectified expression (of the artist), and (3) the appreciation or the states of the mind of the appreciator. This process may also be sub-divided into two sub-processes as their functions are entirely different. The first sub-process may be called the process of the creation of art and the second may be termed the process of the appreciation of art. In the terminology of Bharata, the first one is known as *rasanirmiti-prakriyā* (रसनिर्मिति प्रक्रिया) and the second one as *rasāsvāda prakriyā* (रसास्वाद प्रक्रिया). These processes may be represented in the following schemata:

(1) __________ (2) (2)__________ (3) (It could also be seen that, in some sense at least, the sub-process (1) ________ (2) is an inversion of the process (2) ________ (3) such that poles (1) and (3) may resemble each other in many respects.)

The pole (2), that is the objectified expression (of art) in a sense is independent of the poles (1) and (3). That is though it is dependent on (1) for its creation, it is not dependent on it for its existence. Similarly it is also independent of (3) for its existence though it is related to it for being appreciated. On the other hand pole (3) cannot exist if pole (2) does not exist.

There appears to be an interesting parallel in this account and Sāṁkhya account of knowledge. The pole (2) appears to be similar to the *tanmātra*s of the Sāṁkhya or the world that is absolutely independent of our knowledge, the only difference being that the *tanmātra*s belong to the real world whereas pole (2) belongs to the world of art. The pole (3) appears to be something like the *mahābhūta* of Sāṁkhya, which is a sort of construction of the knower. The sub-process with the poles 1 and 2 is again very similar to the Sāṁkhya process from *tanmātra* to *mahābhūta* with, of course, a difference that the art process of creation is more or less an inverted process of the one that is represented in Sāṁkhya. It is very similar to the process by which the Sāṁkhya philosopher, starting from the world of *mahābhūtas* arrives at an entity called *tanmātras*. The artist also draws his material from the world of *mahābhūtas*, a material which has been transformed into his individual experience. This individual experience starts as a background for the artistic creation and is sometimes known in the Indian theory of Art as *sthāyī bhāva* but should be rather known as *kavi-antargatabhāva*. The problem before an artist is to reduce his "individual" private experience to a medium which will be impersonal, independent of him, and knowable to all people who want to know it. This is pole (2) in our terminology and represents in the world of art a concept which is similar to that of *tanmātra* of the Sāṁkhya. The influence of the Sāṁkhya system on *Nāṭyaśāstra* is well known and several passages from *Naṭyaśāstra* can be quoted for proving that in *Nāṭyaśāstra* the language of Sāṁkhya is used. In fact, the word *rasa* (*tanmātra*) and *bhāva* used in *Nāṭyaśāstra* and the two processes to which I am referring above have been actually mentioned in the *Sāṁkhya Kārikā*. I quote below the fifty-second *Kārikā* from Īśvarakṛṣṇa which will indicate that the words *rasa, bhāva,* etc. are used in Sāṁkhya.

न विना भावैर्लिंगं न विना लिंगेन भावनिर्वृत्तिः ।
लिंगाख्यो भावाख्यास्तस्माद् द्विविधः प्रवर्तते सर्गः ॥

na vinā bhāvairliṅgaṁ na vinā liṅgena bhāvanirvṛtti ।
liṅgākhyo bhāvākhyāstasmād dvividhaḥ pravartate sargaḥ ॥

The *Kārikā* when translated means: without *bhāva* there cannot be *liṅga*, i.e *tanmātras*. Fortunately commentator Gauḍapāda is very clear on this point in his commentary of this *kārikā*. He clearly says that *liṅga* refers to *tanmātras* (*liṅgam na tanmātraḥ na*, लिंगम् न तन्मात्रः न), though in his commentaries on other *Kārikās* he has confused the meanings) and without *liṅga* or *tanmātra* the *bhāvas* cannot come into existence (the word *nirvṛtti* (निर्वृत्ति) also is used in *nāṭya*). Therefore, there are two kinds of creative processes, by name *bhāva* and by name *liṅga*.

Employment of Sāṁkhya Theory in the Indian Theory of Art

I, therefore, think that the Sāṁkhya theory of knowledge is used at some stage in the Indian theory of art in general and the *Nāṭyaśāstra* in particular, in the way I suggest. It thus appears to me that the terms referring to *tanmātra*s in the Sāṁkhya theory of knowledge, such as *śabda*, *rūpa* and *rasa*, were borrowed by the theory of art to designate the pole (2) or nucleus in the media of particular arts. *Śabda* was applied to the medium for literary arts like *kāvya*, *rūpa* for *citra* and *śilpa*, and *rasa* was used for *nāṭya*. There could not, in any real sense, be any fine art connected with *sparśa* and *gandha* as their fields, too, are covered by *śabda*, *rūpa* and *rasa*. I believe, at the time the *Nāṭyaśāstra* was written or edited this triple scheme must have been the basis for the classification of the arts. This is also, perhaps, the reason why we do find a special discussion of *rūpa* in the writings of Abhinavagupta himself. It is evident that the words *śabda*, *rūpa* and *rasa* should stand on the same level, and if one designates a class of media, so should the others. I think it is likely that in the course of history the originally intended meaning of these words were lost, perhaps under the influence of certain schools of philosophy. Thus, *rasa* which was originally intended to refer to an object (or medium or language) of *nāṭya* became, in the post-Abhinavagupta era, a mental state, a pleasure and aesthetic consciousness, and was applied not only to *nāṭya* but also to *kāvya* in general. As late Paul Hacker, of the University of Bonn, pointed out to me, later Sanskrit dramas were most unsuitable for staging and were most likely meant simply to be read. This factor also must have contributed to the change in the meaning of *rasa*. It is said that Abhinavagupta identified *kāvya* with *nāṭya*.[1] I think this is a misinterpretation. But, it should, nevertheless, corroborate the fact that *nāṭya* had lost its distinction from *nāṭaka* and *kāvya* in his time, that is about tenth or eleventh century CE.

Nāṭya and Kāvya

I think the modern followers of Abhinavagupta completely missed the point which Bharata wanted to convey. When Bharata talks about *nāṭya*, it is clear from his use of the word that *kāvya* or poetry was not intended. This is very plain, even from the cursory reading of the text of *Nāṭyaśāstra*. Whenever he wanted to speak of what we now call *kāvya*, he has specifically used the terms, *nāṭaka* and *kāvya*.[2] He also defines *nāṭya* and *nāṭaka* in different terms. This clearly indicates that Bharata did not intend to use these terms indiscriminately. In spite of this clear distinction, the propostition that *nāṭya* is poetry is attributed to Abhinavagupta for his language, *kāvyaṁ nāṭyameva* (काव्यं नाट्यमेव). Of course, it is possible that Abhinavagupta did not have the same concern with the staging of drama (*prayoga*) as did Bharata.

The Meaning of Nāṭya

It is necessary at this stage to dilate further on the meaning of *nāṭya*. Abhinavagupta himself defines *nāṭya* as follows:

यत्तु दशरूपकं तस्य योऽर्थः तदेव नाट्यम्।

---

1. In fact, I do not think that to say *kāvyam ca nāṭyameva* (काव्यम च नाट्यमेव) is to identify poetry and stage drama.
2. (a) *vāgaṅgasattvopetān kāvyārthān*, (वागंगसत्त्वोपेतान् काव्यार्थान्), *NŚ* 7 intro.

   (b) *trayāvasthāḥ nāṭake smṛtāḥ* (त्र्यवस्थाः नाटके स्मृताः), *NŚ* 7.130.

yattu daśarūpakaṁ tasya yo 'arthaḥ tadeva nāṭyam ।

That is, the[3] *artha* of *daśarūpaka* is *nāṭya*. This description, though in a sense correct, is very ambiguous and is likely to be misused unless the primary meaning of *nāṭya* is borne in mind. The object (or *viṣaya*)[4] of *daśarūpaka* may change inasmuch as the artistic medium changes. If the medium is word or ordinary language, this object could be easily identified with poetry; *nāṭya* would thus be equated with poetry. It appears to me that what Abhinavagupta quotes from *Nāṭyaśāstra* is wrongly understood. He says, *yat vakṣyate nāṭyasya eṣā tanuḥ* (यत् वक्ष्यते नाट्यस्य एषा तनुः). The chapter from which this passage is taken, really deals with the importance of speech in acting. In fact, Bharata also says a similar thing when he says.

इतिवृत्तं तु नाट्यस्य शरीरं परिकीर्तितम् ।

itivṛttaṁ tu nāṭyasya śarīraṁ parikīrtitam । — *NŚ* 19.1.

Separated from its context, the quotation is likely[5] to be misleading. The passage runs thus:

यो वागाभिनयः प्रोक्तो मया पूर्वं द्विजोत्तमाः ।
लक्षणं तस्य वक्ष्यामि स्वरव्यंजन-सम्भवम् ।
वाचि यत्नस्तु कर्तव्यो नाट्यस्येयं तनुः स्मृता ।

yo vāgābhinayaḥ prokto mayā pūrvaṁ dvijottamāḥ ।
lakṣaṇaṁ tasya vakṣyāmi svaravyañjana sambhavam ।
vāci yatnastu kartavyo nāṭyasyeyaṁ tanuḥ smṛtā ॥

— *NŚ* 15.1-2

---

3. The word *artha* is again ambiguous. It may mean the content of *daśarūpaka*, or may mean the story; or it may mean the symbolic manifestation, which may also be either (1) verbal or (2) theatrical.
4. *Artha* means *viṣaya*.
5. BOS, 2nd edition.

This passage does not say that *nāṭya* is the same as *kāvya*. Again, R.S. Ramaswamy Shastri, the learned editor of *Abhinavabhāratī*, I think, is wrong in insisting that *nāṭya* should not be regarded as *anukaraṇa*. I feel, on the contrary, it is much better to define *nāṭya* as *anukaraṇa*. Once, however, the distinctiveness of the medium that is employed in *nāṭya* is recognized it can easily be seen that *nāṭya* can substantially be the object or *viṣaya* of *daśarūpaka*. In a sense, even *nāṭaka* (including the representation of it in verbal symbols) may be thought to form a part of *nāṭya*, for it is the *nāṭaka* or the story of *nāṭaka* that is exhibited through the far more extensive resources of *nāṭya*.

Three Stages of an Art

It appears to me that the very crucial point that for Bharata, *naṭya, nāṭaka* or for that matter any art was essentially communicative, should not be overlooked. It should be recognized that any art consisted of three stages: the first stage is that when the art is still potentially in the poet's or artist's mind. The second stage is when the first stage becomes objectified and becomes independent of the artist and that it no longer remains private. It is at this stage that the arts become distinct from one another because their media are different. The third stage is that when the art is experienced by the appreciator, the art, so to speak, becomes a part of the spectator's mind. This stage is the interpretation of the second and is more or less analogous to the first.

Bharata points out:

एकोनपंचाशदिमे यथावद् भावाः त्र्यवस्थाः गदिता मया वः ।

ekonapañcāśadime yathāvad bhāvāḥ tryavasthāḥ gaditā mayā vaḥ ।

and again,

एवं रसाश्च भावाश्च त्र्यवस्थाः नाटके स्मृताः ।

evaṁ rasāśca bhāvāśca tryavasthāḥ nāṭake smṛtāh ॥[6]

The significance of the word *trayāvasthā* does not seem to have been noticed by any commentator. Even Abhinavagupta[7] does not comment on it and in several editions of *Nāṭyaśāstra*, the word is replaced by another word *vyavasthā*. But the word *tryavasthā* is a key word for the understanding of Bharata's theory. Bharata is pointing out that *bhāva*s or *rasa*s have three stages or three transformations. But for these transformations, *rasa* and *bhāva* — a term that will be discussed later — would be identical. What are these three stages? What is it that Bharata wants to convey by the expression *tryavasthā*? As has been pointed out above, Bharata is here referring to three different stages in the theory of *nāṭya*. The theory, however, will hold for any art or for that matter for language.[8] Let me try to explain it further.

Art as Communication

It must be admitted that art, like language, is in a very important sense communicative. This communication is between the artist and the appreciator and is carried on through a certain medium — an art. The state (or content) of mind (feelings) which the artist is impelled to express, as well as the effort on the mind of the appreciator are both mental and perhaps, in some way, similar or equivalent. But, in the

6. *NŚ* 7.107, 130.
7. At least his commentry is not available.
8. I think language and arts are similar in many respects. It must be admitted that the transition from stage 1 to stage 2 is extremely complicated and has problems of its own.

realm of art, there cannot be any direct transmission of the contents of the artist's mind to the mind of the appreciator. There cannot be any direct transition (or transmission) from the artist to the appreciator. The content of the artist's mind must take some form which acts as a medium between the artist and the appreciator and may vary from art to art. It is through such medium that the message of the artist can be carried to readers, spectators or audience. In fact, it is on account of the variations of medium that one art differs from another. *Naṭya* differs from *kāvya* in respect of this medium, the medium of *kāvya* or literature is "ordinary language or word or *śabda*," the medium of drama that is staged (*nāṭya*) is something different, not *abhinaya* or acting alone; it is not entirely *nāṭya*.[9] It is in a sense the stage with all its constituents. A suitable word is to be found for it. To express this idea, I believe Bharata employed the word *rasa* on the analogy of the word *śabda*, borrowing it from the metaphysics of Sāṁkhya and from *Atharvaveda*.

The three Stages of Communication

Before proceeding further, let us note the relations that exist amongst the three stages. Let me call them S1, S2 and S3. S1 refers to the content of the artist's mind, all that he wants to convey or express. S2 represents the public or objectified mental facts or S1 as transformed into symbols. S3 again depicts them

9. The word *nāṭya* is ambiguous. By it, we may understand something less than *rasa*, or something more. We can also use the words *rasa* and *nāṭya* as synonymous as suggested by Abhinavagupta, *tena rasāḥ eva nāṭyam* (तेन रसः एव नाट्यम, p. 267, *NŚ* G.O.S., 2nd edition). But while doing so we must be aware that we are employing them in a sense which is given to them by our definition and that we are not employing them for an art which is distinct from literature, or *kāvya*.

as they are in the mind of the appreciator. S3 again constitutes the meaning that the symbols S2 have for the appreciator. Let this meaning[10] be symbolized by the letter 'M.' The relation amongst S1, S2 and S3 can be expressed in the following way:

$$(1)\ \frac{S1}{M} = S2 \qquad (2)\ M\,(S2) = S3$$

If the above equations are roughly correct, then it will be the object of any artist to put forward his ideas, or the content of his mind in S2. It must, however, be remembered that S2 may differ according to the difference in medium. Let this difference in media be represented by letters D, D', D", D^n. I may then say that the forms of all arts may be expressed by the following notations:

$$D_{S2} \;..\; D'_{S2} \;..\; D''_{S2} \;..\; D^n_{S2}$$

It can be very easily seen that the creative function of the artist ceases with the creation of a member of the series D_{S2} ... D^n_{S2}. Any art must be located only within this series. It is this series which the appreciator knows and when he knows it, knows it with the meaning attached to one or other of the series, that is, knows it as S3. The relation between the D_{S2} series and the S3 could easily be interpreted as analogous to the knowledge process as visualized by Sāṁkhya. S3 is something like the world as we know it — to use Kant's terminology, a phenomenal world. In order to know this world we assume that in the physical reality there must be some datum. This datum can be compared to D_{S2} series. The Sāṁkhya concepts of *tanmātra* and *mahābhūta* can, in exactly the same way, be regarded as parallel with the D_{S2} series and

---

10. Refer to Professor Brough's article on "Some Indian Theories of Meaning," published in *Transactions of the Philological Society*, 1953.

S3. The real world of physical objects consists only of *tanmātras*, though it is perceptible to us as consisting of *mahābhūtas*. Similarly, the world created by the artists consists only of the D_{S2} series though when it is known by the appreciator it is invested with its meaning and is called S3. M is a constant whether it is the first stage or the third and will be present potentially in the second stage also. This is *sthāyī*. When Jagannātha talks of *gocarīkriyamāṇatva*, he refers to this D_{S2} series.

How are we going to interpret and describe the D_{S2} series in the context of *nāṭya* and what name are we to give to this mediatory series? In other words, what will be the *nāṭya* language for expressing the ideas of the artist? What will be the material of such a language?

The Language of Nāṭya

The language of *nāṭya* will differ from that of poetry. The material of this language will consist of visible and audible symbols; it will consist of the cast and action of actors, and also the environment. All these together will form a *nāṭya* language and it is into this language that the thoughts or the ideas of the artists, that is S1 will have to be translated.

Let me illustrate the point. Suppose an artist has to express a love episode between hero and heroine, say Śaṅkara and Pārvatī. It cannot simply be in written or spoken symbols: one party making an offer and the other accepting it. With this mental event, love, certain bodily symptoms are necessary concomitants. The mental content is expressed through bodily expressions and behaviour, very peculiar to the situation. In the actual world too, if a lover expresses his love to his beloved and the beloved accepts the love the whole situation cannot be simply verbal and devoid of proper physiological signs understood as emotion. The beloved's acceptance of love — at least in Indian tradition — will be accompanied by certain bodily postures, or throbbing of the lips, or tremor of the body. The beloved will usually blush. She may not look straight into the lover's eyes, but may look downward and in many cases, may not utter a word but choose to remain silent. Usually, such a scene may occur at some beautiful place near a lake, where there are lotuses. The dramatist, the creator of the art, has to conceive the whole of this complex situation with all its (mental) implications before expressing it in words or symbols. And, in the act of staging of this drama, if the stage director is different from the dramatist, he has to construct on the stage, with the help of the set of actors and situations, all that the dramatist has to convey. The stage director thus makes use of this material in order to give a concrete form to the ideas of the artist, i.e. the dramatist. The set of actors and environment and the acting and the bodily expressions, the direction and the director: all these form the material of the *nāṭya* language, just as the meaningful words and their syntax form part of poetry. I think, it was this *nāṭya* language or rather language medium that was called *rasa*[11] by Bharata, in the same way as the language medium of literature or poetry was called *śabda*.[12] Just as ordinary language or a sentence consists of words, similarly, this language consists of *vibhāva* (i.e. set of actors and environment), *anubhāva* (the expressions) connected with acting (*abhinaya*) which is of three

11. It is possible that *rasa* may be the message (or M/*sthāyī bhāva*) passed through the conductor or *nāṭya* language. But whether *rasa* is M/or *sthāyī bhāva* it cannot be separated from the medium or language.

12. At a later stage *rasa* became a technical word for expressing any art medium.

varieties, *vācika, āṅgika* and *sāttvika,*[13] and *vyabhicārī bhāva* (bodily and organic states, poses and movements). Bharata thought that such *nāṭya* language-patterns would be of eight types and classified them under different *rasa*s like *śṛṅgāra, vīra,* etc.

I have stated that any art can be conceived as having three stages, S1, S2, (or D_{S2}) and S3. I have also stated that S1 is mental and is concerned with the states of the artist's or poet's mind. I have further said that the state of the poet's mind is given a public or concrete form in S2 (or D_{S2}). I have also suggested that S1 is what Bharata thought to be the internal state of artist and M the *sthāyī bhāva*. Now, it may be objected here that this analysis, though adequate for arts like "readable poetry" or painting or sculpture, is not adequate for *nāṭya*. The art of *nāṭya,* unlike other arts, is concerned with a set of four different kinds of persons, (1) the dramatist, (2) the stage director, (3) the actor, and (4) the character played by the actor. Each one of the first three in his turn tries to express what he conceives in his mind and so a problem arises: whose mental state it is that is manifested in D_{S2}. In other words, what is S1? Is it concerned with the mental states of the dramatist, as I have earlier suggested, or with the stage director, the actor, or the character that is being played? In *Abhinavabhāratī,* a lot of discussion is centered round the problem, the problem of "location" of *sthāyī bhāva* as it is called and the theories of Bhaṭṭa Lollaṭa and Śaṅkuka, as they are understood by the contemporary scholars, have contributed considerably to carry the meaning of the discussion on a wrong track.

It is true that in *nāṭya,* each of these four agents in a sense, contribute to the manifestation of D_{S2}. D_{S2} is, in some sense,

13. The fourth type which is known as *āhārya* is also present but its action is unseen.

mentally conceived by the dramatist, the stage director and also in most cases, the actor. But, to "locate" S1, in either the stage director or the actor or the real hero is based on certain misconception. The mistake lies in the fact that the complexity of the human mind was not properly conceived or expressed by the commentators of *Nāṭyaśāstra*. A man cannot only experience some experience, but can also experience that someone else experiences some experience. He can imagine such or more complex situations and try to objectify them. A man who does this is a dramatist. He alone conceives the drama. It is he who conceives that his hero should behave in a particular way in a particular situation. It is not really material whether the real hero has ever existed or if he has existed whether he behaved in a similar way in that situation. It is this creativeness of the dramatist which is accepted and carried out by the stage director and the actor. Their work is not original, but is rather that of expressing the ideas of the dramatist. In this sense, then, both the stage director and the actor are only factors in D_{S2}. Even if they improve on the original ideas of the dramatist, it would mean that they have shown better understanding of the situation and that their mental states were just the improved editions of the original. Both the S1 and M must therefore, be referred to the mind of the dramatist alone.

I believe the interpreters of Bharata like Bhaṭṭa Lollaṭa and Śaṅkuka missed the point that all that Bharata wanted to describe was the language and technique of expressing the ideas in the mind of the artist — in this context, the dramatist. Bhaṭṭa Lollaṭa raised this problem but because of the ambiguity of his expression, ultimately the discussion was carried to wrong track by the commentators who came after Lollaṭa. They centered their attack against Bhaṭṭa Lollaṭa and Śaṅkuka who discussed theories about *sthāyī bhāva* as to whether it was in the mind of the actor or of the real hero. Since *rasa* was supposed to succeed *sthāyī bhāva*, the real notion of *rasa* was misconceived as soon as *sthāyī bhāva* was located at a wrong place. They, therefore, missed the point that Bharata was interested mainly in the production or *niṣpatti* of *rasa*, in the production of D_{S2}. Since they identified *rasa* with the aesthetic consciousness of the appreciator they thought that there could not be any process like the production of *rasa* (*rasa niṣpatti).* They, thus, further missed the point that Bharata distinguished between the process of production of *rasa* (*rasa-niṣpatti*) and the experiencing or testing of *rasa* (*rasāsvāda*). They therefore, thought that *rasa* was intrinsic to the appreciator (*rasikagata*), and manifested only in him, and was mental[14] in nature (*āsvādarūpa*). They totally forgot the distinction between *mental* and *public* and forgot that the creative process of art is concerned with making public that which is something mental or that which is in the mind of the artist (*vide* Chapter VII). They thus completely neglected the keyword in Bharata's theory that *rasa* and *bhāva* and *trayāvasthā*, that is they are manifested in three stages. Bharata, as a matter of fact, clearly distinguished *rasa* from another stage — a fourth one, i.e. happiness, which he called *harṣa.* He talks of *harṣa* while dealing with the process of the experience of *rasa*. It seems clear that the great commentators imposed their own theories on Bharata, oblivious of his profound concern with the actual staging of a drama. Their theories may be important in the history of poetics and aesthetics, but they should not be allowed to replace Bharata's older theory which has its own virtues. It is only by misinterpreting Bharata's intentions and misreading Bharata's texts that a theory like this could be

14. Which indeed it was, but for different reasons.

superimposed on *Nāṭyaśāstra*. The problem before Bharata was relatively simple; it was how to exhibit a drama. All that he tries to do is to explain the different aspects of this technique which concerns the body of *nāṭya*. The problem before his successors was purely philosophic and I believe that Bharata's concern with the technique of production has been sacrificed entirely for the sake of philosophic speculation. Indeed in this process, the theory of art was also lost.

For Bharata state (1) and state (3) or, as I called them, S1 and S3 were definitely mental. For him the state S1 was "internal" as can be seen from his words: *kaverantaragataṁ bhāvam* (कवेरन्तर्गतं भावम्). State S3 was the meaning of, and reaction to *rasa* and could also, in one sense, be termed *sthāyī bhāva*, as the state is similar to it, though Bharata never says so on account of its transformation to M. The state of *rasa* came in between the two, S1 and S3, i.e. it succeeded the meaning in the (dramatist's) artist's mind.[15] But, if the meaning in artist's mind or rather the artist's intention is confused with a *bhāva* in the mind of the appreciator, i.e. S3, then *rasa*, which Bharata says, succeeds *sthāyī bhāva*, i.e. S1, could easily be misunderstood as something succeeding S3.[16] Now this S4 could be a state of pleasure or happiness and all that the present-day scholars say may be perhaps true of S4.

S3 is then taken as a *sthāyī bhāva* and the state of *rasa* which succeeds *sthāyī bhāva* is, therefore, taken as pleasure or aesthetic consciousness. But, this kind of logic is based on a fundamental error that *sthāyī bhāva* was state S3. This in turn is based on the failure to distinguish between the process of production

---

15. In fact, identical after transformation from 1 to 2 and 2 to 3.

16. Since for Abhinavagupta and Bhaṭṭanāyaka there could not be any "production" of *rasa* it could be conceived that S1 and S2 (or D_{S2}) do not exist.

of *rasa* (*rasa niṣpatti*) and the process of tasting or experiencing of *rasa* (*rasāsvāda*). It is on account of this confusion that *rasa*, which for Bharata was not mental at all, became dogmatically mental in later times and was identified with *artha* (meaning) or *āsvāda* which Bharata used for conveying the S3. This paved the way for the condensation or distortion of *rasa-dhvani* theory. The *dhvani* theory is, in fact, a theory about *artha*,[17] i.e. S3. Perhaps, as soon as *rasa* was identified with S3, the distortion could easily take place. It is, however, interesting to note that though the meaning of *rasa* was transformed, the meaning of *śabda* and *rūpa* which belonged originally to the same universe as *rasa*, did not undergo any such transformations.

Evidence from Nāṭyaśāstra

Whether all that I say is right or wrong can be verified from the text of *Nāṭyaśāstra* itself. I, therefore, propose to offer in translation an important passage from Bharata. After giving the list (*saṁgraha*) of all the constitutents of *nāṭya* he says:

न हि रसादृते कश्चिदपि अर्थः प्रवर्तते ।

na hi rasādṛte kaścidapi arthaḥ pravartate ॥ (*NŚ* 6.after 32)

"We shall, therefore, first describe the *rasa*s (for) without *rasa* there could not be any *artha*." This *rasa* is produced there (i.e. on the stage) on account of the combination of *vibhāva*, *anubhāva* and *vyabhicārī bhāva*. This combination (or *saṁyoga* is different *samavāya* but) should not be understood as a just

17. Like all words, *artha* also has its technical and non-technical uses. When we say, "what is the meaning of this word," we simply mean "what is the bearer" of this word. This was evidently in the mind of Abhinavagupta when he commented on the sentence of Bharata — *rasāḥ iti kaḥ padārthaḥ* (रसः इति कः पदार्थः)? by *rasa iti padasya, śṛṅgārādipravartitasya kaḥ* (रस इति पदस्य शृंगारादिप्रवरर्तितस्य कः). But for his modern followers, K.N. Watve, the word *artha* used here stood for S3.

mechanical combination, but should be understood as a combination of parts and a whole or rather of sentence (*vākhya*) and words (*padas*).[18] (The *vibhāvas* are the set of actors and the environment. *Anubhāvas* are different kinds of supplementary states like "smiling," etc. which are useful in acting, and the *vyabhicārī bhāvas* are different bodily and mental states, etc.). How do you explain this process of the production of *rasa*? What is your illustration? It will be explained by us. Just as an account of the combination (chemical) of many spices, medical herbs and things (ores), *rasa* (i.e. either mercury or juice) is produced or from things like jaggery, spices and medicinal herbs *rasas* (essences), *sadava*, etc. are extracted, similarly, the *sthāyī bhāvas* (evidently in the mind of the dramatist), even when they approach the different *bhāvas* (i.e. when they are transformed into different *bhāvas* like *vibhāvas*, *vyabhicārī bhāva* and *anubhāva*) become *rasa*. Here again it must be remembered that the relation between *rasa*, as it occurs here, and *anna* or food is the same as exists between a *tanmātra* and a *mahābhūta*. *Rasa* does not stand for the sensation of tasting but stands for the object of sensation. It is true that the sentence appears ambiguous. But, it is because we are now accustomed to understand by the word *rasa* a taste sensation. Here, it is said, what kind of object is *rasa*? (What is the object of the word *rasa*?, i.e. How do you know what it stands for?) We shall say, because it is that objectified, which can be tasted (experienced) (second process). How is it tasted? Just as good men eating the food prepared with different spices taste the *rasas* (essences

18. This may either mean *kāvyārtha* as some passages show, and as I am inclined to take, i.e. S3 or it may mean an object and in that case, the object or *viṣaya* of *nāṭya*. The verb *pravartate* suggests that *rasa-artha* represents a process and justifies my use. It, however, does not matter for the contention of this essay what you mean by *artha*.

of juices that exist in the food) and attain happiness, so do the good minded *prekṣaka*s (i.e. observers) [Note that the word here is *prekṣaka* which also is necessary for *nāṭya* and not a reader (*vācaka*) or audience (*śrotā*)] taste or experience the *sthāyī bhāva*s which have been special with (i.e. which have been transformed to) different kinds of *bhāvas* (i.e. *vyabhicārī bhāvas*, etc.) and *abhinaya*s and have thus come nearer to (i.e. have taken the shape of) *vāk*, *aṅga* and *sattva*. There are three kinds of *abhinaya* or acting. The spectator perceives or experiences the *sthāyī bhāva*s not in the form that is mental (for this is impossible) but perceives them in public or objectified form or *rasa* and attain happiness, etc.

In this way, the *rasa*s in *nāṭya* are described. Abhinavagupta, however, says that *rasa*s are only in *nāṭya* and not in the actual world, *tena nāṭya eva rasāḥ na loke ityarthaḥ* (तेन नाट्य एव रसाः न लोके इत्यर्थः, *NŚ* p. 291, G.O.S. Baroda).

The passage of *Nāṭyaśāstra* that follows the one rendered above is again of crucial importance.

"Here it is said, whether the *bhāva*s are born of *rasa* or *rasa*s are born of *bhāva*. According to some they are born out of one another. But that is not so. 'Why?' It is seen that *rasa*s are born out of *bhāva*s and *bhāva*s are not born out of *rasa*s." Here, the point to note is that Bharata is referring to the process of creation or production of *rasa*s. It is evident that the *bhāva*s here cannot mean the *sthāyī bhāva* of the spectator or the *sthāyī bhāva*s in the mind of the poet, the *vyabhicārī bhāva*, *anubhāva*, and *vibhāva*s which are stipulated eleswhere as necessary for the production of *rasa*. This is clear from an earlier *kārikā*. Again, the following *kārikā* is significant:

भावाभिनयसंबद्धान् स्थायिभावांस्तथा बुधाः।
आस्वादयन्ति मनसा, तस्मान् नाट्यरसाः स्मृताः॥

bhāvābhinaya saṁbaddhān sthāyibhāvānstathā budhāḥ ।
āsvādayanti manasā, tasmān nāṭyarasāḥ smṛtāḥ ।

— *NŚ* 7.34

Of this *kārikā* too, usually a wrong rendering is given. It is said that because the *rasa*s (i.e. the *sthāyī bhāva*s, which are connected with the other *bhāva*s, such as *vibhāva*, etc. and acting) are experienced by mind, therefore, the *rasa*s are also mental. In the first place everything that is experienced by mind need not be mental. But in this particular case, the experience of the *sthāyī bhāva*s is not a direct experience and so it is quite correct to say that they are experienced by mind. I have drawn a distinction between the state of the poet's mind and that which is a state of the appreciator's mind. I have called them S1 and S3 respectively. I have also said that S3 is similar to S1 and that S3 is the meaning of (S2 or D_{S2}). The stage of S3 should not be confused with *sthāyī bhāva* (*NŚ* 7.5). It appears to me that Bharata is quite conscious of this fact. Whenever he talks of *sthāyī* (the stage S3) he uses the word *artha* for it, e.g. in the *kārikā*: *yo 'rtho hṛdayasaṁvādī tasya bhāvo rasodbhavaḥ* (योऽर्थो हृदयसंवादी तस्य भावो रसोद्भवः), i.e. that meaning which appeals to the heart is produced by *rasa*. It must be noted that the word *bhāva* as used here simply means existence or appearance as is commonly understood in Sanskrit.

Some Confused Interpretations

What Bharata meant by *rasa* cannot be fully realized unless the meaning he gives to the term *bhāva* is properly understood. Perhaps, Bharata used the word in a precise way. But, his commentators have understood it in a loose way. They also interfered with the original text and abused it to the maximum. This has led to the following confused interpretations and all sorts of views have been associated with the doctrine. Some of these mistaken views are:

(1) that all *bhāvas* are mental,

(2) that *rasas* and *bhāvas* are synonymous,

(3) that both of them are mental, but, *rasas* are the effects of *bhāvas* and are synonymous with pleasure of *ānanda*,

(4) that the *sthāyī bhāvas* are the emotions and the *rasas* are the sentiments in the way these terms are understood in modern psychology,

(5) the *sthāyī bhāvas* are the instincts and the *rasas* are the emotions, and

(6) that the *sthāyī bhāva, sañcārī bhāva* and *anubhāva* are psychological terms and stand for sentiment, derived emotion and expression of emotion.

These views have been held by great scholars, ancient and modern, oriental and occidental. At the present time, the names of some very eminent scholars like S.K. Dey, Pandey and K.N. Watve and several others are associated with one or the other of the views mentioned above. The suggested interpretations are ingenious. But, it is not possible to examine them here in detail. In fact, all of them cannot be correct simultaneously, nor in fact need any one of them be correct. I shall, therefore, confine myself to the presenting of what I believe to be Bharata's own theory of *bhāva* as it is found in *Nāṭyaśāstra*, and shall refer to the writings of Abhinavagupta alone, wherever necessary, for it is upon these two that all the differently-held theories concerning *bhāva* ultimately repose.

Bharata on Bhāvas

Bharata discusses *bhāvas* in the seventh chapter of *Nāṭyaśāstra*. It is necessary to bear in mind that by the word *bhāva* Bharata does not necessarily mean something mental as is presently stipulated according to contemporary commentators. In

Sanskrit of Bharata's days, and also in modern usage, *bhāva* means anything that exists. Any existence can be called *bhāva*. Thus, both mental and non-mental existents may be included under *bhāvas*. Moreover it was in this sense, and primarily in a non-mental sense that the word *bhāva* was used in Āyurveda. D.K. Bedekar has very ably brought out this point in his articles on *rasa* and I think this point does not require further elaboration. Bharata starts his whole enquiry with the definition of *bhāvas*. He asks:

किं भवन्ति इति भावाः किं वा भावयन्ति इति भावाः।
उच्यते वागंग सत्त्वोपेतान् काव्यार्थान् भावयन्ति इति भावाः इति।

kiṁ bhavanti iti bhāvāḥ kiṁ vā bhāvayanti iti bhāvāḥ ।
ucyate, vāgaṅga-sattvopetān-kāvyārthān bhāvayanti iti bhāvāḥ iti ॥
(*NŚ* 7 intro.)

He asks whether those that exist are *bhāvas* or those that are created are *bhāvas*, and answers that those which are created (like objects of poetry) or objects which are reduced to (acting of the type of) *vāk*, *aṅga* and *sattva*, are *bhāvas*. There is no doubt that by the phrase *vāgaṅga sattvopetān kāvyārthān* Bharata means *rasa*. Abhinavagupta also accepts that these words refer to *rasas*, but from his quotation of this passage has omitted the words *vāgaṅga sattvopetān*. Only by ignoring the implications of these words can the phrase "objects of poetry" designate *rasa* as a mental concept. Not simply any object of poetry, but that object (of poetry) which has taken the form of acting, etc. Bharata holds to be *rasa*. Without the qualifications *vāgaṅga sattvopetān* the *kāvyārtha* would not stand for *rasa* but would merely be another name for *sthāyī bhāva*. Bharata himself uses the words as synomymous in Chapter 6 (*NŚ* 6.before 33). Of course, Abhinavagupta would have no objection to such an interpretation as *sthāyī bhāvas* and *rasas* are basically the same, one being the transformed state of the other. But if *sthāyī bhāva* and *rasa* are regarded as synonymous by misinterpreting Bharata's text, it would make a world of difference to the whole theory of *rasa*. For, it immediately reduces *rasa* to merely mental status as the meaning of poetry. Thus, instead of designating a member of the DS2 series it comes to designate S3. It is a pity that Bharata's use of language appears somewhat loose. Some interpreters exploit this to the full, but even then this is done only by omitting a crucial part of Bharata's sentence.

There is another defect in Bharata's definition of *bhāva*. It, no doubt, points out that *bhāva*s are the causes of *rasas*. But, even though they are created (*bhāvayanti*), Bharata does not bother to point out that they may still exist (*bhavanti*). There is no contradiction whatsoever in these two positions. But, in emphasizing the creative aspect, Bharata has either forgotten the existence aspect, or his original text has been interfered with. In fact, there are a few places where Bharata himself has used the word *bhāva* in the sense of "that which exists" *bhavanti iti bhāvāḥ* (भवन्ति इति भावाः), e.g. in the *kārikā*, *kaverantargataṁ bhāvaṁ bhāvayan bhāva ucyate* (कवेरन्तर्गतं भावं भावयन् भाव उच्यते). Also in the *karika*, *yo 'artho hṛdayasaṁvādī tasya bhāvo rasodbhavaḥ* (योऽर्थो हृदयसंवादी तस्य भावो रसोद्भवः). Here the word *bhāva* is used in the sense of existence. In fact, all *bhāva*s which Bharata defines as "being created," (*bhāvayanti*) can equally be described as "existing" (*bhavanti*). In fact, *bhāva*s exihibit both the qualities, of existing and manifesting, and the point should not be neglected.

In describing *bhāvas* as the prior conditions of *rasa* Bharata means by *bhāva*s both the mental states as well as the expressions of these in bodily and organic forms. *Bhāva* is a genus to which mental and non-mental belong as species. Unfortuantely, the form of the Sanskrit language makes misinterpretation possible. Only some *bhāva*s are mental. But in the development of the theory if all *bhāvas* are taken as mental a psychological theory can be woven round the *bhāvas* and *rasas* calling them "particular mental attitudes" or *citta vṛttiviśeṣāḥ*. This is what has happened.

Bharata defines the *bhāvas* as *kāvya-rasa-abhivyakti-hetavaḥ* (काव्य-रस-अभिव्यक्ति-हेतवः), i.e. the conditions for the expression of *rasa* in poetry. He enumerates them as forty-nine and classifies them under three categories (1) *sthāyī bhāvas*, (2) *vyabhicārī bhāvas* and (3) *sāttvika bhāvas*. The two points to be noted here are (a) that the list need not be regarded as very exhaustive and scientific and (b) the division need not be regarded as exclusive and trichotomous, though it should be useful.

Sthāyī Bhāvas

Of these *bhāvas*, *sthāyī bhāvas* are certainly the most important and they definitely refer to the artist's (i.e. dramatist's) intentions. I do not wish to conjecture whether they stand for instincts, emotions, sentiments, ideas or imagery or the like. It is most unlikely that this wide range of distinctions which are drawn today would have been known in Bharata's days. At any rate, they would not have been necessary for his purpose. It might well do violence to Bharata's work to identify his concept of *sthāyī bhāva* with anyone of these concepts of psychology. Perhaps this mental gestalt may be much richer and comprehensive than any of the proposed states taken in isolation. *Sthāyī* literally means standing and so its use is in the sense of continuent. I am, therefore, inclined to think that by *sthāyī bhāvas* Bharata meant those *bhāvas* which stand as the ground or primary motives of artistic creation.

Bharata has nowhere defined the *sthāyī bhāvas*. But, it appears to me that he must have defined them in his work as it originally stood. But in the text that has come down to us this passage is lost. This is clear from the structure of the text itself. Bharata in the seventh chapter begins by defining the concepts. First, he defines the *bhāva*s; then he defines *vibhāvas*, *anubhāva*s, etc. He then comes to *sthāyī bhāva*s; but, instead of a definition there follows a discussion of how the *sthāyī bhāva*s are transformed into *rasa*s. After this comes a passage where it is said that the *lakṣaṇa*s of the *sthāyī bhāva*s are already told; i.e. they are already defined and that now the particular *sthāyī bhāva*s would be discussed. In some books the first sentence of this passage (that is *lakṣaṇamkhalu*, etc.) is dropped and instead of the second, another sentence, "that we shall now define *sthāyī bhāva*s" is substituted. Unfortunately, however, this definition is never given. This suggests that some omission or substitution has been made in the original manuscript. In default of the proper definition, we can however infer from Bharata's treatment of *sthāyī bhāva*s in other passages that he meant by them the material of art as they are conceived by the artist in his mind before expressing them in some form. Sentences like *kaveḥ antargatam bhāvam* suggest this. (I am inclined to take it as equivalent to 'M' factor described earlier.)

The second point to note in this connection is that Bharata explicitly states that *sthāyī bhāva*s become *rasa*s; not that they are *rasa*s. This suggests the artistic creation to be a process and that, in some sense, *sthāyī bhāva*s precede the *rasa*s. The words *āpnuvanti* (आप्नुवन्ति) and *labhate* (लभते) suggest this.

The *vyabhicārī bhāva*s and the *sāttvika bhāva*s are those states in which the *sthāyī bhāva*s are expressed. Some of these states, therefore, can be mental and some of them can be otherwise. For this reason, perhaps, in Bharata's list of *vyabhicārī bhāva*s both the mental and non-mental states are included. By *sāttvika bhāvas*, I believe, Bharata meant what we now term as organic sensations. That both the *vyabhicārī bhāva*s as well as the *sāttvika bhāva*s are very useful in *nāṭya* can easily be seen.

From what has been said above, the following characteristics of *rasa* will be clear (1) that it designates a medium just as *rūpa* or *śabda* designates a medium, (2) that it is composite in nature, that it combines characteristics of both *śabda* and *rūpa*, that is to say, both audible and visible symbols form part of this medium, and (3) that essentially it represents movement and is extended in time. The *rasa* has "flow" as one of its basic meanings and the more familiar meanings, juice and flavour, imply this. On account of its peculiar nature it is in fact not possible to translate *rasa* into another medium that is static in nature, or something which only exhibits partial characterstics as do audible or written poetry or pictures. Perhaps, the nearest approach to *rasa* would be a cinematographic film, where several postures and conversations form a new whole. Any momentary glimpse of *rasa* would be *rūpa*, that which you find in painting and sculpture; any non-visual section of it would be *śabda* which is found in poetry. If you could imagine that all the different pictures come together and produce only one dynamic image before you and if you could further imagine that all the images in the picture are living images and that you are able to listen to them, then it would be the nearest approach to *rasa*. This will clearly suggest that it is by extension of meaning that *rasa* can be located either in poetry or in pictures. *Rasa* is the language of staging and it is there alone that its primary manifestations can be observed.

6

Bharata's Rasa Theory (continued.....)
Dharmi, Vṛtti, Pravṛtti and Siddhi

The Element of Communication in Art

In the last chapter I have presented the position of Bharata *vis-á-vis* stage drama. I have, in particular, pointed out that by *rasa* he did not mean joy or some kind of indescribable experience. Such an experience is, certainly, integral to Bharata's theory or drama. But, he discusses this under *siddhi*. Bharata, while giving the *saṁgraha* of *raṅga*, talks of *dharmi*, *vṛtti*, *bhāva*, *abhinaya* and *pravṛtti*. Unless these concepts are understood, Bharata's theory will not be comprehended properly. In fact, a look into how Bharata used these concepts is likely to reveal the context in which Bharata used the word *rasa* and thus supplement my observations about the concept of *rasa* itself.

Any art usually poses two sets of problems; one concerning its creation and the other its appreciation. There is however a similarity between these two sets of problems; for a certain appreciation is invariably associated with experience prior to creation as also with the process of creation. The artist is continuously enjoying while he is creating and his creation, at least partly, is the result of certain appreciation. The process of creation, however, is far more complex than the process of appreciation. Appreciation *qua* appreciation does not lead to creative activity. Creation, on the other hand, is dynamic. It is beset with an urge to express. If, in some broad sense appreciation is an impression, creation is an expression resulting from impression. Impression is essentially private. Expression is public. It takes an objective form and is not governed by private "law," by personal moods and imagination; it follows a public law and exhibits a capacity to communicate. This communicative element is essential for creation and connects the artist with the appreaciator. The (concrete) art object is the medium of communication. I believe that almost all the important writers on Indian poetics recognized these factors and agreed that communication is an important aspect of art. Even Abhinavagupta who, according to existing tradition, has emphasized the enjoyment aspect of art so much, has this element of communication in mind when in the beginning of *Locana*, his commentary on *Dhvanyāloka* he writes:

सरस्वत्यास्तत्त्वं कविसहृदयाख्यं विजयते ।

sarasvatyāstattvaṁ kavisahṛdyākhyaṁ vijayate ।

But although communication is an important element in the theory of art, the complexity of magnitude of this element varies from art to art. In an art like music, communication has no independent status and is dependent on the artist; in arts like painting and sculpture it takes the form of an object and has an independent existence. Both the communication in poetry and the communication in ordinary language are dependent on spoken or written symbols. Thus, the special significance of poetic communication is usually overlooked. In arts like stage drama, the element of communication is not only of primary importance, but its special mode also distinguishes it from poetry. Otherwise, removed from the stage, drama too is a form of poetry. Only the stage part (*prayoga*) transforms *nāṭaka* into *nāṭya*. It is but natural that *Nāṭyaśāstra*, a treaties on stage drama, should be primarily concerned with the art of staging a drama. On the other hand, though the element of communication is significant for poetry, a treatise on poetry cannot analyse with precision the different elements in communication and describe all the details with exactness and accuracy. For, in a sense, there is nothing very special about communication in poetry. The communicated object simply assumes the form of signs and symbols, either auditory or visual; sounds in the case of spoken language and letters in the case of written language. It is just the work of one man, the poet. It is simply a transition from the private to the public. It is translating a private experience so as to make it available to the public. There is hardly any scope for a co-operative effort, as it is in the case of a stage drama, where that which already belongs to the public sphere (viz. the drama), and which is already in one language form is translated into another language, viz. the *nāṭya* language. The essence of successful stage drama lies in translating successfully a piece in ordinary language into the stage language. Success in translating the ordinary language into stage language depends upon how successfully the poet's intentions are translated in the new language and are conveyed to the audience. It should not be forgotten that translating the poet's intentions in the stage language is the essence of (stage) drama. But for this, a staged drama would be only a piece of poetry or a novel. *Nāṭaka* or drama with its text or *pāṭhya* — this will include *itivṛtta* and any of its forms as represented by *daśarūpaka* — is just one element in this stage language, only a part of the stage drama. It is the matter which has to be given another form. It will be worthwhile here to reiterate the distinction between *nāṭya* and *nāṭaka* and to remember that Bharata was primarily interested in *nāṭya*. The difference in the language of *nāṭaka* and *nāṭya* is in fact the difference in the form (of language).

Imitation or Anukaraṇa

This question of form requires further elucidation. A drama is described by Bharata as *anukṛti* or *anukaraṇa* which means imitation. The questions that naturally arise here are: (1) who imitates?, (2) what is imitation?, and (3) whose imitation it is? I have stated earlier that *nāṭya*, like all arts is a kind of creation or production. So it will be relevant to remember here that in Bharata's use of the term it is not the poet who imitates, nor is it the actor who produces (in the sense that the poet produces). I am aware that it can be said that the poet imitates and the actor produces. But, in such constructions the words "imitates" and "produces," are used with a slightly different shade of meaning. Before going into a detailed analysis of the concept of *anukaraṇa*, it will also be relevant to point out that in an art like staged drama there are two distinct processes involved. The transition from the poet or the artist to the art object and from there to the spectator or audience, is one process. I shall call it horizontal process and is common to all arts. The question of creation and appreciation are inter-linked with this process. There is yet another process involved in drama — a vertical process — where something ideal or real is imitated. The word "imitation" can be used in the context of this process, though it can be misused also as it has several usages. The word "imitation" may lay emphasis on the act of imitating, that is, how something is imitated. But it may also indicate a pattern that is created. When somebody imitates, there is the original as also the imitation. In the absence of any other word let me call imitation a *picture* or a copy of the original. The two Sanskrit words *anukaraṇa* and *anukṛti* are better in this respect for they clearly bring out the difference between the two uses.[1] There is no doubt that the element of imitation, as pointed out by Bharata presents a very important dimension of drama.

What is this imitation? I believe that "picture" used above in this sense is only a representation of something, or a situation that is real. Even when it is concrete it tends to reduce the complexity of the original. If it is otherwise, it would be difficult to use it for communication. Let me explain my point with an illustration from cinematography. A person is to be shown running. We do not take snaps of his every single movement and then project them on the screen. We do make a certain selection; we take some snaps leaving out others. But when we project them on the screen the total effect is that of running. In this new presentation there is resemblance, recognition and also the act of running. Even then it is a *curtailment*. This happens in most arts like painting, sculpture and drama. That is why art is regarded as only a partial representation of life. It should be noted that *kalā*, which is a word for art in Sanskrit, literally means a part (*aṁśa*). When Bharata describes *nāṭya* as imitation or *anukaraṇa*, I think he is quite conscious of the implications of imitation. Bharata makes an attempt to explain imitation or *anukṛti* with the help of (1) *rasa*, (2) *dharmi*, (3) *vṛtti*, and (4) *pravṛtti*. It is, therefore, necessary to understand Bharata's use of these terms.

In the first place, as I have stated above, for some reason or the other, not all elements of the original can be reproduced in imitation. One of the reasons is that there is a natural difficulty in the case of imitation. If the hanging of a person or

1. It should not be thought that this process is peculiar to drama alone. It is also found in arts like sculpture and painting as in the case of landscape painting and portrait drawing.

a severe accident is to be described, it is impossible to do so in the ordinary way in which it occurs. Such elements in the drama are, therefore, to be understood only symbolically. In *Vikramorvaśīyam*, Indra's chariot is described as travelling in the air. It was impossible to present it in this way at the time Kālidāsa wrote the drama.[2] Similarly, when the actors speak to themselves, it is heard by the listeners, but it is conventionally agreed that it should be taken as unheard by other actors. Bharata, therefore, classifies all those elements of imitation which can only be imitated symbolically as *nāṭyadharmi*, and the other elements which are common both to imitation and its original as *lokadharmi*.[3]

Two kinds of questions can be asked about imitation. (1) What or who is imitated? and (2) how is it or he imitated? The second question is vague. It may mean (a) the way something or someone is imitated or (b) it may refer to the elements from the original that are combined so as to make a copy or the imitation. In the second alternative of the second question we shall be dealing with some aspects of the first question. But the first alternative of the second question is more important from the standpoint of the staged drama. Having agreed that such and such are the elements of imitation, even then these elements could be presented in a particular style. Just as the same content (of thought) can be spoken in different dialects without making any difference to the meanings, so also the imitation can be presented in different ways. These ways undoubtedly represent a dimension of acting or *abhinaya*. But these particular styles must be present in different individuals in the actual world. Bharata, therefore,

2. With the aid of photoplay it is possible to do so now.

3. *NŚ* 13.65-76; 21.189-93.

enumerates the ways in which the same content is presented by different people in their ordinary life. This is what he calls *pravṛtti* and distinguishes it from *vṛtti*. He writes:

> अत्राह – प्रवृत्तिः इति कस्मात्। उच्यते – पृथिव्यां नानादेशवेशभाषाचारवार्ताः ख्यापयति इति प्रवृत्तिः। प्रवृत्तिश्च निवेदनैः। अत्राह यथा पृथिव्यां नाना देशाः सन्ति। कथमासां चतुर्विधमुत्पन्नं, समानलक्षणश्चासाम् प्रयोगः? उच्यते – सत्यमेतत् आसां समानलक्षणः प्रयोगः। किन्तु नानादेशवेशभाषाचारो लोक इति कृत्वा लोकानुमते अनुवृत्तिसंश्रितं अस्य मया चतुर्विधत्वं अभिहितं भारती, आरभटी, सात्वती, कैशिकी च इति वृत्ति संश्रितेषु अमीषु प्रयोगेषु अभिहिता देशाः, यतः प्रवृत्तिचतुष्टयं अभिनिवृत्तं प्रयोगश्चोत्पादितः। तत्र दक्षिणात्याः तावत् बहुगीतनृत्य-वाद्य-कैशिकी प्रायाश्चतुरमधुर-ललितांगाभिनयाश्च।
>
> *atrāha — pravṛttiḥ iti kasmāt* । *ucyate — pṛthivyāṁ nānādeśaveśa-bhāṣācāravārtāḥ khyāpayati iti pravṛttiḥ* । *pravṛttiśca nivedanaiḥ* । *atrāha yathā pṛthivyāṁ nāṇā deśāḥ santi* । *kathamāsāṁ caturvidham utpannaṁ, samanalakṣaṇaścāsām prayogaḥ? ucyate — satyametat āsām samānalakṣaṇaḥ prayogaḥ* । *kintu nānādeśa-veśabhāṣācāro loka iti kṛtvā lokānumate anuvṛttisaṁśritaṁ asya mayā caturvidhatvaṁ abhihitaṁ bhāratī, ārabhaṭī, sātvatī, kaiśikī ca iti vṛtti saṁśriteṣu amīṣu prayogeṣu abhihitā deśāḥ, yataḥ pravṛtti catuṣṭayaṁ abhinivṛttaṁ, prayogaścotpāditaḥ, tatra dakṣiṇāṭyāḥ tāvat bahugītanṛtya-vādya-kaiśikī prāyāścatura-madhur-lalitāṅgābhinayāśca* ।

Types of Vṛtti and Pravṛttis

But if an action (and so the imitation of the action) can be classified by the special mode of presentation of different people and countries, actions can also be classified by some general mode. For example, a reaction of a woman to a certain situation is bound to be essentially the same in spite of regional variations or differences in *pravṛttis*. A woman in love with a person may be eager to see him, and in the expectation of seeing the beloved may put on beautiful dress and ornaments. The dress and ornaments may vary from region to region and from individual to individual. But the essential idea behind such variations is the same because it is universal. This universal feature when echoed in a behaviour pattern is known as *vṛtti*. Bharata classifies them into four types, and calls them *bhāratī, ārbhaṭī, sātvatī* and *kaiśikī*. The first three refer to the general reactions of men and women. The last refers to reaction of women alone. In the context of drama or imitation these *vṛtti*s may even represent symbolic features of *nāṭyadharmi* elements. For example, the essential feature of *bhāratī* is that it is dialogue-predominated. But Bharata also describes it as that where Sanskrit sentences are used. This only represents the convention of the Sanskrit drama and it cannot be an essential feature of *vṛtti*.

Drama or imitation is not an exhibition of all the *vṛtti*s and *pravṛtti*s, but is an organization and selection of these. In classifying these behaviour-patterns and their regional variations, Bharata admits that the same phenomenon can be exhibited in different ways. The problems connected with *vṛtti*s and *pravṛtti*s are the same. We eliminate the individual variations (*viśeṣa guṇa*s) and confine ourselves to the common features. This is the *sādhāraṇīkaraṇa*. The *sādhāraṇīkaraṇa* applies not only in the case of how a phenomenon is exhibited but also in the case of what is exhibited. If the character of Rāma is to be depicted on the stage, then the pattern of behaviour that is imitated is not necessarily that of the original Rāma; it could be of any virtuous and valorous man or a king. The process of selection and omission operates here as elsewhere. Not only can the pattern of behaviour be different but the actors also can be different. The actors can dress themselves differently, they can act differently, and the environment in which they act can be arranged in different ways. When an actor enacts or imitates Rāma, there is no one-to-one correspondence (resemblance) between the original and the imitation. The actors of different regions and times will not only enact differently, but they will also select different elements from Rāma's behaviour continuum, in order to play Rāma. The first is the *how* element and is connected with *vṛttis* and *pravṛttis*, the second is the *what* element. It is to be noted that usually in drama the imitation is based on the general elements or *sāmānya guṇa* and not on special elements or *viśeṣa guṇa*. For, special elements cannot be known by any other means except perception and this, in almost cent per cent cases, is denied either because the original is an imaginary or a historical person. That Bharata had in his mind only the universal or common elements when he talked of imitation, can be verified from the qualities and powers he expected of an actor.[4]

I mentioned above the "how" and the "what" elements in drama and emphasized that it is only the *vṛttis* and *pravṛttis* which are connected with the expression in a staged drama. But this is not the whole truth. In whatever way the content is expressed, it still has a form[5] which is exhibited through different expressions. In fact, it is the object of any staged drama and of the producer to present the matter (which is usually some story) in some particular form which is of the nature of process. This particular form, the dynamic form, represents the communication element and is the soul of dramatic art. When we talk of imitation we are talking of this form and it is my contention that this form is given the name *rasa*, by Bharata. This form can be studied in two different aspects: (1) the mere objective or passive and the (2) subjective

4. *NŚ* 24.74-79 also *vide* what I have written on *Sādhāraṇīkaraṇa* infra — p. 188.

5. The form represents that "how" element, the matter, the "what element." The drama as a piece of literature is the matter for the staged drama.

or active. In its passive aspect, it is the imitation (*anukṛti*); in the active one it is the imitating (*anukaraṇa*). What I mean would be clear if we compare two different arts, say a painting and a staged drama. A painting is as much an object of art as is the staged drama. But in respect of painting it cannot be meaningfully said that the picture imitates the original. It is only the painter who can imitate, not the picture, for picture is not the agent but the object. In the case of drama on the other hand it can be significantly stated that actors (who are elements in the staged drama) imitate. This is so because a staged drama, so to say, is produced thrice. Its first producer is the dramatist, the second the director and the third the actor(s). In the case of painting, sculpture, poetry or music all these roles are fulfilled by a single agent. Nevertheless, just as in the case of poetry or painting the art object can be treated in its objective aspect, so also in the case of the staged drama the art object — the staged drama itself can be treated in its objective or passive aspect. If the poet is the first producer, say, P1, the P2 (the director) and P3 (the actors) along with accompanying elements, i.e. the exhibited scenes, can be treated as the art object. Thus, as we talk of the *successive* producers the next *successive* elements would be treated as art object. This can be presented in the following formula:

P1 [P2 (P3 (F)]

F represents everything else other than the agent. Thus, for P1, [P2 (P3 (F)] will be the art object, for P2 [P3 (F)] will be the *art object* and for P3 (F) will be the art object. It is necessary to note two points here. First, in staged drama, whereas an art object can be separated from P1 and P2 it cannot be entirely separated from P3. Secondly, F need not be thought of as single indivisible element. It may itself be very complex. I wish to emphasize that in a complex art like staged drama, where, unlike other arts, production continues till the end (even on the stage), the active element can be treated as passive with reference to the previous or earlier stage. Thus, from the viewpoint of the artist, the successive elements could be treated as a passive art object and would represent a picture or imitation of the original, though, in another sense, the actors actively imitate or copy the original. Considered as passive element, this art object — the imitation is the projection of the poet's mind. The objective form is the translation of the projection of poet's mind.

Classification of Arts

On account of differences in emphasis, arts may be classified in two different ways. In arts like painting there is scope for some kind of technical training and the art object, to a certain extent, is the fruit of a certain technique. In such arts, communication or communicability assumes special significance. The artist has to evolve special techniques for communicating his ideas. This is not exactly so in arts like poetry. The communicative capacity of such arts depends on the cultural level of the society and is determined by the general development of the language used. Such arts are symbolic in nature but are not pictographic or concrete and their communicability is regulated by the meaning which the symbolic representation is likely to convey. As a form of art, drama exhibits the nature of both these kinds of arts. Its greatest emphasis is, and ought to be, on the way it is presented or staged. But, as a form of poetry, it does project a certain meaning or meanings. In fact, in every art the symbolic presentation and meaning are very intimately related and one cannot be considered without taking into consideration the other. Unmeaningful presentation will certainly defeat the purpose of any art. Further, it is also possible that one kind of symbolic representation may lead to more than one set of meanings. Sometimes, the secondary or tertiary meaning may convey a more important sense and may lead to aesthetic realization on some kind of happiness which is certainly the purpose of art. Art symbol, thus, produces certain ripples (*taraṅga*) of meaning, which may give birth to the feeling of beauty, happiness, etc. There is no doubt that if an art is to be appreciated it should be appreciated on the basis of these criteria. My only point is that in certain arts, the art object and the meaning of the art object can be clearly distinguished, whereas, in some others, it is not possible. The art like staged drama falls in the first category and pure poetry falls in the second. It is my contention that Bharata clearly distinguished the two elements in art. The one — the art object (or rather the form of the art-object) he called *rasa,* in the other, i.e. the meaning of the art-object he located concepts like *sthāyī bhāva* and *siddhi*.

Purpose of Art: Superworldly Happiness (The Siddhis)

It is alleged that Abhinavagupta and his followers thought that art or poetry is produced for some superworldly happiness, which can be compared to the happiness of Brahma-realization. But this also seems to be the purpose of art according to Bharata. Bharata has stated this in unequivocal terms. He writes: The drama is staged for the sake of *siddhi*.

यस्मात् प्रयोगः सर्वोयं सिध्द्यर्थः संप्रदर्शितः ।

yasmāt prayogaḥ sarvoyaṁ siddhyarthaḥ saṁpradarśitaḥ ।

— *NŚ* 1.27

It is futher alleged that Abhinava does not recognize the distinction between *rasa* and *siddhi* and ignores the element of symbolic representation of art, by identifying them — *rasāḥ siddhireva* (रसः सिद्धिरेव).

It is important to note that Bharata mentions the concept of *siddhi* again and again. The twenty-seventh verse in the seventh chapter of *Naṭyaśāstra*, for example, mentions the *siddhi* as the final stage in a dramatic process. *Vismaya* as the *sthāyī bhāva* is realized in the place of *siddhi*, through *praharṣa* and *pulaka* (on the part of the audience). Similarly, the last verse of seventh chapter mentions *siddhi* though there is a pun on the word *siddhi*. He attains good *siddhi*s who understands (the elements in dramatic process).

य एवमेतान् जानाति स गच्छेत् सिद्धिमुत्तमाम्।

ya evametān jānāti sa gacchet siddhimuttamām । — *NŚ* 7.130

Bharata has clearly mentioned *siddhi* as the most important element in the art process and independent from *rasa* or *bhāva*. Bharata writes:

रसाभावाह्यभिनया धर्मिवृत्तिप्रवृत्तयः।
सिद्धि स्वरास्तथातोद्यं गानं रंगश्च संग्रहः।

rasābhāvahyabhinayā dharmivṛtti pravṛttayaḥ ।
siddhi svarāstathātodyaṁ gānaṁ raṅgaśca saṁgrahaḥ ॥
(*NŚ* 6.10)

This clearly indicates that by *rasa*, Bharata meant something entirely different from what the orientalists usually understood by *rasa*. Both *rasa* and *siddhi* are elements in the same series. But, they appear at different points of time. The current tradition has missed this point and since the tradition accepts the leadership of Abhinava, it is thought that Abhinava also identified *rasa* with *siddhi*. But *rasāḥ siddhireva* does not mean this. Bharata says in unequivocal terms that *siddhi* (the final form of appreciation) arises in the mind of the appreciator or *prekṣaka*. Bharata has separately defined *prekṣaka* (*NŚ* vide 27.6,8,16) and further adds that it (*siddhi*) arises out of happiness in the body (of *prekṣaka*) and it has been evoked on account of several *rasas* (*NŚ* 27.75). It is thus clear that for Bharata, *siddhi* was an element different from *rasa* and was the final purpose of (dramatic) art. Bharata classifies *siddhi* into two sub-classes:

1. that is human or *mānuṣī*, and
2. that which is *divine* or *daivikī*.

The first he sub-divides under ten heads and the second under two (a) *bhāvātiśayopeta* (भावातिशयोपेत) and (b) a stage of complete calm. A dramatic art is exhibited for those two kinds of *siddhis* (vide *NŚ* 27.16-17). One cannot understand Bharata's point of view, *vis-á-vis* (dramatic) art, without understanding the concept of *siddhi*. *Siddhi* is the last element of *āsvāda* (or appreciation) process, which is temporal. Occurrence of different shades of (a) meaning, (b) happiness and (c) *siddhi* seem to form the elements of this process. That this process involves concepts like meaning and appreciation seems to be clear to Bharata. Otherwise, in the beginning of the 6th chapter he would not have talked of *rasa niṣpatti prakriyā* and *rasāsvāda prakriyā* and stated that without the *symbolic presentation* the meaning (of the drama) would not be manifest. *Na hi rasādṛte kaścidapi arthaḥ pravartate* (न हि रसादृते कश्चिदपि अर्थः प्रवर्तते). Unfortunately, some later writers took this to mean that *rasa* is the purpose of dramtic art. Had it been so, Bharata would not have separately mentioned the element of *siddhi*.

Can Rasa and Siddhi be Identified?

Did the great scholar and art-critic like Abhinava identify *rasa* and *siddhi*, the two different concepts in a dramatic process? I earlier thought so. But, on later thought, I think otherwise. But, of course, there seem to be several reasons for such mistaken identification. (1) In drama, a special technique of presentation is required. Without it there cannot be communication. As I have pointed out in the beginning of this chapter, this is not so in the case of poetry where the poet's message is communicated through ordinary lnguage. For those who treat *rasa* in the context of poetry the appreciation aspect becomes more important. (2) Since happiness is one of the most important factors in appreciation and since *rasa* is also used for happiness as in *raso vai saḥ* (रसो वै सः) and *ānandādeva hi imāni bhūtāni jāyante* (आनन्दादेव हि इमानि भूतानि जायन्ते), it is quite natural that some philosophers of art should be carried away and identify the two factors, particularly when they could not separately locate the place of *rasa*, which has been regarded as an important factor in the art process. (3) Perhaps, in the post-Abhinavagupta period, a part of the *Nāṭyaśāstra* might have been lost and the concept of *siddhi* might have been out of focus from the public eye. (4) It is also possible that the editor of *Abhinavabhāratī*, in editing might have identified the two concepts and the identification now goes in the name of Abhinavagupta. Whatever might be the case the fact remains that in the post-Abhinavagupta era, *rasa* was identified with *ānanda* and since the concept of *ānanda* was very similar to that of *siddhi*, *rasa* was substituted for *siddhi* and the notion of *siddhi* was altogether dropped from the theory of poetic appreciation.

One of the reasons which contributed to this *adhyāsa* (अध्यास) must have been philosophic. India, by and large, has been dominated by some form of Advaita philosophy according to which the reality is one and of the nature of *rasa* and *ānanda*. The identification of the two words, *rasa* and *ānanda*, could easily have paved the way for the new theory of *rasa*. The other reason seems to be the existence of certain ambiguous passages in the *Nāṭyaśāstra* itself. Bharata for example, says that it is the *sthāyī bhāva* which becomes *rasa* . . . . *sthāyī bhāvā rasattvamāpnuvanti* (स्थायिभावा रसत्वमाप्नुवन्ति) (*NŚ* 6.after 32).

Similarly, while replying to the question whether *rasas* are born out of *bhāva* or *bhāvas* are born out of *rasa*, Bharata, at one place, has replied that *rasa* comes out of *bhāva*. Another passage which lends support to the above reasoning is:

स्थायिभावानास्वादयन्ति सुमनसः प्रेक्षकाः ।

sthāyībhāvānāsvādayanti sumanasaḥ prekṣakāḥ ।

— *NŚ* 6.before 33

These passages create the misunderstanding that *sthāyī bhāva* is some kind of mental state of the spectator, say, some emotional state and that it develops into *rasa*, a kind of sentiment. Bharata also says that one kind of *daivi siddhi* is *bhāvopeta*, i.e. of the kind of *bhāva* (which is evidently *sthāyī bhāva*). Thus, it is generally thought that *sthāyī bhāva* is a mental state of the spectator and since *rasa* refers to the post-*sthāyī bhāva* stage it could be no other than the stage of "happiness in the mind of the spectator." This is, however, a mistaken logic for the following reasons.

(1) Those who quote these passages mix up the two processes so carefully analysed and separated by Bharata and his successor in that tradition: (a) the process of creation, and (b) the process of appreciation. The statements which refer to the process of creation are cited for proving the process of appreciation. And (2) the statements are usually incomplete. The *avacchedaka* or qualificands of the words are usually omitted. For example, the quotation is not *sthāyībhāvān āsvādayanti* (स्थायिभावान आस्वादयन्ति), but *vāgaṅgasattvopetān sthāyībhāvāna āsvādayanti* (वागंगसत्त्वोपेतान् स्थायिभावान आस्वादयन्ति). The qualification changes the entire meaning of the sentence. Similarly, the other quotation is not *sthāyībhāvān budhāḥ āsvādayanti manasā* (स्थायिभावान् बुधाः आस्वादयन्ति मनसा, *NŚ* 6.34), but *bhāvābhinaya-sambaddhān sthāyībhāvaṁstathā budhāḥ, āsvādayanti manasā* (भावाभिनय सम्बद्धान् स्थायिभावांस्तथा बुधाः आस्वादयन्ति मनसा). It need

not be said that the qualificand changes the meaning of the passage. According to some critics the word *manasā* in the above quotation is very significant and that it suggests a mental state. But this is nonsense for it is not true that the mental alone can be appreciated by mind. This discussion, however, leads to some important questions: what is *sthāyī bhāva*? and where is it to be located? (The nature of *sthāyī bhāva* is discussed in another chapter.)

Vagueness about Bhāvas

Somehow or the other, statements about *bhāva* and *sthāyī bhāva* are very vague in *Nāṭyaśāstra*. This vagueness gave rise to a lot of confusion, and the exponents of different schools of philosophy tried to interpret the theory of *bhāva* and *rasa* so as to suit their own thought. In the first place, in *Nāṭyaśāstra*, the word *bhāva* occurs in the context of certain bodily expressions connected with dance and acting. These are *hāva, bhāva* and *helā*. These are defined as those which manifest the internal *bhāva* of the poet (*NŚ* 22.6-8 and *NŚ* 7.2). These *bhāvas* are technical expressions connected with dance and drama. The *bhāva* is supposed to emerge out of *sattva* (which in its own turn emerges from the body) (*NŚ* 22.7). But Bharata realizes that the word *bhāva* has other usages also. It is not a word from the language of dance and drama alone. The word is significant in the ordinary language and in the context of actual world. Thus, in the verse quoted above (*kaverantargatam bhāvam bhāvayan bhāva ucyate*) the first *bhāva* definitely refers to a real state and not to a dramatic state. It may also be noted here that this state of the poet refers to the mental or internal state as has been clearly stated. But all states, of course, need not be mental. In the beginning of the 7th chapter of *Nāṭyaśāstra* Bharata writes: the root *bhū* has the sense of make (or manifest, fill). Therefore, *bhāva* has the sense as *bhāvita, vāsita* and *kṛta*.

Bhāva, thus, stands for meaning or expression, whether in the drama or any other art or in the real world.

Vagueness about Sthāyī bhāvas and their Meaning

In the *Nāṭyaśāstra, sthāyī bhāva* is not defined anywhere. It is only described with the help of analogies. But the analogies simply indicate that *vyabhicārī bhāva*s and the *sthāyī* are not essentially different in nature (just as a king and his subjects are all men) though only a few of them attain the status of *sthāyī bhāva*. It is, however, necessary to note that Bharata says that he had already defined *sthāyī bhāva (lakṣaṇam khalu pūrvam abhihitam, NŚ* 7.after 8) though this definition does not occur anywhere. In the absence of the definition, the meaning of *sthāyī bhāva* has merely remained a matter of speculation. However, with some effort what is *sthāyī bhāva* can be known. In music too the word *sthāyī* is used. *Saṅgītaratnākara* defines it. Even Bharata makes a reference to the *sthāyī* (of music) — *sthāyī* is a *sthira* — unchanging sound or tune (*NŚ* 29.19). *Sthirā svarā samā yatra sthāyī varṇaḥ sa ucyate* (स्थिरा स्वरा समा यत्र स्थायी वर्णः स उच्यते). On the other hand, a *sañcārī* is that which occurs and which can be withdrawn (*NŚ* 29.36). These definitions of *sthāyī* and *sañcārī* should be a guide in deciding the nature of *sthāyī bhāva. Sthāyī bhāva* should be that *bhāva* cognition or meaning which persists or continues to exist or manifest.

In the context of drama, *sthāyī bhāva* thus should strictly mean that persistent meaning or sense which continues to persist on the stage. It is necessary to remember that as in the ordinary language, in the drama too, there are symbolic expressions and there are meanings of these symbolic expressions. If the two, meaning and symbolic expression, do not go together, the whole thing would be meaningless. It is really strange that most of the writers have completely ignored the fact that Bharata persistently uses the expressions *artha* and *saṁjñā*, and adds that *sthāyī bhāvas* are *rasa saṁjña*, i.e. those (meanings) of which the symbols are *rasa* [*NŚ* 7.after 27]. Similarly, he states that in the dramatic process no sense or meaning could be had without *rasa* — *na hi rasādṛte kaścidapi artha pravartate* (न हि रसादृते कश्चिदपि अर्थ प्रवर्तते।). He again repeats the word *arthaḥ*, in describing *sthāyī bhāva*, in the *Kārikā*, *yo 'rtho hṛdayasaṁvādī tasya bhāvo rasodbhavaḥ* (योऽर्थो हृदयसंवादी तस्य भावो रसोद्भवः, *NŚ* 7.7). If this fact that there must be some kind of correlation between symbol and meaning is taken into account, then alone, the meaning of verse 39 in chapter 6 of *NŚ* that the meanings or *bhāvas* (for the appreciation) emerge from *rasa* would be clear. It is unfortunately thought that *sthāyī bhāva* stands for certain emotional state or sentiment. I too in my earlier writings had thought *sthāyī bhāva* referred to emotional state and ignored the fact that in *Nāṭyaśāstra*, Bharata is not interested in describing the process of poetic creation but is only describing the process of stage communication, though this process would be similar to the first. But in such a process the poetry would be taken for granted and translated into stage language. It is necessary to bear in mind that Bharata gives the list or *saṁgraha* of elements which are connected with stage. Every symbol or art object has a meaning. But on a stage different art objects present one continuum of meaning. This meaning continuum which gives a homogeneous meaning to drama is also a transformed state of *sthāyī bhāva*. Just as in ordinary language a sentence-meaning is different from word-meanings, so in dramatic language a totality of art objects leads to a sort of collective sense. This is the transformed state of *sthāyī bhāva*. Being of the nature of cognition or meaning, it is related with stage symbols on the one hand and with the spectator on the other. (Bharata seems to be aware of this, *NŚ* 27.87). It is this which makes it *hṛdayasaṁvādī*. That the *sthāyī bhāva* as referred to in drama is thus connected with the stage will be clear from the verses 52 and following in chapter 8 of the *Nāṭyaśāstra*.

It is the symbol or art object which undergoes a change from art to art. The meaning of different art objects can remain the same. This happens due to *sthāyī bhāva*. Thus, in the context of drama *sthāyī bhāva* takes the form of the meaning of stage symbol continuum; but, the meaning is essentially the same as the meaning of (dramatic) poetry (*kāvya*) which is exhibited on the stage. Thus, the *kāvyārtha* also can be regarded as the effected form of *sthāyī bhāva*; essentially, the meaning of poetry and the meaning of staged poetry is the same. In one sense then we convert the poetic meanings to stage symbolism, though, in another sense stage symbolism also yields meaning. The concept of *sthāyī bhāva* then is not entirely a concept in drama, nor has it any fixed place; it is persistent meaning or sense concerted with drama, poetry or any expression in the ordinary language. There is absolutely no doubt that Bharata uses the terms *sthāyī bhāva* and *kāvyārtha* as identical. If we look at two passages, one in chapter 6 and the other in chapter 7, this would be clear. In chapter 6 he writes — *vāgaṅga sattvopetān sthāyī bhāvan* (that is *sthāyī bhāva*s take the form of *vāgaṅgasattva abhinaya* on the stage). In chapter 7, he writes *vāgaṅgasattvopetān kāvyārthān* (वागंगसत्त्वोपेतान् काव्यार्थान्) (that is, it is the *kāvyārtha*, which has taken the form of *vāgaṅgastva abhinaya*). The loose use of the two words *kāvyārtha* and *sthāyī bhāva* is unfortunate. For, they have different significance in different arts. Nevertheless, this loose use of the two words gives a clue to the understanding of the motion of *sthāyī bhāva*. In short, *sthāyī bhāva*s being the manifestation of the same *thing and meaning* cannot be of one kind in poetry and of another kind in staged drama. If the essential identity of *sthāyī bhāva* and *kāvyārtha* is taken into account, some of the apparent contradictions in Bharata's writing are removed. The staged drama is essentially a translation of a form of literature into a form of presentation. This is the translation of poetic meaning into stage symbols. The stage symbols again yield a meaning which is equivalent to poetic meaning. *Sthāyī bhāva*, considered as meaning then is both prior and posterior to stage symbols or, as I understand by it, *rasa*. In the process of creation of the dramatic art, *sthāyī bhāva* (*kāvyārtha*) leads to *rasa*, and in the process of appreciation and understanding of staged drama, *rasa* leads to *sthāyī bhāva*. When the *sthāyī bhāva*s (*kāvyārtha*) take the form of different *bhāva*s they become *rasa* (*nānā-bhāvopagatā api sthāyīno bhāvā rasattvaṁ āpnuvanti* (नानाभावोपगता अपि स्थायिनो भावा रसत्वं आप्नुवन्ति *NŚ* 6), and it is these *sthāyī bhāvas* which exist in *vāgaṅgasattva abhinaya* that the spectators enjoy (*vāgaṅgasattvopetan sthāyībhāvān āsvādayanti sumanasaḥ prekṣakāḥ* (वागंगसत्त्वोपेतान् स्थायिभावान् आस्वादयन्ति सुमनसः प्रेक्षकाः . . . ., *NŚ* 6). We have seen that for Bharata, the persistent continuum of meaning, whether connected with poetry or stage, is *sthāyī bhāva*. But understood as meaning of the stage, *sthāyī bhāva* evidently requires some stage symbols or language without which there could be no meaning. In order to appreciate the proposition presented in this thesis, it is necessary to remember that the stage is a temporal continuum with a fixed point at each end. At one end there is *kāvyārtha* or the poetic creation, at the other end there is the artistic enjoyment or *siddhi* which connects the stage with the appreciator. Between these are *vibhāva, anubhāva* and *vyabhicārī bhāva* which form *rasa*. The *rasa* leads successively to *sthāyī bhāva*, the artistic beauty, the pleasure of the spectator and culminates in the indescribable artistic enjoyment or the last of the *daivikī siddhi*.

7

Rasa Theory
(Additional Evidence Continued)

Communication Process: Rasaniṣpatti and Rasāsvāda

We have seen that when we talk of art we are concerned with communication. Communication is a process which starts with the artist and ends with the spectator or audience. Bharata divides this process into two parts and gives them the names:

(1) *Rasa-niṣpatti-prakriyā* (रस-निष्पत्ति-प्रक्रिया)
(2) *Rasa-āsvāda-prakriyā* (रस-आस्वाद-प्रक्रिया)

He says, the *sthāyī bhāva,* through *vibhāva, anubhāva* and *vyabhicārī bhāva* takes the form of *rasa*. So this should be the first process. In the second process, this produced *rasa* is "tasted," evaluated and one accomplishes what is called "fulfilment" or *siddhi* (सिद्धि). What we call *rasa* should, therefore, manifest itself during and at the end of the first process. But those who think that *rasa* is of the nature of happiness or *ānanda* (आनन्द) posit it at the end of the second process. I feel this is against any process of art and in Bharata there is ample evidence against such a thesis. I have already discussed his thesis in the previous chapter. I shall now give some additional evidence to show that according to Bharata, *rasa*s are produced during first process only and not at the end of the second process.

1. In the eighth chapter of *NŚ* Bharata talks of *dṛṣṭi* of *rasa, sthāyī bhāvas*[1] and other *bhāvas*. These *dṛṣṭis* are definitely connected with actors. And Bharata mentions in very clear terms that they arise (8.52) out of *rasa* (*rasajā*, रसजा) as also out of *sthāyī* (*sthāyī bhāva sṛjaḥ*, स्थायिभावः सृजः) *bhāva*. They exist as supported by different *bhāvas* and *rasas* (8.43) *nānā bhāva rasāśritam* (नाना भाव रसाश्रितम्). This is also mentioned in verses 84, 85, 94, 95, 98. Similarly in the same chapter Bharata says that *tārākarma* (ताराकर्म) is to be *used* in *rasa* and *bhāva*/ Re 102, 111, 115, etc. Similarly, the verses 164-67/8 state that the acting which is to be performed through eyes is accompanied by different *rasas* and *bhāvas*. The verses 159-63 may also be referred to. But it is an evidence that *dṛṣṭi* and *tārākarma* are originally connected with the total act of *abhinaya* on the part of the actor resulting objectively in the creation of *rasa*.

2. While explaining the different techniques of stage, Bharata tells us how *music* is to be employed in the drama. *Svara* or vocal music is a stage category (6/10). It is plain that the (stage) music is not in the mind of the spectator. Bharata says that these *svaras* are *obtained* in the *rasas*.

   त एते रसेषु उपपाद्याः।
   ta ete raseṣu upapādyāḥ । *NŚ* 17.before 99

   Similarly in 17.after 118, Bharata *again* mentions: *eṣāṁ ca rasagataḥ prayogaḥ* (एषां च रसगतः प्रयोगः). It is true that from some editions this sentence is dropped. But, it is clear that the editor dropped it, when he did not understand the passage and thought that it was non-

---

1. Although this is also *sthāyī bhāva* of a more complex kind.

significant. Similarly, that the *varṇa*s are *obtained* in *rasa*, is again repeated on next page — *ye varnāḥ raseṣu upapādyāḥ* (ये वर्णाः रसेषु उपपाद्याः).

In the same way, the verse 75 of 27th Chapter clearly states that *siddhi* is evoked by different *rasa*s, suggesting thereby that *rasa* is different from *siddhi*.

3. Most writers on *rasa* unnecessarily make the concept of *rasa* mystical. This is because they forget that *rasa* is a form of the *stage* continuum; (and in its extended use, or the art medium).

   The Chapter 6 of *Nāṭyaśāstra* gives the colours associated with the different *rasa*s. The colour of *śṛṅgāra* (शृंगार) is *śyāma* (श्याम); of *hāsya*, white; of *karuṇa*, brown; of *raudra*, red; of *vīra*, white; of *bhayānaka*, black; of *bībhatsa* it is deep blue; and of *adbhuta* it is yellow (*NŚ* 6.43-44). These verses become mystical and non-sensical as soon as *rasa* is regarded as a *mental state of* the spectator or appreciator. *It is ridiculous to say that a state of mind has a colour*. But, if these *rasa*s are regarded as *objective stage forms*, then different colours can certainly help these forms and the situations. These objective forms can be more effective, if shown in different lights. The modern dramatic techniques make use of coloured lights for certain dramatic effects. Bharata's description too seems to aim at giving the appropriate effects through the use of coloured lights.

4. Again if *rasa*s were emotions, and not the transformation of mental state into behavioural patterns, it would be absurd to say that one *rasa* is produced out of another. Emotions are positively logic-tight and one is definitely different from the other. It is necessary to note that Bharata does not say that a

sthāyī bhāva, *rati* (रति), for example, gives birth to another *sthāyī bhāva*, say, *hāsa*. Such a statement would appear ridiculous. On the other hand, a small variation in the data of presentation will change the whole situation. With a small change in presentation a situation meant for *śṛṅgāra* can easily pass into *hāsya*, *raudra* into *karuṇa* and *vīra* into *adbhuta*. Bharata explains this in verses 40-42 in Chapter 6 of *Nāṭyaśāstra*.

5. Most writers think that the words *rasa* and *ānanda* or happiness are synonyms and quote *raso vai saḥ* (रसो वै सः) as evidence in its support from the Upaniṣads. In the first place this statement does not identify *rasa* with *ānanda*. It only says after obtaining *rasa* one attains the state of *ānanda*. The termination (*cviḥ*, च्विः) clearly says that there is a transformation from something *not existent* to something existent — *abhūta tat bhāve cviḥ* (अभूत-तत्-भावे च्विः). Further, *ānanda*, that is obtained in the stage performance is the effect of "an epistemological" stage of the experience of art presentation. On the other hand, *ānanda* as the stuff (of the cosmos) is ontological. Such a stuff would have nothing to do with the mental state of the spectator. *Ānanda* would be the stuff out of which everything is created and so *nāṭya rasa* also would be produced out of cosmic *ānanda*. To identify *rasa* that is cosmic with the mental state of an appreciator is confusing matters. To talk of *rasa* as *ānanda* on the evidence of Upaniṣads is to use the words *rasa* and *ānanda* ambiguously.

Sources of the Concept of Rasa

However, if the evidence from the Upaniṣads and Śruti is to be cited one ought to be aware of what Bharata says about *rasa*. Bharata says that the concept of *rasa* is taken from

Atharvaveda. So it will be necessary to see how the *Atharva* uses the word *rasa*. The oft-quoted citation *raso vai saḥ* is from *Taittirīya Upaniṣad* which belongs to *Kr̥ṣṇa Yajurveda*. So in the context of drama (and other arts) this quotation should be disregarded. In *Atharva Saṁhitā* the word *rasa* is used several times, but every time it means either juice or essence or some chemical compound, and never does it mean happiness. It should, thus, not be appropriate to use *rasa* in the context of drama as a synonym of *ānanda*. It is my contention that in the 6th chapter of *NŚ*. Bharata uses the word in the sense of juice, essence or a chemical compound and so to follow Bharata faithfully we must also employ it in that sense and in no other.

Sthāyī Bhāvas as Kāvyārtha

In the earlier chapter, I have shown that *rasa* is a basic element in stage continuum; *sthāyī bhāva*s which are the persistent *mental states* of the poet, when transformed into *vibhāva, anubhāva* and *vyabhicārī bhāva* take objective or public form and in this process *rasa*, the basic element in the dramatic process is born. *Sthāyī bhāva* is not just the internal unconscious state of the poet's mind, it is also the meaning of the poet's creation (*kāvyārtha*) and only as meaning of the poet's creation it would be related to the poet's mind. There is, however, one difference between that which is understood by the poet and that which he expresses. The *understanding of the poet* is of the nature of *anuvyavasāya* (अनुव्यवसाय). The *expression* of the poet exhibits the nature of *vyavasāya*. On account of this difference, the poet's understanding is more complex than the poetic expression. Bharata calls it *kavi-antargatabhāva* (कविअंतर्गत भाव). The expression of this in the context of poetry which also is *kāvyārtha* is *sthāyī bhāva* (*NŚ* 7 intro.). There can be several manifestations of the poet's understanding, the poetic expression is one which can again be translated into another kind of expression, say, a dramatic one. Just as the poetic expression takes the form of language, the dramatic expression takes a different form which requires a separate name. Bharata calls this *nāṭya-rasa*, is something which flows through the poet's mind to this *nāṭya*. It is also the medium. What I say would be clear if we examine the aphorism of Bharata. Bharata writes:

vibhāvānubhāva vyabhicāri saṁyogād rasa-niṣpattiḥ ।

विभावानुभाव-व्यभिचारि-संयोगाद् रसभनिष्पत्तिः ।

This aphorism when translated means that *rasa* is produced when *vibhāva, anubhāva* and *vyabhicārī bhāva* are combined. There cannot really be any difference of opinion about the meaning of *vibhāva, anubhāva* or *vyabhicārī bhāva.*

It cannot be denied that their orbit is the *stage* (or art). So the advocates of *ānandavāda* state that the combination of *vibhāva, anubhāva* and *vyabhicārī bhāva* leads to a certain state in the mind of the spectator or appreciator. I feel that in the first place this situation is covered by *siddhi* in Bharata's theory and secondly, it is necessary to recognize a behavioural *situation* on the stage in order to make the explanation of stage drama meaningful. It is, therefore, necessary to examine carefully the two concepts namely that of *niṣpatti* and that of *saṁyoga*.

THE CONCEPT OF NIṢPATTI

What is *niṣpatti*? Is there any difference between *niṣpatti* and *utpatti* or are the two concept identical? It appears to me that *utpatti* essentially denotes an effect, which is temporarily, that is, in terms of time sequence, separated from its cause. A bullet is fired and a man is killed. The firing of the bullet is the cause, and the death of a man is the effect. The death of the man is not present in the firing of the bullet. The *meaning of a sentence* on the other hand is contained in the sentence though it is obtained from a sentence. It is not, strictly speaking, *successive* to a sentence. It is in such cases that we can meaningfully employ the word *niṣpatti*. Oil is produced from oil seeds. By pressing oil seeds we get oil. Though oil manifests a form different from that of the seeds, still oil is present in the seeds. Only it has not been transformed in its later form. In *niṣpatti*, thus, the effect is already present in the cause, there is a co-presence of cause and effect.[2] *Niṣpatti* means separating the co-presence either physically or mentally and making it possible to view one apart from the other. In a *situation* denoted by *niṣpatti* the so-called "cause" and "effect" are not logically bound by a temporal relation of earlier than and later than; they are really simultaneous though the separate manifestation may occur at a "later" stage. It is necessary to note that I am not entering into the philosophical dispute about the theories of causation, denoted by *satkāryavāda* and *ārambhavāda*. For any situation can be interpreted on either theory. There is, however, a sense in which in one case the "effect" is present in the "cause" whereas in another case the "effect" is not present in the "cause." For example, oil is present in the oil seeds whereas curds is not present in the milk. I am not concerned with the theoretical discussion where a philosopher would agrue that the effect is always present in the cause in some microscopic way. I am only concerned with macroscopic concepts. It is my contention that the word *niṣpatti* in the above aphorism, *tatra vibhāvānubhāva vyābhicārī saṁyogāt rasa niṣpattiḥ* (तत्र विभावानुभाव व्यभिचारिसंयोगात् रसनिष्पतिः), only indicates that *rasa* is present and contained by *vibhāva, anubhāva* and *vyabhicārī bhāva*. It, thus, does not convey the idea of "leading to" but conveys the idea of "contained by." This will be clear even from the illustration of Bharata. Bharata says that *rasa* is produced when different peppers and medicines are combined together. It is

2. For, in the strict sense they are not cause and effect.

plain that the combination does not lead to *rasa* but is *rasa* itself.

THE CONCEPT OF SAṀYOGA

What is the meaning of *saṁyoga* in the above aphorism? *Saṁyoga* means contact and denotes an external relation. Such a relation can exist only between two or more substances. In sentences like, "this man is intelligent" or "that thing is yellow" or "that woman is weeping and miserable," there is no external relation between the man and intelligence, or a thing and yellow or the woman and miserableness or weepingness. Such a relation is some kind of internal relation and is usually known as "inherence." When a person is really *weeping*, weepingness is an expression of his *self*, and his self is modified by it. The expression cannot be separated from that person. This is what is known as *svabhāva*. *Bhāva* in the real world denotes an expression of the self. Bharata points this attitude when he says, *ātmābhinayanaṁ bhāvāḥ* (आत्माभिनयनं भावः, *NŚ* 25.40). But when a person *pretends* to *weep*, the enacted weepingness cannot be said to belong in a straightforward sense to the person who pretends. This is more so when the person not only pretends to weep but also impersonates some other person. The person impersonating someone else cannot have the same feeling as the person impersonated. When a person impersonates another person the impersonating person is not really transformed into the person who is impersonated. In a person who is not pretending, all these behavioural elements are originally assimilated with his self or personality. They have become parts of his personality and do not merely remain external parts as is seen in the case of *saṁyoga*. In this connection it would be interesting to consider the meaning of words like *vibhāva*, *bhūmikā*, *anubhāva* and *vyabhicārī bhāva*. The first two appear only in the situation of pretense. I shall confine myself to *ālambana vibhāva* only. But what is true of *ālambana* will be equally true of *uddīpana vibhāva*. In a real situation there is neither *vibhāva* nor *bhūmikā*, there is only the real self with all its expressions, etc. But when somebody is pretending to be another person, the person who is pretending gets rid of (temporarily) all that is really connected with himself, and claims to own something that does not belong to him but belongs to someone else. He, as it were, puts on or reflects someone else's personality. A person who does so has his own body as substratum and the other person's behaviour or personality as qualities *temporarily* connected with his body. This substratum, which has temporarily got rid of his own personality is known as *vibhāva* and the personality that this substratum reflects is known as *bhūmikā*.

The *ālambana vibhāva* is also sometimes known as *pātra*, pot or a substratum. The *bhūmikā* can be successfully carried out when the *bhāva* which really belongs to the person represented by *bhūmikā* is associated with the *vibhāva*, with the help of bodily expression or *anubhāva*. Thus, in any drama, which, in a sense, is an imitation, it is necessary to get together the *vibhāva*, *anubhāva* and *vyabhicārī bhāva*. The technique of drama requires this without exception. One drama may differ from another drama on account of a particualr content, but the form of representation is universal and the form becomes the form on account of the contact or *saṁyoga* of *vibhāva, anubhāva* and *vyabhicārī bhāva*. It is the object of every stage director to give this form to drama, which in the beginning is only a piece of literature. And so this form is the soul of stage or dramatic art. Without this *imitation and pretending*, *bhūmikā* would be impossible and a drama could never be staged. It is, therefore, absolutely correct that Bharata should insist on the combination of *vibhāva, anubhāva* and *vyabhicārī bhāva* and call the combination of *rasa* or *nāṭyarasa*, which is the essence of *staging*. In a particular drama, this form and the content together make it meaningful and produce *favourable* or unfavourable reactions in the minds of the spectators. These favourable or unfavourable reactions represent the *utpatti* but the mere combination of the three elements *vibhāva, anubhāva and vyabhicārī bhāva* gives us only *niṣpatti*. It is, therefore, desirable to say that for Bharata, *vibhāva, anubhāva* and *vyabhicārī bhāva* do not *lead to rasa*, but they are themselves *rasa* when they are *combined*.

I have already stated that the staged drama is an *imitation, anukaraṇa*. It is either an imitation of that which is or was existent or is an imitation of something imagined and conceived by the poet (or God). *Devānāṁ mānasī sṛṣṭiḥ* (देवानां मानसी सृष्टिः, *NŚ* 2.5). We have seen that in imitation, different elements are only compounded, or externally related. Thus, whereas the original would present a harmonious and homogeneous organic whole, the imitation would only appear so on account of *abhinaya*. Every element in this imitated form, therefore, is to be treated as a part (which exists in its own right) which can be combined with similar parts to make a whole. Such a combination of parts exists in its own right and can be treated on par with *dravya* or substance. A *saṁyoga* or external contact is possible only between substances. In the context of drama, therefore, *vibhāva, anubhāva, vyabhicārī bhāva* — all these are to be treated as *independently* existing entities without which the staging of a drama would be impossible. The combination of these which is *rasa* is a *dravya* or a substance — a substance (at least a *viṣaya*) which can be appreciated (*āsvādyate NŚ* 6.before 33).

Rasa — The Audio-Visual Language

It is my contention that the word *rasa* refers to audio-visual language. Abhinavagupta himself has in his *Tantrāloka* thought of visual language and called it *rūpa.* I have elsewhere stated that most probably these words were borrowed from Sāṁkhya system, where they stand for *tanmātras*. Scholars admit that the *nāṭya* system and Kāśmīra Śaivism have sprung out of Sāṁkhya system. This may or may not be so. But in either case it should not affect my assertion that the term *rasa* stood for audio-visual language, particularly, in the context of staged drama. In fact, the audio-visual art language becomes the field for the operation of *rasa*.

The word *rasa*, in the early *rasa* theory primarily referred to audio-visual art. This will also be clear if we carefully scrutinize how Vāmana and early rhetoricians or Alaṁkāravādins used the word *rasa* even in the context of audible poetry. The significance of Vāmana's aphorism, *dīptarasattvaṁ kāntiḥ* (दीप्तरसत्वं कान्तिः) has been thoroughly misunderstood in recent times. According to Vāmana *kānti* is one of the qualities of good poetry. It is either a quality of sound, *śabda* or a quality of meaning. In either case the quality *kānti* is associated with poetry as an art object and is not a pure state of the appreciator's mind like *ānanda* or so. It is necessary to note that according to Vāmana, when *rasa* is *dīpta it becomes kānti*, that is, *rasa* and *kānti* are related by the temporal relation, "earlier than" and "later than." Thus, at least in the system of Vāmana, *rasa* cannot be a state posterior to *kānti* and a synonym of *ānanda*. Bharata also mentions *kānti* as a quality of a dramatic text and also uses the word *dīpti*. He defines *kānti* as *dīpti*, a visual image felt for a *long time. Kānti-revātivistīrṇā dīptirityabhidhīyate* (कान्तिरेवातिविस्तीर्णा दीप्तिरित्यभिधीयते, *NŚ* 22.26). *Dīpta*, literally means "lighted" and stands for strongly evoked visual sensations. Thus, *kānti* is a strongly felt visual image or picture and *rasa* also would be a visual image. There

the she-bird. Though each part of the situation has an independent meaning or sense, the total situation also has an independent meaning or sense. This is *sthāyī bhāva*; if the *sthāyī bhāva* is of the kind of *pratyaya* or *vyavasāya* — the cognition, a reaction to this will be of *anuvyavasāya*. This is the case when an outside observer reacts to the total situation. It may be admitted that in some situations an *anuvyavasāya* and the *vyavasāya* may be identical. But, it may not always be the case. Sometimes the sense of total situation will enter the *anuvyavasāya*, sometimes it will not. In fact, it is on account of the possibilities of variations that an art object takes different forms. We have seen that even the *anuvyavasāya* or the reactions of observers to the total situation might be different. It is, therefore, the reaction of a disinterested person that is important. But, even the reaction of different (originally) disinterested person may be different. An observer may, for example kill the hunter, and take the bird for nursing; that is, an originally disinterested person may get interested and become a part of the situation which would now become still more complex. Another observer may have the same kind of mental reaction. But it may not translate itself in an action of this kind. The essential detachment may still exist and the observer may not make himself a part of the total situation. The poet's mind essentially depicts this situation. But, it is even more complex than this. It is essentially filled with creativeness. So, his reaction does not merely remain a passive part of his mind. It is again projected outside in some form. And that is what we call art or poetry. In the case of the poet Vālmīki, this projection came out in the form of a curse:

मा निषाद प्रतिष्ठां त्वं अगमः शाश्वतीः समाः ।
यत् क्रौंचमिथुनादेकं अवधीः काममोहितम् ॥

mā niṣāda pratiṣṭhāṁ tvaṁ agamaḥ śāśvatīḥ samāḥ ।
yat krauñcamithunādekaṁ avadhīḥ kāma-mohitam ॥

This complex state of a poet's mind is more complex than that of *sthāyī bhāva,* and is called by Bharata as *kaviantargata bhāva.* It is to be noted here that what the poet observes is a particular situation or situations. His reaction is certainly evoked by particular situations. But, even in the process of reception and conception, his reactions tend to have a general form or what Abhinavagupta calls *sādhāraṇīkaraṇa* (साधारणीकरण).

It should be clear that the reaction of the spectator to the art object should be very similar to the reaction of the poet to the *total situation,* particularly, when the total situation represented in an object of art is the imitation of the real situation. Emotionally, the two states can be equated. However, objectively, the two states may not be similar. This is for two reasons. (1) The art object, to which the spectator or appreciator reacts, may be less or more complex than the object to which the poet has reacted, (2) secondly, any art situation, like any language, may result in several secondary and tertiary meanings — *lakṣaṇā* and *vyañjanā.* The process might actually start in the poet's mind, as a process of generalization. But it may not stop and complete there. On account of time and environment and according to the capacity of the spectator, the total situation may have different meanings for the spectator.

8

Rasa Theory
(Bhaṭṭanāyaka and Abhinavagupta)

Rasa as Ānanda

WE have seen in the last chapter that Bharata who is supposed to be the author of *rasa* theory talks of *rasa* in the context of a stage-drama. Bharata's theory, however, was foisted, generally, on every work of art and poetry in particular. But in this process the interpretations of the text by later scholars like Bhaṭṭanāyaka and Abhinavagupta were however, understood in some different ways and the tradition emerged generally after seventeenth century CE, that is in post-Jagannāth period, when the concept of *rasa* was understood as feeling, emotion, sentiment, etc. that was supposed to arise in the minds of the appreciators while experiencing poetry or a work of art. The poetic or artistic appreciation was regarded as an artistic enjoyment and was equated with some kind of non-worldly (*alaukika*) happiness or *ānanda*.[1] It was compared to the realization of *Brahman* which was also regarded as of the nature of happiness, bliss or *ānanda*. *Rasa* was identified with *rasāsvāda*. It is this concept which R. Gnoli well brought out in the first edition of his book *Aesthetic Experience According to Abhinavagupta* and called it beatitude, rest, lysis. The passage

1. It was indeed *alaukika*, but in a different sense.

not only represents Gnoli's view but also represents the views of the galaxy of scholars in India and perhaps outside. Such a view was shared by Śaṅkaran, Raghavan, Vijayavardhan, Mulk Raj Anand, Gokak, G.T. Deshpande, K.N. Watve and several others. Manmohan Ghosh's translation of *Nāṭyaśāstra* also propounds such a view, because he translated *rasa* as emotion or sentiment. Today, it is almost an accepted view that by *rasa* was meant happiness arising out of poetic or artistic enjoyment. It has given rise to a tradition that *rasa* was connected with the *āsvāda prakriyā* or process of appreciation and referred to the concept of *ānanda*. The works of Mammaṭa and Viśvanātha were thus read with a prejudiced mind. This change of gear was due to the application of *rasa* theory of stage-drama (*nāṭya*) to poetry in general. Rudra Bhaṭṭa, the author of *Śṛṅgāra Tilaka* clearly says that he was going to apply to poetry the theory of *rasa* which Bharata had applied to stage drama.[2]

प्रायो नाट्य प्रति प्रोक्ता भरताद्यैः रसस्थितिः ।
यथामति मयोप्येषा काव्यं प्रति निगद्यते ॥

prāyo nāṭya prati proktā bharatādyaiḥ rasasthitiḥ ।
yathāmati mayopyeṣā kāvyaṁ prati nigadyate ॥

The verse clearly shows that the theory of *rasa* was at some stage being explained in the context of poetry in general. Similarly, in connection with the explanation of the relation of *rasa* and *bhāva*, Abhinavagupta mentions four different views, the views of Bhaṭṭa Lollaṭa, Śaṅkuka, Bhaṭṭanāyaka and his own preceptor, Bhaṭṭatauta, whom he sometimes calls Upādhyāya. Abhinavagupta's view is a synthesis and perhaps (at places) improvement over Bhaṭṭanāyaka's views. The views of Bhaṭṭa Lollaṭa and Śaṅkuka, though different, are of one

---

2. In the course of time the scope of *rasa* theory was further extended and it was applied to all arts.

kind and Abhinavagupta rejects them *in toto*. He largely accepts Bhaṭṭanāyaka's view but he criticizes it and suggests improvement on it by adding something of his own to it and substracting something else which according to him is not relevant.

Bhaṭṭanāyaka's View

What exactly is the view of Bhaṭṭanāyaka? Bhaṭṭanāyaka says *rasāḥ na pratīyate, na utpadyate na abhivyañjyate* (रसः न प्रतीयते, न उत्पद्यते, न अभिव्यंज्यते). It means, it is not experienced empirically, is not created, is not manifested. At least superficially this view is different from that of Bharata who talks of *rasaniṣpatti* (of course, *niṣpatti* is different from *utpatti*; but they are at least similar). A little later Abhinavagupta explains the view of Bhaṭṭanāyaka who explains *rasa* in terms of *bhāvanā* and *bhogīkaraṇa* and attributes to it the status of a (hypothesis) presupposition (*tat abhyupagamyate*, तत् अभ्युपगम्यते).

Of course, Abhinavagupta differs from Bhaṭṭanāyaka when he says "It is of the nature of *saṁvedanā* and *vyaṅgya parisaṁvittivedanā* (व्यंग्य परिसंवित्तिवेदना), of the nature of *āsvādana* and gives the purpose or meaning of *kāvya* or poetry. "He, further, attributes to Bhaṭṭanāyaka that this is enjoyed by *bhogakriyā* which is very similar to *Parabrahmāsvāda* (*parabrahmāsvāda-savidhena-bhogena paraṁ bhojyate iti*, परब्रह्मास्वाद-सविधेनभोगेन परं भोज्यते इति). Bhaṭṭanāyaka seems to have said further that actual experience felt in art leads to its *sādhāraṇīkaraṇa*, i.e. the particularity of the experience is replaced by its generality. I think, I have not distorted that which is attributed to Bhaṭṭanāyaka. First, one thing seems certain: Bhaṭṭanāyaka's concept of *rasa* does not seem to have any bearing on Bharata's concept of *rasa* directly. Bharata's concept of *rasa* or *rasa*s is concerned with particular experience[3] (though not with particular *guṇa*) which is experienced there and then, when we are concerned with the stage performance. For Bharata, *rasa* is brought into existence (*niṣpadyate*). For Bhaṭṭanāyaka it does not exist in any empirical form. It is our experience of the empirical that leads to *rasa*. So now the question is what is it that is referred to when Bhaṭṭanāyaka talks of *rasa* which is neither experienced nor created nor manifested? Bhaṭṭanāyaka seems to answer this by saying that it is *abhyupagama*, i.e. it is a hypothesis which is to be accepted in order to explain *rasa*s.

First Bhaṭṭanāyaka distinguishes between *rasa* in singular and *rasa* in plural. He says, *tena rasa eva nāṭyaṁ* (तेन रस एव नाट्यं) and then adds *yasya vyutpattiḥ phalaṁ iti ucyate* (यस्य व्युत्पत्तिः फलं इति उच्यते). *Rasa* and *nāṭya* are the same but *nāṭya*[4] is of the nature of *phala*, i.e. it is the (resultant) effect of *rasa*. Through *nāṭya* you arrive at *rasa*s as they are understood in plural by Bhaṭṭanāyaka. When we say *rasādṛte rasa* is understood in singular. Bhaṭṭanāyaka, as he is quoted by Abhinavagupta, says that it is the case of singular number. He regards it as *mahārasa* and this is not only presupposed but is the central idea. It is from this *rasa*, as is understood or presupposed in singular, that through *sphoṭa* or explosion we get the *rasa*s in plural. They are of the nature of *kāvyārtha*, i.e. the poetry or art becomes meaningful through them. Nevertheless, these *rasa*s, in plural, are in a way an expression of a singular *rasa* which is presupposed by the *rasa*s in plural.

---

3. But Bharata also does not talk of *viśeṣa guṇa*. He says *sāmānya guṇa yogena* (सामान्य गुण योगेन) . . . . . . *NŚ* 31. f.n. on 63, verse 26 also 7.before 7.

4. For Bharata, *rasa* was something like a precipitate of *vibhāva*. *anubhāva* and *vyabhicārī bhāva*.

This whole thought of Bhaṭṭanāyaka as expounded by Abhinavagupta is likely to express something very important, if it is taken along with what he has stated earlier, viz. that it does not "show" itself, it is not created, nor is it manifested, it only "is" in the sense that it is presupposed. This singular *rasa* is of the nature of *mahārasa* and its experience is like the taste of the ultimate *Brahman* (*Parabrahmāsvāda*). It is revealed in this way by *bhāvanā*, i.e. it is merely sensed or felt. What is this concept of *rasa* (in singular)? What is it that is felt when you are explaining the different kinds of the poetic experience? From what is said above I feel that Bhaṭṭanāyaka has in his mind the parameter of measuring the aesthetic "quality" of poetry or art. A parameter is a kind of a *pramāṇa* or a measure or scale. It is that by which we measure. Between that *by* which we measure and that which we measure there must ordinarily be something common, some similarity although this measure is not separately seen, separately experienced; it is seen or experienced through the object which we experience. I am sitting in a room. I experience the room in all its dimensions. If the room is to be measured it has to be measured by some spatial parameter, i.e. by length, breadth, height. This measure may be of the form of three-dimensional volume. But each dimension has a length which also can be measured by some measuring rod of the nature of metre or foot. This is the scale by which we get the knowledge of the room. Similarly, the different *rasa*s are to be measured by one *rasa*. If this measure is removed, measuring will be impossible. In Bhaṭṭanāyaka's thought, Bharata's aphorism *na hi rasādṛte kaścidapi arthaḥ pravartate* (न हि रसादृते कश्चिदपि अर्थः प्रवर्तते) is now understood in the way that if the scale of *rasa* is removed we will be groping in the dark regarding the nature of the appreciation of the art-object, i.e. poetry. This scale by which we measure does not reveal itself directly, it is not created, it is also not manifested or expressed. It "is not" in the sense material objects "are"; *nevertheless "it is"* and it is only after presupposing such a scale or parameter that we are able to explain any particular poetry or art. The scale, is, therefore, *alaukika*, is not worldly, it is our ideal. Of course, there will be such ideal scales for different arts and the actual artefact (or particular poetry) is only an approximation of the scale that is presupposed by these arts. Since this scale is concerned with the understanding and/or appreciation of a particular form of art it will be of the nature of taste itself and not of the nature of any material object. So although we talk of art object as object the stuff or the body of this object will be the resultant constituent of taste. The universe of discourse, in which all this happens is the universe of taste. Of course, in this universe, we will distinguish between the object and appreciation of the object.

The Process of Appreciation

But, both the object and the appreciation of the object will be of the nature of taste. (We will illustrate this with examples.) Bharata, in his *Nāṭyaśāstra*, talks of the two processes concerned with *rasa*: one is concerned with the emergence of the *rasa* (*niṣpatti prakriyā*) and the other is concerned with tasting or appreciation of *rasa* (*rasāsvāda prakriyā*). He has before him something like a knowledge model. There is a thing or an object and there is a knower. When the knower knows the object the resultant is knowledge. The object is called *jñeya* and this *jñeya* is different from knowledge or *jñāna*. In the appreciation process we have to distinguish between the appreciation which is either the act of appreciating or the result of the act of appreciating. But what you appreciated is different from the appreciation itself. The object of appreciation is evidently not appreciation. He, therefore, distinguishes between appreciation and the object of appreciation. The object of appreciation is called *āsvādya* and the actual appreciation is called *āsvāda*. He clearly states this in the text, *Rasaḥ iti kaḥ padārthaḥ? Ucyate, āsvādyatvāt* (रसः इति कः पदार्थः? उच्यते आस्वाद्यत्वात्). *Rasa* is *āsvādya padārtha*. The merit of Abhinavagupta who tried to streamline Bhaṭṭanāyaka's theory, lies in regarding *rasa* as of the nature of *āsvāda*. But this has led people to think that Bharata and Abhinavagupta did not distinguish between *āsvāda* and *āsvādya* and thought that Bharata implicitly and Abhinavagupta explicitly were talking about *āsvāda* or appreciation only. But, first Bharata clearly distinguished between *āsvāda* and *āsvādya,* and Abhinavagupta also distinguished *āsvāda* and *āsvādya* (see footnote no. 1, p. 291 BOS, *Abhinavabhāratī* also p. 280). As stated earlier, Abhinavagupta does say that whether it is appreciation or the object of appreciation, they belong to the universe of *āsvāda* only. But, it does not follow from this that there is no object of appreciation, nor does it follow that the atoms or molecules of appreciation cannot be brought in the focus of our understanding as the object of appreciation.[5] Just as one distinguishes between the object of knowledge and knowledge, similarily one can also take appreciation itself as the object (of knowledge) and appreciate it by reflecting on it. The reflection of appreciation could again be of the nature of appreciation only. It should be realized that in the epistemic world the object of knowledge need not always be some material object. When we are talking of language, and are concerned with meaning of language we must know that the meaning is never of the nature of crude material object; but, we can make such language or the meaning of such language as an object of appreciation and appreciate it. Language does not have existence in the same way as material things have.

---

5. Op. cit.

Similar is the case with laws, norms and so on. They do not exist in the way tables and chairs exist.[6] On account of our ability of self-consciousness we can sucessively bring such norms and laws in the focus of criticism and treat them as "existing." But this existence is not of the same kind as the existence of material objects. So, it is possible to talk of appreciation of appreciation itself, just as it is possible to talk of knowledge of knowledge itself, and, in arts and in poetry we are concerned with such objects. When Bharata talks of universe of *deva*s he has such a thing in mind. He says, *devānāṁ mānasī sṛṣṭiḥ* (देवानां मानसी सृष्टिः, *NŚ* 2.5). On account of our self-consciousness and *pratyabhijñā* this world of appreciation itself can be subjected to further appreciation. While staging drama, this philosophy of appreciation is only in the background, only implicit, and, therfore, Bharata might not have explicitly stated that *nāṭya* is essentially concerned with something that is mental. Abhinavagupta who is a profound philosopher, while streamlining Bhaṭṭanāyaka's theory, expounded that which was implicit in Bharata's theory and reconstructed his own theory. But in his theory he has distinguished between the object appreciation or experience itself taken as objects and the appreciation of "these appreciations." Bharata was concened with staging of a drama and in this act of staging he was concerned with what is called as *ālambana vibhāva* or *pātra* and these *pātra*s have bodily existence. In drama you try to transform that which is an idea into something that is concrete, i.e. you superimpose the mental over the body and make it living. This *pātra* which literally means a pot is basically a body

6. *Nyāya* talks of *viṣayī* and *viṣaya*. Every *viṣaya* is not a thing, as we ordinarily understand. When we are self-conscious, consciousness or self is not a thing. But it still is the object of self-consciousness or *viṣaya*.

and Abhinavagupta says that even if it is of the nature of appreciation or *āsvāda* it should be regarded as *āsvādya*. Abhinavagupta says (*NŚ* p. 291, Baroda Oriental Series):

> अतएव च नटे न रसः। कुत्र तर्हि विस्मृतिशीलो न बोध्यते ?
> उक्तं हि देशकालप्रमातृभेदनियन्त्रितो रसः, केयं आशंका।
> नटे तर्हि किं आस्वादनोपायः। अतएव च पात्रं इति उच्यते . . . नहि पात्रे मद्यास्वादः।
>
> *ataeva ca naṭe na rasaḥ* । *kutra tarhi vismṛtiśīlo na bodhyate?*
> *uktaṁ hi deśakālapramātṛbhedaniyantrito rasaḥ, keyaṁ āśaṅkā* ।
> *nāṭe tarhi kiṁ āsvādanopāyaḥ* । *ata eva ca pātraṁ iti ucyate . . .*
> *nahi pātre madyāsvādaḥ* ॥
>
> (The *āsvāda* of liquor is not in the glass).
>
> अपितु तदुपायकः। तेन प्रमुख पात्रे नटोपयोगः इत्यलम्।
>
> *apitu tadupāyakaḥ* । *tena pramukha pātre naṭopayogaḥ ityalam* ।

Abhinavagupta ramifies his position further by saying that this whole thing belongs to the world of consciousness (of the nature of idealism). He says (ibid., p. 280), *bhāvānugamitayā karaṇāt viṣayasāmagryapi bhavatu vijñānavādāvalaṁbanāt* (भावानुगमितया करणात् विषय सामग्र्यपि भवतु विज्ञानवादावलम्बनात्).

Bhaṭṭanāyaka's View — Continuation

This also seems to be the position of Bhaṭṭanāyaka. Bhaṭṭanāyaka is branded as a Mīmāṁsaka by many. In his metaphysics of epistemology or in his propounding the act of rituals he could be a Mīmāṁsaka. He must have certainly studied Mīmāṁsā, without that he could not have used words like *bhāvanā* and *bhogīkaraṇa*. But his position *vis á vis* the theory of art and poetry is not that of Mīmāṁsaka. We have seen that when we talk of standard its existence is *presupposed* or *felt*, this is what is conveyed by *bhāvanā*. In his pursuit of the theory of art, his basic position is not different from that of Abhinavagupta though Abhinavagupta might have rejected something and stated something more. On page 390 and Index of *Abhinavabhāratī*, Abhinavagupta states the position of Bhaṭṭanāyaka in the following words:

> भट्टनायकस्तु ब्रह्मणा परमात्मना यदुदाहृतम् अविद्याविरचित निःसारभेदग्रहे यदुदाहरणीकृतं तन्नाद्ट्यं तद् वक्ष्यामि। यथाहि कल्पनामात्रसारं तत् एव अनवस्थितैकरूपं क्षणेन कल्पनाशतसहस्रसहस्वप्नादि-विलक्षणमपि सुष्ठुतरां हृदयग्रहनिदानम् अव्यक्त स्वालम्बन-कल्पनया परचितं रामरावणादिचेष्टितं कुतोप्यभूताद् भूतवृत्त्या भाति। तथा भ सनपि च पुं अर्थोपदेशोपायताम् एति। तथा तादृग् एवं विश्वमिदं सत्यनामरूपं प्रपंचात्मकम्।
>
> *bhaṭṭanāyakastu brahmaṇā paramātmanā yadudāhṛtam avidyā-viracita niḥsārabhedagrahe yadudāharaṇīkṛtaṁ tannāṭyaṁ tad vakṣyāmi* । *yathāhi kalpanāmātrasāraṁ tat eva anavasthitai-karūpaṁ kṣaṇena kalpanāśatasahasrasahasvapnādi vilakṣanamapi suṣṭhutarāṁ hṛdayagrahanidānam avyakta svālambanakalpanayā paracitaṁ rāmarāvaṇādiceṣṭitaṁ kutopyabhūtād bhūtavṛttyā bhāti* । *tathā bha sanapi ca puṁ arthopadeśopāyatām eti* । *tathā tādṛg evaṁviśvamidaṁ satyanāmarūpaṁ prapañcātmakam* ।

Rasa as a Norm

I have earlier suggested that when Bhaṭṭanāyaka distinguished between *rasa* in singular and *rasa* in plural, he was distinguishing between the norm by which one would evaluate poetry or art and the particular norms which are just applications of the basic norm. For example, Vāmana has suggested in his *Kāvyālaṅkārasūtra* that art or poetry had two parameters or two co-ordinates: one of them is called evaluative or acceptance principle (*grāhyatātattva*) and the other is called constitutive principle or *ātmatattva*. The two co-ordinates would have a certain relation such that the constitutive magnitude could be a determinant of the evaluation and the evaluative norm could be a determinable of this constitutive condition. The constitutive condition is something which is concerned with the actuality or the subject matter and the evaluative norm is to be connected with beauty. Nevertheless, the constitutive condition will also have a scale of its own by which we measure the matter that constitutes the art. Thus, the constitutive scale will be concerned with the positive and not the normative. But, the scale will be a pointer to either the maximum in that scale or the best in that scale. The first will be the quntitative measurement, the second will be the qualitative one. Thus, for example if we are concerned with painting we may be concerned with the colour of the painting, and the composition of the colour of the painting; and also, with the curve and the texture of the colour of the painting, etc. All these will be concerned with the particular norms in those areas. The painting would be judged according to these subject norms and when the painting is completed it would be intuitively judged not by these constitutive norms but by evaluative or appreciative norms. We could, for example, say that the painting was beautiful or otherwise. There could be a certain relationship between the subject norms and evaluative norms. It could also be that these subject norms which would help us in describing artefacts could sometimes be used for indicating the evaluation. The descriptive language could be understood in an evaluative way. Take, for example the words *tanvī* (तन्वी) and *surekhā* (सुरेखा). They really mean slim and good line respectively. But, they could be understood as something standing for beauty. *Dhvanī* or *vakrokti* are also such words. *vakrokti* means an expression which is not straightforward, which is *vakra*, i.e. one which has curvature. But, it stands for the norm which according to some, determines the beauty of poetry. While dealing with subject norms one could compare a lyric poem with a social novel. In lyric poetry the subject norm determining the poem may be softness of word and its meaning and can be concerned with softness of individual feelings. When we go to social novel in addition to norms determining the lyric poetry one may have to consider the relations of individuals in the society and their relevance to each member of the society. Thus, the positive norms determining the subject matter of each art would have a tendency to become more and more complex. In addition, at each stage and at the stage of each complexity, if the artefact is well determined by the norm, it would result in some kind of satisfaction or happiness. If the artefact is in this way perfect it would be evaluated by the acceptance norm and would be judged whether it was beautiful or otherwise. The resultant of this process also will be some kind of satisfaction or happiness. Thus, there will be a relationship between the subject matter, the resultant arising out of it due to the subject matter norms and beauty and satisfaction arising out of this evaluative norm, if the artefact comes to a certain standard. The norm, standard or parameter or *pramāṇa* would be running through the veins of the artefact, but it would not be explicit, it would only be felt. One would not be able to say that the parameter exists in the way the subject matter exists. Perhaps, Bhaṭṭanāyaka has this in mind and therefore he says that they are not produced, they are not experienced, they are not expressed, they are only presupposed. For Bhaṭṭanāyaka the subject matter norms are expressed by the word *rasa* or *rasa*s. A point may be clarified at this stage. When we talk of norms we do not talk of them in a negative manner. They are always positive, e.g. if we are talking of the colour norm, we would talk of perfect colour and never of a non-colour or a perfect non-colour. A perfect non-colour will have no relevance whatsoever with the colour, and to talk of such non-colour norm will be irrelevant and meaningless. This will be equally true of other subject norms. (This will also be true of evaluative norms.) Thus if we are talking of happiness or a feeling of satisfaction we would be concerned with satisfaction or happiness in its positive aspect only; we could never be concerned with dissatisfaction or unhappiness. I could take two illustrations here, first could be from compassion and the other could be from *bībhatsa*. Compassion is certainly concerned with the situation that is miserable. But, when we reflect on this situation in art, the reflection would never be miserable. So would be the case with *bībhatsa*.

Summary

Let me recapitulate what I have said above. First, I have very crudely said that any art requires two axes. To take an example from geography, I should say that one axis could be called longitudinal and the other latitudinal. Longitudinally, all possible arts could be placed on one longitude but at different latitudes intersecting the longitude; one above the other or below the other; and all these arts located on the longitude could be judged by one norm, viz. the beautiful, for example. Latitudinally, one could say that on each latitude there would be only one art and the nature of the art could be explained in this way. First, the art would be an expression of the artist's experience. The experience in one sense of the term would be mental. It would be, in some sense mental, sometimes of the form of feeling, emotions, sentiments mixed with the cognitions of some external or internal objects. But when expressed the privacy of this would disappear and it would become public and assume certain shape or form. This objective form will vary from art to art. It would be a transformation of something mental to something objective (material or non-material) such that several people could experience the same. The complexity of this would vary from art to art, e.g. it would vary from lyric poetry to social novel and to dance and drama. What we call art at this point is the "objectivity" which makes the inmates of the artist's mind public. Of course, in this process they will be transformed into some form of sound or colour or curves or organic sensations, etc. But evidently this objective representation would have the relation of identity with the artist's experience that is mental. It is this experience which the artist has transmitted to the audience or listeners. One of the objects of the artist in creating art in fact is to communicate his experience to the audience or spectators. So in a sense the artist intends to communicate his experience. Of course, it would not be possible to certify whether the experience of the artist while taking the objective form or in the transmission to the spectator or the audience is communicated in equal measure and that there was no deviation in any way from that which was intended by the artist. It is possible that nothing is communicated or something is over-communicated, or something unintended or something different is communicated. But, what is intended to be communicated can be roughly regarded as the intention or the meaning which the artist has intended while communicating. So, the artefact, which is the creation or outcome of the artist's intention and experience, and that (i.e. the art object) which is experienced by the spectator or audience will be basically of the same kind. If the artefact is poetry in the form of sounds or signs we shall be concerned not with sounds or signs, but with the meaning which oozes out of it, and it would not be of the nature of things, but would be of the nature of experience (which in some sense would be mental). This will also be the case with what audience or spectator would experience from the artefact. Thus, the inmates of experience in the poet's mind, the objective form it takes in the artefact and the experience that the spectator or audience has, will be in some way related to or continuation of the mental or of the nature of *cittavṛtti*. If we are talking of *rasa*, then *rasa* would be of the nature of *āsvāda*, and, it would still be of the nature of *āsvādya*; because, it is *āsvāda* which takes the form of *āsvādya*. When it takes the form of an artefact, this artefact would, thus, have two different kinds of properties: (1) it would be of the nature of *artha*, and (2) it would be of the nature of *kāraṇasāmagrī* of *artha*. In the case of drama, it would be a combination of *vibhāva, anubhāva* and *vyabhicārī bhāva*. In the case of poetry it would be a *viśiṣṭa* of the combination of different words (*viśiṣṭapadaracanā*, विशिष्टपदरचना). This whole process is referred to by Abhinavagupta in the first verse of *Locana* as *Sarasvatītattva*, having two prongs, one in the poet and the other in the *sahṛdaya* (and the transition is due to the medium which may differ from art to art). But whatever the form each art takes it is bound to be the experience of the artist, and, therefore, it would be of the nature of taste or *āsvāda*. This *āsvāda* itself (i.e. of the artist) would become *āsvādya* and would allow the spectators or audience to have its taste or *āsvāda*.

I have said earlier that there are two parameters or axes: one is the positive and the other is the normative. But, in the positive parameter again one could locate two different currents: one would be that of *artha* and the other would be *kāraṇasāmagrī* of *artha*. The *artha* itself would be in some sense mental or at least non-material, non-spatial; but the *kāraṇasāmagrī* would not be non-material, it would vary from art to art; in the case of painting it would be concerned with colours, curves, lines and the squares of the canvas. In the case of music it would be concerned with the pitch, timbre, the tone of the sound and the rhythm and *laya*. In the case of drama, it would be concerned with *vibhāva, anubhāva* and *vyabhicārī*s, etc. And, when we would be considering parameters (i.e. the norm of the scale), we would be concerned with the best of the *sāmagrī*. But if we are concerned with *artha* we would be concerned with the mental effect which the *kāraṇasāmagrī* (कारणसामग्री) produces in the minds of the spectators or the audience. This effect would not be a real effect as we get in actual experience. Nevertheless, it would create in us some kind of experience with some kind of (emotional) tone. This (emotional) tone would be of eight kinds in drama[7] and in poetry it could be of nine (or more) kinds. The word *rasa* could be used for the experience of the poet's mind, *kavi antargata bhāva* or the *kāraṇasāmagrī* or *sahṛdaya antargata bhāva*. And apart from or isolated from the *kāraṇasāmagrī rasa* would be of the nature of *cittavṛtti*, of the nature of *āsvāda*. In *kāraṇasāmagrī* it would be of the nature of *āsvādya*, but this *āsvādya* also would be the result of something that is *āsvāda*. Abhinavagupta takes note of both these stages, *āsvādya* and *āsvāda* and also states that even as *āsvādya* it is the result of *āsvāda* which the artist or the poet has experienced. When the spectator or the audience experiences this *āsvādya* which is the resultant of this *āsvāda* he has to pass through two stages. In the first stage his experience would be toned by *śṛṅgāra, vīra, raudra, bhayānaka, karuṇa*, etc. These are different kinds of experiences. But, since the spectator or audience knows that these experiences have nothing to do with reality, that they are not *laukika*, in the second stage, he would reflect on them and such a reflection would be of the nature of approval (*anukūlatayā vedanīyaṁ*, अनुकूलतया वेदनीयं) or happiness. Its counterpart in actual experience in the form of misery or unhappiness would be absent there, because the understanding of the reality through such artistic or unreal models would itself be pleasant (*hṛdayasaṁvādī*). It would help him understand reality better, and understanding the reality itself is an experience which cannot be regarded as unpleasent. Bhaṭṭanāyaka calls such experience similar to *parabrahmāsvāda*. Abhinavagupta accepts this and later on this particular aspect

7. Indicating a range from substantives real or pseudo from concrete to abstract.

of this experience is accepted by later writers like Viśvanātha. Viśvanātha, for example, talks of such experience as *Brahmāsvādasahodara.* It is not an experience of *Brahman* or *Brahmāsvāda,* but it is an experience similar to that of *Brahmāsvāda.*

I have earlier suggested two parameters for art following Vāmana (or Kant). Bhaṭṭanāyaka's sentence,

रसः न प्रतीयते। नोत्पद्यते। नाभिव्यज्यते।

rasāḥ na pratīyate । *notpadyate* । *nābhivyajyate* ।

makes me think that Bhaṭṭanāyaka has these parameters in his mind. But, Abhinavagupta does not seem to expound the theory of parameters openly. He only says that *rasa* is *sarvathā rasanātmaka vīta vighna pratīti grāhyo bhāvāḥ* (सर्वथा रसनात्मक वीत विघ्न प्रतीति ग्राह्यो भावः) and he also says that the *viṣayasāmagrī* in the form of *vibhāva, anubhāva* and *vyabhicārī bhāva* is also in some sense akin to the mental because it arises out of *bhāva* (perhaps *kaviantargata bhāva*); and, therefore, in final analysis this *viṣayasāmagrī,* in the context of art, particularly, drama and poetry, is mental, i.e. of the nature of experience itself. He says, *bhāvānugamitayā karaṇāt viṣaya sāmagryapi bhavatu vijñāna-vādāvalambanāt* (भावानुगमितया करणात् विषय सामग्र्यपि भवतु विज्ञानवादावलम्बनात्).

He also says that although the experience is of different kinds, the reflections on these experiences are bound to be pleasant:

तत्र सर्वे अमी सुखप्रधानाः स्वसंविच्चवर्णरूपस्यैकधनस्य प्रकाशस्य ॥
आनन्द सारत्वात्.....
इत्यानन्दरूपता सर्वरसानाम्॥

tatra sarve amī sukhapradhānāḥ[8] *svasaṁviccavarṇarūpa-syaikadhanasya prakāśasya* ॥

8. The *śānta rasa* could be in the background of the other *rasas.*

ānanda sāratvāt.............. ।
ityānandarūpatā sarvarasānām ॥

It does not mean that *rasas* are constituted of *ānanda*. It means that *ānanda* is reflecting through, it is flowing through all *rasas*; it is *ānanda* for which *rasas* are used.

Experience vis-á-vis-Language

Our experience, I understand, is always a kind of a process. "Process" can be explained by a verb or verbs which point to a certain continuity spreading over a time length, short or long. But when our experience is expressed in language it takes the form of "parts of speech." This experience in language form would be of (1) nouns or pronouns[9] (2) adjectives of the nouns, indicating the norms and/or categories,[10] (3) verbs, with their modifiers in the form of adverbs,[11] and (4) syntactical connectives in the form of *kārakas* and *vibhaktis*.[12] Perhaps, on account of the analysis of our experience into the three main parts, (1) substantives, (2) actions (or happenings) perfomed and (3) the process of action, three theories about the meaning (or performance indicated) have come into existence in Indian thought. These three views are represented by Nyāya, Mīmāṁsā and Vyākaraṇa in the form of *śābdabodha*. Nyāya theory is known as *prathamānta mukhya viśeṣya*, the Mīmāṁsā theory is known as *bhāvanā rūpa vyāpara* and Vyākaraṇa theory is called *ākhyātārtha mukhya viśeṣya*. The

9. *NŚ* 17.107-118.
10. Either of the nouns or our viewpoint from which you look at them.
11. As a matter of fact the action part cannot be separated into the actual verb and its modifiers. But in the language structure this is done.
12. Indicated in some language by prepositions, etc.

Mīmāṁsā and Vyākaraṇa theories are concerned with the action part. But, when we actually experience something and store it in our memory it has three distinct categories indicated by substantives, actions and immediate action.[13] The adjectives are again of different types. Some of the adjectives are really the inseparable parts of the things, some of them relate them to other things and some of them are our observations on or judgements of the things. This, I think, is the picture of our experience; though rough and incomplete. In this analysis, the mainstay of our experiencing is the substantives for they could be objects with flesh and blood, and our interests blossom around them. In Nyāya-Vaiśeṣika language these parts (of our analysis) are indicated by *padārtha*s — *dravya, guṇa, karma, sāmānya, viśeṣa, samavāya* and *abhāva*. The "old" Nyāya also regarded the first three, *dravya, guṇa* and *karma* as having existence (i.e. whose existence could be felt by anyone who is able to perceive them). *Sāmānya* and *viśeṣa* are again two limiting points of our scale of (perceptive) knowledge. Our experience is always specific and so is always an experience of a particular. But, in this experience, it is possible to know the *jāti* or *sāmānya* or the species of the substratum which is the object of experience. This object is the *dravya* and is known to us through the *guṇa*s. The *sāmānya guṇa*s are shared by all particular objects and perhaps due to this we are able to discern the class of the thing. But each thing is differentiated from every other thing on account of its specific or *viśeṣa guṇa*s. These specific *guṇa*s make that thing a specific thing. In arts (except perhaps to a certain extent in portrait painting and sculpture depicting a specific individual) the artist tries to strip off the specific qualities of objects so that its identity gets

13. The actions and the acting parts are also sometimes transformed into substantives artificially.

established by some kind of "description" which is attempted by the artists to make it definite, an attempt which cannot be carried to perfection. This process is clearly seen in a stage drama. The actors, who play certain roles, play the roles only. They are never the original "characters."[14] The identity of the original is only thrust on them. *Śakuntalā* played by different actresses would be different but we regard them as *Śakuntalā* by common consent. In this process some specific characters of "the original *Śakuntalā*" are ignored by us. This is done by removing (some of) the *viśeṣa guṇa*s. It is this process which Bhaṭṭanāyaka called *sadhāraṇīkaraṇa.*[15] It must be remembered that *sādhāraṇīkaraṇa* is not *sāmānyīkaraṇa* or abstraction. Old Nyāya talked of *vyakti, ākṛti* and *jāti* as necessary for recognition of an object. When we accomplish the abstraction, the elements of *vyakti* and *ākṛti* are done away with retaining only the *jāti* part. In *sādhāraṇīkaraṇa* only some part of *vyaktitva* is stripped off. The *ākṛti* and *jāti* are kept intact. This is how anyone endowed with talents can play a particular role. This *sādhāraṇīkaraṇa* is attained in stage drama and dance only. In different arts there will be only degrees of *sādhāraṇīkaraṇa*. And in literary arts the identity is established through *sāmānyīkaraṇa* and through the Syntax only.

Sādhāraṇīkaraṇa and Knowing

But the concept of *sādhāraṇīkaraṇa* has a wider significance. It gives us the clue for finding out the different elements in the restructuring or constituting of the art objects through the elimination of a few elements and retention of a few others.

---

14. That is why the actors fall in the category of *vibhāva* and are not *svabhāva*s.

15. The *viśeṣa guṇa*s also form a hierarchy such as some *viśeṣa guṇa*s are nearer, some slightly distant, some accidental and some inseparable.

In fact, this is done in our knowing process also. What is knowing? In our knowing we are contrasting our experience with something ideal, some parameter. This is how we are able to recognize objects. This is what perhaps was in Plato's mind when he talked of his theory of ideas.[16] The *sāmānya guṇa*s the *sāmānya*, etc. supply us the *māna* or *upamāna* against which we test our *meya*s or *upameya*s. The process of (conscious) knowing is a continuous process of testing our experience against some parameters. The theory of *pramāṇa* is implicitly present here. Thus the theory (of *pramāṇa*) is further tested on the theory of *prāmāṇya*. In this process, a proper noun is tested by a common noun, abstract noun and an adjective. It is also evaluated by some types of adjectives. Let me ask as to what is meant by *pramāṇa*. It is defined as an instrument of knowledge. In Sanskrit the root *mā* is used both for knowing and measuring. In fact, knowing is a kind of measuring and indeed measuring is knowing. This knowing or measuring can be of various types and at a certain stage a question can be asked as to whether our instrument of measurement is a bona fide instrument. In fact, what is known as *prāmāṇyavāda* in Nyāya aims at determining whether our *pramāṇa*s are right *pramāṇa*s. That which determines the *prāmāṇya* of *pramāṇa*s is *prāmāṇyavāda*. The knowing process is in a sense a sea-saw of *prameya* and *pramāṇa*.

Knowing Qua Measuring

But, if we carefully look into the problem of measuring or knowing we will see that at each step we are measuring something by something. The first such stage is that of naming. Although we say that we give the names arbitrarily the procedure in social life is not that arbitrary. Even from names

16. This is also indicated in the process of *pratyabhijñā*.

we do usually understand whether the child is a male or a female. The next comes the stage of predication. When we predicate something of a subject (say a noun) we are actually measuring the subject against a norm supplied to us by the predicate. The predicate is the meter or sub-parameter in this context. But, this is usually the case when we go from a proper noun to a common noun, abstract or collective noun and adjectives of different kinds and even verbs. Verbs are only predications, functional predicates which give us the potentiality of the function and how far this potentiality can be used. The concept of measurement also persists when we move from one level to different levels and also talk of categories. In fact, even at the adjectival level, that is, when we judge something as something, the judgement can be at different levels. For example, "X is a thing," "X is beautiful," "X is sublime," "X is good" indicate different kinds of propositions. "X is a thing" tells us something about the constitution of a thing. The other judgements are evaluative and do not tell us anything about the nature or constitution of the thing. But all such cases are the cases of balancing, weighing, measuring. In this process we are in fact eliminating the special characteristics of the thing weighed. This is what is called *sādhāraṇīkaraṇa*. Bhaṭṭanāyaka who used this concept evidently had the concept of parameters which he expresses in terms of *mahārasa*. It is in a way a deviation from Bharata, but in a way it is making Bharata's idea explicit. For Bharata was also measuring the different terms in the *nāṭya* process by the concept of *rasa*.[17] Bhaṭṭanāyaka's concept of *sādhāraṇīkaraṇa* has in the background this concept of balancing. Of course, *sādhāraṇīkaraṇa* does not give us abstraction. But, it does eliminate the specific characteristics which go with stage

17. In fact, the term *alaṁkāra* also literally stands for parameter.

drama. Unless such characteristics are eliminated, *rasa* would not be used effectively as a parameter for all arts. In this process the word *rasa* lost its original narrow context of drama, and it was still used for measuring the dynamism and essence of arts. *Rasa* was also used for describing the evaluative character and perhaps in this process the concept of *rasa* was vulgarized. For, it lost some of its distinctive features. First, it became the constitutive parameter of arts and then it became the evaluative parameter of arts. In this transition the distinctive difference between the constitutive and evaluative processes was either lost or ignored. In fact, even in the Western tradition we find a parallel development. From the Biblical tradition the two words "existence" and "essence" were used. The existentialists also use them in contemporary times. But the word "essence" is sometimes used in the sense of existence, resulting in confusion regarding the two concepts.

9

Post-Abhinavagupta Development of Rasa Theory

Meaning of Vijñānavāda

It may be admitted that during the post-Abhinava period *rasa* theory was treading an idealistic path and the ground was ready for wrongly identifying it with either savour or happiness. Perhaps the use of some words by Abhinavagupta himself led to the misinterpretation of the *rasa* theory. In his commentary, *Abhinavabhāratī*, Abhinava uses a certain phrase. He says, *vijñānavādāvalaṁbanāt* (विज्ञानवादावलम्बनात्). In contemporary idioms *vijñānavāda* is understood as idealism. In fact, according to me this Western distinction of realism and idealism is not very useful for classifying the Indian philosophical concepts. Philosophers in India were not strictly materialists or idealists or realists or pragmatists. In a way, whether a philosopher belonged to Advaita school or Viśiṣṭādvaita or Pratyabhijñā school, he was in certain respects leaning towards idealism of the Western thought. But certain elements in these thoughts also took him away from idealism. In a way, Pratyabhijñā (प्रत्यभिज्ञा), Viśiṣṭādvaita (विशिष्टाद्वैत) and Dvaita schools accepted God and so the followers of these schools could be classified under Deism or Theism. Similarly, many of the elements in these thoughts brought them near realism. So merely because Abhinavagupta used the word *vijñānavāda* his thought as pointed out in the previous chapter should not be classified under idealism. He, in fact, belonged to the Pratyabhijñā school of Śaiva thought. He did not regard that the world was illusory. (In fact, to my mind even Śaṅkara and *vijñānavādī* Buddhist philosophers also do not regard the world as illusory, in the sense the word illusion is understood in English. If some of them have used the word *māyā* (माया), it was only to describe that aspect of the world which regarded that the things in the world have beginning, duration and end. Perhaps, only those philosophers who believed in *dṛṣṭi-sṛṣṭivāda* (दृष्टि-सृष्टिवाद) or *esse est percipi*, could be strictly brought under idealism.) What does *vijñānavāda* claim? It says that by our apparatus of knowing we get only *vijñāna* or particular *knowledges*. This means that we are able to build only a coherent universe of knowledge (or knowledges). This is idealism certainly. But, when Abhinavagupta uses the phrase *vijñānavādāvalaṁbanāt,* he says that by making use of *vijñānavāda*, it would be easier to explain the theory of art. Thereby he suggested that there was some similarity between the procedure of knowledge and art creation and art appreciation.

What is art? One can answer the question by saying that it is some kind of human creation. How does an artist create? With what material? Perhaps the answer to these questions would be (1) by his creative power (or *kārayitrī pratibhā,* कारयित्री प्रतिभा) (2) by using the cross-sections or slices of his experience. Is this experience constituted of the same elements as that of the common man in the world? Obviously not. The experience is basically mental, of the nature of knowledge, feeling, emotions, desires, etc. These elements are rearranged in artistic creation. The analogy that can be suggested here is that of *pratyabhijñā*. We do not have merely the knowledge of things or objects; we have the knowledge of the knowledge also. That is, the first knowledge becomes the predicate of the second knowledge if put in a proportional form. That is, in the second instance we are able to *handle* knowledge, as in the first instance we *handle* or use things or objects in the knowledge situation. In fact, knowing this intricacy of the transition from the first order knowledge situation to the second and some other order knowledge situations, the knowledge obtained in the first perception itself can be used in the second perception as if it was a thing. We also find this in self-consciousness. Ourself, who is the knower in the knowledge situation, can be made the object of our knowledge. Abhinavagupta says that this ability of ours is and can be very successfully used in the process of art creation, and he uses it. I should like to point out that the phrase, *vijñānavādāvalaṁbanāt*, has nothing to do with whether one is a realist or idealist. He points out that this is the relevant process of art, for art is not concerned with the first order creation. It is concerned with the second and other order creations. I also should like to point out that in order for *resorting to vijñānavāda* in art explanation, one need not always be a *vijñānavādin* or an idealist. The word *avalambana* suggests that it is *resorting* to something temporarily. The very fact that he talks of *avalambana* suggests that he does not want to adhere to the techniques of *vijñānavāda* irrespective of the context.

Āsvāda and Āsvādya

The material which is used in the process of creation is of the nature of experience. It is of the nature of the taste or *āsvāda* (आस्वाद). But, when used in the process of artistic creation, it cannot be used as taste *qua* taste or just pure *āsvāda*. The atoms of *āsvāda* now become *āsvādya*. (Shall I use the word, taste-datum or tastum, following the pattern of sense-datum sensum?) For, it is this first order *āsvāda* which becomes the "raw material" in the further process of creation and appreciation. If it is forgotten that we are now concerned with the *āsvāda* of *āsvāda* (experience of the experience atoms) we are likely to miss the most essential point in the theory of Abhinavagupta. Abhinavagupta, for example, clearly accepts the status of *rasa* as *āsvādya* as was originally suggested by Bharata when he asked the question, *rasa iti kaḥ padārthaḥ* ? (रस इति कः पदार्थः ?) and answered it by saying, *ucyateḥ āsvādyatvāt* (उच्यतेः आस्वाद्यत्वात्). It should be realized that the *āsvādya*(*tvā*) is different from the (first order) *āsvāda*, although it is made out of *āsvāda* atoms itself of the first order. In this second order *experience* situation, the knower or the *āsvādaka* would be the same as the knower or *jñātā*, in the first order experience-cum-knowledge situation. But the first order *āsvāda* would now become *āsvādya* or (*jñeya*) and the knowledge or rather the appreciation of this *āsvādya* would become the second order *āsvāda*. This second order *āsvāda* is important and significant in artistic process. In fact, Abhinavagupta brings out this distinction between this second order *āsvāda* and the second order *āsvādya* clearly. He illustrates it by comprehending a situation, where there is a glass (of alcohol), alcohol, the taste of alcohol and the taster of alcohol. He explains the relationship by saying, *pātre na madyāsvādaḥ* (पात्रे न मद्यास्वादः). He says *āsvāda* (आस्वाद) is not in the *āsvādya* (आस्वाद्य) but in *āsvādī* (आस्वादी) or *āsvādaka* (आस्वादक). Although in case of a drama, the *pātra* or the actor himself is a conscious being, as an actor, he is merely the container of the datum (*rasa*), and the *āsvāda* experience belongs to those who experience, that is to the spectators only. It is necessary to note that Abhinavagupta does not confuse the first order ***āsvādya*** with the second order ***āsvādya***, or the first order ***āsvāda*** with the second order ***āsvāda***.

The Post-Abhinavagupta Period — The Period of Decadence

It appears to me that the post-Abhinavagupta period is the beginning of Indian cultural decadence. In this period were also narrowed down the areas of different arts and they were mostly restricted to, and stabilized in, the theory of poetry. This was due to the influence of Ānandavardhana. The last and the most important treatise on architecture, *Samarāṅgaṇa Sūtradhāra* (समरांगण सूत्रधार) attributed to king Bhoja must have been written either by Bhoja or his ghost writer in the eleventh century only. According to M.M. P.V. Kane other writings like *Śṛṅgāraprakāśa* (शृंगारप्रकाश) attributed to Bhoja also appear like a compilation. This period is connected with the invasions from ouside — first by Hūṇas and, then by Afghans, Turks and Persians, etc. These invaders destroyed the existing architecture and it must have become a problem for an artist to save his technological literature on art and architecture. Round about CE 1215. Kutubuddin Aibak established his Slave Dynasty in Delhi and within the next 50 or 60 years the invaders found their way to Orissa in the east, Kanyākumārī in the south and Kashmir in the north. In Sanskrit Literature the name of Allauddin of Khalaji is mentioned perhaps by Viśvanātha, the author of *Sāhitya Darpaṇa*. Viśvanātha quotes a verse which speak of a Muslim king named Allauddin.

सन्धौ सर्वस्वहरणं विग्रहे प्राणनिग्रहः ।
अल्लावदीननृपतौ न सन्धिर्न च विग्रहः ॥

sandhau sarvasvaharaṇaṁ vigrahe prāṇanigrahaḥ ।
allāvadīnanṛpatau na sandhirna ca vigrahaḥ ॥

— P.V. Kane, *History of Sanskrit Poetics*, p. 298

Allauddin's deputy, Malik Kafar, after the conquest of Devagiri or Daulatabad, also went up to Rameshwaram and destroyed some temples there and built a mosque. It is during this period that it was difficult for the Kashmiri paṇḍits to save the literature on philosophy and on the theory of art. Most of the Sanskrit paṇḍits who wrote on the theory of art came from Kashmir, but very soon a large part of literature on drama was lost to them. Bharata's *Nāṭyaśāstra* was found somewhere in south India after three hundred years or more and *Abhinavabhāratī* was a discovery of the late Ramkṛṣṇa Kavi after several hundred years. Bhartṛhari's commentary of *Mahābhāṣya* was also lost and was ultimately found in Berlin. Bhaṭṭanāyaka's work *Hṛdayadarpaṇa* (हृदयदर्पण) which is quoted by Abhinavagupta and others is found only in fragments in the writings of later Sanskrit philosophers of art. This was also the period when Vijayanagar Empire came into existence. Similarly, this is also the period when Koṇārka and Khajurāho temples were built in Orissa and Central India respectively. Perhaps the paṇḍits in order to preserve their learning must have taken shelter in such kingdoms, and as the invaders went more and more to the south the arts must have receded to the southernmost states. It is important to note that *Bharatanāṭya* in its original form as given by Bharata continued its existence in Kerala and Tamil Nadu only, the southernmost State of India; for its continuation it had to travel from Kashmir to Kerala. Perhaps, during this period of upheaval the theory of *rasa* also got a shake. Hemacandra, a great Jain philosopher and art critic, still talks of *rasa* in the idiom of Bharata and anticipates Jagannātha. He describes it very clearly. He says, *rasa* is *sthāyī bhāva* which is expressed in terms of *vibhāva*, *anubhāva* and *vyabhicārī* (*Kāvyānuśāsanam*, 1:2)

> विभावानुभाव-व्यभिचारिभिः अभिव्यक्तः स्थायिभावो रसः।
> *vibhānubhāva-vyabhicāribhiḥ abhivyaktaḥ sthāyibhāvo rasāḥ* ।

Similarly, 1:2 (*Kāvyānuśāsanam*) states,

> रसस्योत्कर्षापकर्ष-हेतु-गुणदोषौ भक्त्या शब्दार्थयोः।
> *rasasyotkarṣāpakarṣahetu guṇadoṣau bhaktyā śabdārthayoḥ* ।

the commentary says (*rasavakṣyamāṇasvarūpaḥ*, रसवक्ष्यमाणस्वरूपः) that *rasa* is that which is made expressible. This description very much agrees with that given later on by Jagannātha who describes *rasa* in terms of *gocarīkriyamāṇatā* (गोचरीक्रियामाणता) [*Kāvyānuśāsana* edited by Rasiklal Parikh and V.M. Kulkarni by Mahavira Jain Vidyalaya, Bombay]. It should be noted that of the three important critics on poetics, Mammaṭa, Viśvanātha and Jagannātha, it is Viśvanātha alone who includes *rasa* in the definition of poetry — *vākyaṁ rasātmakaṁ kāvyam* (वाक्यं रसात्मकं काव्यम्).

It should not be forgotten, however, that Viśvanātha does not forget to include *vākya* in the definition of poetry. But for Viśvanātha, *rasa* appears to be a source of happiness or beauty. Mammaṭa talks of *rasa,* no doubt, but he does not define poetry in terms of *rasa*. Following in the footsteps of Ānandavardhana, he distinguishes three types of poetry (1) *citrakāvya,* (2) *guṇībhūta vyaṅgya* (गुणीभूत व्यंग्य), and (3) *dhvani*. Under this *dhvani* he talks of *rasadhvani* (रसध्वनि) but, he does recognize *citrakāvya* also as poetry. Perhaps, Jagannātha carries this further and says that poetry should be expressive of meaning that is beautiful, but does not make poetry dependent on *rasa* which according to him is concerned with expressibility (of medium and message).

Post-Abhinavagupta Theories of Poetics

The successors of Abhinavagupta like Hemacandra, Mammaṭa, Viśvanātha, Appaya Dīkṣita and Jagannātha were important philosophers of aesthetics. Although there are differences in their thinking so far as the emphasis is concerned, all of them accepted the basic syncratism of all the six theories of poetry. None of them defined poetry in terms of *rasa* though all of them gave due importance to the concept of *rasa*. They all regarded, like Bhāmaha, that *alaṁkāra*s or embellishments were necessary for beautifying poetic art. By extension of the concept, one could also say that for every art some kind of ornamentation was necessary, although the ornaments would differ from art to art. Naturally in the case of architecture, the ornamentation would depend on proportion, similarities and contrasts and on the relation of parts and whole. But, in a sense this was true of all arts including poetry. None of them did define art in terms of happiness, although it was recognized that happiness was the objective (or a necessary resultant) of all arts. They also thought in terms of parameters of arts, and also recognized that the parameters of the subject matter were different from the parameters of evaluation. They further recognized the transition and significance of the process of making the subjective experience or idea transform into objective or public and regarded this as the *process* of realization of *rasa*. Of course, they did differ from one another as regards the nature of transformation and the stages in this transformation. Bharata tradition had recognized all elements in this process of transition from *vibhāva*, *anubhāva* and *vyabhicārī bhāva*, etc. leading to *rasa*. But, some of them emphasized, as Shri Madanmohan Jha pointed out, on some element or the other. I shall try to discuss them in detail so far as the development of the theory is concerned. But, I would like to point out that none of these defined poetry in terms of *rasa* as happiness, as was interpreted by nineteenth and twentieth century interpreters of poetry in particular and art in general. Neither Viśvanātha nor Mammaṭa nor Jagannātha did anything of this kind. In fact, while discussing poetry, Jagannātha did recognize the possibility of poetic creation (i.e. of any art) even in the absence of *rasa* that the process of *rasa* was operative only when the *sthāyī bhāva* came into play, took the objective form and became perceptible to our senses. The process of *rasa* according to them lay in making the subjective state of *sthāyī bhāva* assume an objective and public form.

But, in this process and in the translation from one to another the concept of *rasa* and *rasa* theory assumed some kind of idealistic form and something exactly oppostite of what was originally intended came into existence. Jagannāth was perhaps the ony exception who expounded his theory of poetry with great clarity.

Pre-Jagannātha

In the poetic tradition of India the culminating point was reached in Jagannātha. Those who came before Jagannātha did make several contributions to poetic thought and the concepts in poetics had become so important that they were adopted by the theorists and critics of other arts. The chief concept was that of *rasa*. This, of course, does not mean that they did not introduce other concepts. Bhāmaha, for instance, introduced *alaṁkāra*. Daṇḍin and everyone also accepted the concept of *alaṁkāra* and incorporated it in their own theory. But, Vāmana added to this the concept of parameter and also said that the parameter of art in general and poetry in particular was that of *saundarya* or beauty. Bhāmaha insisted on the equal significance of *śabda* and *artha* in poetics which in a more general form would mean medium and intention. Vāmana who followed Bhāmaha developed this theory in the form of *rīti* and added to it the concept of *guṇa* as an evaluative characteristic. He pointed out that every art object is characterized by some *viśeṣa* which he defined as *guṇātmā*. Kuntaka accepted what Bharata, Daṇḍin and Vāmana had said but introduced the concept of *vakrokti* as an evaluative concept. In poetry it means speaking in an elliptical manner. But, *vakrokti* was used by Bhāmaha also and he had pointed out that exaggeration is the basic quality of *vakrokti* and is a blanket characteristic of all poetry. Vāmana talked of *rīti* but Bharata had also introduced the concepts of *vṛtti* and *pravṛtti* which were the counterparts of *rīti* in drama. Kṣemendra talked of propriety but the germs of this concept, in some sense, are found in all the writers on poetics. But the concept which became most important and was thus used as a parameter was, as pointed out earlier, that of *rasa*. It was generally used for *āsvādya*. It, gradually, gathered more and more meaning around it and was not regarded as a private idea which could not be shared by others. It was connected with another psychological concept *sthāyī bhāva* and it was accepted that *sthāyī bhāva* which was the private property of an individual cannot be, without objective transformation, shared by others. By such transformation, it changed its form and acquired a shareable property in the form of *anubhāva*, *vyabhicārī bhāva* or its combination or product. In this transformation, *rasa* became all important and arts and poetry were defined in terms of *rasa*. It was Jagannātha alone who while recognizing the value of *rasa* concept pointed out that it could not be the defining property of poetry. He thus introduced another concept, *ramaṇīyatā* (रमणीयता).

Jagannātha

In fact, this concept was mentioned by Bharata who called it *śabdā*. But it was Jagannātha who clearly defined *kāvya* or poetry as a structure of language which demonstrates or expounds beauty:

रमणीयार्थप्रतिपादकः शब्दः काव्यम् ।

ramaṇīyārthapratipādakaḥ śabdaḥ kāvyam ।

He says that the description of poetry by Bhāmaha that it is an inseparable pair or a couple of *śabda* and *artha* is incorrect for it cannot be proved by any parameter. [For example it could be said that *though* I have read a certain poem I did not understand its meaning (I however feel that the word *artha* (in *ramaṇīyārthapratipādakaḥ*)] appears even in the definition given by Jagannātha)]. But what according to me is necessary, is the meaning and not the particular person's understanding of meaning. I further feel that Bhāmaha suggests here only the necessary condition of poetry and not the sufficient condition which is perhaps given to us by *alaṁkāra*. We may ignore Jagannātha's critisism of Bhāmaha but accept his definition of poetry as more accurate. It is more accurate than the definition of poetry given by Mammaṭa or Hemacandra.

अदोषौ सगुणौ सालंकारौ शब्दार्थौ काव्यम् ।

adoṣau saguṇau sālaṁkārau śabdārthau kāvyam ।

This definition of poetry is merely a combination of several things propounded by the earlier doyens. I feel that when our masters criticize their contemporaries of other masters they base their criticism more on quibbles. Jagannātha's criticism of Viśvanātha, who defined poetry as *rasātmakaṁ vākyaṁ kāvyam* (रसात्मकं वाक्यं काव्यम्) is again very important. But, Jagannātha points out that there can be poetry even in the absence of *rasa*. What Viśvanātha says in *Sāhityadarpaṇa* about poetry (that which has *rasa* in it) is incorrect, for on this definition, that poetry which describes nature or *alaṁkāra* would be excluded from the locus of poetry. This indeed is incorrect.

In his *Rasaprakaraṇa*, Jagannātha does describe *rasa*. But from this description, it appears that while discussing *rasa*, Jagannātha is not concerned with happiness, which is traditionally given as the meaning of *rasa*. On the other hand, he regards, and regards, rightly, that *rasa* is the communication-continuum in visual arts. For this purpose Jagannātha, like Bharata and Mammaṭa, takes stage drama as a paradigm. For, it is in the stage drama alone that *vibhāva*, *anubhāva* and *vyabhivcārī bhāva* have a straightforward use. The *sthāyī bhāva* is transformed into *rasa* through *vibhāva, anubhāva* and *vyabhicārī bhāva,* and *sthāyī bhāva* becomes *vyakta* or expressed and becomes public. (In other non-visual arts *vibhāva*, etc. are only imagined and not directly experienced in some visual concrete form.) Jagannātha states this explicitly in these words —

निजस्वरूपानन्देन सह गोचरीक्रियमाणः प्रग्निविष्टावासना रूपोख्यादिरेव रसः।

nijasvarūpānandena saha gocarīkriyamāṇaḥ pragniviṣṭāvāsanā rūpokhyādirev rasāḥ ।

Even Mammaṭa also says the same thing when he says,

व्यक्तः स तैर्विभावाद्यैः स्थायिभावो रसः स्मृतः।

vyaktaḥ sa tairvibhāvādyaiḥ sthāyībhāvo rasāḥ smṛtaḥ ।

It should be remembered that it is only in the drama that *vibhāva*s, etc. have a direct role. And it is only indirectly that these concepts are utilized in other arts, on account of the common element in all arts. This common process has been clearly stated by Jagannātha in the words *gocarīkriyamāṇatā* (*Rasagaṅgādhara,* Prathamanand, p. 80, edited by Shri Madanmohan Jha). The transformation from subjective to objective, or from private to public, is what takes place in all arts and this is the dynamic element required for transformation from *sthāyī bhāva* to *rasa*. For Jagannātha it is not *rasa* which is the essence of poetry (and so of arts). It is the *camatkṛti* (चमत्कृति) which is of essence. This creation of *camatkṛti* is due to the power of imagination or *pratibhā* of the poet. When the poet is able to visualize his imagination in pictographic image form, it is *rasa* (which is directly visualized in stage drama). But where it is merely a description of nature or *alaṁkāra*, no *rasa* is required for its obtaining the status of poetry. One can easily see that it is not on visual images that poetry is dependent (ibid., pp. 23-34). But, it could also be seen that this *gocarīkriyamāṇatva* itself was taken to be *rasa* by most writers after Rudrabhaṭṭa. In fact, there seems to be non-difference between *gocarīkriyamāṇatva* and *camatkṛti.*

The World of Creation

The distinguishing feature of the human world is its activity. It starts with knowing. It is taken for granted here that what is known is different from the knower. This is the process of exploring the object of the objective world. Even when our knowledge is illusory, its form is objective, i.e. it behaves as if it is independent. Our entry into the field of knowledge is due to mind, which itself might be of the nature of function of the organism. Without operation of such functions, the presence or existence of the *states of mind* or mind would not be felt. This feeling of *cittavṛtti* or knowing the things through *cittavṛtti* is the process of objectification. Through *cittavṛtti* we know the outside world, and we know that the outside world presupposes *cittavṛtti*s. Mind or something that is mental is known by its movement making it perceptible to sense. This is *gocarīkriyamāṇatā*. Mind or any state of mind is complex. (Perhaps, because it is related to other states.) We do not seem to isolate a simple mental state. It can be cellular. But even a single cell is a complex of many. It is like an integrated circuit (IC); it does not behave like a part of a whole. It behaves like a whole, which is micro-cosmic or even nano-cosmic. Usually, such states are not artificial. They arise naturally. But such naturally arisen states can be made to flow artificially. It is like changing the flow of a river and making it pass through a canal of the reservoir made from the river itself. Such artificially induced mental state (*bhāva*) is *rasa*. But, whether it is naturally induced or artificially, a mental state cannot be *known* or *felt* unless it is subjected to a process that is either objective or public. This *objectivity* may be bodily, physiological, physical or even mental. Without such substratum a mental state would not be known. But, its ultimate substratum or support would be the body (living) itself. The *sthāyī bhāva* thus passes through natural (or artificial) *bhāva*s, depends upon *vibhāva* (or *svabhāva*) and takes the form of *anubhāva*s (and/or *sañcārī bhāva*s). But, unless the *sthāyī bhāva* is transformed into these it cannot be known. It is so not only for others; but, also, for him whose *sthāyī bhāva* is under consideration. It is so, because, although we regard *sthāyī bhāva* as mental, it cannot be separated though distinguished from bodily or neurological states. Artists in general, and drama directors in particular, make use of this technique.

Misinterpretation of Rasa-Theory in the Post-Jagannātha Period

While interpreting our Masters, I do want to be faithful to them. But, I believe that there is some relationship between the authors' intention and the readers' understanding. If what I understand is sensible and necessary to the theory, I would say that I was successful in interpreting the author. If the analysis that I give and the concept I project is necessary for the rational understanding of the theory, I presume that it was also the intention of the author in propounding the thesis.

I believe that in the post-Jagannātha period *rasa* theory has been completely misunderstood and misinterpreted. Let me reconsider the problem. I take two pairs of words (1) moment, point, *kṣana* and (2) continuum, fibre, *santāna*. How shall I differentiate between the two sets? Perhaps, mathematical moments, points, *kṣana* do not exist in the objective world. They "exist" only in our ideas, in our mind. But we postulate them for they supply the background for our thought in general and mathematical thought in particular. What we get in actuality is length in time or space. But we are able to "divide" actually or mentally a temporal or spatial length into parts, the minutes of which we think (though wrongly) consist of points and moments. But our thinking at the other end has also similar difficulties. We also talk of infinite length and infinite duration. But like a mathematical point or moment, the infinite extension and duration also is beyond the grasp of our practice, and, in thought infinite extension or duration is ever increasing. Our thought proceeds between these two extremes. Our grasp is always finite. Of course this finite grasp is either static or dynamic. If it is dynamic, it is of the nature of process. But, even if it is not a dynamic one, if the moments or points are arranged in some order they look "dynamic." Here, perhaps, the dynamism is mental, supplied by the thinker. A series of points looks like a line and a series of moments "becomes" duration.

In the light of the above observation let me look at words like fibre or sound (resonance of a sound). In our actual practice we deal with *thread and not with fibre*. But a thread is made up of *fibres*. It is never made up of points. The length of fibres may vary, the fibres may be long or short. But, they always have a length. What about a sound? Can it exist without a pitch or duration? We move our finger on a string instrument. It gives a certain note. Is it just momentary? I feel, it is like a temporal "fibre." The resonance gives us the idea of duration. The same seems to be the case in the sphere of thought. It may be of a short or long duration. But, it must have a duration and to have a duration, there must be a continuous sequential transition from the beginning to the end. Of course, such a transition can break also and in that case we may say that the thought is broken in the middle. We may use this gauge for understanding the transformation from *sthāyī bhāva* to *rasa* or vice versa. Is it merely a static transformation, just a translation or encoding of the one into the other? or is it like an electric current which continuously "moves" from one end to the other with the object of completing the circuit? Of course, it is possible to think of different parts in the process, if we demarcate them. But while the parts can be demarcated the *elan vital* of the process cannot be demarcated. It is continuous. From Bharata to Jagannātha, through Daṇḍin, Vāmana, Bhaṭṭanāyaka, Abhinavagupta, Mammaṭa and Viśvanātha, etc. everyone talks of different items in the process. But, they have also talked of the *dynamic process*. Jagannātha, for example, talks of *gocarīkriyamāṇatā* element. Bharata talks of this element by using the *bhāva*s like *sañcārī* and word like *āpnuvanti/upaiti*, etc. Even Viśvanātha says,

> रसावस्थः परं भावः स्थायितां प्रतिपद्यते ।
>
> *rasāvasthaḥ paraṁ bhāvāḥ sthāyitāṁ pratipadyate* । (p. 72)

and also

> विभावेनानुभावेन व्यक्तः संचारिणो यथा ।
> रसतामेति रत्यादिः स्थायिभावस्सचेतसाम् ॥
>
> *vibhāvenānubhāvena vyaktaḥ sañcārīṇo yathā* ।
> *rasatāmeti ratyādiḥ sthāyī bhāvas sacetasām* ॥ — 1, *SA.DA*

All this, I think, should be understood properly. I feel that all these masters basically agreed that *rasa* was the essence, the *sara* (सार). Viśvanātha quotes from Dharmadatta —

> रसे सारश्चमत्कारः सर्वत्राप्यनुभूयते ।
> तच्चमत्कार-सारत्वे सर्वत्राप्यद्भुतो रसः ।
>
> *raśe sāraścamatkāraḥ sarvatrāpyanubhūyate* ।
> *taccamatkāra sāratve sarvatrāpyadbhuto rasāḥ* ॥ — p. 73, *SA.DA*

To my mind, Mammaṭa also expressed the same thing, when he said *vyaktaiḥ sa tairvibhāvādyaiḥ sthāyibhāvo rasāḥ smṛtaḥ* (व्यक्तैः स तैर्विभावाद्यैः स्थायिभावो रसः स्मृतः). So to my mind it appears that at the macroscopic level they might have demarcated certain stages. But at microscopic level they thought of some dynamic principle to which they gave the name *rasa*. The original sense of *rasa* as *sāra*, essence or flow, is thus kept intact. Jagannātha clearly brings this out when he uses his phrase *gocarīkriyamāṇa*. This process, in the end, is bound to have some affective tone, which may be expressed by such words as *viṣāda* (विषाद), *harṣa* (हर्ष), *ānanda* (आनन्द), *camatkāra* (चमत्कार), etc. But this is not of essence to *rasa*.

Almost every writer has made a distinction between *rasa* and *rasāsvāda*. Even in the quotation from Upaniṣads, *rasa* does not point to *ānanda*, which is the after effect of *rasa*. For, the quotation clearly says *tameva labdhvā ānandī bhavati* (तमेव लब्ध्वा आनन्दी भवति). Even Viśvanātha and, before him, Bhaṭṭanāyaka have clearly distinguished between *rasa* and its taste (*āsvāda*). As Abhinavagupta pointed out, even *rasa* may be constituted of taste (*āsvāda*), but even then we have to distinguish between taste (*āsvāda*) and the object of taste (*āsvādya*). The nature of this *āsvāda* will be of the form *āsvāda* of *āsvāda*. When Viśvanātha talks of *Brahmāsvādasahodaratva* (ब्रह्मास्वादसहोदरत्व) he is talking of *rasāsvāda* and not of *rasa*. He clearly mentions that in the words,

अस्यस्वरूप कथनगर्भः आस्वादन प्रकारः कथ्यते ।

asyasvarūpa kathanagarbhaḥ āsvādana prakāraḥ kathyate ।

— ibid., p. 72

सत्त्वोद्रेकादखण्डस्व प्रकाशानन्द चिन्मयः ।
वेद्यान्तरस्पर्शशून्यो ब्रह्मास्वादसहोदरः ।
लोकोत्तर-चमत्कारप्राणः कैश्चित् प्रमातृभिः ।
स्वाकारवद् अभिन्नत्वेनायम् आस्वाद्यते रसः ।

sattvodrekādakhaṇḍasva prakāśānanda cinmayaḥ ।
vedyāntara-sparśāśūnyo brahmāsvādasahodaraḥ ॥
lokottara-camatkāraprāṇaḥ kaiścit pramātṛbhiḥ ।
svākāravad-abhinnatvenāyam āsvādyate rasāḥ ॥ — ibid., p. 72

It should be noted that in this context *rasa* and *rasāsvāda* though made of the same stuff are clearly distinguished. It should also be noted that while defining *rasa*, it is defined in terms of *sthāyī bhāva*s and other *bhāva*s alone and not in terms of *ānanda*, *camatkāra*, etc.

Paṇḍitrāj Jagannātha on Poetry

Paṇḍitrāj Jagannātha was perhaps the last but not the least important scholar who contributed to the aesthetic theory. He was a poet, a grammarian, a Mīmāṁsaka and a rhetorician. He also wrote on different subjects. His work *Rasagaṅgādhara* (incomplete) is admittedly an original and important work on poetics wherein he discusses the theory of *rasa* in particular. That is why his book is called *Rasagaṅgādhara*. Gaṅgādhara is a name of Śiva, who held the holy Gaṅgā in his matted hair. Here, in this book, Jagannātha is not concerned with river Gaṅgā, he is concerned with *rasa-gaṅgā*. As a poet, he adorned the court of Shāhajahān. There are many stories about his unorthodoxy. He married a Muslim lady called Lavaṅgī, and, therefore, he was ex-communicated by the Hindu paṇḍit class led by Appayya Dīkṣita, who was also a great scholar, poet, grammarian, rhetorician, etc. But he was deadly afraid of the scholarship of Jagannātha. There are many stories about Paṇḍit Jagannātha and Apayya Dīkṣita. But, I shall not be concerned with these stories here. I shall be concerned only with a few sentences which are relevent to the definition of art and art parameter. It must of course be pointed out that when I talk of art, the paradigm before me is that of poetry. And it is only by some kind of analogy that we can talk of the theory of art because some kind of things which are applicable to poetry are also applicable to art.

Jagannātha redefined the concept of poetry and thereby in a way he redefined art also. He says,

रमणीयार्थ प्रतिपादकः शब्दः काव्यम्।

ramaṇīyārtha pratipādakaḥ śabdaḥ kāvyam ।

Poetry (art) is a word (a language) that is symbolic representation of that which opens before us the experience of the artist in the form of his intentions, which gives us the meaning that is beautiful. Literally, *ramaṇīya* means that which has the ability to please. Here there are three words: *ramaṇīya, artha*, and *śabda*.

If this definition is to be applied to all arts, then we will have to say *ramaṇīyārtha pratipādakaṁ mādhyamaṁ kalā* (रमणीयार्थ-प्रतिपादकं माध्यमं कला). He is trying to point out that our experience of the beautiful correlates three co-ordinates: beauty, meaning that is intuitively flashed experience and the medium in which it is represented. These three different elements were not explicitly pointed out by earlier writers. Viśvanātha, for example, says, *vākyaṁ rasātamakaṁ kāvyam* (वाक्यं रसात्मकं काव्यम्).

Poetry is a language which incorporates in it the *rasa*. Apparently, in this definition, *kāvya* gives us a diadic relation having two relata; *rasa* and *vākya*. Whether *rasa* itself is a composite concept or not is not clarified in this definition. Jagannātha's definition clearly indicates that poetry or art is concerned with three constituents :

1. *Ramaṇīyatā*,
2. *Artha*, and,
3. *Śabda* (or medium).

What kind of triadic relation is in the mind of Paṇḍitrāj Jagannātha? First, he distinguishes between meaning *qua* meaning and its relation to the word. Such relationship is concerned with word and meaning in ordinary language. Here meaning is what the word connotes. But, poetry or art is not concerned with such meanings. Just as word or symbol connotes to us its meaning; similarly, the symbol and its meaning lead us to a further concept — that of beauty. It is not word leading to meaning and meaning leading to beauty. It is the word or symbol leading to meaning and the symbols and meaning together leading to beauty, i.e. here the symbol and its meaning appear as a *compound symbol*, which together give rise to the experience of the beautiful. This according to me is a very important step leading to aesthetic experience. The ripple 1 is a symbol. The ripple 2 is a product of the ripple 1. Ripple 3 is not just a product of ripple 2, but a product of 1 and 2 put together. If there is a ripple 4 then it will not be a product of 3 or 2 and 3, it will be a product of 1, 2 and 3 together. When we feel happy our happiness is due to the symbol, the meaning of the symbol and the aesthetic experience that we get on account of the symbol and its meaning.

The Development of Rasa Theory

Let me now summarize:

Bharata, while developing the technique of the performance of stage drama used the word *rasa*. This is pointed out in the first chapter of *Nāṭyaśāstra:*

जग्राह पाठ्यमृग्वेदात्सामभ्यो गीतमेव च ।
यजुर्वेदादभिनयान्रसानाथर्वणादपि ॥

jagrāha pāṭhyamṛgvedātsāmabhyo gītameva ca ।
yajurvedādabhinayānrasānātharvaṇādapi ॥ — *NŚ* 1.17

It means that in the beginning *nāṭya* consisted of four elements — (1) *pāṭhya,* the text or the subject matter which was to be presented, (2) the *music* which was to be recited, (3) acting or that by which something is communicated (to the audience) and (4) the *rasa*. The first three elements are mechanical. The lively principle which made *nāṭya* one whole, one unit, something living, which related all these three parts and which ran through all these was *rasa*. At this stage, it was the *pāṭhya* which was borrowed from earlier works like Vedas was recited. This recitation had two dimensions: (1) one was supplied by the *form* or the manner by which it was recited and (2) the other was given by presenting it in the lyrical musical form. They could be got from *Yajurveda* and *Sāmaveda*. The followers of *Yajurveda* sing the Vedic hymns with all articulations, gestures and in a picturesque form Sāmavedins sing them. In *Sāmaveda* we find the beginning of music. But, all these elements have to be *conjoined* into one whole, into something organic, so that all the elements would make an *organic* harmonic whole. This was the task of *rasa*. It was the essence, flow and living principle which lay the different elements together and made the presentation interesting. This task always remained the objective of *rasa* in its stages of development and application.

But, in the early stage, when Druhina narrated the subject to Bharata, it was confined to stage drama. But, gradually, its scope was widened. The whole of poetry became the field of its operation. This was pointed out by Rudrabhaṭṭa in the first 25 verses of first canto of *Śṛṅgāra Tilaka*. The most explicit of this is,

प्रायो नाट्यं प्रति प्रोक्ता भरताद्यैः रसस्थितिः ।
यथामति मयाप्येषा काव्यं प्रति निगद्यते ॥

prāyo nāṭyaṁ prati proktā bharatādyaiḥ rasasthitiḥ ।
yathāmati mayāpyeṣā kāvyaṁ prati nigadyate ॥ — *ST* 1.5

Still the question remained as to what the nature of *rasa* was, and people gave different answers to it. According to Vyākaraṇa, *rasa* means that which is tested. It is thus, the *āsvādya*. Even in *Nāṭyaśāstra*, this is acknowledged.

Rasaḥ iti kaḥ padārthaḥ ucyate, āsvādyatvāt (रसः इति कः पदार्थः उच्यते। आस्वाद्यत्वात्). *Āsvādyatva* is different from *āsvāda* (*NŚ* VI). But, in the dramatic presentation, everything is concentrated round *vibhāva*s or rather *ālambana vibhāva*s and *anubhāva*s and *vyabhicārī*s are centred round *vibhāva*s. So *rasa* for some time was identified with certain state of *vibhāvas*. *Bhāvyamāno vibhāva eva rasāḥ* (भाव्यमानो विभाव एव रसः). It is in some sense a transformation of some "function" of *vibhāva* which takes the form of *rasa*. But, how is this realized? Without *anubhāva*s this cannot be done. It is the *anubhāva*s which have the ability to operate. So, as Madanmohan Jha pointed out, for some time *anubhāva*s were regarded as *rasa*. And in a similar way even the *vyabhicārī* were regarded as *rasa* for some time. For it is *vyabhicārī* which develops in this direction (*vyabhicāryaivatathā tathā pariṇamati*, व्यभिचार्यैवतथा तथा परिणमति). And, in this way, at a certain stage all the three *vibhāvas, anubhāva*s and *vyabhicārī*s (*vibhāva, anubhāva, vyabhicārī bhāva*) were together regarded as *rasa*. In *Nāṭyaśāstra* itself this is observed —

विभावानुभावव्यभिचारि-संयोगाद् रसनिष्पत्तिः।

vibhāvānubhāvavyabhicārī saṁyogād rasaniṣpattiḥ ।

In any art two *things* are important. One is the dynamic principle which runs through the art object or artefact and makes all the parts or the process act as one unit[1] and the other is the culmination of this process which *brings* satisfaction, happiness, enjoyment, fulfilment, etc. which Bharata called *siddhi*. Though an end part of the art process, siddhi cannot be separated from the other parts of the process. The result was that sometimes *rasa* was identified with *siddhi*. Abhinavagupta's statement, *rasāḥ siddhireva* (रसः सिद्धिरेव) helped this identification. But had *siddhi* been identical with *rasa*,

1. *śarīram vyāpyate tena suṣkam kāṣṭamivāgninā* — *NŚ* 7.7

Abhinava would not have used the word *eva*. *Eva* suggests that *rasa* and *siddhi* form a process and that they are intimately and inseparably related. But, it does not make them identical. *Rasa* was also identified as taste or *āsvāda*. Now, it is certainly true that *āsvāda* is the *viṣaya* of the art-universe. But as *viṣaya,* it is *āsvādya* and not *āsvāda*. It is the *āsvāda* which becomes *āsvādya*. Such a thing happens when man makes his knowledge or his experience, the subject matter of his investigation and this is either due to *anuvyavasāya* or *pratyabhijñā*. Nevertheless, the role of *āsvāda* as *āsvādya* is different from that of *āsvāda* as *āsvāda*. But, this distinction was forgotten and *rasa* was regarded as *āsvāda*, pure and simple. It also happened that *āsvāda* and happiness were identified with the result that *rasa* was identified with happiness or *ānanda*. The Upaniṣadic statement *raso vai saḥ* (रसो वै सः) helped this development. But, while the emphasis shifted from *āsvādya* to *āsvāda*, it was recognized that not *vibhāva, anubhāva,* or *vyabicāri* was *rasa*. All of them draw their strength from *sthāyī bhāva*. It is the *sthāyī* alone which takes the form of *rasa*. Mammaṭa recognized this —

व्यक्तैः स तैर्विभावद्यैः स्थायिभावो रसः स्मृतः।

vyaktaiḥ sa tairvibhāvadyaiḥ sthāyibhāvo rasāḥ smṛtaḥ ।

Jagannātha also recognized this. Bharata had also said this in *Nāṭyaśāstra*. But, all the three, Bharata, Mammaṭa and Jagannātha clearly say that *sthāyī bhāva* has to be modified in the art process. Only then it becomes *rasa*. But Jagannātha emphasizes the process which is running through and regards the *sthāyī bhāva* as passing through the whole process as *rasa*. His emphasis is on *gocarīkriyamāṇatā*. *Gocara* means that which is perceptible. By *gocarīkaraṇa* is meant, that which is not perceptible becomes perceptible — *abhūtatatbhāve cviḥ* (अभूततत्भावे च्विः). This is the process of *objectification*. It should be noted that it is a continuous process. *Kriyamāṇa* is present passive participle from *kṛ*. Therefore, it means that which is not objective is now made objective. *Rasa* is this. The *sthāyī bhāva* in this process is turned dynamic. *Rasa* is thus not the end product, but this dynamic form, which *sthāyī bhāva* takes. But in this discussion it is pointed out that *rasa* (understood an *ānanda*) is neither the necessary nor the sufficient condition of poetry that it is not a defining characteristic of poetry, although, it may be important for its exalted position which the process of experiences gradually and steadily acquire.

10

Abhinaya

Bharata's Theory of Abhinaya

ABHINAYA is not just a theoretical concept. Bharata discusses the meaning of *abhinaya* and then gives instructions as to how *abhinaya* should be performed. I shall illustrate Bharata's theory from my reactions and then shall relate it to the philosophical problem of name, form and identity.

Once, I had been to Udaipur and there I had an occassion to visit a very beautiful puppet museum. I feel, everyone ought to visit that museum. One of the puppets in the museum was giving a performance of dance. A scene from a drama was also enacted. I was wonder struck by these two scenes and was completely hypnotized. Both these appeared to be absolutely real and living. How could these scenes appear so real? "What is a puppet after all?" I asked myself. It was only a doll made of some material. The different joints, which a human being also has, were somehow or the other joined together by some strings which could be controlled by somebody. For this manipulation somebody who had the capacity to control, adjust and order the movements was required. This man, behind the show, must, of course, have known and directed drama and dance and must have been acquainted with rhythm, beats and temporal continuum or *laya*. When I was viewing all these a thought came to my mind as to whether all that I was seeing could be regarded as of the dolls acting. The dolls' actions seemed to be actions but they were only happenings. When a man or a woman acts in real life or in a drama, could we really say that his or her actions are self-controlled actions? Or is some "God" directing and controlling these actions? In fact, the Bible says that not a single leaf in this world can shake without God's wish. If there is no difference between the so-called "actions" of the doll and the actions of men, how are we going to differentiate between the behaviour of man and the behaviour of a doll? But, evidently, we do distinguish between the two behaviour patterns. In the case of the so-called "action" of the puppets the author of the action is the man who controls the movements of the doll. So, what appears to be the "actions" of the doll are merely the movements without any awareness on the part of the doll. In fact, on account of the controller's action of the dolls' movements appear to be actions. The doll neither has any will, nor any desire, nor any urge for the action. Its movements are only mechanical; although, they appear to be action-like. In fact, in our life also, many of the so-called actions are not actions. We have no control over them. These things only happen to us. When a man breathes his breathing is ordinarily not voluntary. Similarly, the internal actions of the brain or the beating of the heart, or circulation of the blood or nervous reactions are not actions. A man is merely subjected to them. Similarly, although, what to eat and what not to eat is dependent on us, the digestion of what we eat is not dependent on us. However, some events in man's life are controlled by him. They are dependent on his urges, wishes, etc. I, for example, ask Megha whether one would take the dictation. She agrees and I dictate. In this action-game my asking Megha, Megha's willingness to take dictation, my giving the dictation — all these are voluntary actions. But Megha could have said "no" when I asked her whether she would take the dictation. The real difference between action and happening is that no authorship can be attributed to happenings. What is the difference between a living man and a statue? Suppose, there is a statue made of stone. It means that, that which was earlier a stone has now become a statue. It means that the stone has the potentiality and "ability" to "become" a statue. But a stone doesn't have the potentiality to bring about this change. This ability belongs to a third person, the sculptor. The trees grow, but neither the seed nor the seedlings make them grow. It is dependent on several other factors. But none of these factors is comparable to the human factor which is operative, when we say it is an "action." There are some insects which are sensitive to light. They always move from darkness to light. This action is an action of a living body. But it is still mechanical. This doesn't happen when somebody decides to go to somebody's lecture. The behaviour of the insects is called *tropism* and the particular instance which I gave is an instance of phototropism. The insects follow a certain path which they cannot resist for they have no power to resist. When animals cohabit, is it voluntary? Or is it instinctive? But sometimes when we milk a cow, it does resist milking sometimes and one is not able to milk it. The pet dog of Shivaji Maharaj called "Waghya" is said to have jumped in the Shivaji's funeral pyre. Its action was voluntary. But, voluntariness also seems to be a hierarchical. I, for example, visit somebody's place and I am offered some snacks. I am actually in need of snacks. But I say, "no" out of etiquette. On another occasion, I go to a friend of mine. He says, I should keep company with him for dinner. I do not have any appetite, still I accept his offer for he is persistible. Not to eat when one is hungry and to eat when one is not — both these kinds of behaviour exist in the case of man alone.

This experience can be an eye opener for determining the status of acting and the status of the person who acts. In some drama there is a scene of weeping. The scene of weeping is different from actual weeping. This is only a scene because it has been enacted and the spectators see it. Is it real weeping? It is not. But this pseudo-weeping is also of two types: (1) where the actor consciously takes out tears from his eyes, that is, of his own accord creates the impression that he is weeping. But he may not do that at all. (2) The director at that time may put some glycerin in his eyes and paint his face in such a way that it would give the impression of the actors having wept. The actual process of weeping is mental. But, even in actual weeping, that which is mental, is encoded into something physiological. Now, this encoding is natural or instinctive. But on account of his ability, the actor may induce such a behaviour on his own and act in such a way that others would get the impression that he was weeping. When the actor is not doing anything, he is not the author of his weeping. The author is the director, who induces the necessary behaviour in the actor by means of some chemicals.

In fact, all this presupposes that there is no direct communication between one mind and another. Communication or dialogue has to pass through some physiological means or changes. This is how, although the puppets cannot act, their movements can be made to appear as acting on account of the ability and dexterity of the man behind the scene. In a stage drama also something of this kind takes place. The stage is removed from reality, and so are the actors. In this sense, their stage personality would have a different appearance. The theme of the drama has nothing to do with any happening in the actor's actual life. But the dramatist, the director and the actors bring these unconnected things and events together, co-ordinate them and create a parallel world. This feat is achieved through a continuous encoding and decoding of mental into physiological and physiological into mental. This translating is also not concerned with the actual. It is only artificially created and the authorship of this transformation or pseudo-change is shared by the author, the director and the actors. But, the actor can also control the quality of acting on his own. Thus, what an actor does on the stage goes by the name of acting and what the puppet is made to do in the show is not regarded as acting.

Acting as Pretending

Wherefrom does a man get the ability to act, which, in a way, is a kind of pretending or pretense? Some man "A" acts like another, say "B." He shows to others that he acts like B, that he can imitate what B has already done. This is regarded as acting. In acting, a man does not carry on his natural behaviour, he is impersonating someone. And, if his behaviour corresponds to the natural behaviour of the person impersonated we say that he is a good actor. In the Marathi drama "Ekach Pyala" Bālagandharva used to perform a female role — the role of Sindhu. To perform this role he was to act like Sindhu. If Sindhu was a real lady in a real world, we could have said that Bālagandharva imitated her. But Sindhu is merely a creation of the dramatist's imagination. Before Bālagandharva enacted this role, it was Gadkari, the author of the drama who "*wrote* this role." In writing a role he was performing that role though it was performance in his individual mental world. Had it not been so, he would not have been able to write this role. But, reducing such a role to writing is also making it public, in the way the actor does it on the stage. But in any drama there is not just one role. One can say that the author performs all the roles on his mental stage. The author has to enter into the role of every character in the drama. Ordinarily, an actor performs only one role. But the author has to perform all the roles. When the actor plays a role, he not only mentally enters the body and mind of that particular character, but he has to perceive other actors also not in their original form in the real world but in the role which they are performing. He has to behave as if the others are also different persons. It is only when the actor understands this that all the roles in the drama would cohere with one another.

Many a time, this world is regarded as a stage. But, the content of the sentence is richer than what we ordinarily understand. When somebody is born, he is not born with a name. Naming is an act which we thrust on "somebody." When we address him by the name, he reacts to it. He accepts the name given to him and he acts in such a way that in all these contexts where his name is mentioned he acts by identifying himself with his name and the situation. That is, the individual born enacts the role of the name given to him. But the name is not the individual. When the individual dies it is not the name which dies. Had it been so, it would not have been possible for us to talk about a dead individual. One may say that when the individual is alive, he plays the role of "his name." The possibility of acting is connected with the possibility of the actor's identification with some other name of the person or role he is playing. It is also not just limited to the name. The language, the dress, etc. of that individual are all dependent on the way he is conditioned. If a male child is, for instance, trained from a very early age to behave like a girl, he starts speaking like a girl. One of my friends was longing for a daughter. She started treating her male child as if he was a girl for nearly ten to eleven years. The boy was dressed like a girl and he started living like a girl. His behaviour from morning to evening was like that of a girl. He used to tie his hair like a girl without fail, even his bodily gestures were like those of a girl. Today, this boy is an engineer and he behaves as a normal man. But, on account of the early conditioning, even today his bodily gestures are sometimes feminine. The behaviour which we learn right from our childhood is called our *svabhāva*, i.e. manifestation (of the self). This manifestation is like our dress. (If we leave "this dress" and for sometime wear another person's dress, it will not be our permanent dress.)

In the theory of drama this is called *vibhāva*. It is possible for a man to enact the role of someone else because his own role is also imposed on him; he can identify himself with another role. This identification is due to his ability to pretend. To alienate ourselves from our natural role and identify ourselves with some other role is, what is called, acting. Thus he can shed pseudo-tears, he can behave like Shivaji and can also move like a woman. When the actor accepts this other role, he, so to say, has shed his original role (though for sometime) and "married" another role. When he divorces himself from this role, he returns to his original, natural role. It is possible for a man to shift his roles because his nature or states of his mind can be "replaced." This acting is in fact possible on account of our being able to control the mind or the states of the mind. Acting also requires *cittavṛttinirodha* (चित्तवृत्तिनिरोध). Is acting temporarily suspending our own frame of mind and identifying ourselves with some other frame of mind? Sometimes we use the word "aping" or "monkeying." It is, in fact, behaving as monkeys do. It means that monkeys also can act to a certain extent. For a monkey shows his teeth, when we show him our teeth. But other animals are not able to act in this way. It is because they cannot suspend their (own) nature and assume another nature even for a very short time. Perhaps they are not even aware that they have a nature? In order to impose such a frame of mind on ourselves, evolution in our consciousness is necessary. It is necessary to evolve ourselves from consciousness to self-consciousness and in self-consciousness also there must be an evolution gradually from one stage to another. When this happens a person starts using the expressions in the first person singular. I see a chair in front of me. But when I see the chair, I am not conscious that I am seeing the chair. That I am seeing the chair is here taken for granted. It is only in the background. But when I say "I am seeing the chair," that I am seeing the chair becomes clear. I can for example say "I was in fact seeing the chair but at that time I didn't realize that I was seeing the chair." In this second sentence, I am acting two roles. That this "myself" can play different roles can be seen in the following sentences:

1. It is this.
2. I know that it is this.
3. I know that I know that it is this.
4. I know that I know that I know that it is this.

The fourth sentence tells me that I am performing three roles. In my first knowing I was not aware that I knew this. The two other roles are, however, consciously played. This shows that I can play more than one role. This also shows that I can put my first "me" in some nook and corner, for some time. The possibility of acting lies in this particular role of the mind.

Abhinaya and Communication

Bharata has used the word *abhinaya* in the context of drama. Ordinarily we suppose that actors acting is perceived by the spectators and they react to it. But Bharata uses the word *abhinaya* in a wider sense. For Bharata, *abhinaya* is the cause of communication. It is at the back of something that is conveyed. As a matter of fact, as said earlier, there is no direct passage from one mind to another. The message that is mental has to get translated into physiological and bodily signs before it is conveyed. These bodily signs are perceived by us, but they are retranslated into a mental messsage. This is how the message of "A" is carried to "B" and vice versa. If two persons are talking to each other then these messages and the counter-messages take the form of a dialogue. When the message from the dramatist passes to the spectators, it has to pass through the director of the drama, the actors and through them to the spectators. But at each stage, it is transformed from something mental to something physiological and again re-transformed and re-re-transformed from physiological to mental. This kind of *abhinaya* takes place in actual life also. But in drama instead of actual transaction there is some fake transaction. Even if this message is not conveyed to the other man he knows that he has to react in some particular way to the sounds and movements of others. It is predetermined. But the fact is that he is listening to the first part of the dialogue and then reacting to it. In order to bring about the facial changes and bodily changes, the actor has to understand what the first actor has said. Without that the second actor would not be able to act in the appropriate way. Acting is not concerned merely with speech. Like all other drama theories, Bharata talks of four kinds of *abhinaya*s: *vāk, aṅga, sattva* and *āhārya*. Our speech acts are concerned with *vāgabhinaya*. *Āṅgika abhinaya* is concerned with our bodily movements and facial changes. *Sattva abhinaya* is more difficult. For example, if one has to enact weeping and has to do the acting of shedding tears, it is very difficult to act without the aid of artificial means. By using glycerin in the eyes, one can produce some tears and for practical purposes the spectators may think that the actor was weeping. But those who are really good at *abhinaya* are able to change their mood and produce tears. Changing the mood naturally and producing the tears come under *sāttvika abhinaya*. Similar will be the case in changing the mood to anger or love. Good actors are able to produce facial changes without any artificial aid. *Āhārya abhinaya* is connected with the greenroom. Perhaps, "prompting" which is necessary for all actors might be connected with it. Similarly, make-up or drapery which becomes an important factor in the dramatic situation may come under *āhārya abhinaya*. In fact, this is something which is not directly connected with acting. But as these are aids to acting, Bharata includes them under *abhinaya*. In fact, this follows from the etymology of the word *abhinaya*.

There are limitations to acting, however efficient the actor may be and many artificialities are to be resorted to. In our dramas and movies many a time the actresses and actors are shown as dancing and singing when their desires are fulfilled. This seldom happens in actual life. But, such artificialities can be justified in one way. For instance, if a man is in a jubilant mood, although he doesn't do anything physically, one can, for example, say that his mind is singing and dancing. Perhaps, with a view to externalize these mental acts the directors make the actors and actresses sing and dance. Many a time our wishes are unfulfilled. We do long for their fulfilment. And when we see that they can't be so fulfilled, we get the satisfaction if we see that they are fulfilled in someone else's actual life, or at least in a drama on stage. This is called transference in psychology. When we see others doing the acts which we want to do but which we cannot do, we get such vicarious satisfaction. In acting this can be done. A man, on account of his capacity to hide something, pretends something and impersonates someone. He, thus, succeeds in acting.

11

Medium, Language and Parameters

Experience, Thought, Language and Models

RIGHT from the time of our birth we continuously experience something or the other. This experience, at least in part, is stored in our memory and sometimes can be recalled. When it is recalled, and expressed, it takes the form of language. With the aid of language, we also compare one experience with another. The two experiences are different, but they are characterized by similarities and contrasts. How do we measure the similarities or contrasts? More importantly, how are we able to convert our experience into thought and the thought into language? Are there any similarities among these three? Or even without there being any similarity are we able to convert the one into the other? That we are able to convert one into the other is a fact, and so the question arises as to whether we are able to convert one phenomenon into another without there being any similarity amongst them. Comparing is like measuring. When I say that "this room is 12 feet long," there is some relationship between the measurement in terms of feet and the length of the room. We cannot, for instance, say that this room is sleeping. But if a poet says, "this room is sleeping," then we think that the poet has found out some similarity between the act of sleeping and the way we think the room behaves or does not behave. Ordinary we do not say that the room is sleeping; but we do say that it is 12 feet in length. Length is a spatial property common both to the measurement and to the room. So we take it for granted that our measuring is done on the basis of similarity. Our measuring is a kind of evaluation. We can, therefore, say that evaluation is based on similarity. This is how poets talk of simile, metaphor, etc. But when we go from a simile to a metaphor, we, so to say, go beyond comparison and identify one with the other. In a simile, for example, the poet says that somebody's face is like a lotus. Then he steps further, drops the word "like" and says, it (the face) is lotus. In Sanskrit, this is what is called *rūpaka.*[1] But suppose a certain thing 'x' cannot be compared to anything else, and is incomparable to anything, then its comparison is done in a negative way; 'x' cannot be compared to anything else or 'x' can be compared with itself alone. Poets give instances of such cases. If a certain thing is incomparable, it is called *apratima* (अप्रतिम). There are other more positive instances too. How is the sky? The sky is like itself *gaganaṁ gaganākāram* (गगनं गगनाकारम्). How is the sea? It is like the sea itself, *sāgaraḥ sāgaropamaḥ* (सागरः सागरोपमः). On this background, let us see how we go from a proper noun to a common noun. A proper noun is a name, an identification mark given to a particular thing. We see, say, a particular cow. When we see a second cow, how do we recognize that it is a cow? From the particular characteristics of the first cow, we go to the general characteristics and since these general characteristics are shared by the first and the second cow, we cognize or recognize that the second entity is also a cow. From cow, we go to another animal, say, a horse. The horse is not a cow. But there appear to be some common characteristics between a cow and a horse. We now ignore the special characteristics and emphasize on the common ones. We say

1. Literally it means "a little less than identical." *Rūpa* means identical and *ka* means "a little, less than."

that a cow is an animal and so is a horse. In this way we go from an individual to a class concept and from a class concept to a wider class concept.

But like the similarities between one animal and another, and between one class of animals and another, is there a similarity between thought and language? If not, even without there being a similarity, are we able to convert one into another? What happens in codification? Is not language a codification of thought? Literally, language means speech (*bhāṣā*, भाषा) the spoken language. It means that thought is codified into sound patterns.

Language and Thought

Let us leave the matter here and come to the basic experience again. Let us say, we are perceiving a lotus flower. It has petals, fragrance, stem, colour, etc. We understand this, but if we want to explain a specific fragrance or a specific colour, how do we do it? We cannot, for example, say that blue colour is like red colour or the fragrance of lotus is like that of saffron or sandalwood. Ultimately, we have to stop at certain points which cannot be explained further. They are not based on likeness/contrast. They are based on their innate nature, their own identity. It is itself. It cannot be further analysed. But although it cannot be analysed further, it can be converted into some other medium. It can be codified. There is no "known" relationship between thought and language and still we require a language to express a thought. Nay, unless we have adequate language, not only is the thought not expressed, it does not also arise at all. The expression of thought is always through some form of language. I therefore feel that the basic instrument of measurement or evaluation is *not similarity but identity*. We understand a thing if it is simple and we symbolize and codify it. The relationship between thought and language is similar to this. That is why language is a conductor of thought. Without language our thought or whatever arises in our mind cannot be conveyed to others. Language can also act as a non-conductor or an insular of thought. If a proper language is not found out, either the thought becomes inexpressible or the language acts as an obstacle or hindrance to the expression of thought. Language and thought are thus distinguishable from each other, and at the same time are inseparable from each other. It may also be pointed out that language is a sound pattern and can be a conductor not only of one thought but of different thoughts. Just as out of the same wire parallel circuits of electricity can be formed, similarly, from the same language or its cross-sections different ideas can be expressed. This, however, makes the language ambiguous and sometimes even obsolete. Ultimately, the meaning of language is at least partly determined by its usages. So, although language is the conveyer of thought, usages also become useful in determining the nature of thought. This is particularly so when we try to interpret the thought from the language that is available to us. This has happened in all literature of the world and that is why philosophers have insisted on the analysis of language. The grammar and the idiom under reference when the literature was produced, thus play an important role in the whole game. How to interpret the text, thus, becomes an important task. There could be a wide gap between what the writer has to say and what the reader understands. A poet, for example, writes something and we, so to say, understand it as poetry. But, can we ever say that what the poet has to convey and what we receive is exactly the same?

Language and Dialogue

Nevertheless, there is a safeguard, for we also know that communication among men is possible. This possibility of communication suggests that the sphere of language is determined by certain limits and certain fields of operation. Had it not been so, each one's language would be his private language. But this does not happen. We can learn a language, express in that language and can convey our thoughts in that language. The other person also understands our thought expressed in that language and a dialogue becomes possible. All these possibilities make room for a correct interpretation of the text. But all these also throw light on the nature of language itself. They make language a form of expression, a form of communication, a form of a possible dialogue and a form of a possible potentiality. It is because of this potentiality that one can learn a language which one does not know and this is possible because the potentiality of knowing other lanugages already exists in him. This again is possible because there is some rudimentary language present which members of the same species understand. For example, if we point to a thing it means that we are showing the thing. If we move our fingers in one particular way, it means that we are calling a person, moving the fingers in some other way indicates that we want him to go away. We also are able to discover some common elements in the human nature.

The concept of *tāla* and *laya* and beats of *tāla* are everywhere the same because such concepts seem to be tuned to the human nature. Sometimes they go beyond the species also. For example, when a dog wags its tail, we understand it. The dog also understands some of our signs and sounds. If we make a shrill cry, it is reacted to in a particular way by some animals. We do think that some kind of language, some sign language, is understood by some animals. Of course, the situation could be far more complicated than what we understand. For language, understanding is a must. But some kind of tropisms, reflexes and conditioned reflexes may also participate in this communication process and the understanding which presupposes some kind of self-consciousness, may not always be operative. But these are the limiting cases, and, by and large, one can say that within the limits of the same species, the languge is either understood by the speakers and the listeners or there is a potentiality in man to speak and understand the language. I may not know the Svaihili language today. But I can learn it and converse in it with those who are conversant with that langauge. Thus, in addition to the language that we speak or write, we have assumed that there is a universal potential language on which all languages are based. In addition, we have to assume further that the language we speak or write has also to go through some forms without which it would not be possible for us to converse in it. The language that we speak will also have to be connected with our memory, and our experience will have to be stored. Finally, it should be possible to convey our stored experience to others. This experience (that which is conveyed) will be each one's individual experience having the potentiality to become public. Otherwise it could not be conveyed to others. Thus, our language would take, in all, four forms :

1. That which we experience but do not express;
2. Experience that we store in our memory or brain in the forms of mental, electromagnetic signs (by codifying our experience);
3. That which we express orally or by written signs, to convey it to others; and
4. There must be a possibility of such a language for the whole species, though it may not always be expressed explicitly. Our forefathers in the past have talked of such possible languages. They have perhaps mystified them. It is equally possible that not they but we might

have mystified them, ourselves not knowing the language and their purpose. I have a feeling that our forefathers have called these languages as *parā, paśyantī, madhyamā* and *vaikharī*. Whether they have considered the same elements as I have discussed above, or not, it is certain that the four different kinds of languages or forms of languages and the language sphere can be discerned. The ancient scholars have not only used such language forms for communication but have also used them for creating and evaluating art patterns. (What is true of thought and language seems to be true of all mediums and perhaps whether it is thought and language or a medium for something they believe like means and ends.)

Language as Expression of Experience

Let us understand the concept of language from a different perspective. We saw that it is the expression of experience, and also an expression of thought. Since our thought may also be related to our experience of the outside world, language is the expression of internal and external experience. When we experience something we distinguish between the *object* of experience and *our experience* of it. The object of experience is the stimulus and our experiencing it is the response. Experiencing means the *storing* of responses. The process of language activity is just the opposite of it. Here, the stimulus *starts from* us although it may be in regard to experience already collected. But it may not be just the reaction to already collected experiences. When I "express...." it is presupposed that the other should share the experiences. It is communicating to others. Communicating is the end or object and expression is the means by which we communicate. Of course, communicating need not be to others only. We can communicate to ourselves as well. But although the one who communicates and the one to whom something is communicated are one, they should be regarded as two. This is the beginning of dualism.

In *Chāndogya Upaniṣad* (छान्दोग्य उपनिषद्), this process is described — *vācārambhaṇaṁ vikāro nāmadheyaṁ mṛttikā ityeva satyam* (वाचारम्भणं विकारो नामधेयं मृत्तिका इत्येव सत्यम्). (By *mṛttikā* is not meant the word *mṛttikā*, it really means the bearer of the word *mṛttika*.)

Expressing in the word(s) is the first *vikāra* (विकार) which the object has. But with this *vikāra* or modification, we are able to convey our thought or feeling to others. Metaphorically speaking, when we express something, we are, so to say, holding the object of our experience in our clutches. Language is the mould in which we pour our thought regarding the object. It is in this sense that "the limits of (my) language are the limits of (my) thought." If the language is the mould of our experience, then in a way, in a practical way, language acts as a standard, as a parameter of our thinking. Ordinarily, when we measure something by another thing there is some similarity between the measure and that which we measure. When we say that sugar is one kg., what is common and similar between sugar and kilogram is the weight. Unless there is something common through several differences, measuring is not possible. The concept of parameter is the concept of measuring. Mammaṭa describes *upamā* (उपमा) or simile as *sādharmyaṁ upamā bhede* (साधर्म्यं उपमा भेदे). In brief, we now can say that language is the first parameter by which we hold or measure our thought. But, if what we say is correct, there will be a hierarchy of measures or parameters. On account of this hierarchy we are able to divide or classify the world into several categories, in different classes. If we have to describe a certain thing, we should say, and give its conceptual latitude and longitude and determine its place in the conceptual geography. If we have to say what a horse is we should determine the class of horses and try to show the place of "this" particular horse in that class. The ancient Nyāya instead of giving two constituents *jāti* (जाति) and *vyakti* (व्यक्ति) added one more constituent, the *ākṛti* (आकृति) and gave the aphorism *jātyākṛti-vyaktayastu padārthaḥ* (जात्याकृतिव्यक्तयस्तु पदार्थः).

This concept of language as mould or standard and its break-up into *vyakti*, *ākṛti* and *jāti* should be of use to us in understanding the concept of parameters in art.

First, any art belongs to a particular class of art and every piece of art or artefact requires a particular matter or subject matter. Poetry, painting and dance may also have something different and something common amongst them. All these arts will have to be subjected to different kinds of appreciation (due to subject matter, forms and mould or style).

Language as Expression of Self-Consciousness

Let us look at this problem from still a different angle. The question was what language was, and the answer given was that language was an expression, that whatever we express was a kind of language. This expression must be a means for communication, for conveying our thought to others. Such language therefore would have to be meaningful and cogent. Such language would not merely be an expression, it would belong to the species of action and since action is different from happening, language would have to be an expression of our self-consciousness. The change from mere happening to action occurs because of self-consciousness. Acting is a product of self-consciousness. Self is the author of action. But such expression which is an outcome of our self-consciousness must have its base in our experiencing, which would not be just a passive reception as in the photographic image. It would be a self-conscious action of some kind. We cannot experience anything without demarcating the details of what we experience. To know the details is perhaps the beginning of rudimentary language. I have quoted above from *Chāndogya Upaniṣad, vācārambhaṇaṁ vikāro nāmadheyam* (वाचारम्भणं विकारो नामधेयम्) — the process of *vikāra* or modification of the original is the beginning of language. There may or may not be one-to-one correspondence between the details of our experiencing and the details of our expressing. Nevertheless, in experiencing and expressing we would be able to discern a few common elements. These elements form the basic structure of experiencing and expressing. The main source of expressing lies in *expressing itself*. Expressing itself is a kind of rudimentary language. Of course, in both the cases, it is our self-consciousness which is at play. In between our experiencing and expressing there is a stage where we receive and store our experience. This storing of experience is neither experiencing nor expressing. In this storing also the separately discerned elements are properly arranged and are known to us independently when we try to recollect them. Thus, experiencing, storing and expressing, all these three could be regarded as forms of language. The basic relationship in all these three is the relationship of our realization of experience and putting it in a symbolic form. Thus, separately discerned experience is stored in a certain symbolic form which we may call thought-form, and this thought-form is again expressed in the form of sounds, signs, lines or colours. We usually express this in terms of symbols and also in terms of what we understand from symbols. But the process is not that simple. It is not merely a relation between symbol and its meaning. Its next stage would be predication, which is in fact a comparison of the subject with predicate on the basis of similarity and difference; and in this way the sentences become more and more complicated. But what is important to know is that the relation between thing and thought, or symbol and its meaning, or the relation between the predicate and the subject are not just a static relation. In fact, all these pairs form a continuum and the whole languge process is a continuum, which is a continuous transformation going from one level to other levels. In fact, this process of transformation is also the process of transformation from subjective to objective and making our private thought something objective. This also makes its evaluation possible. This process of objectivity is attained in two stages. The first is the stage of symbolization and the second is what may be described as continuous dynamic process. In literary arts, the first such process was marked by *śabda* and *rūpa*, and in dramatic art it was marked by *rasa*. But, it appears that later this term *rasa* was used for denoting the dynamic process of all arts. In this dynamic process, the medium and the message like conductor and current (of electricity) could be distinguished but not separated. It may also be pointed out that the dynamic process begins with the subject, then becomes more and more objective when it suggests different kinds of meanings and values, but finally, it tends to become subjective again inasmuch as it gives satisfaction and happiness to the spectators, etc. *Rasa* perhaps was used for denoting all these stages.

Language as Human Activity

All animals act through bodily organs. Man acts in addition through his "mental acts." For all that happens in and through mind is relevant for human experience and expression. I should like to mention that I am using the words experience and expression in a very wide sense. They include different things like knowing, wishing, desiring, expecting or the urge for doing something. These different elements of mind are called *bhāva*s in Sanskrit and they can be classified under *bhāvanā, vedanā, codanā, karuṇā, kalpanā, icchā, preraṇā*, etc. All these are fleeting states of mind and sometimes they are known by the name *sañcārī* (संचारी) or *vyabhicārī bhāva*. Bharata thinks that they are 49. But they could be more. Bharata, for instance, does not talk of urge or *codanā* (चोदना) under it. He does not explicitly discuss the role of *codanā* in his *Nāṭyaśāstra* nor does he classify *codanā*s under *bhāva* in general. He does talk of *sthāyī bhāva*s but under this also he does not discuss some of the mental states like *āsakti*. It was not necessary to discuss such states in the context of *Nāṭyaśāstra*. They are discussed elsewhere. In the *Yogasūtra*s, for example, they are discussed under *cittavṛtti*. Anyway, activities or actions in a living man are concerned with these and all of them belong to (the class of) consciousness. In addition, man and the higher vertebrates act in varying measures on another aspect of consciousness called self-consciousness. This gives man the power to think about what he does and also evaluate his actions. This state of consciousness is more or less a blanket term and covers what is termed in Sanskrit as *anuvyavasāya*. It is on account of self-consciousness that one can also have the knowledge of knowledge or *pratyabhijñā*. All these manifestations of consciousness make man living and active and distinguish him from a dead person and matter. In the above paragraph, I have used the word "man" which is a common noun. This shows that I do not have the individual "I," i.e. only myself, in my mind. I do think that there are other individuals and they are also like myself. I also have a desire of exchanging my ideas with others. I believe and assume, though unconsciously, that the other men also must have ideas like mine, that they would have a nature or behaviour like mine on the basis of analogy or *upamāna*. I have used the word "belief" but in fact, this is not a matter of belief, but of fact.

Men are able to exchange their ideas. How is this transmission possible? The ideas are without wings. If the ideas are subjective, they would originate and die in the body of the individual. But this happens, and happens through an instrument called language. Ideas are mental and subjective. Language, in so far as it consists of sounds or some other symbolic form, is material or at least objective. Unless our ideas are encoded in mediums like sounds, they would not take the form of language. It is through language that one can communicate to others, correspond and exchange ideas with others. Language is an instrument of transforming the subjective ideas into objective and give them a form which can be shared by several individuals. It is a mould in which our ideas are moulded. Theoretically, there could be ideas without languge. That is, even a dumb man could think, desire, expect, etc. but without languge the ideas would be only at a rudimentary germinating level. As we go on finding and defining and making our thought definite we do require a languge form without which it would be impossible to store the multitude of ideas. Unless, for example, we are able to state the arithmetical numbers in languge, it would not be possible for us to make higher calculations. Some aborigines know numbers up to five, because they can hold the numbers 1, 2, 3, 4, 5 onto their memory; when they have to express something more than five they use the word "many" (in their language) which can stand for any indefinite number. As the form becomes finer and finer we are able to think in more and more subtle ways. When such a language form comes to a standstill, we invent and start using the word "infinite." One can easily see the similarity between the aboriginal concept of "many" and the civilized man's concept of "infinite." In fact, the mathematicians's concept of infinite is also not the same as that of the common man, although it is similar. I have already expressed that language is the mould in which our ideas are fitted or moulded. But this makes language also a standard of measuring our thought or ideas: language itself becomes a parameter. It is a linguameter for measuring our ideas or rather, the inmatess of our mind. Language is the measuring rod of our ideas. And so language gives us the limit of our thought, at least in so far as it is expressible and communicable to others. This also gives us another measure which could be termed in language as inexpressible, indescribable, wonderful, unimaginable, etc. Both that which is expressible in language and the inexpressible are points in the parameter scale (like a boundary and a sixer in the game of cricket). Language itself is a standard, a parameter, and within this parameter there are several sub-parameters suggesting different levels and dimensions. For example, value is such a dimension, beauty another. But unless these different dimensions are brought within the scope of language, we would not be able to measure our ideas. We all knew what heat was. But we could talk of it in different indefinite terms. Before heat could be measured with instruments we could not talk of it in terms of degrees of temperature. With the introduction of mercury in measuring heat, this could be actualized. Heat came to be measured in additive terms and this led to the invention of the thermometer. This is also the case with what arises in our mind as ideas and what is turned into language. Our ideas are like *upameya* and language is like *upamāna*. It is, however, not an actual or perceptible case of *upamā* or simile. Although there is no identifiable similarity, *sādṛśya* (सादृश्य) or difference or *vaidharmya* (वैधर्म्य) between language and thought, still they are "identified." The relation between the ideas and language has a greater and continuously increasing similarity with *rūpaka* (रूपक) and *ananvaya* (अनन्वय). Language is again decoded by men on the receiving end and turned into ideas. These ideas are also of different types. They may stand for something or may express some ideas alone without suggesting a bearer. Ideas and language thus become more or less inseparable though they can be distinguished. This thought and language relation is termed by Sanskrit linguists and rhetoricians as a relation between *vācya* and *vācaka*. The words in language are *vācaka* and the thought which is behind it is called *vācya* (वाच्य). *Vācya* in return may be of two types — one having bearers and the other without bearers, that is of the nature of *vikalpa* (विकल्प).

We have talked about the ideas (in the mind) and their relations with language. But what are the sources of these ideas? Although the ideas are processed in the mind and through this processing new ideas emerge, basically ideas are recollections, nay, impressions that the knower or man receives from outside (they are also modified in our mind). If there were nothing to receive, I wonder, whether man would have any ideas at all. It appears that none of the ideas are without any empirical base. Pure imagination, *qua* imagination, is like a myth, i.e. in imagination the spatial properties in our experience are either expanded or narrowed down (even to the limit of zero). Similarly, its temporal properties are also utilized in the same way. We may, for example, talk of a ghost. We conceive the ghost in the fashion of some living creatures with the additional properties like the capacity of entering or going through solid things like walls. Sometimes, when the spatial or temporal properties are reduced to "zero," the things become concepts. In this way, we can also talk of "and," "or" "not" "if then," etc. But without any support or experience not a single idea can emerge. One may experience them in a finite, discrete form but this experiencing is different from the thing experienced in this process of experiencing. The experiencer "reduces" the things to ideas and the experience of this, primarily, takes the form of "asserting." If there is a thing, table, and we know it as a table, we express it in some assertive form. This is the miracle of the verb "is." That is, even the rudimentary and basic form of language is one of a sentence. Suppose we say, "table." Even then it is a cryptic way or a shorthand technique of saying, "it is a table." Although the things may be in the form of some (material or non-material) substances, when thus expressed they take the form of sentences. But, what we experience is an image or some kind of mental photograph of things. It is some kind of "that" which is sensed. Either it is seen or it is "heard" or it is "felt" by touch or pressure, taste or smell. All these basic sensed objects are objects belonging to the world of things. But when expressed in language, they take the form of nouns, adjectives, adverbs (or other predicates), etc. In this relationship of the outside or inside objects, with the mind, the things are as it were, stored in some kinds of signals, like electromagnetic signals. Thus when we express our experience in language we pass through three kinds of processes — (1) the process of seeing or experiencing, (2) the process of registering in the form of signals in (the mind or in) the brain, and (3) expressing. This last could take the form of ordinary languge or *vaikharī* as it is also seen in other art-form like music, painting, dance, etc. Our experience can undergo another kind of processing also. We may not only express what is, but may also express wishes, desires, etc. and in this way, our intellect and will can act. Thus, between our experiencing and expressing there are three different things involved. In some sense, they could be regarded as different forms of language. I wonder whether Indian thinkers particularly grammarians and philosophers of Kāśmīra Śaivism had all this in their minds when they talked of three types of languages — *paśyantī, madhyamā* and *vaikharī*. KS also talks of a *parā*, the fourth and the basic language. This problem also raises another issue, that of the potentiality of a man or a living animal in creating different languages and their relationship to one another.

Man is a speaking animal. He speaks language and communicates with others with the help of language. But there are different people in the world who speak different languages. There does not seem to be any apparent connection between one language and another, but unless these languages have some common known or unknown ancestor no communication between people belonging to different language groups would be possible. For example, those speaking Hindi, Marathi, Gujarati, Bengali, Oriya, Assamese or Maithili understand something in other languages because these languages are from the same group. Similarly, those who speak the slav group of languages, like Serbian, Croatian, Slovanian, Czech, Polish, Russian and Bulgarian may understand each other's thought. But those who speak Marathi may not understand anything in Chinese or Swahili. But still even those who belong to different language groups are able to communicate with each other and soon they are also able to talk in each other's languages. How do they learn such languages? It may be said that human beings are after all human beings, and there may be many things common in their gestures. Two men, for example, from different parts of the world may nod their heads in one way for saying "yes" and in another way for saying "no." Similarly, they may move their hands in a particular way in order to call someone. A person can know whether someone is angry without knowing the other person's language. This sign language might have given rise to performing arts like dance. Even pictographic language or script arises from such natural signs. But the question that arises here is this: "How do two men understand these (each other's) signs?" Similarly, how do two men from two language groups, learn each other's language? In fact, if we go deeper into the problem we could be confronted with as to how a child starts learning from his parents. Indian tradition speaks of the *uttamavṛddha* (उत्तमवृद्ध) and *madhymavṛddha* (मध्यमवृद्ध) and other Nyāya methods. How does he go from *not knowing* to *knowing*? Is there really a *passage* from not knowing to knowing? (There may be, we assume, a passage from knowing to knowing.) Let us dilate on the subject with the help of some more examples. In a game of cricket, a batsman may hit a ball in the air. The ball takes a certain path, a certain trajectory. A fielder notices the ball and runs in a particular direction. He takes a certain position and tries to catch it. Whether he is successful or not in so doing is a different question. But, how does he *know* that the ball is going to a particular place? Someone may say he anticipates it. But what is the analysis of this anticipation? Has he calculated the speed of the ball, the trajectory of the ball, the mathematics of the ballistics of the ball's path and speed? Has he learnt this anytime in a mathematics class? Shall we be able to say that he knows all about the ball, its speed and path, etc. without knowing its speed and path? or shall we say that he knows it intuitively and it is intuitive knowing which takes the form of calculations? In fact, that which is potentially present in him alone is manifested in the analysis, and takes the form of a discipline. Shall we not say that it is like a folded "Japanese" fan having some picture painted on it? When unfolded the picture is clearly seen. But unless it is already there on the fan, it would not be seen by anyone at all. All this is what is called *niṣpatti*. Oil is already present in oil seeds. Only when the seed is pressed we get oil.[2]

2. Sometimes this is called *"kārya"* But since it is translated by most people as effect the entire process is called the theory of causation. I do not think that this can be called a causal theory.

Nevertheless, it is a peculiar experience operating in several areas of life. This gives us a possible explanation of the language phenomenon. Although the common nexus among several languages may not be perceptible, potentially the languages should have a common nucleus inbuilt in human nature and the cosmos; and this may take the form of language. Because of this common nucleus people may be able to understand languages even when they are entirely different.

Let me take one more example. Suppose two infants are lying near each other. They are so young that they cannot speak, they cannot even walk. They can either weep or play, make some instinctive gestures with their eyes, and move their hands and feet. It will have to be admitted that they play with each other. Evidently, they do not know each other; they cannot know each other, but unless there is some basic "acquaintance" can they play? Perhaps we would have to posit some pre-empirical knowledge guiding them. The situation is somewhat like this — they know each other without knowing each other. In such a case we have to say that *knowing each other* is in-built in these children. *Satkāryavāda* (सत्कार्यवाद) would say that all that becomes explicit later, is already there, present in the mind or consciousness of the babies. This capacity gives them the ability to learn different languges. But, in such a case, this capacity itself would be a languge unmanifest. Perhaps we would have to presuppose some such potential language. Could such a language be called *parā*? a language of which Kashmir Śaiva school talks. In all probability, such a language could be at the back of all human languages. It would be concerned with natural law and order. It need not be supposed that the fourfold[3] classification of the languages *parā*,

---

3. Infra .... Also see *Ṛgveda Maṇḍala* 1.164.45 *catvāri vāk parimitā padāni tānividurbrāhmaṇā ye manīṣinaḥ* (चत्वारि वाक् परिमिता पदानि तानि विदुरब्राह्मणा ये मनीषिनः)।

paśyantī, madhyamā and *vaikharī* has anything mystical about them, although the so-called *parā* language is today fused with some form of *kaulavidhi* (कौलविधि).

Parā, Paśyantī, Madhyamā and Vaikharī

Our cultural tradition talks of these four types of languages, *parā, paśyantī, madhyamā* and *vaikharī*. But in the ancient and medieval thought all these languages were not mentioned as a part of one system. Vyākaraṇa discusses only *vaikharī*, i.e. our ordinary language. Bhartṛhari, however, mentions three languages, *madhyamā* and *paśyantī* in addition to *vaikharī*. Kashmir Śaivism in the context of *kaul* rituals talks of *parā* (perhaps in oral *yoga* tradition and saint literature also *parā* is mentioned). All these "languages" are not languages in the sense Sanskrit, English, or Swahili are languages. Our ordinary languages can be classified under *vaikharī*. *Vaikharī* is a language which uses sound symbols for expressions. But in this sense, the "language" of dance, etc. is not language. The only common point between the medium of arts like dance, painting or architecture and ordinary language is that all of them are manifestations and expressions of our thought and feeling. They are expressions or vehicles of our communication. In this respect the task assigned to language is also fulfilled by "art-languages." In a way art-languages are "filled with" natural expression.

But language has more intricate and extended dimensions than are given to us by expressions. For, basically it is an expression of experience. Our utterances in ordinary language are responses to certain *stimuli* which can be stored if necessary. Like the silk worm our ordinary language has to go through three stages: first is the incubation stage, or the stage of experiencing, the second is the "larva" stage which stores the experience in memory of nervous system, and the third is the stage of expression. To my mind, it appears that these three stages are described in terms of *paśyantī*, *madhyamā* and *vaikharī*. Right from our childhood we look at the Universe and understand the environment and the world part by part. The world may be one but after seeing or experiencing the world, we experience it as if it were made up of different parts. The experience of the Vedic seers when they talk of *ekaṁ sat viprā bahudhā vadanti* (एकं सत् विप्रा बहुधा वदन्ति) equally applies here. Perhaps *paśyantī* refers to the multitude of experiences. *Paśyantī* is something that is received. Man receives experiences, classifies them and determines them in specific groups and individual experiences. But it has to be preserved further in memory or in some medium, may be nervous or psychic. In fact, nervous and psychic are not two different media. Our experiences are stored with the help of some electromagnetic or nervous apparatus. But, at this stage, there is neither sound, *svara* or *nāda* and it has not taken the form of any language by way of expressed signs. But at this stage, selection and formation of ideas received from the experience have taken place. Our experience is now reduced or converted to a certain medium. *Madhyamā* means the middle but it also means that which is concerned with *mādhyama* or medium. *Madhyamā* could be the stored language, not reduced to any sound, etc. and therefore people might think that it is *anāhata*. These sounds, at proper time, with the help of certain movements of the mouth are expressed and take the form of ordinary language. I do not know whether all this is a fabrication of my mind but this is what I have understood in my study of philosophy of language of Indian origin. Again, all this according to me is an empirical apparatus and it presupposes some inbuilt language which is beyond experience and this I think refers to what tradition calls *parā* language. This *parā* language is recognized by Kāśmīra Śaivism and is also current in Yoga and Tantra Tradition. But many a time it is discussed in the context of something that is mystical and, therefore, I am not sure of what the ancients thought about it. for example, Kashmir Śaiva philosophers talk of it in the context of Bhairavanātha. This, I think, is not necessary to discuss here.

Evaluation and Parameters

I have said earlier that to put our ideas in ordinary language is, in a way, to measure our ideas, to put them into a mould, to measure them on a certain scale, to weigh them against a certain standard, to evaluate them against certain parameters. But to put our ideas in language, is, for example, not the same as evaluating our ideas against some parameters. It means that putting our ideas in a linguistic mould is a continuous process both quantitatively and qualitatively, from giving them a linguistic form to evaluating them. If I say, "It is a flower," even then I am putting my ideas, my experiences into some kind of mould. I am describing my ideas in language. I am passing a judgement on my ideas and evaluating, in a way, all these varieties of expression.

Reviews and Evaluation

We ought to make a distinction at this point between reviewing and evaluating. A review emphasizes on certain points, magnifies some points, ignores and criticizes some points. Such reviews may help the readers to understand the work. But this is neither evaluating nor appreciating. Sometimes reviewing and appreciating or evaluating may go together. But still the two concepts are different. When a man reviews a certain work of art, he, so to say, is standing on the same ground on which the writer is standing. Only he sees it under a magnifying glass. But, when he is commenting on it, passing a judgement on it, making a favourable or unfavourable remark and appreciating the work, he is passing his opinion on it. Appreciating something is passing an opinion, although passing an opinion may not remain a personal opinion. In evaluating one has transcended the mere description of art objects. Amongst Indian aestheticians Vāmana has clearly distinguished them. While discussing the *alaṁkāra*s he says that poetry becomes acceptable, on account of *alaṁkāra* and by *alaṁkāra* he does not mean ornamentation but an evaluative parameter against which it is weighed. Poetry reaches a certain standard when it adheres to certain norms. A norm is a parameter. *Alaṁkāra* literally means the last limit, a threshold beyond which there is nothing further (in that game). According to him, such a limit is given to us by beauty. But this norm or parameter is a norm of appreciation. Poetry has also to follow certain descriptive norms by which our poetic ideas are expressed in language. Poetry is a gestalt of the expression of our ideas. Of course, the appreciative and descriptive parts or standards are not necessarily independently located and unmixed. But even if they are mixed, they can be distinguished. They belong to two different parameters but when we are engaged in the appreciative activity, we are, so to say, lifted up from the descriptive level to the evaluative one. It is possible that the evaluation may also not be of one type. One may for example, talk of beauty and also of propriety although they may overlap. Perhaps one may not be able to define them but still one may understand them. When we describe something we, so to say, analyse them by separating their parts. It is only a complex thing which can be so described. If it is simple, we may not be able to describe it at all. Perhaps, "beautiful" and "appropriate" may be such notions. By using these notions we may be able to evaluate some objects. We should also realize that such notions may be indescribable and might not be fully comprehensible.

Appreciative norms have to be of two kinds: (1) definite and (2) non-comprehensible. When we talk of comprehensible norms we describe things under them as "just touching the threshold." The non-comprehensible norms would naturally be out of the threshold, out of bounds. The descriptive norms also are of two kinds. Either they are about the subject matter, or they are about the form. Their parameter will be based on the nature of the form but will have to be related to the subject matter.

Naming, Describing and Explaining

Naming, describing and explaining *have different status*, but they have one thing in common, viz. in some sense, they are instruments of measuring. It is usually supposed that we cannot measure anything unless there is something common between that which we measure and that by which we measure. This commonness between the measure and the object that is to be measured is described by the *Oxford Dictionary* as the *quantity constant*. But it need not be a quantity constant. It could be a constant of different varieties and even when it is a quantity constant the lower limit of the quantity can tend to be "zero." In the case of naming we make use of this lower limit. We think that there need not be any similarity between the name and its bearer, that is, that which we measure and that by which we measure. What is necessary is *not similarity but taking it for granted that there is similarity.* In naming we impose a certain similarity although there may be nothing common and this imposing of the "similarity" is sufficient to identify the object with its name. That is why we say that a proper name has no connotation. Although the identification is only imposed it tends to become natural. This operation of identification continues not only during the existence of the object but also after the "death" of the object. That is why when something,

X, is dead and is no more, we can say that X is no more. We would have occasion to see that several models in arts and science are dependent on these varying degrees of similarity, both quantitative and qualitative.

A relation like "longer than" indicates some common co-ordinate between the terms in which this relation exists. This co-ordinate is a quantitative co-ordinate. The relation between two predicates, if there is a relation, or a relation between the subject and predicate of a logical proposition in the strict sense of the term, is a qualitative co-ordinate. But barring such extreme cases it can be said that there is some natural similarity between the instrument of measurement and the object that is measured. This is how the concept of measurement or parameter or *mānadaṇḍa* comes into operation. That which is measured is determinable and that by which it is measured is something already determined, at least conceptually determined. It is because of this that it attains the status of a standard or a parameter. Ordinarily this relation between determinable and the parameter is quantitative and linear. But we can extend this relationship to non-quantitative and non-linear areas. In quantitative measurement the two co-ordinates are measured in terms of groups. I feel that out of the two co-ordinates if one is a quality and the other a quantity you get a class, and in the case of value the determinable may have a quality or a quantity or both and the value itself may not have anything of these. It would be a measurement on altogether a different plane. Thus at the lowest end the process of measurement starts with naming and in the end it ends with evaluation.

Status of Parameters

While talking about the nature of art, art medium and language the problem about the status of a parameter becomes significant. Parameter is that with which we compare our experience of creation and standardize it. Parameter literally means measurement. It is the final measurement. This raises a question about the status of a parameter. Does a parameter necessarily exist? Is it necessary that it should exist? Do we experience the existence of a parameter? Does a parameter become manifest? If we want to measure a room and say it is 20 metres in width, have we experienced the metre? Is it merely our idea or does it have existence? We talk of width. It is also a parameter. Is ideal width given to us in experience? According to me such problems about parameters, at least about constitutive parameters were raised by Bhaṭṭanāyaka. He thought that *rasa* was a parameter, perhaps a constitutive parameter of at least some kinds of arts. He classified *rasa* into two categories, *rasa* and *mahārasa*. Incidentally, Bharata has also used the word *mahārasa* at some places in *Nāṭyaśāstra*. Bhaṭṭanāyaka says that in the use of such sentences as *na hi rasādṛte kaścidapi arthaḥ pravartate* (न हि रसादृते कश्चिदपि अर्थः प्रवर्तते) the reference is to *mahārasa*. The use, he says, of the word *rasa*, in singular shows that when *rasa* is used in plural (as for example *nāṭye aṣṭau rasāḥ smṛtāḥ*, नाट्ये अष्टौ रसाः स्मृताः), the plurality indicates merely the illustrations which are measured in terms of the basic concept of *rasa*. Perhaps he thought that *rasa* as used in singular is a parameter. He says, *rasaḥ na pratīyate, na utpadyate, na abhivyañjyate* (रसः न प्रतीयते। न उत्पद्यते। न अभिव्यंजते). Bhaṭṭanāyaka's work *Hṛdayadarpaṇa* is not available. The fragments, one of which I have quoted above, are available in *Abhinavabhāratī* of Abhinavagupta and a few other works. But here Bhaṭṭanāyaka's position is assumed as that of *pūrvapakṣa* and his statements are used only for criticizing him. He said that *rasa* is not produced, is not perceived and is not distinctly manifested. Instead of trying to understand him, people have tried to find fault with him. But is it not the description of a parameter? It is true that Bhaṭṭanāyaka does not use the word parameter or its equivalent in Sanskrit. But the context in which he has used this description is kept away from us, and he has been criticized by his successors. People have even gone to the extent of saying that he has contradicted himself. Since Bhaṭṭanāyaka's writings are not before me, I cannot positively say as to what was in his mind, when he described *rasa* in these terms. But evidently this description properly fits in the concept of parameter and I do think that *rasa* was one of the constitutive parameters, first used in the performing arts and then used in fine arts including the plastic arts. In fact, I believe that in our use of language and medium we are continuously using some rod or some meter and describing some ideas in terms of some mini parameters. I call them mini parameters, for we see and create them in terms of *upamāna* (उपमान). All that we convey to others is in terms of *upamāna*. The theory of parameters will certainly lead us to the basic theory of medium and I look to language as a medium only.

Use of Language

When we use language we are certainly doing some activity. But this activity consists in naming, describing and explaining. It may be concerned with many other things but we need not bother about them. When we describe something we are, so to say, explaining one name in terms of several other names or actions. When we explain something in terms of some other thing there is bound to be some kind of overt or covert comparison.[4] In explaining we are expanding our description. But basically description itself is an explanation, and it can't be done unless we compare one idea in terms of another idea. I believe that the model which is at work in this activity is

4. I have assumed this point earlier; I am repeating it because it is on this base that the further developments were made.

that of simile or metaphor. Poets and scientists have made use of these kinds of models and metaphors. But is it the basic model? Of course, some Alaṁkārins start their theses with similes. But, I believe that the basic model is not that of simile or *upamā* which requires two constituents, one *upameya* and the other *upamāna*. To me description or explanation model seems to be basic. Starting with this model we create two other samples which the rhetoricians regard as the special cases of the basic model. Indian rhetoricians call them *rūpaka* (रूपक) and *ananvaya* (अनन्वय) respectively. "Her face is like that of the moon" is a simile model. "Her face is the moon itself" is a metaphor model. "Her face is like her face" (it cannot be compared with anything else). This is regarded as *ananvaya*. The other cases of *ananvaya* are "The sky is like the sky," "the ocean is like the ocean."[5] In such descriptions we are misled by the word "like." The word "like" is redundant. We could instead say "ocean is ocean," "sky is sky," "her face is her face." In logical symbolism it is A is A (A = A). "A" is the name model.[6] There is hundred per cent *identity* between the first and the second A, in "A is A" or the subject and the predicate. But this hundred per cent identity arises not because it is a name or a symbol but because the name or symbol points to the same object or *vācya*. While explaining or naming, our philosophers have said that "naming" is due to our desire, (or God's desire) *icchā* or *Īśvarecchā*. It means that it is arbitrary. But it is the "arbitrariness" which gives complete identification. Any word in a language basically stands for the medium, i.e.

5. In fact, the whole theory of *alaṁkāras* like *upamā, apahnuti, bhrāntimān, rūpaka, upameyopamā* etc. can be looked at as a theory of language models applied to poetry.

6. But the similarity or identity is not in fact between the symbols or the symbol and its bearer. The identity (or similarity) is always between the object denoted by the same symbol. The identity is always between *vācaka*, which may be mentioned twice.

for the word itself as well as for the object denoted by the word. It stands for *vācya-vācaka* relation. Is this relation on account of similarity that is found in nature? Perhaps, this is thrust on it and is experienced in any symbolization. I believe that this is the basic model of communication. Of course, I have talked of *vācya* and *vācaka*. They are like the two wings of a butterfly. Jagannātha uses the word *yugala* for it. Of course, the concept of the bearer and the concept of meaning are different and sometimes there could be a meaning without bearer. But I believe that the basic model of every word is "name model" and it is from the name model that the description and explanation models arise. It is this understanding of languge or medium which is at the back of developed languages of art. I think Indian philosophers also have made use of the same ideas. Basically, Indians had developed the name theory or what Ryle called Fido-fido theory. But Indians had distinguished between the bearer and the knowledge that we get when we utter a name. Patañjali of *Yogasūtra* clearly means this when he says, *śabdārtha pratyayānām itaretarādhyāsāt saṅkaraḥ* (शब्दार्थप्रत्ययानाम् इतरेतराध्यासात् संकरः). The word *artha* is used in Indian philosophical literature in a very ambiguous manner. It stands for (1) the object indicated by the name, (2) the meaning indicated by the name, (3) purpose, (4) human and (as in *puruṣārtha*), (5) polity, (6) money or wealth, and (7) value. All these are important senses in which the word *artha* is used. But as pointed out above the word *artha* here stands for (a) the object indicated, and (b) meaning (of the word). In the above *sūtra* the very fact that Patañjali distinguishes between *artha* and *pratyaya* shows that the word *artha* stands for the thing indicated, and the *pratyaya* stands for its meaning which is of the nature of *pratīti* or flash. Patañjali himself might have used the word *artha* ambiguously. But at present it should not concern us. He points out that *śabda* may not always have a bearer since the basic model is that of a name and its bearer. When a word is used we might think that it has some bearer. This kind of delusion gives rise to several philosophical problems which are, in fact, pseudo problems. But this is also at the back of imagination, fiction, literature and scientific hypotheses. While describing what he calls *vikalpa* (विकल्प) Patañjali of *Yogasūtra* says, *śabdajñānānupāti vāstuśūnyo vikalpaḥ* (शब्दज्ञानानुपाति वस्तुशून्यो विकल्पः), i.e. when the word is uttered the idea (or the bearer) arises in our mind immediately. But corresponding to the idea there is no bearer. This is what is called *vikalpa*. Poets and artists, I feel, have made use of this concept in all their creations. In fact, the very concept of *nāṭya* where one plays the role of another person who is either imaginary or has the so-called historical reality is of this kind. An actor performs a role by impersonating the other character in the drama. This impersonation is *vikalpa*. In drama the medium is concrete, this is generally true in all arts. Instead of using the medium in its accepted way, the artist uses it in some untraditional way. I have said above that every activity of language is an activity of understanding with the help of a model. In our ordinary language such models are used. But when use of such models becomes routine, one forgets that it is the source of poetry. If a poet uses the same model again and again we say that he has no originality. When Kālidāsa or Jñāneśvara graphically describes a certain situation we admire their originality. But, when we find that the same simile which was used by Kālidāsa was earlier used by Aśvaghoṣa, we are shocked to some extent and then we begin to think that it is possible for two great poets to think alike. This is also found in regard to imitation of great painters like Vermeer. For an ordinary man, imitations of his paintings are as good as the originals at Louvre in Paris. But we satisfy ourselves by bringing in the concepts of originality and imitation. Originality lies in expressing something afresh and which is not the repetition of the work of the earlier masters. This is what Kuntaka perhaps wants to say when he propounds the theory of *vakratā*. He gives several instances of *vakratā*. Since he is concerned with poetry he talks of *vakra ukti* (vŕ̥ %iKt). In the larger context we should understand by *vakrokti* some kind of untraditional expression whether it is spoken or performed. The essence of poetry according to him lies in expressing our ideas in an untraditional or curved way. Since every word or medium has two wings, the one of "medium" and the other of meaning — *vācaka* and *vācya* — it is possible to use unusual *vācaka* and also possible to comprehend unusual *vācya*. This unusual *vācaka* would be of two types (at least). In our poetic theory this unusual *vācya* is either of implication type or of suggestion type (it could also point to some after-effect in the form of beauty). Similarly, the word which stands for medium can be unusual. The word *sudhāṁśu* (suxa<zu), for example is the synonym of moon or *candra*. This unusual name is given because we have a belief that rays of nectar spring from the moon. This is unusual and certainly very attractive. But, in course of time, this beautiful description of the moon becomes a matter of routine and is reduced to the status of pure symbol or name. It does not remain an *incomplete symbol*. But when one describes *sudhāṁśu* as *vyomagaṅgāsaroruha* (Vyaemg<gasraeṜh) we are going further from something traditional to something *absolutely untraditional*. This again is of two types. The description in its semantical mode is certainly very untraditional since we are describing it as a lotus bloomed in the galaxy or heavenly Ganges. But in its sound patttern also there is some kind of unusuality as we go from *kamala* to *sudhāṁśu* and *sudhāṁśu* to *vyomagaṅgāsaroruha*. According to Kuntaka all theories of poetry or art are covered by this concept of *vakratā*. He has described it in the following way.

शब्दार्थौ सहितं वक्र-कविव्यापारशालिनी ।
बन्धे व्यवस्थितौ काव्यं तद्वदाह्लादकारिणी ॥

śabdārthau sahitaṁ vakra-kavivyāpāraśālinī ।
bandhe vyavasthitau kāvyaṁ tadvadāhlādakāriṇī ॥ — 1.2

शब्दो विवक्षितार्थैक-वाचकोन्येषु सत्स्वपि ।
अर्थः सहृदयाह्लादकारिस्वस्पन्दसुन्दरः ॥

śabdo vivakṣitārthaika-vācakonyeṣu satsvapi ।
arthaḥ sahṛdayāhlādakārisvaspanda-sundaraḥ ॥ — 1.9

The followers of Kuntaka, Ānandavardhana and Mahimabhaṭṭa have raised a hue and cry against one another. But there is no doubt that the artistic expression has to be untraditional and unusual if it is to be attractive. Suppose a painter paints a landscape and in this landscape he paints a cottage. The painting of a cottage, giving the idea of human habitation, is itself somewhat novel in regard to painting because the realm of nature has already been crossed and we have entered the human realm. But when we come down to its details, we find that the painter has painted the grass not with the usual green or gray colour but has painted it with some shade of red or something else. We know that it is not the natural colour, that grass is never like this. But even then, the painting attracts us.[7]

The Meaning of Beauty

What shall we understand how shall we analyse and when we say that something is beautiful? It cannot be denied that we do say something is beautiful and when we say so, we need not be wrong, for, a few other persons would say that the object that we judge as beautiful is beautiful. What is the

7. I owe this to my friend late M. B. Chitnis, the founder Principal of Milind Maha Vidyalaya, of Aurangabad and the first Registrar of Ambedkar Marathwada University.

status of this "beautiful"? Is beautiful a natural characteristic of the thing that we perceive? Just as we can say that the object is round or oblong or square or red or green or variegated (in the sense that what we *see* in perception constituted the thing), can we say that something is beautiful? The paradox is that we do *see* something as beautiful and still we do not see something as beautiful. There is some tricky and immediate transition from something that we see to something that we judge as beautiful. It is something like this: we see certain ornaments. We say that they are ornaments and in saying this we have ignored that they are made of gold. But if we have to make ornaments of other designs we would have to melt the ornaments (into gold). In the strict sense of the term it is not the ornament that we melt nor is it the beauty that we melt. But one could say that the metal has the potentiality of ornaments being formed of it, as also to be beautiful. In Nyāya language one could say that this is possible because the *samavāyī* cause is the same. Transformation takes place only in regard to *asamavāyī kāraṇa*. If we have to explain this with the help of an analogy at least on some interpretation it is the *tanmātra* or a combination of a few *tanmātra*s which appears as *mahābhūta*. Of course, this does not mean that *tanmātra* and *mahābhūta* are the same. It is to my mind a difference between "being there" and "knowing it to be there." Both of them in a sense "are." But one has the context of the ontological world and the other has the context of epistemological world. We do not recognize, although it should be recognized, that a large part of our experience is in the epistemic world. In fact, what the phenomenologists talk of, is about this epistemic world. Perhaps there is a hierarchy in the epistemic world which may add layers after layers to the thing-in-itself and become richer and richer by added properties. But in the matter of transformation it is the original that is of significance and the added properties are merely functional. In Bhartṛhari's language, as I understand it, it is merely a *vivarta* (विवर्त). Of course, *vivarta* does not mean that it is unreal, it only means that it has become richer on account of the added properties and it makes the original inhabitants of ontology to reside in the epistemological world. This is perhaps what happens between creation and its appreciation. We are, to put in a light way, continuously passing from *annamaya koṣa* (अन्नमय कोष) to *ānandamaya koṣa* (आनंदमय कोष) through *prāṇamaya* (प्राणमय), *vijñānamaya* (विज्ञानमय) and *manomaya koṣa* (मनोमय कोष). We do talk of some beautiful object. But beautiful is not just any material of which the object is made. If it is a town it is made of buildings "planned" in a particular way: if it is a sculpture, it is made of some material like clay or marble or bronze, if it is a painting it is made of some lines or curves and colours. None of these is beautiful and the object completed is also an object only, in the ontological world. But in the world of epistemology or rather in the epistemic world it is not only *an object* but a *beautiful object*. This "beautiful" is not only a "characteristic" of the object, it also acts as a "parameter" of the object. It is something like this. In the world of physics (chemistry) there are elementary particles or basic elements. One could say that there are oxygen and hydrogen and so on. One could also say that some of these can be combined and finally when we come across two parts of hydrogen and one part of oxygen, we see this as water. Everything except the basic structure is only functional. I may take one more example. We take out ore from a mine. Taking out the ore from the mine is due to human labour. We send this iron ore to a melting foundry and turn it into pig iron. This is also due to human labour and processing. This pig iron is further turned into some finished object. But all these transformations are of the ore and they take place on account of human labour and processing. But human labour and processing (and ore in its original form) are not seen anywhere. Similar is the case in regard to a beautiful three-dimensional object like the Tajmahal. If we try to go to the material aspect of it, we may come to the conclusion that the material is not beautiful. The marble and the shape given to them is due to a certain process. The artisan makes an object and leaves it to others to see whether it is beautiful or not. A landscape painter may see some object, but he reduces it to two-dimensional lines and curves and colours. If he is not able to decode his experience and encode it into lines and colours, etc. he would not succeed as a painter. Objects are objects. They become beautiful or otherwise when they are subjected to certain operations. The operation part too does not make the object beautiful. Rather only a judgement on the finished product "makes" it beautiful. The relationship between the original material and the finished product as beautiful, has an intimate relation. But this intimate relation is brought about on account of the operations which require some author. He works on the material with a certain insight. He can tell us about the complexity of the structure but he cannot say anything about the beauty of the finished product. The beauty of the finished product cannot be analysed either in operational parts or in structural elements. One could say that it has potentiality but the potentiality cannot also be termed as beauty. The transition from potentiality to actuality is possible and can be described by a dictum, *śaktasya śakyakaranāt* (शक्तस्य शक्यकरणात्). There may not appear any similarity between the original and the finished product. But still unless there is a similarity between the original and the finished product, the finished product cannot come into existence. The existence of the original is in the ontic world, the existence of the finished product is in the epistemic or human world. This according to me is the basic problem between the medium and its expression. This also reflects in language and its meaning or a thing and its beauty. This is basically a problem of structure and function. Finally, this is a problem of insight and not of analysis. This is, perhaps, in the mind of the Indian aestheticians from Bharata to Jagannātha or amongst the sculptors, *sthapatis*, painters, etc. They give the description of constituent parameters and also talk of evaluative parameters. But they do not give any analysis of evaluative parameters and only describe them either with the help of *upamāna* or with the help of *ananvaya*. "It" is beautiful like the *lāvaṇya* of a pretty maid. "It is *ucita*." But what is *ucita*? *Ucita* is like *ucita*. It cannot be further analysed. The relation between *śabda* and *artha* is also unique in the same way and cannot be further analysed.

It may be objected that the analysis which I have given may be true of art objects but may not apply to objects of nature. A woman is beautiful. What makes her beautiful? My answer would be that the epistemic processing applies to all structure and so it applies to a woman also. For it is ultimately a judgement on the structure. An artist draws a picture and an observer discerns the specific characteristics of the picture. An observer need not be an artist. When we know we know something in terms of design. We look at the clouds in the sky, we do not see merely the clouds, we also "shape" them in some figures. These figures may evaporate in the course of time and other figures may be created. But the discerned figures are superimposed on the structure. The structure here is carved out by the artist, i.e. the observer from the nebulous material. Even in the absence of the artist the structure is there. The transition from structure to function is also functional and is due to our insight. It is epistemic. Ordinarily, just as one who is not a trained proof reader does not discern the mistakes in the proof, similarly, the observer does not discern the form of such structures or the forms of the parts of such structures. A painter is able to discern them, a sculptor is able to discern them, a *sthapati* is able to discern them. In fact, any keen observer can discern them. This makes him different from the ordinary observer. We see the picture of a certain scene. A painter not only sees a picture-*qua*-picture. He also sees lines, curves and colours of the picture. Although we say, he draws a picture, he does not draw a picture. He only paints lines, colours and curves.[8] Any artefact is merely a symbolization of something that is in the mind of the artist, but which has also evolved and developed during the process of creation, i.e. in the process of encoding or symbolization. The symbolization arouses in the spectator or the audience. Some reactions and finally takes them to that region which can be regarded as the region of meaning, judgement or ideas. The symbols are usually understood not as symbols *qua* symbols. They are understood along with "coatings" which are so to say "inherent" in the symbols but which primarily belong to the region of ideas. Ultimately the problem is concerned with the relation between symbol and its meanings, interpretations and judgements which arise as ripples from the symbols. In this context it would be interesting to see what Nyāya, Mīmāṁsā and Grammar schools think about the problem.

Relationship Between Śabda and Artha

In Nyāya and Mīmāṁsā philosophy the relation between *śabda* and *artha* is accepted as constant or *nitya* (नित्य). Mīmāṁsā *sūtra*

---

8. The essence of creativity lies in filing the gap between what he does and what he effects by his imagination. It is this which makes him different from the appreciator. It is in this special capacity to reduce the figures, etc. to lines and so on that his *kārayitrī pratibhā* lies. What is true of a painter is equally true of all artists.

says, *śabdasya arthena autpattīkavastu sambandhaḥ* (शब्दस्य अर्थेन औत्पत्तिकवस्तु सम्बन्धः). According to Nyāya philosophy the relation between sound-symbol and its meaning or intended meaning is regarded as *nitya*. The other name which Naiyāyikas give to this relationship is called *samaya* (समय). On account of this inseparable relationship two kinds of inferences are possible. If we have the meaning pattern, we could infer that *probably* such and such would be its sound pattern. Such inference is certainly not deductive, for other sound patterns also could have a similar relation with the meaning pattern. But, as I have pointed out earlier, we could distinguish symbols from their natural signs, and also from their artificial signs. In the case of natural signs or symbols there would be a greater probability of a particular set of symbols going with a particular pattern of meaning. I have already pointed out that something that is in our mind is displayed in our face in the case of emotions like anger, love, etc. The individual *anubhāva* may be *common* to different emotions but their combination is unique and, therefore, there is almost no possibility of misinterpreting the emotion of love for the emotion of anger. Perhaps, on this account, the Mīmāṁsakas might have modified the concept of *nitya sambandha* slightly and used the name *autpattika sambandha* instead of *nitya sambandha*. *Nitya sambandha* means the continuent or permanent relationship which exists between the word and its meaning. The *autpattika sambandha* means the continual relationship which starts from the point of time the word (or sound) is uttered. It is nevertheless a permanent inseparable relation after that moment. Perhaps the grammarians might not agree with this if by *śabda* and *artha* they understand two different or alternative "names" of the same "thing." I am not sure whether they really mean so. But, as I pointed out above Patañjali and Bhartṛhari seem to have a slight variation in their views, one emphasizing on the *pratyaya* part (the immediate cognition of the meaning) as primary, and the other emphasizing on the sound pattern itself as primary. Bhartṛhari says that the *śabdatattva* (शब्दतत्त्व) exhibits itself or appears (itself) as *artha bhāva*. Perhaps Pāṇini also has to say a similar thing when he says, *svaṁ rūpaṁ śabdasya aśabdasaṁjñā* (स्वं रूपं शब्दस्य अशब्दसंज्ञा).

In the case of natural signs or symbols, as soon as the sign is expressed it leads to some kind of meaning, understanding or *pratyaya*. It converts itself (*vivartate,* विवर्तते) into *artha bhāva. Vivarta* means a continued production of ripples. If the idea is to be expressed by a simile it is like this. In a reservoir of water, if a pebble is dropped it disturbs the water by creating involutes (ripples).[9] There are a number of ripples seen by our eyes one after another; (and then) they gradually become indistinct before they finally disappear. The meanings behave like ripples. One meaning could be followed by another meaning, which in its turn could be followed by still different meanings. Perhaps, Ānandavardhana's *Dhvani Siddhānta* has this kind of thought in the back ground. But his thought is restricted only to *abhidhā, lakṣaṇā* and *vyañjanā*. But, there could be other kinds of ripples also like the ones emerging in beauty, another emerging in happiness and still an other creating the feeling of numbness or inexpressibility. Bharata mentions this as the reaction which the spectator has to the drama or dance performance. He mentions this in *Āsvādaprakriyā* when he says that *rasa* leads to *harṣādīṁśca* (हर्षादींश्च) in the minds of the spectators and talks of the *siddhis, mānuṣī* and *daivikī* and again under *daivikī siddhi* talks of *bhāvātiśayapeta* (भावातिशयोपेत) and *sampūrṇa* (सम्पूर्ण). He has described *sampūrṇa siddhi* as inexpressibility or absence of all actions.

9. Involute is a part of a point which travels around the fixed point with increase in radii at equal intervals of angles. [This is a term used in engineering drawing.]

न शब्दः नैव क्षोभः न चोत्पातनिदर्शनम् ।
सम्पूर्णता च रंगस्य सा सिद्धिः दैविकी स्मृता ॥

na śabdaḥ naiva kṣobhaḥ na cotpātanidarśanam ।
sampūrṇatā ca raṅgasya sā siddhiḥ daivikī smṛtā ॥[10]

Perhaps, all these possibilities are potentially present in the symbol itself and like ripples created by small pebbles are induced to different kinds of manifested meanings. Indian art critics have restricted themselves to poetry and have therefore talked of sound symbols and their meanings. But, in fact, this would be the case in regard to every art and artefact. Each art and artefact would lead to different kinds of reaction patterns which have all these possibilities. The symbol patterns and the reaction patterns could be regarded as parameters of different kinds and there could be a certain ultimate relationship between the two kinds of parameters — one concerned with matter or the constituents, the other with evaluation of these constituents. In fact, even in the first kind there would be two types of patterns. One would be concerned with the matter of the constituent and the other with the form of the constituent. On these forms (or the constituent) will depend the reactions which we call appreciations. Since the reactions would be spontaneous and unique, it can be said that it is not a sum of different reactions. This pattern would be simple and if analysable, not analysable on the same level. Thus, it would be possible, e.g. for an architect or a *sthapati* not to talk of beauty but to talk of symmetries, contrast, balance, etc. and understand thereby that a particular structure would lead to beauty. Beauty would be a universal *a priori* concept arising in the presence of certain structural designs.

Aesthetics: An Anthopocentric World

Kant in his three critiques talks of three kinds of *a priori*

10. *NŚ* 27.17.

synthetic judgements. In the case of pure knowledge, he says that the forms of intuitions are, for example, *a priori* synthetic. Of course, in the first critique also he does distinguish between the knowledge of *a priori* concepts in relation to geometry and the knowledge of *a priori* concepts in relation to arithmetic. He relates one to Space and the other to Time. As soon as a certain figure, say, e.g. an equilateral triangle, is put before us, we know that it is equiangular and also that any other equilateral triangle will be equiangular. The same is the case with arithmetic $7 + 5 = 12$. This is *a priori* synthetic judgement and he thinks that it follows from the nature of Time. Perhaps, such arithmetical sums are dependent on original number series and Kant might be thinking that this series is dependent on succession and, therefore, might be linking it with Time. Russell, Reichenbach and others do not accept that these are synthetic *a priori* judgements. They think that they are *a priori* analytic propositions (one must, of course, distinguish between a judgement and a proposition and must know that Kant has never used the word proposition in this context. On the contrary, philosophers like Russell have not used the word judgement). I am not contesting what Kant or Russell has said but I want to point out that the judgements about geometry arise only when geometrical world is present before us. The observer does not add or supplement anything of his own when he has the knowledge of properties of geometrical figures. This is not so with regard to the arithmetical phenomena. One could know the properties of arithmetic *a priori* without reference to the properties of outside world; paradoxes in such cases may arise when the geometrical and arithmetical concepts are blended in one, or are confused with one another, or mistaken as belonging to one category.

Descartes in particular did this by introducing co-ordinate geometry, where problems of geometry were solved by algebraical methods. But here a difficulty arose. Mathematicians did not merely talk of series of cardinal or ordinal numbers. They also talked of number squares and number cubes. I am afraid that this was a geometrical concept applied to numbers. Square is a figure of a particular kind which has two dimensions and cube is a figure of three dimensions. A figure of n-dimensions might not exist at all. It may be just a generalization of one, two and three dimensions. Mathematical formula of n-dimensions may apply to all cases of 1, 2, and 3 dimensions. But, such formulae give rise to paradoxes, e.g. the square root of number two. The square root of one is plus minus one and the square root of four is plus minus two. But what is root 2? It is not possible to work it out by algebraical method, for a square, in the strict sense, is not an arithmetical number. If we take a series of squares it would not be a series of cardinals 1, 2, 3, 4, etc. It would be 1, 4, 9, 16, 25. But that is because we are regarding them as areas of geometrical figures. Only by confusing the geometrical with the arithmetical that this kind of confusion can arise. In the case of geometrical figures, one has a prior knowledge in the presence of the objective geometrical world. In the case of pure arithmetical numbers, perhaps the geometrical world acts like a neutral background and the knower manipulates the numbers. But, whatever may be the case, the cosmological world is present before us. But, from this cosmological world when we come to the world of ethics and try to understand the rules or dicta of ethics, this cosmological world, except man, can be completely ignored and the knower could react only to the anthropological world. What is good or bad can be known *a priori* only in the presence of the anthropological world. Since the presence of the anthropological world is in the background all such ethical norms could be regarded as *a priori* synthetic. When we go to the province of aesthetics, the cosmological, as also the anthropological world is presupposed. It is not discovering something from the cosmological world nor is it discovering something from the anthropological world. It is any knower's reaction, both to the anthropological and the cosmological worlds. He is, so to say, creating a new world, an anthropocosmic world. Beauty is a quality of this world. It is known in a flash but requires the presence of both these worlds, may be in different proportions. Beautiful as a norm therefore is on a different level. It arises in the mind of man but applies to physical and non-physical objects alike. In Indian literature, the varieties of beauty, of course, are accepted and different words are coined to express these varieties. For example, Vāmana uses the word *saundarya*, Bharata uses the word *śobhā*, Kālidāsa uses the words *manojñātā* and *cārutā*, and Māgha and Jagannātha use the word *ramaṇīyatā*. These four different words are, in fact, representative words of different concepts, although from the same family. Indians have used these different words or concepts as parameters of beauty in different arts like painting, drama, dance and music, both vocal and instrumental.

Relationship Between Mind and Body

In discussing the development of aesthetic theory in India, we will have to deal with relation of mind and body, the concept of medium and language, the relation of different arts to aesthetic theory and the relation of different arts to one another.

In Bharata's *Nāṭyaśāstra* there are references to arts like poetry, musical instruments and lighting arrangements in the theatre although most of the people did not notice the reference to lighting arrangements.[11] Bharata, of course, directly refers

---

11. Vide supra/infra the *Chapter concerned.*

to arts like drama and dance. Both in regard to drama and dance Bharata gives us the steps in its organization. This is concerned with the dancers' and the actors' bodily movements. What is the relation of body and mind?

In the West, three theories have been current regarding this relation for the last some centuries. According to Descartes, mind and body are two substances which are independent of each other, but which nevertheless act on each other. Gilbert Ryle describes this phenomenon as the "ghost in the machine." According to this theory of Descartes one substance acts on the other substance or vice versa. This is what is known as the theory of body-mind interactionism. The other theory is known as body-mind parallelism. In the naïve form, the theory asserts that there are two independent substances but on account of some pre-established harmony, with a change in one substance there is a similar change in the other substance. Tradition attributes this theory to Spinoza. Perhaps this theory leads to Leibnitz's theory of pre-established harmony which says that there are many windowless monads having no communication amongst themselves. But, on account of the pre-established harmony they live together without colliding with one another and without any conflict amongst themselves. According to me, there is no real conflict between Spinoza and Leibnitz. The multitudes of monads are nothing but modes for Spinoza. Spinoza did not accept body and mind as two substances. For him they were merely the attributes of one substance, the cosmos or the cosmic God. So his parallelism is a correlation between body and mind. But, since the substance is one, the parallelism theory would in fact get reduced to only one process with twin parallel expressions instead of two parallel processes. Thus, the body-mind parallelism could be only illusory. Ryle perhaps thought in a similar way and asserted that the so-called parallelism of body and mind was concerned with two languages — the physiological and the mental, where the alternative expressions of the one language correspond in one-to-one relation with the other and so can be called as two linguistic processes. But, they are not two real processes running parallel to each other. Perhaps, while interpreting Bharata one has to keep in the background this type of relationship between body and mind or *śarīra* on the one hand and *manas* (*antaḥkaraṇa*, *jīva* or *ātman*), on the other. Bharata, of course, did not theorise the body-mind relationship. But, he noticed that whatever be the internal feeling or phenomenon, it is known to others only by our facial expressions and bodily movements. These two he termed as *anubhāva* and *vyabhicārī bhāva.*[12] *Bhāva* in ordinary language is anything that is or that exists. It is anything that is projected. It could also be a feeling, desire or a cross-section of movement or action. It could also be a sentiment or emotion. To narrow down the meaning of *bhāva* is incorrect. Ordinarily we say *bhavati iti bhāvaḥ* (भवति इति भावः). Bharata says that in the context of drama it should not be *bhāvati iti bhāvaḥ*, it should be *bhāvayanti iti bhāvaḥ* (भावयन्ति इति भावः). The point we should understand is that although the two senses of *bhāva*s are different *these senses* do not conflict with each other. In dramatic art the actor is always concerned with some form of doing. It is never just a form of happening. But every form of doing is ultimately a happening. *Anukaraṇa* is certainly a form of doing. Nevertheless one can say that what he does also happens. It is a causal sense or *nijanta* of *bhū* ("भू" का "निजन्त"). Bharata says: *bhū iti karaṇe dhātuḥ* (भू इति करणे धातुः). *Abhinaya* is that happening which the actor does. But in so doing what happens is the

12. This has already been considered while dealing with *bhāvas*, vide chapters *Bhāva Vicāra* and *Abhinaya*, op. cit. But I am repeating it here.

happening of a specific facial expression or the movement of the body. It may be pointed out here that there is a difference between a whole and parts which are related to one another due to chemical action and the whole and parts, which are united in a facial gestalt, due to some change in psychological attitude. In the case of facial expressions we can see that the changes which occur on the face on account of changes in our emotions or responses to others are finite and can be counted. There may be many similarities of facial expressions between two different emotions or responses. For example, whether a man is angry or in a mood of love the reaction on the cheeks could be the same. They may become reddish, similarly there may be a quivering of the lips in both the cases. The movement of the eyes or the eyebrows, however, may be different. But, these different emotions or emotional moods are composed of only a limited number of facial changes. Bharata calls them *anubhāva*s and he has given a list of *anubhāva*s in *Nāṭyaśāstra*. Perhaps in our final analysis one may add to the list of facial expressions and changes. But that is strictly irrelevant; for we are not here concerned with the listing of *anubhāva*s but with the fact that the internal state of the mind of man is revealed in and through the bodily movements or expressions on the face. To use modern language, I may say that the internal experiences and expressions are encoded in physiological expression. I need not point out here that these encoded physiological expressions are decoded and interpreted by the observers into mental language. Thus, to me it appears that the language which is symbolized in physical expression or mental expression is one and the same, only its mode of expression is different. I could thus say, using the language of Spinoza, that when we go from the mental language to the physiological or vice versa we are thinking of the parallelism of modes and nothing else. In the hypothesis of parallelism the body and mind are not regarded as different and independent substances. They are rather regarded as one thought expressed in different modes.

Communication in Arts

In fact, like language the object of art also is to communicate. But this is done not in a straightway. Sometimes a game of hide-and-seek is resorted to and that which is to be conveyed is kept away with the result that a suspense is created. Sometimes what is conveyed can be interpreted in different ways giving rise to some kind of ambiguity. In fact, this seems to be the very nature of language. Where some things which are not identical are to be connected, such a thing is bound to happen. Perhaps, unless something of the original is concealed something new cannot be attributed to it. Attributing something new is grafting something different on the original. Thus, in simile, metaphor and puns this technique is used in greater and greater progression. In drama a dramatic effect is achieved by this technique by using a certain expression in one context and thereby making audience aware of a different situation. This is called *patākāsthāna* (पताकास्थान). It is described in the following way:

यत्रार्थे चिन्तितेऽन्यस्मिन् तालिंगोन्यः प्रयुज्यते ।
आगन्तुकेन भावेन पताकास्थानकं तु यत् ॥

yatrārthe cintite 'nyasmin tālliṅgonyaḥ prayujyate ।
āgantukena bhāvena patākā sthānakaṁ tu yat ॥

It is an intimation of episodical incident, when instead of the thing thought of or expected, another of the same character is brought in by some unexpected circumstances. In fact, concealment of something to reveal something else seems to be one of the features of art. The rhetoricians have used this concept in their theory. It is *camatkṛti* which is regarded as *alaṁkāra*. In *vakrokti* also the same idea is used. It is certainly used in *dhvani*. But I think, it is also used in sculpture. I have seen a very beautiful sculpture of a woman in Salarjung Museum where the artist attempts to conceal the face of the woman by a marble screen through which the face is nevertheless visible. Such concealment gives a marvellous effect to the artefact.

Upamā and Types of Parameter

When we talk of art object, we are unconsciously comparing an art object with some standard or the other. This concept of standard is the concept of parameter, and usually when we pass a judgement of appreciation on the art object the parameter is in the background. When for example, we say that X's face is like the moon, the parameter is not the moon; parameter is the beauty and the moon is an instance of this parameter. Beauty is the *māna* and the moon which is an instance of this parameter is, therefore, called *upamāna* a substitute of the *māna* or the parameter. Similarly 'X' is not the *meya*. The *meya* is any art object. But this particular art object is called *upameya* — a substitute or an example of *meya*, and *māna*.

The *māna* is that by which we measure. And *meya* is that which is measured. Unless there is a possibility of measurement of the *meya* by the *māna*, *māna* will not act as a parameter. This possibility of measurement of the *meya* by the *māna* is due to some "similarity" between the *meya* and the *māna*. This similarity is rather hidden. It appears only in the form of *upamāna*. When we say that a certain lady's face is like the moon, the concept of beauty is not made explicit; but it is present, nevertheless. The *upameya* is, in some sense, identified with *māna* and because of this identification, the similarity or identity between the two things *upameya* and *upamāna* is not clearly stated. The paradigm here, is that of metaphor and in uses like *mukhakamala* or *mukhacandra* this is clearly seen. Both *mukha* and *kamala* or *mukha* and *candra* appear as belonging to the same language, but instead of *candra* or *kamala* if we substitute beautiful, which is the real measure, we will immediately see that the two concepts belong to different levels.

The parameters can be of different types. One kind of parameter, for example, may belong to the same class as the object which is measured but it may give us the last possible limit of that class, and so it attains the status of parameter. But a parameter may altogether have a different status, and may not belong to this world at all. It may be merely our appreciation of the object which belongs to this world. Beautiful is such a parameter. It may not have any characteristic of the object but when we say "great" or "grand" or *bhavya*, it may have the characteristics of the object; nevertheless, it may have quantitative excellence whereby it attains the status of parameter. When the object which is to be measured by a parameter has multiple dimensions it would follow that it could be subjected to different parameters. Finally, it may also be pointed out that whether the parameters are descriptive, i.e. belonging to the nature of the object itself, or evaluative, there may be a stage when we go from "the limit" to "limitless." Such parameters cannot be properly described. For, here the concept of parameter itself breaks.

In every art or craft varieties of parameters are thus used. If we are concerned with lyrical poetry, for example, we may talk of softness of the poetry or we may talk of the beauty of the poetry. But we may come across a certain creation which we cannot express in words and we look at it with wonder or awe and cannot express anything about it. Such parameters will be indescribable and could be compared with such concept as *Brahma* or *Parabrahma* (परब्रह्म). Indian philosophers have talked of some parameters in this way and they say that their appreciation is similar to the experience (or appreciation) of *Brahman* which cannot be described.

There could be other kinds of parameters also. Propriety and utility are parameters of this kind and if the art object has a social dimension then some moral or social parameters also would be required for describing, understanding and appreciating such objects.

There are various kinds of art objects. Till now, our paradigm was that of literary arts. But, we may, for instance, talk of sculpture or architecture. Here, we will have several parameters which could be used as measures, both evaluative and descriptive. Indian writers on architecture, for example, have talked of various such parameters. Here, we shall enumerate parameters from *Viśvakarmā Vāstuśāstram* (विश्वकर्मा वास्तुशास्त्रम्). In the case of building, for example, we require bricks and stones and wood, iron, nails, etc. All these are material. But, it will have to be found out whether it would be *useful*, durable and whether it would be the *appropriate* material to be used. It will thus have to be tested against some actual or ideal parameters. Where the concept of "better" occurs one has consciously or unconsciously made use of the concept of parameter. When we test the quality of gold, we test the gold on the touchstone by comparing our gold with the standard gold. Thus one material itself can, in some sense, be the parameter for determining the standard of other material. Thus, the concept of parameter is itself based on similarity (also difference) and the idea of relative betterness. This betterness may be of the same kind or of different kinds. In the books of architecture some parameters are given. In fact, they are not different from the material to be used.

The author of *Viśvakarmā Vāstuśāstram* very rightly says that one who doesn't have the knowledge of parameter is not competent to do any work.

मान-ज्ञान विहीनस्तु कर्मकर्तुं न शक्यते।

mānajñāna vihīnastu karmakartuṁ na śakyate ।

This parameter is to be gauged by a microscopic eye, because it does not belong to this world. That they belong to the *heavens* is told to us by our preceptor. It is very important to point out that the author of the work says that the relevant parameters should be used for the relevant sculptures and architecture. Unless the parameters are kept in mind, from actions neither beauty nor the strength (of the work) will be achieved.

मानाभावे क्रियादीनां। न शोभा न बलादिकम्।

mānābhāve kriyādīnāṁ । *na śobhā na balādikam* ।

12

Observations and Remarks

Distinction Between Rasa-Dhvani and Rasa-Siddhī

Rasa, saundarya and *ānanda* are some of the important concepts in Indian aesthetic theory. But, in the post-Jagannātha period, they are, more or less, regarded as equivalent, and a new *rasa* theory came into existence in the late nineteeth and twentieth century. But, to my mind, this was due to some confusion of thought. I think it is necessary to distinguish synonyms, symbol-meanings, sequential occurrents in the same process or series and completely different concepts where time sequence is irrelevant. Thus, the pair *rasa-dhvani* or the pair *rasa-siddhi* refer to sequential occurrents in the same series; and *rasa, saundarya* and *ānanda* refer to different stages though in the same series. Similarly *rasa* and *siddhi* refer to sequences in the same series, whereas *vācya* and *vācaka* refer to meanings and symbols. But none of them stands for equivalence or identity. All such distinctions were overlooked in the recent past.

This resulted in further confusion regarding the status and meaning of the word *rasa*. Earlier, it was *sthāyī bhāva* which was regarded as mental and *rasa* was the objective and public form given to it. But, with the new interpretation of the concept of *rasa* and its successive identification with beauty and happiness it, gradually, was reduced to the status that was subjective. This change has given rise to some further problems. In the following pages, I intend to study the conceptual geography of such problems.

Nature and Kinds of Judgement

The world in which man is born exists in its own right. This world at least at macro-level consists of beings and things. Beings are conscious but all of them are not self-conscious and, even the self-consciousness of those who are self-conscious also may be of varying degrees. Earlier, I have stated that there are man and the world. But, in the strict sense, man is also a part and parcel of this world. He is not outside the world. But on account of consciousness, he can project himself as outsider and view the world from outside. This gives rise to pluralism and epistemology. It goes without saying that it also results in continuous interaction amongst beings and also between beings and things. These interactions are mixed, they are cognitive, affective, conative and also evaluative. A man may observe certain other man's behaviour and remark that it is immoral. A man may also observe a certain thing or a certain fellow being — man or woman and say that he or she is handsome or beautiful. He may experience, for example, a sunset or cataract and remark that it is beautiful or sublime. His remarks may be either discursive and come within the purview of logic, psychology or physics or they may be evaluative and may be concerned with ethics or aesthetics. It is on account of his ability to pass such evaluative remarks that a judgement like, "something is beautiful or otherwise" can be made. I have earlier remarked that there are things in the world and they exist in their own right. They are physical or ontological, but, our remarks can be in the form of judgements and take the linguistic form. The words used, for example, in this context may take the form of substantives, adjectives, etc. This may delude us from differentiating between those elements which are part and parcel of things of the world and which are thrust by us on the things in the world. Of course, we do distinguish the area of ontology from that of epistemology, but there are sensitive elements in the epistemological areas which are not usually distinguished. Consider for example the case of pain or anger or any state of mind. What kind of existence does pain or anger have? Can it be said that they exist in the same way a stone exists? Can it be said that this wall is angry? If the wall is to be angry then the anger of the wall has to be felt by others, that is it has to be public. Without public and meaningful interaction between at least two men (or a man and the object) the objectivity of such states cannot be assessed or decided. There has to be a linguistic interaction also in regard to our experience. In the absence of such expressions statements like "wall is angry," have to be brushed aside. What happens when we say that a man "A" is angry. How do we become aware of his anger? Unless this anger is correlated with other symptoms, will it be possible for us to say that A is angry? That which is not expressed, regarding it we cannot make any remark. If there can be pure mental phenomena or states, they have to be felt and recognized by others. This cannot be done unless it is observed by "some" "second person." (Even when the same person says he is angry he as an observer is the second person). A self-conscious person can be the second person. This is not the case with things that are given to us or which are made of material given to us by nature. We can then say that tables, chairs, and anger, love, etc. exist; but they exist in two different ways.

If the logic in the above argument is correct, what would we say when we remark that something is beautiful? I think we will have to say that such judgements which pertain to beauty, etc. exist in man's world of awareness. I am not using the word "knowledge." I am using the word "awareness" because both beliefs and knowledge are covered by the word "awareness." I therefore, think that my judgements like, "this is beautiful" are determined by the orbit of epistemology, though it may be pertaining to some ontological areas. When I say that the sunset is beautiful, I get some stimulus from the heavenly object, the setting sun, and then remark that it is beautiful. But I may also say to B, "O, B, look at the sunset." "Don't you feel it is beautiful?" And he (B) may agree (or disagree) with me. How do I know that this sunset is beautiful? This may be known intuitively and I also know that it cannot be known in a discursive manner? How do I know that it cannot be known in a discursive manner? How do I know that it is beautiful? Perhaps because (and this "because" is not the because in ordinary sense) it appeals to me or to my heart. Appealing to me or to my heart is in some sense related to the sunset and its being beautiful. My judgement is based on my intuition and B's judgement is based on his intuition and may be we are able to compare our judgements because the word "beautiful" has some objective core and probably both of us use the word in the same sense. Does the same thing happen when I say to someone that this poetry is beautiful or this painting or this musical composition is beautiful? In all these cases, I carry my judgement to the other person. He understands me. He goes through the same kind of experience and then agrees (or disagrees) with me [that it is beautiful]. Here the procedure is that which is laid down by Buddhist logicians. My knowledge is *svārthajñāna* (स्वार्थज्ञान) and other's knowledge is *parārthajñāna* (परार्थज्ञान). (Buddhists would call *svarthānumāna* (स्वार्थानुमान) and *parārthānumāna* (परार्थानुमान).) Here, I am assuming that the other person is going through the same kind of experience. But although we assume such things, "such things" might not happen. Once a student of mine presented to me a painting of an ancient Egyptian lady. I thought it was beautiful and hung it in my lounge. When a certain senior colleague of mine saw the same, he spontaneously remarked that it was "ugly." He judged it in the way we judge a woman as beautiful or otherwise. Evidently, the features painted in the portrait were of an ugly woman. If the portrait had presented beautiful features and gait, etc. the painting would have been regarded by him as beautiful. But in painting if a painter paints an ugly old man or woman do we not say that it is beautiful and artistic? Some kind of agreement has to be reached between the painter's intention and our judgement. Unless one is in agreement with the painter and, in some sense, knows his intentions and thinks that there is the agreement between his intentions and what he has depicted we would not be able to say that it is beautiful. The same is the case with poetry. In fact, the case of poetry is far more complicated than the case of painting. But the criterion that something is beautiful in both the cases is my agreement with the artists. The ugly woman would not be beautiful but the painting of the ugly woman could be beautiful because there is an agreement between what the artist intends and what I understand from what is exhibited. What he exhibits becomes objective and is known to others and this paves the way for agreement between the artist and the observer. Of course, there are a few variations here and there. For example, in dramatic performance, someone plays "Rāma." Neither the actor nor the spectator knows the actual traits of the actual Rāma. His traits are unknown. But we are not concerned here with his specific characteristics. We are concerned with general characteristics. Bharata suggests this by the phrase *sāmānya-guṇa-yoga* (सामान्य-गुण योग) and Bhaṭṭanāyaka and Abhinavagupta use the word *sādhāraṇīkaraṇa* (साधारणीकरण) for this (as against *viśeṣīkaraṇa*, विशेषीकरण). The beauty of a certain art object is then based on such agreement about the art object between the artist and the spectator. This agreement is something which is achieved by the spectator's intuition while he is evaluating. At least such an agreement is assumed in such situations.

I have used the word agreement in regard to what occurs to the artist and the appreciation by the spectators or readers. But can we be certain about the agreement between the artist and the spectator or the reader? This cannot be verified. So, although we talk of agreement it can only be of the nature of appeal, re: the creation of the artist. If what the artist creates appeals to the spectator or reader that is enough. So far as the agreement part is concerned it cannot be measured; but we can be certain whether the art object appeals or not. In the case of natural object like the sunset there is direct experience of the beautiful, but in the case of art object like poetry, drama or painting the stress is on the appeal, and if it is agreeable, the art object is regarded as beautiful. In the case of art object there is in fact a double appeal; something appeals to the artist and also appeals to the spectators or readers. If the experience is appealing to an artist and induces him to create, and what is created is appealing to the appreciator then the appreciator calls it beautiful. Appealing to the heart seems to be the basic criterion of appreciation re: something beautiful, sublime, etc. There does not seem to be another criterion by which we can judge something as beautiful. Evaluating something is dependent on our appeal only. This is, I think, recognized by Bharata when he talks of *hṛdayasaṁvāda* and uses the phrase *hṛdayasaṁvādī* (which appeals to the heart). Bharata uses the phrase, *yo 'rtho hṛdayasaṁvādī* (योऽर्थो हृदयसंवादी). Here the word *artha* is ambiguous. *Artha* stands for meaning (the bearer of the meaning and also the artistic intention). But all these senses have something common and when we talk of art perhaps all these senses are equally important. If it is literary art, *artha* could mean "meaning." If it is plastic art it could mean "object." But in every case of art, intention of artist and his isomorphic correspondence with the appreciator has to be taken into account and from this point of view the verse in the seventh *adhyāya* of *Naṭyaśāstra* should be interpreted. The verse is as follows.

योऽर्थो हृदयसंवादी तस्य भावो रसोद्भवः ।
शरीरं व्याप्यते तेन शुष्कं काष्ठमिवाग्निना ॥

yo 'rtho hṛdayasaṁvādī tasya-bhāvo rasodbhavaḥ ।
śarīraṁ vyāpyate tena śuṣkaṁ kāṣṭhamivāgninā ॥ — *NŚ* 7.7

I think this verse fully illustrates the art process.

The creative stimulus starts from *sthāyī bhāva*. It is interpreted as feelings, emotions or sentiments (also instincts) by some writers but this does not appear to be the case. *Sthāyī bhāva* only means some mental state or a complex of mental states. I should regard it as a quantum of experience which an artist has. *Sthāyi bhāva* is called *cittavṛttiviśeṣa* (चित्तवृत्तिविशेष) (some specific states of *citta*). If these experiences or mental states which are private (as they belong to the experiencer) are to be transformed into an art object, they would have to be made public, that is, they would have to get transformed and appear in a form which could be experienced by more than one individual. They would have to take either some linguistic or object form, but while taking such a form the intent of the *sthāyī bhāva* which is also the message of the artist and which induced him to create an artefact would have to be manifested. Thus, *sthāyī bhāva* would have to be converted into a form with two co-ordinates: one represented by medium and the other represented by a message. It would be like a living being where livingness or soul and body cannot be separated, though they could be distinguished. The medium-cum-message would be a transformation of *sthāyī bhāva* and would pass from stage to stage (if necessary). This happens in painting, music, poetry and drama. It may be pointed out that even under natural conditions, this happens. How do I know that someone is angry? If it is just a mental state nobody would ever know it. But it gets expressed in its bodily form and appears in quivering of lips, redness of cheeks, frowning and a peculiar utterance of words, walking style and various gestures. In fact, these are known as *anubhāva*s and *vyabhicārī bhāva*s and these are used in acting. But they are also used in different arts like poetry, painting and sculpture. The drama producers use these in acting. In fact, *abhinaya* means this. It literally means that, that which takes us (or the actors) from one stage to another.

यस्मात् प्रयोगं नयति तस्मात् अभिनयः स्मृतः ।

yasmāt prayogaṁ nayati tasmāt abhinayaḥ smṛtaḥ । — *NŚ* 8.6[1]

A certain mental state is cognized by us on account of *abhinaya*. It is not just the acting but the natural transformation also. When a painter paints, he intends to paint a certain figure, but the actual painting shows forms of lines, points and colours. Similarly, those lines and colours express certain gestalts of expressions and are understood as gestures, etc. Thus the object of painting is accomplished. Similar is the case in every art.

The mental states are private unless they are made public, i.e. objectified. Objectification standardizes the mental states and gives them some kind of objective standard. On account of this change they can be measured. Measurement implies parameters as well as (some kind of) uniformity, which is objective. Unless we have these, we cannot judge anything as good or bad, beautiful or otherwise. The most important stage

1. Another reading is as follows —
yasmat padārthān nayati tasmāt abhinayaḥ smṛtaḥ (यस्मात् पदार्थान् नयति तस्मात् अभिनयः स्मृतः).* I should like to coin such a technical word.

in this connection is a transformation from something, which is restricted to a single mind or which is subjective, to something which is objective and public. Even when we talk of psychological states we are able to do so by inferring them back from the expressed objective states. We further infer that the basic psychological states also would be similar in different individuals. In this process the mental states have to flow from one person to another and that which is private has to become public. The concept of *rasa* indicates this process. I think, this was the earlier meaning of *rasa*, and it indicated flow, liquid, etc. It is only the objective or public form which can be tested. It can become *āsvādya* and can be appreciated.

Such transformation will have two layers, one would be signified by medium, the other by message. It is two in one. I therefore take it that the original basic experience now passes through another stage and assumes either material form or a linguistic form (i.e. some kind of bodily form). This form is due to *rasa*.

तस्य भावो रसोद्भवः ।

tasya bhāvo rasodbhavaḥ । — *NŚ* 7.7

Its form or manifestation is due to *rasa*.

In this way that which is mental now becomes objective in some sense. This transformation is in the form of a process and depends on the capacity of the *conductor*. If there is some insularity or if there is no proper conduction, the process will not be accomplished. This I think is explained in *Nāṭyaśāstra* in the stanza:

शरीरम् व्याप्यते तेन शुष्कम् काष्ठमिवाग्निना ।

śarīram vyāpyate tena śuṣkam kāṣṭhamivāgninā ॥

According to me *tena* refers to *sthāyī bhāva* or message which takes the form of and is conducted through the medium.

The efficiency of carrying out this transformation is expressed in the form of simile, *śuṣkam kāṣṭhamivāgninā* (शुष्कम् काष्ठमिवाग्निना) (just as the dry firewood is completely and quickly enveloped by fire). Just as the dry firewood is a good conductor of fire and quickly envelops the whole body of the dry wood and makes a quick transition possible, similarly the *sthāyī bhāva* gets transformed into *rasa* and *rasa* again into *hṛdayasaṁvādībhāva*. In those days, when the properties of electricity were not known Bharata or his predecessors had to use the simile of dry firewood and fire enveloping the body, but this can now be explained in more modern idiom by using the example of electricity. Electricity can pass from one pole to another, only if the circuit is complete. This completion of circuit is suggested by *saṁvāditva* of *hṛdayasaṁvāditva* (that is, passing from one heart to another heart, the heart of artist to that of the appreciator) and the ability of passing depends on the medium. If the conductor is good, circuit is completed immediately but if there is obstruction or insularity then the object is not accomplished. For electric current to pass we require a proper conductor and also an electrical pressure itself. In the case of art it is supplied by the medium and intention of the artist (or *sthāyī bhāva*), but it has to have two manifestations, one in the form of message and the other in the form of medium. When this transformation is complete the spectator or the reader is able to appreciate it and the stimulus of the message creates in him certain reactions which might lead to enjoyment, happiness and even misery. This is Bharata's theory of drama. But it is applicable to all arts and therefore in the course of time it was applied to arts ranging from poetry and music to architecture.

Nature of Art

I assume that art is for enjoyment. I believe this is an intuitive proposition. But, there are many other things which are for enjoyment. One may say that art consists in *creating* the enjoyments. Other enjoyments are for simply experiencing and appreciating. They are created by nature. A scenic landscape, a sunset, an expanse of water may be given as instances. Art is created by man, experienced by man and also appreciated by man. But, this also does not seem to be the differentia of art. For any theoretical research, inventing something new, discovering something new satisfies the conditions attributed to art. Sex activity of humans leading to furtherance of race also satisfies these conditions. In fact, that is the basic human activity and all other creative activities are only metaphorical, that is, based on the model assumed from the basic sex activity. Man enjoys the sex activity for, in some sense, it is for him a self-conscious activity. He is fully aware of what he wants and does. Of course, if other animals are also equally self-conscious of what they want and what they do, their enjoyment would be of the same kind and complexity. In fact, it could be said that sex activity is a paradigm or some kind of parameter of enjoyment. That is perhaps the reason why the Vedāntins have expressed the *Brahman*-realization in terms of co-habitation with thousand times greater intensity. So the definition of art could not be given in terms of just creativity. Nevertheless, it would be a necessary condition of art and in trying to understand the nature of this activity of creativity one might be able to distinguish the art from other activities. The analysis may lead to further refinement of our understanding of the nature of art. In fact, the history of art is the history of the human attempts towards such refinement.

Let me ask what art is. Although we use the word "art" in singular, there are *different* arts. Indian tradition talks of fourteen types of *knowledge* or achievements and sixty-four types of arts. In fact, many of these fourteen *vidyās* would have to be classified under arts and skills, and several of the sixty-four *kalās* would be out of the locus of the present concept of art. They would be merely crafts. However, in all these 78 types (14+64) there is one thing common. In the strict sense of the term they are not just "creating." They are *re-creating*. The material or the stuff used in this process is that of *human experience*, one might receive from the moment of one's birth and so long as one is living. The experience that man receives is stored from time to time as layers of experience units, one over the other, but the total experience is a process of continuous symbiosis. This stored experience is in the physical, physiological or electromagnetic form, and may be called memory. When it is expressed, it is thought to be mental. The expression may be due to some (inside or outside) stimulus or reaction, may be in the form of thought or language and might further take some objective form, some concrete form, using some material from the outside world. One art is distinguished from another art on account of these varieties of material used and the medium. Again the experience that is stored in our memory need not be of one type. Also, what is reproduced is a *replica* (*kalā* literally means a replica) of what one has experienced and what is modified by our experience and personality. So it is necessary to realize that the contents of our memory are not samples of one kind. They could not be, for example, just emotional, or just cognitive; they would be as complex as human life is. But this complex memory-material is the raw material for further processing and producing them in the form of finished goods. This processing could be of various types and these variations would give birth to different arts. This road from memory to the actualization of art-objects is also paved with several complexities. It will be marked by some flow, some dynamism and the flow will have some constituents which will flow from one place to another. The flow will indicate some urge, some vitality and would help the transformation from one form to another, from something material to something concrete, visual, auditory, *factual,* etc. or all together. It is this transformation of form which makes them objective and capable of being experienced by others. It is this transformation which gives them the capacity to express and capacity to communicate. But, the transformation is effected on account of the urge of the artist. This urge leads him from point to point and helps him "achieve" the creative process. Herein lies the creativity of the artist. Each step in this process, he enjoys, and gets satisfaction when the process is completed. This process and its resultants are also complex. First there is transformation from something mental to non-mental. The resultant "non-mental" may be of different material or stuff. The material might take different kinds of forms and each form may give rise to varieties of shapes, etc. The medium of their expression may also differ from art to art. Nevertheless it would be the same thought, "expressed" in different languages, mediums, etc. This urge to transform is at the back of the ability of the art object to express itself and communicate. It should be remembered that the whole process is very complicated and cannot just be stated in terms of medium or language or material. However, the same experience (admitting the individual variation) in the hands of a painter, would take the form of painting, in the hands of a poet a form of poetry and in the hands of a dancer or a musician a form of dance or music performance. Similarly, the source of similar experience of two painters or two poets may take different forms. Nay, even an artist at two different points of time may look at the experience in a different way. Milton's two poems L'Allegro (1632) and Ill Penseroso (1637) are instances of such creations. This attitude of the artist is bound to have a print on the art object.

The accomplished art object is no more an inmate of the artist's mind or memory. It can be experienced by anybody, perceived by anybody. The only point is whether it can be perceived as art object by everybody and in the same manner. To my mind the answer is that it cannot be a straight "Yes" or "No." Human beings also are of various types. And to know an art object is different from knowing an object.[2] To know an object as a piece of art is a specific activity and everyone might not have enough attainment to accomplish it. And even if one has ability to appreciate an art object, he might not have the point of view of the artist. All this is possible. This will certainly make the communication complicated and blurred. Nevertheless, the communication will not be entirely obstructed.

Have I explained the process of creativity in arts? I think in a way I have. But, I feel, no one can really explain the whole procedure of artistic creation; for, every element in artistic creativity is not likely to be identical in every art. Staging of a drama is a process which can be perceived and organized *consciously* but composing a poem cannot be so organized. One cannot go into steps in the field of organization, the poet or a litterateur takes or comes across in achieving the theme of a poem or novel. It may be that good deal of it might have been worked out at the unconscious or subconscious level. So the process of creation of poetic art cannot be completely explained. But, the process of transformation of mental into

2. Bharata discusses the concept of *prekṣaka* in *Nāṭyaśāstra* Chapter 27, verse 51-53. The main quality of the spectator is that he must be sympathetic to what he observed.

यस्तुस्टे तुष्टिमायानि शोके शोकमुपैतिच ।
दैन्ये दीनत्वमभ्येति स नाट्ये प्रेक्षकः स्मृतः ॥

yastuṣṭe tuṣṭimāyāni śoke śokamupaitica ।
dainye dīnatvamabhyeti sa nāṭye prekṣakaḥ smṛtaḥ ॥ — *NŚ* 27.52

non-mental or the private into public which starts with the artist and ends with the art object is common to all arts. At each step of such creation the artist is consciously or unconsciously enjoying. When the art object is complete and the spectator or hearer (audience) also enjoys the art-object, can this enjoyment of the spectator, etc. be compared to the enjoyment of the artist? I think it is not comparable. For, whether the enjoyment is of the artist or the appreciator, it is not enjoyment *qua* enjoyment. Artist's enjoyment is a part of the total complex of creativity-cum-enjoyment. The appreciator's enjoyment is a part of a different whole, understanding the art-object-cum-enjoyment. It is a different enjoyment arising in a different context, and of a different concept. Indian writers say that at the back of both these enjoyments there is *pratibhā* — a flash. But they distinguish between two types of *pratibhā*, creative or *kārayitrī* and cognitive or *bhāvayitrī*. There will be one more difference in the two types of enjoyment. The first enjoyment is connected with the whole process of creation, there may be steps in it from stage to stage. In the case of the appreciator he is confronted with the end-product. Further the appreciator is *vividly* self-conscious. The artist may be self-conscious, but he is completely absorbed in his creativity. He is not looking at it as a third person. He is a part of the process. So his action and his consciousness of his action cannot be looked at in isolation.[3]

One more word. The first process proceeds from the subjective to the objective. In this process, thought or something mental is getting transformed to something objective. In the

3. Further, if the artist is to enjoy the completed art object as an appreciator, even then the enjoyment would be modified by the curiosity he would have as to how the others appreciate his art. Bhavabhūti's remark: *utpaddyatesati mama ko 'pi samāna dharmā* (उत्पद्यतेसति मम कोऽपि समान धर्मा) is very significant in this context.

second process something objective is tending to become subjective. Also one must distinguish art object as symbol and the art object as meaning or intention. But the process from the "mental" to art object is both the process of symbolization as also that of the retaining of intention. This process is common to all arts, and could be given one name. From the art history of India it becomes clear that the name *rasa* became current for this process. The word is able to express this richness of complexity than can be expressed by *śabda*, *rūpa*, *sparśa* or *gandha*. That is perhaps the reason why the word which was originally used in the context of stage drama began finally to dominate all arts. Writers like Jagannātha distinguished between *śabda* and *rasa* and used the word *śabda* in the definition of poetry; but, in order to depict the process of objectification and, particularly, the dynamism and flow in the process used the word *rasa* and called his work *Rasagaṅgādhara* (रसगंगाधर). The word *śabda* which is *vācaka* as pointed out earlier, has its twin or counterpart in *vācya* (which may be of various varieties). This *vācya* stands for meaning which might again be of various types. It can also be neutral or beautiful. If the *vācaka* points to *vācya* which is qualified with beauty, then alone the symbol stands for poetry (or with the extension of meaning for art).

Nature of Appreciation

We see a certain landscape, we observe the sunset, we come across a woman. We are agreeably moved. Such objects attract us and we say they are beautiful. They are not created by any human agency. No human intention is involved in the creation of these objects which we perceive or sense. (The woman is also not an exception.) They are given to us. On the other hand our act of sensing or knowing starts with me and the process of appreciation ends in me. But this phenomenon is also present before *us*. When I say, "present before *us*" it can be present before me alone and it need not be before me, in the sense that it is spatially distant and situated outside me. But, if it is an inhabitant of my mind, it would be my idea, my dream and would be incapable of being experienced by individuals other than me. Nevertheless, the object that is sensed and appreciated would be (ideally) different from my sensing and appreciating. The existence and appreciation of such objects will be confined to me alone. But, in the case of objects like the sunset, a landscape or a woman, the case is otherwise. They can be known (and, perhaps, appreciated) by anybody. For, they have acquired an objective form, may be of more or less duration. In all these above cases, I have assumed that the knowing and appreciating starts with me and ends with me. The knower or the appreciator is the same man. It is, of course, possible that we may compare our notes with others and be satisfied that the experience of others is also similar to ours. But, here too, it is taken for granted that each one's experience is confined to himself.

But, like the sunset or a landscape or a woman, if one's experience can assume an objective form, then it can also be experienced and appreciated. The art activity (like many other scientific activities) consists in giving such objective forms. For, essentially, creating an art object is like inventing something (new). This process starts in the mind of the artist, whether he is a painter or a poet or dramatist and takes some objective form, whether it is of the nature of language or any kind of art object. Creation of an art object is the creation of a medium, a conductor through which the current of the idea of the artist can pass successfully. The current (or message) and the medium are different. But in most cases they cannot be separated. Without the proper medium or conductor the current or the message would not pass. (Instead of a conductor, there would be only some insulator.) The art activity mainly consists in giving appropriate medium to the idea of the artist, and allows the current to pass successfully. If the message successfully reaches the appreciator and the rapport is established (or supposed to be established) between the artist and the appreciator, the artist is successful in his mission. The problems of art are, therefore, mainly concerned with the medium, with giving the idea of the artist an objective form. When the message reaches the appreciator and we say that the rapport is established, the idea of the artist is, so to say, measured by a parameter present in the mind of the appreciator. The activity of measuring is present all through. In fact, it is present even while the idea is taking the objective form. Assuming the objective form is perhaps the most important step in art activity. I think the idea of the artist is mental. Similar is the case with a parameter, which is objectively non-existing. The most important thing is to give the idea the objective form, which is corrected from moment to moment by the parameter. The whole process of art creation, I think, is explained in the seventh chapter of *Nāṭyaśāstra*.

योऽर्थो हृदयसंवादी तस्य भावो रसोद्भवः।
शरीरं व्याप्यते तेन शुष्कं काष्ठमिवाग्निना।

yo 'rtho hṛdayasaṁvādī tasya bhāvo rasodbhavaḥ ।
śarīram vyāpyate tena śuṣkaṁ kāṣṭhamivāgninā ॥

Nature of Beautiful

Sometimes when we see some natural or art object we pass a remark that it is beautiful. How are we to understand this "beautiful"? Philosophers think that it is a property of the object. Some philosophers even distinguish it from the primary or secondary qualities and regard it as a tertiary quality. Alexander, for example, thinks so. Suppose someone asks a question, "why is this object beautiful"? Philosophers may answer this question by saying "because. . . ." That is, they try to bring out a *causal* relationship between the "cause" and the objects being beautiful. Some philosophers even think that *to be beautiful* means to be proportionate, to be blended with something else, harmonious, symmetrical, showing a certain contrast or balance. Such philosophers try to formulate the rules "about beauty." For example, they would say that if the object followed a certain pattern prescribed by them then that object would be beautiful. Here, their paradigm seems to be that of moral or legal behaviour. Just as we can formulate a rule that nobody should trespass or if any one trespassed he would be prosecuted, similarly, we could also formulate a rule which would supply criteria for regarding something as beautiful. In a way, if we observe some particular (beautiful) thing, we could certainly say that what we have observed is beautiful. But, are we sure that between what we observe and beautiful there is either a causal relation (or even an identity relation). I am inclined to think that none of these relations can possibly exist between these two phenomena. My reason for thinking so is that we can pass a *judgement* on a certain object, whether it is beautiful or not, but we cannot fomulate a *rule* that such and such a thing would be beautiful in the absence of that thing. Of course, although one might not be able to define or conceptualize the object, one might be able to picture the object, plan the object, "observe" some imaginary object and judge it as beautiful. The relation between the actual and/or imaginary object and beautiful is not that of either causality or identity.

I may point out that while dealing with inference Dharmakīrti observes that inference is of two types — (1) *svabhāvānumāna* (स्वभावानुमान) and (2) *kāryānumāna* (कार्यानुमान), that which is based on identity relation and that which is based on casual relation. These two relations he named as *tādātmya* (तादात्म्य) and *tadutpati* (तदुत्पत्ति) and the inferences based on these two were named by him as *svabhāvānumāna* and *kāryānumāna*. However, the relationship between the object and our judgement on it, that it is beautiful, does not follow any of these types. To explain this I may take resort to a third type. Buddha says that "Everything in the world is misery." The problem then is how to remove misery. He does not use a causal model for this. Instead of *kāraṇa* (कारण) or *svabhāva* (स्वभाव) or *tādātmya* (तादात्म्य) he uses the concept of *nidāna* (निदान) and calls his explanation model, *dvādaśanidāna* (द्वादशनिदान). It is a model used by physicians to diagnose a certain disease from the symptoms observable. When the doctor says that somebody is suffering from, say, tuberculosis, he has not given the cause of the disease. He has identified (explained) the disease on the basis of some symptoms. If we go to the genesis of the disease, we might be required to go to the bacteria which caused the disease. That would be a process of finding out the cause. Diagnosing something is not necessarily finding out the cause. When we say that something is beautiful, we are only observing the object and "diagnosing" it as beautiful. This diagnosing is something like "seeing" the phenomenon under a "microscope," with this difference that the microscope gives us only a quantitative magnification and does not give us the qualitative or, better still, aesthetic dimension. When we observe a certain object under a "human microscope," this microscope adds something to it and we call it beautiful. Perhaps, the nearest approximation to it would be that of a symbol and the meaning of a symbol. When we observe certain symbols or signs, we understand by that some meaning. Meaning is something which "emanates" from the symbol and overpowers in a flash; perhaps, because one who uses the symbols has ability to acquaint us with the flash. The speaker codifies his intention in the symbol and communicates what is in his mind. It may not be that, what the speaker intends to communicate is actually communicated. But, that is strictly irrelevant for our purpose. Ordinarily, when we understand the relationship between the symbol and the meaning, we ignore the subjectivity or the speaker's shadow fallen on the symbol. Encoding is objectifying and in such encoding the speaker is practically ignored. Our ordinary meanings, which we obtain from symbols are thus bereft of subjectivity. They are like the blood-plasma, which we may classify into different groups but we are not concerned whether it is the blood of A or B or C. But, while observing some meaning, we colour it with our own judgement. The impression of the observer is not eliminated from such judgements. The meaning, which is a flash, is or could be subjected to further flashes and such succeeding flashes or at least some of them could go by the name beautiful. In ordinary symbol-meaning relationship, the relationship which is triadic (because the third element is the intention of the speaker) tends to become diadic (for we get used to ignoring the intention part). But, when we judge something as beautiful, this diadic relation again becomes a triadic relation. The observer becomes one of the relata in this relationship. However, the relationship that is manifested in the form of a judgement that "it is beautiful" is still objective, as it is in regard to the object and not in regard to the observer himself. Suppose the observer as a consequence of seeing the "beautiful" object (or its opposite) feels happy (or miserable) about the object then it would depict the *state* (that is mental) of the observer and not the object. That would be a further reaction and it would be subjective. We can, therefore, say that the judgement that something is beautiful is objective judgement and that someone is happy or miserable is subjective. They cannot be equated.

In Indian languages, that something is beautiful is described by words like *cāru, sundara, manojña, lāvaṇyavatī, ramaṇīyā, rūpavatī*, etc. No author on art has ever discussed the status of these concepts. They are merely taken for granted. They are taken to be of the nature of *pratīti, sphoṭa* or flash. A writer on Sthāpatya Śāstra describes how a building is to be built. How many pillars, there should be, what should be the measurement of these pillars, etc. A writer on dance would describe the *mudrā* and *abhinaya* and the poses of *aṅga, pratyaṅga* and *upāṅga* and the movements of different parts of the body. A writer on music would discuss the *laya*, the *tāla*, the *sura* (*svara*) the *rāga* and the style, the volume, etc. Similar is the case with a painter. But, none of them discusses the status of beauty. All of them take it for granted that if certain parameters are adhered to *the* beauty would automatically follow. The model is, according to me, that of word and meaning. Or one may also say that the aesthetic theory is merely an extended theory of symbol and meaning, for it is a theory of *pratīti*. Perhaps, it would be desirable to point out what Pippalāda of *Vāstusūtropaniṣad* says on the point. He says that the artist or architect can bring the picture of his design before his mind's eye and that makes it possible to decide whether the projected design is beautiful or not — *dhyāna-prayoge rūpa sauṣṭhavaṁ bhavati* (ध्यानप्रयोगे रूप-सौष्ठवं भवति, *VS*, 4.5-14.3).[4]

Beauty and Artistic Communications

Indian writers on *śilpa* and *sthāpatya*, unlike the authors on poetics, do not talk of evaluative parameters like beauty. They only talk of the constituent conditions, as to how the artefact or aesthetic object is to be created. They do not discuss what

---

4. *dhyānaprayoge rūpasauṣṭhavam bhavati* (ध्यानप्रयोगे रुप-सौष्ठवम् भवति, 14.3 *Vāstusūtropaniṣad*).

are the concepts behind their creations which make them art objects, which are beautiful or sublime. They do not talk of concepts like beautiful and sublime. Even the writers on music do not talk of these concepts. However, in the *Vāstuśāstram* of Viśvakarmā, I came across a quotation which says that unless the artist has some parameter (in his mind) the art object (*vastu*, वस्तु) will neither have strength nor beauty.[5] From this one can conclude that whether they have expressedly stated or not about the evaluative standards they must certainly have the visualization or image of beauty in their mind. In the absence of such a thing it would be impossible for a musician to create a composition and present it, for a painter to draw a definite picture (although in the process of painting, the original idea may undergo a change) and for a *śilpī* or architect to imagine the beauty of his future creation. I feel that values or parameters like beauty are certainly before his eyes. He is certainly conscious of them. But he cannot have a certain common concept of beauty. If he is a painter or a sculptor he can certainly imagine a pattern and bring it before his mind's eye and he can evaluate that pattern. If he is satisfied with his evaluation he would give it an objective form, otherwise he would reject it. From this I should like to conclude that artistic communication proceeds not by using the concept but by using images. The images can be many but they would have one characteristic, viz., they should appear beautiful. It would be, as Bharata puts it, *hṛdayasaṁvādī*, i.e. agreeable to two or more hearts. That is, perhaps, the reason why writers of these subjects do not explicitly consider the parameters which are aesthetic.

---

5. *Viśvakarmā Vāstusūtra* :
mānābhāve kriyādīnām na śobhā no balādikam (मानाभावे क्रियादीनाम् न शोभा नो बलादिकम्).

Concepts are evolved in human life, for, usually without them it would be difficult to communicate. Concepts are abstractions of experience. They are, so to say, symbolic representations of experience. If there is a thing then we abstract the different features of the things and call them qualities, universals, classes, etc. These abstractions are common to different particulars and so they can be used for describing different particulars. Take for example, the word "flower." There is nothing like "a flower" in the world; each flower is a particular flower — a lotus, a rose, a daffodil, but flowerness is taken away from these different flowers and made into a unit for the sake of communication. Again, in the roses there may be white roses, red roses, yellow roses, the natural roses. But, we can think of different colours and its symbolic representation (in the form of word) not only for describing the roses but for several other things. We can also think of several shades of red and in short in this way communication becomes possible.

We also use the word beautiful while passing such a judgement as *"X is beautiful"* and so on. Is beautiful a concept? Kant said, it is not. I think Kant is right. Beautiful and a few other words concerning judgements look like concepts but they are not concepts. Kant has discussed this in his *Critique of Judgement*. I have also discussed it as to why beautiful cannot be regarded as a concept. But a question arises as to how communication without concept is possible? I think, though I would not like to generalize my statement, the aesthetic communication can be done without concepts. The reason seems to be the following. First, concepts can be used only where language is the medium of the communication. Every art is language-like but is not a language. So we will have to classify art into (1) where language is used and (2) where language is not used. But, in both the cases art will be symbolic representation of experience. So, every concept would be a symbol but every symbol would not be a concept. I should agree that in the expression of art there is a symbolic representation of experience, there is a reconstruction of experience. Artistic creation means such a reconstruction. In this representation, not the symbols but some things which stand as bearers of the symbol are used. These bearers of the symbol are also symbols, but they are not the concepts. Some kind of material is used for creating an artefact, for creating a model, for reconstructing experience like a concrete model, the artefact or the art object. But this material that is concrete (or a picture of concrete something) is not abstract (even an abstract art is not an exception). Here there is a representation, a symbolization but not a conceptualization, not an abstraction. In this re-construction the artefact, which is a medium for communication, itself becomes the object of appreciation. Although the artefact may be a symbol for indicating the intentions of the artist it is the symbol which is appreciated. We do not say that the intentions of the artist are beautiful, we say that the art object is beautiful. The difference or distinction between the symbol and the bearer of the symbol vanishes here. The symbolic whole itself becomes the concrete object; it becomes the bearer of itself. This is so even where language is used. The poetry or drama itself becomes the art object. It becomes both a means of communication as well as an end in itself. Just as an individual becomes a proto-universe on account of the awareness; similarly, the art object also becomes a proto-universe. It begins to have individuality and uniqueness. It exists in its own right as an individual and is enjoyed for its own sake. It communicates no doubt but it also becomes incarnation of all the intentions. It no more remains a symbolic representation, it attains the status of an object which presents itself in its own right. It becomes an object of perception; it becomes *vāstutantra* (वास्तुतंत्र) and it is for this reason that the concepts are no more required for this communication. If you appreciate this object as beautiful or otherwise your judgement also becomes a kind of object, not through which, but about which, you communicate. When things or words are used for "communicating about" they no more are, or remain, concepts. Only when we "communicate through," concepts are required. When we are talking of fire, fire is a concept and the word fire is a symbol which indicates that concept. But when we are talking about the word "fire" itself, neither is the word "fire" a concept nor does it indicate a concept. So also is the case with the word beautiful, or any word or image which behaves as a parameter.

Ryle once said that investigation about the nature of meaning is the disease from which philosophers of this century are suffering. The reason, perhaps, for making this remark is that philosophers of later nineteenth century and early twentieth century tried to investigate hectically the nature and status of meaning. In a way Meinong and Husserl, Frege and Russell asked the question about meaning, and the problem of philosophers of the Vienna Circle, with their insistence on the principle of verifiability, was centered around the problem of meaning. Early Wittgenstein was also overpowered by the same problem. Richards and Ogden wrote a book entitled *Meaning of Meaning*. These investigations led people like Wittgenstein and Ryle to advise people not to ask the question about meaning or define meaning but rather find out how we use the words. Grammarians talk about the change in usages of words, and pragmatists and utilitarians talked about the utility (of words). On the face of it, usage, utility and use appear to be belonging to the same species but there is indeed a difference. Usages and utility presuppose use. Whether it is one usage or another, it is still a use. Perhaps, the ancient

Indian grammar philosophers had recognized this. They had said that whereas we can distinguish between a structure and function of a pot we cannot distinguish the structure and the function of a word. Patañjali says that "If you want a pot you'll go to a pot maker and say "make me a pot so that I can use it for such and such a purpose." But if you want a word you don't go to a maker of the words (grammarian) and say to him "make me a word so that I can use it for such and such a purpose." The word and its use are not different. "Frege's distinction between Sinn and Bedeutung or Mill's distinction between denotation and connotation are also concerned with the problem of meaning. When we ask for use of a certain word, we are in a way, ignoring the bearer of a word. The use of a word is concerned with the sense of a word or rather, the sense of a word is concerned with the use of a word and it may be that each word may not have a bearer. The words like "ghost" *śaśaśṛṅga* of logical connectives like "and," "or" and "if then," do not denote anything. Patañjali the author of *Mahābhāṣya* and others in the East cognized this. Patañjali of *Yogasūtra* also cognizes this and gives the name *vikalpa* to such words which do not have bearers, *śabdajñānānupāti-vastuśūnyo vikalpaḥ* (शब्दज्ञानानुपाति-वस्तुशून्यो विकल्पः).

But, he further recognizes that words may have a bearer and/or a meaning (without a bearer) and it is not proper to identify the meaning and the bearer. *Śabdārtha pratyayānām itaretarādhyāsāt saṅkaraḥ* (शब्दार्थ प्रत्ययानाम् इतरेतराध्यासात् संकरः). This is refutation of the theory that meaning is concerned only with the bearer. Indian *alaṅkārins* talk of *vācya* and *vācaka*. *Vācaka* stands for a word or some sign signifying some *vācya* but *vācya* may not be a bearer but only that which the *vācaka* signifies.

But, the problem still remains as to what meaning is. Usually, when we use a word, we use a certain sign, oral or written. This oral or written sign acts as a medium for something that is conveyed. Ordinarily, we think there is a diadic relation between the sign and that which is signified. But, the word and what it signifies has a relation with a self-conscious living being. If there were no living beings the whole inquiry regarding the sign and other meanings would be meaningless and irrelevant. So, perhaps, one could say that the relationship between the word and its meaning is not diadic but triadic. The intention of the user is also imprinted on the sign although it is not directly felt. The relationship of a word and its meaning is, therefore, a game played by someone with the help of a sign and that which is experienced through the sign. Nevertheless, it cannot be denied that the sign reveals something, may be due to constant practice or tradition. So, the problem of meaning has two important prongs, one concerned with the user's intention and the other concerned with the sign revealing something. It may not reveal some things, some bearer always. But, it may reveal atleast some sense. The problem of meaning is, therefore, concerned with the relationship of symbol, the intention of the user and the sense that is conveyed. The sense that is conveyed may have its origin in the intention of the user but the subjectivity that is involved, gradually lapses in the background and what we get is some direct revelation, some oozing of "meaning" from the symbol itself. If we take a more complex situation what I want to say would be clear. A poet may write a certain poem and the reader may appreciate it. But, it is not necessary that there should be one-to-one correspondence between the thought of the poet and the understanding of the reader, the possibility of (gradual) transition from subjectivity to non-subjectivity. The person who uses the words or signs to convey something, therefore, acts more or less as a catalytic agent only; and for all practical purposes, we can regard this relation between the symbol and its sense as a diadic relation. Meaning may be concerned with use but it is in one important sense that the symbol reveals. But, does this revealing stop at first revealing? Or just as water is disturbed when a pebble is dropped in it and gives rise to ripples; similarly, does the revealing continue to have some kind of successive revelations one after another?

Bhartṛhari, the author of *Vākyapadīya* says that sound which takes the form of words, manifests itself in the form of meaning. Patañjali too says that the real "*śabda* is *sphoṭa*," i.e. the exploded meaning or *sphoṭa* itself is the *śabda*. Here, the problem is whether the process ends with the first explosion. Could there be a series of explosions? And in such a case would not there be several meanings revealing themselves one after another? Ānandavardhana the propounder of *dhvani* theory says that the words have three types of meanings manifesting through *abhidhā*, *lakṣaṇā* and *vyañjanā*. Some authors on Sanskrit poetics have talked of *dīrgha abhidhā*, i.e. one after another different *abhidhā*s get manifested. I am not interested in pointing out at this stage whether the continued manifestation is of *abhidhā* or of *lakṣaṇā* and *vyañjanā*, etc. I want to point out that just as ripples are produced in the water (on account of dropping of pebbles in the water) different manifestations of meaning reveal to us one after another. There may be different *abhidhā*s one after another or *abhidhā*s, *lakṣaṇā*, *vyañjanā* one after another. But, it may not stop at this point also and may proceed further.

Let me discuss what that "further" is. Let me point out some other aspect of the problem. I have said that the relation which is ordinarily supposed to exist between the word and the meaning really exists amongst the *users* of the word, the *word, symbol* and the *meaning*. It is the intention of the speaker which is encoded in sound symbols or signs and it is this encoded something that gets decoded when we understand the meaning. However, when the intention of the user or speaker is encoded in signs, it no more remains private. The encoded symbols are public, even if the script in which they are encoded is a secret script. This change from the private to public shows that the navel chord which existed earlier between the speaker and the listener has now disappeared and for all practical purposes the relation now becomes a diadic relation. Such a diadic relation is objective or at least epi-objective, where subjectivity can be ignored. What we call meaning is characterized by such objectivity. When one perceives an object the reactions which are produced can be both subjective as well as objective. But, it is only the objective reactions which we connect with meaning. Suppose we see an object "X" and we feel happy about it, then we do not regard our happiness as the meaning of the object. But, if we say it is beautiful it has a direct reference to the object although it may be connected with my reaction. I do not say, I feel beautiful about it. Feeling happy, primarily, belongs to the person. Being beautiful or looking beautiful is attributed to the object; although, in either case the role of experience is not overlooked. This makes me think that whereas my feeling happy is not the meaning of the object, the object looking beautiful belongs to the orbit of meaning. Or, it could be an extended meaning of the object. Earlier, I have discussed the *vācya-vācaka bhāva* and although the first *vācya* of the symbol is a referent or bearer of the symbol, *vācya* need not always mean the referent or denotatum. We have also seen that there cannot be any rule which governs the judgements of the form "'X' is beautiful." Unless we see "X" we are not able to say that 'X' is beautiful. We cannot, for example, say that the object of such and such a form could be beautiful, even if it does not exist. This is because the relation between the object or its constituent properties is not related to its being beautiful or otherwise by a causal relation. The relation that exists between the symbol and its meaning is given a special name by the Nyāya philosophers. They call it *samaya saṁbandha* (समय संबंध). I would suggest that an object and its being regarded as beautiful should also be regarded as being bound by *samya sambandha* at least in its external form.

Of course, we will have to make one more amendment. It need not be the case that the object on which we pass the judgement "beautiful" should be actually present. But, if we are able to bring that object, the image of the "concrete" object before the mind's eye, even if we do not have arguments for our judgement, it will be possible for us to know whether the object which is not yet produced could be beautiful. (For "beautiful" is not known by inference, it is known only in perception.) I think this would be an important clue in understanding the aesthetic theory that "beautiful" is something which reveals to us. It is with the help of parameters like "beautiful" and the like that we judge or measure an object to be beautiful whether the object would be poetry, painting, or sculpture. If we want to make some sculpture or painting our first concern is to make an object; but somewhere in our mind is linking the idea that it should be a *beautiful object*. We want to produce an object which would be beautiful. It is possible for us to bring before our mental eye the object and judge whether it is beautiful or not. This makes the creation of aesthetic object possible. As soon as we bring before our eyes an object which is a symbol, its meaning in all *directions* including the direction of beauty will follow. What an artist does is the activity of bringing before his mind the object and judge the mental object whether it is beautiful or not. A poet composes poetry, a painter paints a picture, a musician composes music, an architect plans a design. All these artists, before they begin their art activity bring before their mind's eye the picture of their art and continuously modify their artefact in their process of making. It is like imagining a drama even in the absence of a stage. It is not a conceptual activity, it is a perceptual activity done in the field of imagination. The designed art object and its possible meaning are presented before the artist perhaps in a richer way than when they are presented before the audience. This is the difference between creativity and appreciation.

Most of our artists and theorists of art talk about the constituent conditions of those particular arts but do not talk about the relationship between the art object and beauty or any other parameter. The reason, according to me, is that even the parameters are in-built in the art and they make it possible for the artist and the critic to judge an art object. This is, perhaps, the reason why we do not get any theory or analysis of beauty in the treatises on art and architecture.

Beauty: Natural and Artistic

"Beautiful" is indeed a value word and its Sanskrit synonym, *sundara* is used by Vāmana in the value sense. Beauty or *saundarya* which is formed from *sundara* or its other equivalents behaves like a blanket-term. Nevertheless, in different contexts they have different shades of meaning. Many critics, thus, distinguish between natural beauty and beauty in art. Indeed, they are different. But, is there no common point or thread between them, such that they can be brought under one roof? When we talk of beauty in nature, we have before us such objects as the sunset or a cataract or a stormy sea or a sea that is calm or some scenic beauty of mountains or a beautiful woman or a handsome man and the like. When we talk of beauty in art it may be springing from some musical recital or from the observation of a certain painting or a statue or from a certain pattern of a certain colour combination or certain dance-poses and performance. These indeed are different and, therefore, many people assert that beauty is a very complex notion. Nevertheless, our cognition of beauty comes in a twinkle of an eye. When the beauty is known or grasped, it does not take more than a moment for knowing or grasping. I believe that beauty is epistimic in nature. It arises in the world that is anthropocentric only. In the absence of an anthropos, the natural beauty will not only be not known to us; but, also, will not have any existence of its own in its own right and independent of the knowing of the cogniser.

Let me take an instance of the sunset or a blossoming rose flower. What happens when I say it is beautiful? When I look at it, I feel its image falls on my retina, or in the case of a flower its touch and appearance gives me a feel. This experience is carried to my mind or brain and some kind of rapport is established between me, that is the observer, and the object. Can I convey my experience to another man say, B? I feel I can convey my reaction to him, but, I cannot convey to him the complete process of my experiencing. My experiencing is private and is my own. Like me B also experiences the (same) phenomenon; and, perhaps, comes to the same conclusion and regards the sunset or rose flower as beautiful. His experience is also private. My experience while conveying it to B or his experience while conveying it to me does not penetrate the object and through it reach the other person. My experience is, so to say, a rebounding of my vision which comes in contact with the object; and so is B's. It is this after effect that becomes the object of communication between me and B. Since we accept that there is communication, we take it for granted that I am able to convey my experience to B and B is able to convey his experience to me and somehow we are able to tally these experiences with the result that we agree that the object of our experience is beautiful. This, perhaps, is the case if "A and B" observe a certain painting at different times or hear a musical recital. But this does not seem to be the case in respect of a communication between an artist and an appreciator. A's and B's experience of a certain natural or the artistic object is the experience of the appreciators, but in the case of art objects there can also be communication between the artist and the appreciator even if they are different points of time. When Kālidāsa or Shakespeare composed literary pieces or when dramatic pieces are enacted, the intention of the dramatist takes the form of symbols or signs and it is these symbols or signs, which are experienced by the appreciator. Is there any guarantee that the appreciator experiences the same thing, which is intended by the artist? Evidently, there is no guarantee or any logical proof but the fact remains that something is conveyed to the appreciator and that which is conveyed is appreciated by the appreciator. What is conveyed, so to say, touches or takes the grip of the appreciator's heart. This minimum is certainly there. The same is the case with the artist. Whether he intends to convey anything or not; evidently what he is able to convey is a certain feel.

This can be illustrated from an *electricity-model.* In electric phenomenon, if the circuit is complete and if it is connnected with an electric bulb, there is light. Similarly, in the case of art also, the circuit has to be complete. Out of the two ends (of circuit) artists is one and the appreciator is the other. Understanding or appreciation comes like a spark. This ignition of the spark is understood both by the artist and the appreciator. This, of course, requires a medium. The medium transforms the experience of the artist which is private into something that is public, and this experience is intuitively known. I have assumed that at one end, there is an artist, but, once the intention of the artist is reduced to a medium, the circuit can be complete even in the absence of the artist. This is how the feel of art, whether it is of Shakespeare, Kālidāsa, Bethoven or Vermeer is conveyed to us. In the case of natural objects, the circuit starts with me and ends with me. In the case of artistic objects, the circuit is completed when the message is carried from the artist to appreciator and in the absence of the artist, the circuit completes through some kind of *earthing*. The appreciation is either of the nature of light or of the nature of a shock, but, in either case it is quick and certain. This is how Bharata calls it *Hṛdayasaṁvādī*.

The Artist and the Appreciation

How are we to distinguish the role of the appreciator? Are their experiences identical? What is the nature of the aesthetic object which the artist creates? In what consists the aesthetic quality of the aesthetic object which the artist creates? It may be said that when an artist creates something, it is some idea in his mind to which he gives a form. Pippalāda in *Vāstusūtra Upaniṣad* points out that it is the *bhāva* in the mind of the artist which he imposes on or transforms into a form or a figure, i.e. creation consists in transforming something mental (or private and personal) into something objective, or public. Therefore, one could say that objectivity of art is based on the experience that is mental. Aesthetic experience consists in the transformation of this mental into objective. The artist enjoys this creation and in this process of enjoyment-cum-creation beauty is superimposed on it. Beauty is imagined or created in the transformation of something mental into something objective or something which can be sensed. The insight of the artist (*pratibhā*) lies in his ability to transform something that is mental into something objective. This is not the case with one who observes the object and looks at it with satisfaction or appreciation. The experience of the observer or appreciator lies in reacting to something mental. So, although the experience of both is connected with the object one consists in the transforming of the mental into objective and the other consists in transforming the objective into something mental (*pratibhā*, प्रतिभा is regarded as of two types, of the artist and of the appreciator). Pippalāda says that the artist is, so to say, grafting the *bhāva*s on the objective form. *Rasa* is the substratum of these *bhāva*s. By *rasa* he understands this objective form. While taking a certain form or *rūpa*, the *rasa*, so to say, spreads over the whole form.

अरूपाद् रूपं तस्य फलम् ।
भावस्य आरोपणं रूपकर्माणि विधेयम् ॥

arūpād rūpaṁ tasya phalam ।
bhāvasya āropaṇaṁ rūpakarmāṇi vidheyam ॥ — *VSU*, 21.5

Bharata also says a similar thing: *rasa* is the base on which the superstructure of *bhāva*s is erected.

तथा मूलं रसाः सर्वे तेभ्यो भावा व्यवस्थिताः ।

tathā mūlaṁ rasāḥ sarve tebhyo bhāvā vyavasthitāḥ ।[6]
— *NŚ* 6.39

I have earlier said that of the two processes in art, the process of creation and the process of appreciation, the process of creation cannot be observed or experienced in the case of poetry, as it is done in the case of drama. Nevertheless, all processes of creation whether they belong to dance, drama or poetry, music or painting are concerned with the transition from something mental to something objective. The name *rasa*

---

6. *Vāstusūtra Upaniṣad*, 13/3, 14/3, 1/5, 2/5, Also *NŚ* 7.39.

which Bharata gives to this process of objectifying is therefore equally true of all arts like poetry, whether they are manifestly seen or not. The standard or parameter by which arts like poetry, drama or painting are measured, are therefore concerned with this process of objectification. What characterizes an aesthetic experience? We see a rose flower and pass a judgement that it is beautiful. Our second reaction (to it) is that we are (get) pleased. We see a painting and our reaction to it is again positive. We read a certain piece of poetry and we either like it or are passive to it. We also see a certain drama or dance or music performance and react to it in a similar manner. When we see a certain flower we are not concerned with who created it. It might have been, for example, "created" by God. But we are not bothered how God, if he has created it, felt about it. But in the case of poetry, drama, painting and other art objects we are not only concerned with our reaction but we are also concerned with the reaction of the creator or the author of the artefact. Again, just as I may experience all these, similarly there might be other men like me who might have similar reactions. It might be that the reaction of every experience is different. But it is possible to think that two persons who observe the same object might have identical or similar reactions. We can, therefore, treat this experience as objective in some way. But like ouselves (the observers) will this also be true of the reactions of the creator or author of the art object who experiences the art object of his own creation? The author creates the art object and in some sense, we experience the "same" art object. But is the object that we experience really the same as one experienced by the author of the art object? Is it not the case that the object that experiences is the end-product for the author and that the author has to experience a certain process of creation itself? Is not the process of creation a series of the author's creation-components? It is true that the author enjoys this whole process of creation and he "describes" his experience as beautiful or fine; but his judgement that his experience is beautiful is a judgement passed on the entire creative process. It is the process of creation due to his creativity on which the judgement is passed. This process of creation is rooted in the transformation or translation of the author's earlier experience which is stored in his memory and later brought out in the form of some art object. The distinguishing feature of this process is creativity which lies in giving objective form to some earlier mental experience. Creativity lies in giving objective form to something that is mental. This process is spread in time. It starts with something mental and ends when it is experienced not only by the author but by others also. This objectivity might be different in the cases of different arts. This is however not the case in the process of appreciation. In this case we get the ready-made art object — the end-product of the artist — and we try to reduce it to something mental just as the artist had earlier experienced something (in the world) before he reduced it to mental experience. The author's experience is concerned with objectification whereas the appreciator's experience is concerned with giving this objectivity a mental status or form. So although we may say that the frame of reference of the artist and the appreciator is the same, in actuality it is not so.

When a person composes a piece of poetry he is reducing his thought to sound-sign patterns. When the appreciator reads a poem he is replacing the sound or sign patterns by something mental. This is the case in all arts. Sometimes it may be said that the artist enjoys the art object in exactly the same way as other appreciators do. But if this is so it is because at this particular time the artist is not the author but is the appreciator only. When Bharata talked of the techniques of dramatic performance he was pointing out to the process of reduction of something which was already created in objective form, in the form of *pāṭhya* or *itivṛtta*. This literary form was again translated into theatrical form and this process of flow was called *rasa*. But later, the word *rasa* was used in the context of poetry and other arts. In the case of poetry the creative process (except the end part) cannot be observed by others. But this is not so in performative arts and painting, sculptures, etc. In the case of stage drama the process of creation is fully seen by the observer (except when it is *āhārya*) but the actors might not be able to perceive fully the whole process. I have stated earlier that in the case of literary arts this process should be named as one of the *śabda* or *vākya* or even *prabandha*. Similarly in the case of painting, sculpture and architecture it should be called *rūpa*. *Śabda* or *vākya* is used by Viśvanātha and Jagannātha in this regard —

> वाक्यं रसात्मकं काव्यम् ।
> रमणीयार्थ प्रतिपादकः शब्दः काव्यम् ॥
>
> *vākyaṁ rasātmakaṁ kāvyam* ।
> *ramaṇīyārthapratipādakaḥ śabdaḥ kāvyam* ॥[7]

Both Viśvanātha and Jagannātha use the words *vākya* and *śabda* respectively. Similarly in the case of visual arts Abhinavagupta and the author of *Vāstusūtra Upaniṣad* talk of *rūpa*. Perhaps the technical terms like *śabda, rūpa*, etc. were chosen from Sāṁkhya system, from *tanmātras*, and used for objectification process in arts. I have earlier stated that *rasa* was also chosen from the *tanmātras* and was used to express

---

7. It is true that Viśvanātha uses the word *rasa* in the body of his definition. But this is perhaps because the word *rasa* by this time was used in the context of all aesthetic experience. Of course, any word can be technically used but it has also its non-technical uses and these non-technical uses are subjected to different usages.

the objects of audio-visual arts. But in the course of time the word *rasa* became more important and it was used for expressing any art object. In the course of history we find an evidence of it. I have earlier quoted a verse from Rudrabhaṭṭa's *Śṛṅgāra Tilaka* which clearly stated that Rudrabhaṭṭa wanted to extend the use of the word *rasa* to arts like poetry. I have earlier stated that in the case of poetry the process of creation cannot be experienced except by the author. But we know that it is connected with reducing something mental to something objective. So I conjecture that when the use of *rasa* was extended to different arts it was used for expressing this process in every art.

The Knowledge by Gestalt of Art Experience

In the second Kārikā of *Dhvanyāloka*, there is an important statement regarding the concept of meaning in poetry. But what Ānandavardhana says in *Dhvanyāloka* about the poetic meaning is perhaps equally true of the essence of art; I am using the word "essence" because in the context of art usually we do not use the word meaning. Ānandavardhana says: "that meaning which wins the admiration of *sahṛdaya* is called the soul of poetry."[8] This is of two types: *vācya* and *pratīyamāna*. *Vācya* is the direct meaning and is related to what it stands for. It gives us the relationship between *vācya* and *vācaka*. But, in addition to this meaning, there is another meaning, which flashes across us and takes us to some new region of meaning. Meanings are, therefore, to be grouped under two heads *vācya* or direct and *pratīyamāna* which is like a flash. This meaning shines in its own light and is different from and independent

---

8. योऽर्थःसहृदयश्लाघ्यः काव्यात्मेति व्यवस्थितः ।
वाच्यप्रतीयमानाख्यौ तस्य भेदावुभौ स्मृतौ ॥
yo 'arthaḥ sahṛdayaślāghyaḥ kāvyātmeti vyavasthitaḥ ।
vācya pratīyamānākhyau tasya bhedāvubhau smṛtau ॥ — *Dh.L* 1.2.

of the meanings which the parts of the object suggest. It is over and above that which is given to us by the parts. It is like the *lāvaṇya* or beauty of a woman or the bashfulness or shyness of a woman.

This classification of meanings may lead us to think that the first meaning is the meaning of the object and the second meaning is due to our understanding of the object in some particular special way, i.e. the first meaning is what follows from the symbol and the second meaning is what is super-imposed by us on the symbol. But, this kind of over-simplification would not do, for, even in the case of first meaning, it is not something which is necessarily in the nature of the object. Although Ānandavardhana distinguishes between *vācya* (वाच्य) and *pratīyamāna* (प्रतीयमान) (meanings), according to grammarians, like Patañjali and Bhartṛhari, even the *vācya* meaning is like a flash or explosion. Whether in this explosion, man's understanding is also a constituent or not, is not made explicit. But, in all probability, the relationship is not diadic, that is, between the symbol and its meaning. It is triadic, i.e. in addition to the meaning and symbol, the observer or knower is also one of the relata. Without the observer, the meaning of the word or symbol would not be understood in the peculiar and particular way. In this case, also, the meaning is given to the symbol by the observer. Again when the observer "imparts" the meaning to the symbol, the meaning may be either related to the object of which it is a symbol or it may just be meaning, i.e. something understood by the observer, even in the absence of the bearer of the symbol. In such a case the meaning would belong to the region of epistemology and not ontology, and then even this direct meaning would only be a *pratīyamāna* meaning, although for practical convenience, we may regard the first *pratīyamāna* proper. It may also be pointed out here that the followers of *dhvani* theory further classify the *pratīyamāna* meaning into two sub-classes, one that is implied and the other that is suggested. In Sanskrit they are called *lakṣyārtha* (लक्ष्यार्थ) and *vyaṅgyārtha* (व्यङ्ग्यार्थ) or *dhvani.*

That the meaning of a sentence or a word is really something which comes as a flash or explosion, has been held by the grammarians and philosophers of India from the very ancient times. Pāṇini mentions, in this context, one *sphoṭayāna,* in his *Aṣṭhādhyāyī-Avan* (अष्टाध्यायी अवन्).[9] *Sphoṭayāna* is one who propounded the theory of *sphoṭa* (which means a sudden, instantaneous explosion). Grammarians have consistently held the theory of *sphoṭa.* Bhartṛhari talks of *vākyasphoṭa, padasphoṭa* and *varṇasphoṭa.* In his *Vākyapadīya, sphoṭa* is concerned with something which happens suddenly. Maṇḍana Miśra too talks of *sphoṭa* in his *Sphoṭasiddhi.* As pointed out earlier, the later grammarians and Mīmāṁsakas modified the *sphoṭa* theory and put it in two different forms:

(1) *Abhihitānvayavāda* (अभिहितान्वयवाद), and

(2) *Anvitābhidhānavāda* (अन्विताभिधानवाद)

One theory says that the letters are joined together in a sentence and, finally, the meaning of the sentence emerges or flashes suddenly. The other theory says that the letters get joined into words (along with their meanings), but, only when the syntax of the words is complete, the meaning comes as a flash to us. We need not concern ouselves with these theories. But, we must know that both these are gestalt theories. But, we must, further, know that these gestalts are auditory gestalts and even if they are visual (as when we read the sentence) they are successive, i.e. they are temporal and, unless, the sensation is complete, the gestalt will not follow.

---

9. अवङ्स्फोटायनस्य (*avaṅgasphoṭāyanasya*) ।

But, what about the arts other than the literary? We may think of arts like painting, sculpture and architecture. They are different from arts like music (instrumental and vocal), dance and drama, and also literary arts which either we perceive gradually or hear gradually. Where there is succession and graduality, we cannot comprehend the whole at the first moment and sight. But, in the case of the first kind of arts like painting, the very first act (perception) could be the total apprehension in so far as it is concerned with the span of attention. Even the word "com-prehend" suggests this. Such apprehension is different from the apprehension of parts. And so it is called *avayavātirikta* (अवयवातिरिक्त), i.e. other than the apprehension of parts. It does not mean that on the second look we would not get the view of the objects in detail. But in a visual gestalt we move from whole to whole and not by adding part to part. Such an apprehension of the whole is very important for understanding the nature of art, at least some arts.

I may also point out that our perception and thinking are also not of one type. When we perceive an object with our eye, the first glimpse is a total glimpse. It is what our span of attention can hold. And, this can make a difference to our conceptual thinking also when we think *through* concepts (and our language is the best instance of such a procedure). We proceed in an abstract manner. But it is possible that when we *see* an object, we may retain the whole image in our memory and recollect the whole image at a later time. I think in the context of painting and architecture this is what happens. We are able to reproduce the image, as a reaction to the symbols presented to us. This also will have an important effect on the aesthetic theory.

I have tried to explain how the meaning can be of two types. One, the direct meaning, and the other that we experience by way of a flash. We have also seen that what we call direct meaning is also a kind of a flash. But, on account of its occurrence again and again it becomes stereotyped and it is forgotten that it also arose as a kind of a flash. We have also seen that whether it is the direct meaning or *pratīyamāna* meaning it is a product of a triadic relation, although it tends to become diadic. It is conveniently forgotten that there was somebody who spoke or uttered or wrote these words as symbols leaving it to someone else to interpret them. X means Y in its fully expanded form means A intended[10] X to mean Y. When the part "A intended," is dropped or is not expressed, we get the present form, X means Y. But in this case also its form would be X means Y for B. When this tailpiece is dropped, what remains is, X means Y. Here, X is revealed as Y. This revealing is our concept of meaning and it comes in a flash.

Does this mean that the process stops here? And, if it does not stop, are we to say that the successive flashes are merely the "continuation" of the first flash? Bhartṛhari, the author of *Vākyapadīya*, while explaining the relation between the word (in the form of sound) and meaning, says that the eternal sound which is beginningless appears to us in the form of ripples.

अनादिनिधनं ब्रह्म शब्दतत्त्वं यदक्षरम् ।
विवर्तते अर्थभावेन प्रक्रिया जगतो यतः ।

anādinidhanaṁ brahma śabda tattvaṁ yadakṣaram ।
vivartate arthabhāvena prakriyā jagato yataḥ ॥ — *VP* 1.1

---

10. योऽर्थो सहृदयश्लाघ्यः काव्यात्मेति वयवस्थितः ।
वाच्य प्रतीयमानख्यौ तस्य भेदावुभौ स्मृतौ ॥

yo 'rtho sahṛdayaślāghyaḥ kāvyāmeti vyavasthitaḥ ।
vācya pratīyamānkhyau tasya bhedāvubhau smṛtau ॥ Dh. 1.2

It is a common experience that the sound stimulus is understood by us in some sensible form or meaning but our response continues further and we, for example, react by saying whether it is beautiful or otherwise. This response of ours, although it arises in us, is not subjective. Let us look at it again — for us it is the object which looks beautiful. The flash makes us see the object as beautiful. The object can be a painting, a piece of poetry, a scene in a drama or a landscape, etc., etc. This kind of reaction as *beautiful* is also a flash though altogether of a different kind. What is wrong in supposing that it has the same kind of status as one possessed by direct meaning or *pratīyamāna* meaning? What we understand as beauty is also a kind of *pratīti*. It can be pointed out here that our response can be further prolonged and we may be pleased or displeased on account of our experience. Our experience may end in either our pleasure or happiness or displeasure or misery. There is, however, a difference between this ultimate reaction and the penultimate and the earlier ones. The reactions except the final are the reactions to the object itself; the final reaction is the reaction of the subject only where the reference to the object becomes insignificant. When we are pleased, it is not the object which is pleased, just as when we say that the object is beautiful. It is not our intention to say that one who experiences is beautiful. The last reaction is not in regard to the *pratīti* of the object, whereas all other reactions are so. This is how A's happiness may not be the same as B's happiness in the same situation. By happiness we mean happiness or its opposite.

A certain school of Indian rhetoricians propounded the theory of *dīrgha abhidhā* which means direct meanings coming one after the other. They said that we need not have different kinds of *pratīti*, but only one kind of *pratīti* is enough to understand the different experiences and this *pratīti* is only of the nature of *abhidhā*. They give instance of a shot arrow. When a warrior shoots an arrow, it passes through the air. It hits the target, say, for example, another warrior, breaks his armour, enters his body and kills him. They appear to be different functions but it is one, long extended function. Mammaṭa criticizes this theory which tries to explain everything in terms of *abhidhā śakti* and Mammaṭa could be right. But there could be a chain reaction in the form of *abhidhā*, giving rise to *vyañjana pratīti* or *abhidhā* giving rise to *saundarya pratīti*. When we talk of *saundarya*, we talk of *pratīti* (of *saundarya* only). The first *pratīti* is in regard to the symbol. The other *pratīti*s are in regard to the symbols and also the meanings of the symbols as they are understood by us. There can be different *pratīti*s one after another just as dropping of a pebble in water may give rise to different ripples successively one after another. In fact, the different ripples may not be of the same order and our judgement about them may be based either on our description of the experience or the evaluation of the experience. When we are talking of meaning, we are, so to say, explaining or describing the symbol. When we say it is beautiful, it is evaluating the symbol along with the meaning generated by it. The *pratīti* of evaluation may be far more complex than the *pratīti* of the symbol. Nevertheless, the evaluative *pratīti* is also *pratīti* and we may be enlightened by this *pratīti* instantaneously. Mammaṭa, while talking of *alaṁkāra*, says *camatkr̥tiścālaṁkaraḥ* (चमत्कृतिश्चालंकरः). *Camatkr̥ti* is instantaneous happening or realization and *alaṁkāra* could mean not ornaments or embellishments, but a parameter of evaluation. In fact, Vāmana has said this (op. cit.). It will now be easier for us to understand as to why Indian aestheticians do not discuss the evaluative process though they talk of evaluative standards, like beauty or *pārabrahmasvāda savidhatā*. This last standard is tuned with indefiniteness, infiniteness.

Pratīti is like a tool box which can accommodate different tools. We do not know what exactly it is. We can be dumb-founded by it and look at it aghast or wonderstruck like the last ripple where we do not know where the ripples are beginning or ending. The most important part, however, is that the realization of meaning or evaluation is instantaneous.

Arts: Auditory, Visual and Audio-Visual

In India while there are lots of works on *śilpa* and *sthāpatya* the paradigm which is kept by art critics before their mind is the theory of poetry and drama and here also the parameter is that of *rasa*. The word *rasa* is found in Bharata's *Naṭyaśāstra* and some authors say that people earlier than Bharata have used the word, *rasa*, in the sense Bharata has used it. The original reference to *rasa* was in the context of stage drama; but, later, it was predominantly used in the context of poetry. Sometimes, we do find that the word *rasa* is used in the context of *kalā* or art. (In a recently found Upaniṣad, *Vāstusūtra Upaniṣad*, we do find the word *rasa* used in the context of *śilpa* also.) Perhaps, on account of the tradition that followed, people used *rasa*, particularly, in the context of appreciation of poetry and it was on the analogy of poetry that it was used in other arts.

Indians have classified poetry into auditory, visual and audio-visual. Drama, if staged, belongs to audio-visual; *śilpa sthāpatya* would belong to visual; and poetry, drama-text, and other literary forms would belong to auditory, if heard, and visual, if read. But even if they are visual, in Sanskrit it would be classified under *śravya* ('श्रव्य').

The literary forms of art have two prongs. One is called *śabda* and the other is called *artha*. *Śabda* stands for sound and *artha* for its meaning. Elsewhere, in this work I have talked of words, language and meaning. Here, I may point out that Sanskrit critics of poetry have talked of three meanings. One, the direct which is given to us by *abhidhā* or which in its original form could be called the denotatum of the word, the other is *lakṣaṇa* or implied meaning and the third is *vyañjana* (व्यंजन) or suggested meaning. Among the poetic critics a person who dominated the scene of poetic criticism was Ānandavardhana who has unique ranking amongst the poetic critics. His work *Dhvanyāloka* gives us a theory called *dhvani* theory, and just as *rasa* theory dominated the scene, so also was the *dhvani* theory, and finally in the hands of Abhinavagupta, the two theories were amalgamated in one and was called *rasabhadhvani-siddhānta.* (रसभध्वनि सिद्धान्त) Abhinavagupta says *rasāḥ dhvaniḥ eva* (रसः ध्वनिः एव).

By this I understand that although these two are different, even then both of them have the same reference. I have, further, pointed out that a word has two wings, one is concerned with *vācya* and the other with *vācaka* and it is this *vācya* wing which leads to different meanings like *lakṣaṇa* and *vyañjana*.

In my preface to *Dhvanyāloka* written by Vīrkar and Patwardhan, I have suggested that the authors should enlighten us on one important point. In the second verse of the first *udyota*, Ānandvardhana says:

योऽर्थः सहृदयश्लाघ्यः काव्यात्मेति व्यवस्थितः।
वाच्यप्रतीयमानाख्यौ तस्य भेदावुभौ स्मृतौ॥

yo 'rthaḥ sahṛdayaślāghyaḥ kāvyātmeti vyavasthitaḥ ।
vācyapratīyamānākhyau tasya bhedāvubhau smṛtau ॥

(That meaning which wins admiration of refined critics is decided to be the soul of poetry. *Dhvanyāloka* by K. Krishnamoorthy.) *Vācya* (वाच्य) and *pratīyamāna* (प्रतीयमान) are regarded as its two aspects. I asked the question that if the meaning is of two types, how is it that in the text and in the commentary they talk of three meanings. I should however like to explain this anomaly by pointing out that the meaning is of two types. But under the second are included the *lakṣaṇa* and *vyañjana*. Here, again, I would ask: Is not the first kind of meaning also something which is of the nature of flash? I would say "yes." But as Ānandvardhana points out this meaning is in common use and so, that it is also a kind of flash is overlooked. But the *pratīyamāna* is something which is comprehended as a whole in that particular context; and in this concept I find an important truth — meaning is a kind of a flash and it is known as a whole — that it cannot be explained in parts and joined together. This is the basic feature of the visual gestalt.

If we take two types of perception, auditory and visual, we find that there is a basic difference in them. Auditory perception is due to stimulus occurring on account of successive sensations. But visual perception is a single comprehension. There is no succession in it. That is, it can't be known part by part. It is always simultaneous. This is experienced in plastic arts like painting. In music for example, it is otherwise. The succeeding sounds come together and have a kind of blending which, so to say, gives us a different type of gestalt. Ānandvardhana in the fourth verse explains this in the following way. The *pratīyamāna* aspect is quite different from this. In the words of great poets, it shines supreme and stands out over and above the parts like the beauty of a woman.

Aesthetic Experience and the Nature of Originality

Many a time we talk of aesthetic experience. This experience may be in the context of art-objects or nature. We connect art experience with beauty. But this also raises a question about the nature of art. Though the words "pleasant," "beautiful" and "artistic" are not synonyms, we certainly feel that they belong to one family. These words can be used meaningfully in respect of the natural objects as also in the case of objects which are created by man. What we call art, comes under the second kind of objects. Although all objects created by man may not be art objects, in some sense artistic character (or aesthesis) of these objects is certainly connected with man's creation of these objects. That is why when we ask questions about art we also talk about the originality of the artist. If another man creates merely a copy of the first object we do not value the maker of this second object as a great artist. Nay, in an important sense we do not regard "that" art object or artefact as a piece of art. We rather regard it as a piece of craft. It means that in our idea the originality of the artist is also a constituent of the art object and it is perhaps one of the most important constituents in our evaluation or appreciation of the object.

What is the function and value of this originality? First, the word originality requires (1) that art or art object is some kind of transformation from something A to something B. That is, whatever be the art object this transformation from A to B is bound to characterize every art object. And, (2) the art object which is a process and also a product of the process, is of the nature of idea at one end and of the nature of a thing at the other end. If we are able to transform whatever comes to our mind into something which can be experienced not only by us but by all those who either open their eyes or lend their ears, then only it can become an art object. Artist's genius consists in transforming the ideas giving them an objective form. We should be able to say that the objective form is the mould in which we cast our ideas. When our ideas take the shape of this objective mould then alone they can become art-objects. Of course, everything that takes such a form is not an art object. But taking such form is a necessary condition for art objects also. Otherwise our ideas would remain only as our private properties and there would be no possibility of others perceiving or enjoying these properties. This objectification is in a way encoding of our ideas. Reducing the ideas to a certain medium is something which is absolutely essential for its becoming an art object. Although we talk of art and its medium, it would be more correct to say that the medium itself (along with the *elan vital* running through it) is the art object. Sometimes, the medium would be concerned with time, sometimes with space, and sometimes with both. In addition, it would have some matter which is to be given form in space, time or space and time; and above all, it is the idea of the artist, which is given this form and the creative power of the artist which has given this form to his ideas.

I have, elsewhere, said that *sthāyī bhāva*s are *cittavṛttiviśeṣa*, and in staging the drama these *cittavṛtti*s, with the help of *vibhāva*, *anubhāva* and *vyabhicārī bhāva*s are transformed into *rasa*. It is the *rasa*s which give objective form to the "inhabitants of our mind" or *sthāyī bhāva*s. I have earlier said that this transition in respect of stage drama can be experienced and measured. This transition is not possible to experience or visualize in respect of poetic creation, although in poetry-making, we are reducing our ideas to words. But, in the course of time, the word *rasa* became a blanket term to explain this transition from the subjective to the objective; and once we know that an art object is concerned with the transition from the subjective to objective, it would also be understood as to why they used *rasa* as a blanket term for explaining this process from the subjective to objective. So far as the subjective element is concerned, every art is concerned with *sthāyī bhāva* alone. It is the persistent idea. On account of the different media our *sthāyī bhāvas* take the form of different arts. Thus, the same *sthāyī bhāva* can be transformed into music, painting, sculpture, drama or poetry by the respective artists.

The Meaning of Beautiful

It is necessary to state my position *vis-á-vis* the concept of beauty. It cannot be denied that in some sense the beauty concept is connected with all arts. Bharata calls it *śobhā,* Vāmana calls it *saundarya* or *alaṁkāra*, and Ānandavardhana finds a manifestation of it in *dhvani.* All these great masters are in a sense right. No art can be conceived without the concept of beauty. Every art is concerned with it. All arts are communications though all communications are not arts. The reason is that in arts there is a double communication. First, as in language there is the usual communication. But, there is another type of communication also. That is communication of *beauty*. It is this element that distinguishes *art* from other kinds of language. All great masters like Bharata, Vāmana, Abhinavagupta, Kṣemendra, Ānandavardhana, Rājaśekhara seem to be aware of this. Paṇḍit Jagannātha has clearly stated this even in the definition of poetry. Poetry is for him a language pattern which conveys *beautiful meaning* — *ramaṇīyārtha pratipādakaḥ śabdaḥ kāvyam* (रमणीयार्थ-प्रतिपादकः शब्दः काव्यम्, *Rasagaṅgādhara*). This, however, creates a fresh problem about the nature of beauty. I have stated earlier that though "beauty" is a name it does not denote anything existent. I, therefore, hold that the primary sense conveyed by the noun "beauty" is that of adjective beautiful. I believe that there are adjectives which convey a meaning without standing for any bearer. It should not be thought that for every word that conveys meaning, there should be a thing — a bearer. It can be that beauty is not a single concept, but a family of concepts and all these variations of concepts are known as beauty because of *the family resemblances*. I believe that "beautiful" essentially belongs to the category of *cognition* or *pratyaya*. It does not belong to the category of things, but to the cognition of things. A cognition of thing is not a thing. Most philosophical mistakes arise because of equating "a thing" with a cognition of a thing. It, therefore, falls into the same class as *meanings*. Therefore, though we may use a phrase like "a cognition of beauty," the "cognition of beauty or beautiful" is not in any way different from "beauty"; it is just in the same sense that we may talk of "myself," though it does not mean that "my" is different from self. I believe, our ancient masters were quite aware of this nature of beauty. Otherwise they would never have thought of it as *saṁvit*. As soon as it is realized that the concept of beauty belongs to the class of meanings and cognitions, another aspect of it becomes clear. For, a cognition or *saṁvit* must always be single, unanalysable and indivisible, though it may arise in a complex situation. This is how our masters have described it. The concept of beauty, being a different order-concept, is unanalysable and does not denote any object. The recognition that beauty belongs to the concept of cognition should bring before us other aspects of beauty. A cognition has been regarded by Indian thinkers — particularly of Nyāya school as a quality of *ātman*. But there is an essential difference between *cognition* or *jñāna* and other qualities of the self. There cannot be cognition without an object. So cognition is *related* on the one hand with the object or *viṣaya* and on the other with *ātman*. Thus, a cognition "is neither purely objective nor purely subjective." It is a relational concept which exists with a *samavāya* relation with the art object on the one hand and the *cogniser* or the appreciator on the other.

Describability of Beauty

How is the describable beauty described? When we explain

the beauty of a flower, we describe its shape, arrangement of petals, its colour, its agreeable smell, etc. But does all such description make the flower beautiful? It is true that we are evaluating the flower in terms of descriptive language. But the descriptive language *qua* descriptive language does not give us the evaluation. Although the description leads us to the evaluation point, the description and evaluation cannot be equated. One cannot say that something is beautiful because it has symmetry or contrast or balance or a combination of all such qualities. I, therefore, suggest that the beauty is cognized only intuitively. This is also the case with all evaluative parameters. What we can do is to create an art object and then examine whether the object is really an art or merely a craft. We can only create a field or situation in which the art object can be located.

It is possible that while we describe an art object we may create an impression that the object goes beyond a certain point, for example, a static object may give the impression that it is moving. In the case of dance, it may be just a posture, but it may give an impression that the dancer is moving. (It can be observed in a greater degree in the case of painting. A certain tree dipicted, leaning in a certain direction, may create an impression of a blowing wind.) The paradox is that although we make a distinction between describable and indescribable parameters, even the "describable" parameter is not really describable. We can only describe the constituents. The constituents may give rise to the evaluative aspect intuitively. But through the constituent parts of poetic or other forms of art structures, we do not arrive at any definition of the evaluative parameter such as beauty.

Ānandavardhana says that we know the "beauty" of a beautiful woman and there the matter ends. Bhaṭṭanāyaka in the work *Hṛdayadarpaṇa* (which is lost but of which some fragments are found here and there) finds another parameter which he called *mahārasa*. He describes its evaluation as *brahmāsvādasavidhā*, i.e. the experience of *rasa* is like the experience of *Brahman*. Viśvanātha repeats the same thing and says that *rasāsvāda* is like the sibling of *brahmāsvāda* (*Brahmāsvādasahodara*). Mammaṭa also says the same thing when he says that it is reckoned instantaneously. It is a *camatkāra*. *Camatkāra* means "miracle." If one asks why is it a miracle, Mammaṭa would answer, because it flashes instantaneously like the lightning, it dazzles us. Bhaṭṭanāyaka makes a distinction between *mahārasa* and *rasa*. He says that each *rasa* is an instance of *mahārasa*. In my opinion, Bhaṭṭanāyaka's *rasa* theory is basically different from other *rasa* theories and that he uses the term *rasa* in the sense of a parameter. He says:

रसः न प्रतीयते। न उत्पद्यते। न अभिव्यंज्यते।

rasāḥ na pratīyate, na utpadyate, na abhivyañjyate ।

Rasa is not perceived, not produced, nor vividly expressed. His critics think that this is a mythical concept of *rasa*. But we have seen that the concept of parameter fits in the description. A parameter is not produced nor perceived nor is expressible. It is only taken for granted. It is just a presumption. If Abhinavagupta's text is read further in the light of what Bhaṭṭanāyaka says, we get a positive explanation, which students of Abhinavagupta have not taken note of. One can easily find that the passage ends with *apitu abhyupagamyate evaṁ* (अपितु अभ्युपगम्यते एवं). *Abhyupagama* is a technical term for hypothesis. So it means that although we do not know how it is produced, whether it is perceptible and expressible, yet it is taken for granted. It is a hypothesis.

Indescribability and Parameters of Art

We have seen that Indian art critics offer several standards for measuring the quality of art. Roughly, they can be classified under two kinds of scale. One is the scale which measures the subject matter with the concepts pertaining to the subject matter. *Rīti*, for example, is one such scale or standard. The other is the evaluative standard. Beauty certainly is such a standard. Both these types give us the last limit either in regard to the subject matter or the evaluation. In fact, this is the meaning of the term *alaṁkāra*. But is it not possible to imagine a state where such parameters break? As pointed out in the previous section, at least Bhaṭṭanāyaka and Viśvanātha talk of this when they say that the experience of *rasa* is like the experience of *Brahmāsvāda*. Bharata too, in classifying *siddhi* under *mānuṣī* and *daivikī* and again distinguishing two types of *daivikī siddhi,* the ultimate one being *sampūrṇa siddhi* (संपूर्ण सिद्धि) hints at this. Such a standard or parameter which suggests the breaking of all parameters is bound to be indescribable or *anirvacanīya*. Philosophical (metaphysical) discussions talk of such *anirvacanīya* both in the context of *māyā* and *Brahman*. When it is used in the context of *māyā* it points to the status of "neither being true, nor being false" and so in a sense it cannot be properly described. But although *Brahman* is regarded as real, it too cannot be described. An expression falls short in such cases, *yato vāco nivartante* (यतो वाचो निवर्तन्ते). Such a state would occur both in dealing with the perfection of the subject matter as also in evaluating it. So the standards or parameters which point to indescribability will also be of two kinds. But can the parameters which keep to the ordinary limit indicated by parameters be described? To me it appears that they too cannot be described. I have suggested elsewhere that Bhaṭṭanāyaka suggests this in regard to *rasa* (used in singular) or *mahārasa*, when he says, *na pratīyate, na utpadyate, na abhivyañjyate*. But, I think this is true of beauty also and in fact, all standards. Sanskrit rhetoricians only describe beauty functionally by giving examples and by suggesting that art is an outcome of *pratibhā*. When I say "functionally" I mean that the poets and critics try to describe it in terms of relations positive or negative. Only the examples of beauty are given. Kālidāsa, for example, describes beauty as that which results in the accomplishment of that which is desirable,

प्रियेषु सौभाग्यफल हि चारुता — कुमारसंभवम्

priyeṣu saubhāgyaphala hi cārutā । — *KS*

His another *description of beauty* is found in such verses as:

सरसिजमनुविद्धं शैवलेनापि रम्यम् — अभिज्ञान शाकुंतलम्

sarasijamanuviddhaṁ śaivalenāpi ramyam ।
— *Abhijñāna Śākuntalam*

Māgha also describes it as that which appears to be new every moment, *kṣaṇe kṣaṇe yannavatām upaiti tadeva rūpam ramaṇīyatāyāḥ* (क्षणे-क्षणे यन्नवतामुपैति तदेव रूपं रमणीयतायाः). But, many a time beauty is merely stated as a unique notion which can be understood and accepted, but which cannot be described. Ānandavardhana uses this technique in *Dhvanyāloka* when he says, *lāvaṇayamivāṅganāsu* (लावणयामिवांगनासु). He also describes it on the basis of analogy when he compares the standard with the bashfulness of ladies (*lajjā*).

An Epistemology of Art

Earlier, I said that (1) there is a world which exists in its own right and (2) we are able to know it. When we know it, we know it in pluralistic forms; and (3) we are able to express these forms in language. This transition is continuously subjected to categorization and abstraction. It is reducing the complexity of the dimensions of the world. We now start knowing the universe in categories or *padārthas* like *dravya, guṇa, karma, sāmānya* and *viśeṣa,* which are like the chips of the original stem. (We extend this categorization by including in our scheme of categorization, *samavāya* and *abhāva.*) We also talk of *vikṛti* of *prakṛti* and *māyā, saṁsāra* and *jagat*. All this brings in the process of our knowing and expressing. To separate the knower from the known and regarding it as proto universe, outside the universe itself is the beginning of categorization and abstraction. In this process, what we call imagination is born. But imagination, universalization, and generalization including all abstractions are not synonyms, although they are some kind of choppings of the Universe. In this act of peeling the universe we get concepts, notions, universals and so on. Indian grammar school calls this the process of *apoddhāra* (अपोद्धार). From a well when we draw water, the bucket-water, isolated from the water in the well is *apoddhāra*. The relation of the bucket-water with the water in the well is broken although it is water from the same well. Like the water in the pot the categorized objects are isolated items and are called *apoddhāra padārtha* (अपोद्धर पदार्थ). Space, time, substance, qualities, quantities, etc. are such isolated forms of the universe. Man's understanding lies in the understanding of these parts and establishing a relation amongst them. But, man, with his intelligence can group these different parts the way he likes. Thus, he can group two or more parts (percepts) of one and relate them with anything with which it is not naturally related. The hare has no horns, a cow has them; but, he can think of an hare with horns. A horse has head and so has man. A man through his power constructs in his mind an animal with man's body and horse's head, and calls it *tumbaru.* Man takes the parts from the world and with his skill and power joins them together and such an object is called a product of imagination. The skill is the power of imagination and the product is the imagination. But, in fact, whatever he produces, houses, streets, towns, weapons, machines, televisions, computers, all these are due to man's imagination. In fact, through his imaginations he can create a parallel world. Like the world of nature it is man's world, created from material, taken from the world, giving it a form obtained through images cognized. Today we use the word *imagination* or the Sanskrit word *kalpanā* for it. It will be interesting to see the etymological meaning of these words. *Kalpanā* has come from the root *kḷp*. The word *imagine* and the word *image* have the same etymology. In *Ṛgveda* and Upaniṣads we get passages like *dhātā yathā pūrvaṁ akalpayat* (धाता यथा पूर्वं अकल्पयत्) and we also use the word *kalpa* for denoting a certain specific strand of time. We also use the word *kḷpti* for device, which is some kind of planning and is mental. In later Indian thought the word *kalpanā* was used not for the constructions but for the form that is given to parts of the Universe by mind. But mind can give a form in many different ways. When we use language, we certainly give a form to what we observe and what we also add to it. But, language proceeds through words or concepts. Man can also bring the picture of his experience before his mind's eye and create a world similar to the world which is given to us, but where physical existence is absent. There is nothing actual, there are only mental images. In dreams we get such images. Our knowledge process also follows this path just as it also follows the path of abstractions. I have earlier stated that just as there is knowledge through concepts, similarly, there is knowledge through images. In Indian philosophy the school of Nyāya recognizes this. Nyāya philosophers talk of *jñāna lakṣaṇa pratyāsatti* (ज्ञान लक्षण प्रत्यासत्ति) and also *sāmānya lakṣaṇa pratyāsatti* (सामान्य लक्षण प्रत्यासत्ति). In *sāmānya lakṣaṇa pratyāsatti* our knowledge proceeds through concepts. But, even before the concepts are formed knowledge can proceed through images. Such knowledge is at the level of perception. It is not conceptual knowledge and is called *jñāna lakṣaṇa pratyāsatti.* I think this happens in painting, sculpture and architecture directly. But this also takes place in music and poetry. Stage drama is a pictorial visualization of our ideas and experience. But even in poetry, sometimes when the words are heard the images appear before us in some concrete form. In fact, there are many types of words. Some words do not "provoke" images. But some words do. For example, when the word *chariot* is uttered the picture of the chariot stands before us. The poetic genius lies in using such words and creating such images. Many of the similies, metaphors and other figures of speech and also description used by Kālidāsa and other poets are of this type. Kālidāsa is sometimes known as *Dīpa Śikhā Kālidāsa* on account of his verse, *sañcāriṇī dīpa śikheva rātrau* (संचारिणी दीप शिखेव रात्रौ). This verse has the ability to create before us the whole scene as if it was living and real. The same is true of the description of the deer in the 1st act of *Śākuntalam-Trīvābhaṅgābhirāmam* (शाकुन्तलम् त्रीवाभ ंगाभिरामम्), etc. The artist who indulges in performative or plastic art uses this method. In a drama an actor plays a certain role. What is playing a role? For sometimes he forgets his own nature, withdraws his *svabhāva* from his body and turns himself into a *vibhāva* and artificially puts someone else's *svabhāva* in it. This is playing a role. This happens on account of his imagination, as well as the imagination of the director. But such things also happen in music, paintings, dance and sculpture. Art is some kind of artificial grouping and it is possible to do it on account of man's capacity to re-arrange things in the world, even by abstracting existencne from it. If I am allowed to use an analogy, I would like to say that it is illusion or delusion and I would like to give its explanation on the basis of *anyathākhyāti* (अन्यथाख्याति) (or other *khyātis*) discussed by Indian philosophers.

In Indian aesthetic theory they use the word *pratibhā* and explain it as *nava nava unmeṣaśālinī* (नव नव उन्मेषशालिनी). This capacity gives something newer and newer every moment. It is on account of this capacity that an artist is able to create something and the appreciator is able to appreciate it. I have explained this concept elsewhere in this monograph and have also pointed out that in all art process or the process of re-creation the images that we form in perception are "presented forms" after removing from them the specific qualities or *viśeṣa guṇa*. But still their pictographic form is retained. It is, of course, possible to express our experience in concepts. But many a time these concepts produce a pictographic effect. The greatness (and the originality) of the artists is measured by his ability to produce such suggested effect. I shall give a few instances of such effect which enhances the beauty of the poetic creation. In the Ancient Mariner, Colridge describes the incident when the ancient mariner's ship gets stuck up and does not move. This incident is described in the words: "a painted ship on a painted ocean."

This expression of the poet is able to bring before the reader the picture of an ocean along with a ship which could not move, as a painted ship cannot have any mobility. Such expressions are also found in Kālidāsa. Consider for example the following lines in *Kumārasambhava*:

मार्गाचलव्यतिकराकलितेव सिन्धुः ।
शैलाधिराजतनया न ययौ न तस्थौ ॥

mārgācalavyatikarākalitevasindhuḥ ।
śailādhirājatanayā na yayau na tasthau ॥

(When Śiva embraces Pārvatī who wanted to get away from (Śiva in the form of) Batu she looked like a river which dashes against a mountain and is not able to move further nor stay at the same point.)

One can also get instances of such pictographic descriptions in:

इति गमिष्याम्यथवेति वादिनी
चचाल बाला स्तनभिन्नवल्कला।
स्वरूपमस्थाय च तां कृतस्थितः
सोमाललम्बे वृष राजकेतनः॥

iti gamiṣyāmyathaveti vādinī ।
cacāla bālā stana-bhinna-valkalā ॥
svarūpamasthāya ca tāṁ kṛtasthitaḥ ।
somālalambe vṛṣa rājaketanaḥ ॥

But in such descriptions the pictographic effect is produced on account of the words with pictographic ability. But sometimes the poetic genius creates such pictographic effect even if the words in themselves do not exhibit such phictographic nature. When Keats says: "My heart aches and drowsy numbness pains." It can be seen that no word here has pictographic characteristic. Still the combination of these words has the power to create a *picture* although of indefiniteness. It is such characteristic of description which tends to make an imaginary mental picture take a realistic form and look as if it was a canvas of emotion.

There is no doubt that we are able to measure and grade instances or types of imagination. We are also able to discriminate the higher and lower types. These types of course are dependent on the ability of the artist. Two artists use almost the same material but by making a slight change the effect that is produced by one artist is far greater than the effect produced by the other. There is an anecdote about the compositions of Bhavabhūti and Kālidāsa, the two great poets and dramatists of India. The anecdote says that Bhavabhūti composed a line:

> अविदितगतयामा रात्रिरेवंव्यरंसीत्।
>
> *aviditagatayāmā rātrirevaṁvyaraṁsīt* ।
>
> (In this way, while we were engaged in talk the night passed away.)
>
> Kālidāsa merely removed the *bindu* (dot) from *rātrirevaṁ* and said:
>
> अविदितगतयामा रात्रिरेवंव्य रंसीत्।
>
> *aviditagatayāmā rātrirevaṁvya raṁsīt* ।
>
> (While engaged in talk the night passed away — but the talk remained lingering.)

Evidently some appreciator of Kālidāsa wanted to show Kālidāsa's superiority over Bhavabhūti. Nevertheless, the change shows the difference in the ability of imagination underlying the expressions.

Evidently this ability is the *ability* of the artist and is described by Rājaśekhara and those who came after him like Hemcandra and Jagannātha as *kārayitrīpratibhā*. The greatness of the artefacts does depend on such capacity of the artist; such abilities manifest in the environment of wishes and take the form of wish fulfilment when they are presented. So in a way the *horizons* of the artists also play an important role in the artistic creation. Like all other objective factors, the subjective factor, the ability to perceive the Universe and the ability to present it to the readers, audience and viewers also is vital to art creation.

13

Epilogue

In the previous chapters, I discussed the concepts used by Indian rhetoricians in their aesthetic thought. There is no doubt that the stage drama was woven around *rasa* and the concept of *rasa* was gradually extended to other arts also. So far as literary arts are concerned the concept of *dhvani* or suggestion also came in the arena; and very soon the need of *aucitya* was also felt. But since the social outlook did not dominate the Indian literary horizon the concept of *aucitya* lagged behind. Vāmana emphasized on the concept of *alaṁkāra* as parameter (constitutive and normative), but in actual use it was restricted to figures of speech. Even in this respect the essential link between the concept of figure of speech and the development of language as vehicle of thought and expression was ignored. The concept of *vakratā* as a means of expressing or indicating beauty was introduced by Bhāmaha and later by Kuntaka. But since it was coupled with *ukti* or *speech* it was restricted to literary arts and soon it was reduced to the secondary position on account of the dominance of *rasa* and *dhvani.* In fact, the concept of *vakratā* could have been very usefully used in all the plastic and performing arts. But this did not happen.

I have a feeling that the concept which is basic to arts and in fact, which is in-built in all other aesthetic concepts — the concept of *laya*[1] — was not given attention at all except in music. Sharadchandra Gokhale, who is both a physicist and a theoretician of musical theory brought out the significance of *laya* by writing a unique book, *Laya-Tāla-Vicāra*. But the book is in Marathi and artists and philosophers of art did not take notice of the same. In this book he discusses the basic ideas governing the concept of *laya*. But he discusses them only in the context of music (and dance).

But concepts get developed as people use them in different spheres and I think the concept of *laya* is so used. The concept of *laya* is basically a temporal concept. But its use is extended to other areas also. There cannot be music without *laya*. But music also requires *tāla* and *sura*. But *sura* also gets developed into words and meaningful sentences. This gives birth to language and theories of language. We thus talk of *laya* in poetry, *laya* in thought, *laya* in physical shapes, etc. In fact, in practical life, *laya* is equated with *coherence* and harmony (not in the sense in which Western music talks of harmony). The *laya* is noticed by us in symmetry, contrast and balance and we also talk of slow *laya* (*vilambita*) and *fast laya* (*druta*). *Laya* is concerned both with continuity and occurrence or movement. But this is because *laya* acts as a background of all arts. It assumes a greater generality than is given to us by *vakratā*. For just as *vakratā* creates beauty, similarly in some cases its opposite also may lead to beauty. Art, like life, is not governed by one concept, it is governed by different concepts which might appear as contrary or contradictory. *Laya* incorporates

1. *Laya* is variously translated in English. Some people think that its English equivalent is rhythm. I think the concept of *laya* stands for temporal continuum incorporating both continuent and occurrents. But, in its extended use I should like to drop the epithet "temporal" also. For, I feel, in its extended form it also refers to motion and space.

such opposites. It gives equal emphasis on occurrence and continuance. But in fact, it goes beyond this also. *Laya* literally means extinction — *pralaya*, and it is concerned with creation and destruction.

The central idea of Indian philosophic thought is that cosmos is the ocean of eternal calm. Buddhist call it *śūnya*,[2] Sāṁkhyas *prakṛti*, Vedānta-Brāhmaṇa and even Nyāya refer to it through their concept of *apavarga*. We get a glimpse of this calm or silence in music when the singer arrives at *sama*. What we call "the world" is temporarily built or superimposed on this. The world of our experience is like the tides, waves or *taraṅga*s of the ocean. There is no difference of opinion that an artist is a creator. The world that he creates is, of course, out of his experience, which is mental. Bharata says that the world of Gods is mental — *devānām mānasī sṛṣṭiḥ*.

So is the case with the world of artists. Ānandavardhana, in his *Dhvanyāloka* quotes a verse:

अपारे काव्यसंसारे कविरेकः प्रजापतिः ।
यथास्मै रोचते विश्वं तथैवं परिवर्तते ॥

apāre kāvyasaṁsāre kavirekaḥ prajāpatiḥ ।
yathāsmai rocate viśvaṁ tathaivaṁ parivartate ॥

What is true of a poet is equally true of any artist.

What would (the status of) reality be before the world is created? One could say that there would be *abhāva* (*prāgabhāva*)

2. This *śūnya* has two aspect(s) denoted by (1) *anityatā* or *kṣaṇikatā* and (2) *santānatā*. The *santānatā* itself is *śūnya*. The *Oṁ* or *praṇava* of the Indian thought also exhibits the same nature. It is both eternal and novel from moment to moment — *praṇava*. It should not be forgotten that the Buddhist thinkers express this *śūnyatā* in terms of *sarvam santanam*. The concept of *sarva* in music also suggests this original state — the state of silence.

of what is created. That is, in some sense what is created is created out of nothing, although it may be created from some material, some *upādāna*. In other words what is created would be the *counter-correlative or pratiyogī* of *abhāva* and the *abhāva, laya* (or *pralaya*) would be the *anuyogī* of the relation which connects the *laya* with things created. In *Nāsadīyasūkta* this is stated in these words:

नासदासीत् नोसदासीत् तदानीनासीत् राजो नो व्योमा परोयत्।

nāsadāsīt nosadāsīt tadānīnāsīt rājo no vyomā paroyat ॥[3]

There was neither the *sat* nor *asat*. At that time there was not *rajas*. There was no *vyoma* or sky. There was nothing except *void*. The artistic creation also presupposes such background of nothingness. It is on this background that the artist creates his own world. We get a glimpse of this void, this silence when the musician comes to *sama*. *Sama* means the state of balance — the original state.

In the 30th verse of *Śivamahimnā stotra*, four different functions of the artist are pointed out obliquely. The first three of them are manifestations of the *sattva*, *rajas*, and *tamas*, respectively. But the creator transcends these three functions and is concerned with something which is other than the *sattva*, *rajas* or *tamas*. The author of *Śivamahiman stotra* says :

बहलरजसे विश्वोत्पत्तौ भवाय नमो नमः
प्रबलतमसे तत्संहारे हराय नमो नमः
जनसुखकृते सत्त्वोद्रिक्तौ मृडाय नमो नमः
प्रमहसिपदे निस्त्रैगुण्ये शिवाय नमो नमः ॥

bahalarajase viśvotpattau bhavāya namo namaḥ ।
prabalatamase tatsaṁhāre harāya namo namaḥ ॥
janasukhakṛte sattvodriktau mṛḍāya namo namaḥ ।
pramahasipade nistraiguṇye śivāya namo namaḥ ॥

3. (*Ṛgveda*) (*NS* Maṇḍala 10).

Bhāva, Hara, Mṛdu and Śiva are the names of the same God, Śiva, which depict different functions.

(1) creation, (2) destruction, and (3) happiness of the people, but it also transcends all these, and is concerned with non-wordly prosperity or goodness. In fact, this is the most important function, an artist should strive for. An artist has to create the world of his dream, destroy the (earlier) world that has become obsolete and also endeavour for the happiness of the world. In addition he has to act for the preservation of value or goodness. An artist does all this on account of the ability or *pratibhā* with which he is endowed. In some measure this is also required for appreciating the artist's creation. That is why *pratibhā* is classified under two heads : (1) *kārayitrī* and (2) *bhāvayitrī*. The idea of such a theorization takes it for granted that the artist creates his world from a void and again transforms it into a void. For that is the state of eternal calm and a real substratum of all creations. *Laya* stands for all this. It is used differently in different contexts. It stands for concentration, the path or trajectory of thinking (process), the gradual and coherent emergence of notes, etc. But *laya* literally means *pralaya*. This is *prakṛti. Prakṛti* and *vikṛti* are two forms of the same thing. They are like different *guṇa*s or *doṣas.* But in the end a balance of all these is attained. Iśvarakṛṣṇa describes this evolution-involution in a picturesque way and compares it with the performance of a dancer — *raṅgasya darśayitvā nirvatate nartakī yathā nṛtyāt* (रंगस्य दर्शयित्वा निवर्तते नर्तकी यथा नृत्यात्). After the performance of dance, the dancer returns to her original state. Similarly after the performance or creation of any art the artist returns to the original state. All the other states which are imposed on the original state are inbuilt in this original state itself and all of them together form harmony. All this is at the back of *laya.* Any artistic performance is like drawing lines on an expanse of water. But that is only a

temporary state. The eternal state is the state of nature. Space, time and everything constitute this harmony. *Laya* points to such kind of harmony. We draw from this reservoir and present the experience with different characteristics and different forms. Art is *saguṇa* and *sākāra* form of this nature which has no definite form or no definite characteristics. It is *nirguṇa* and *nirākāra*. That is why the savour or the taste of this state is like the taste or *āsvāda* or experience of *Brahman*. This outlook regarding arts seems to have been taken by everybody whatever be his philosophic vision.

A large part of modern Western music is based on the principle of harmony. On the other hand Indian music whether Karnataki or Uttar Hindustani is usually described as based on melody. According to *Oxford Dictionary*, melody is the arrangement of *single notes* in musically expressive succession. Are the concepts of melody and harmony mutually exclusive? We are told that *melody is present as a principal part* in harmonized music. Early European music was also based on melody. Is harmony totally absent in Indian music? It is certainly absent in so far as different notes, two or more, are not harmonized simultaneously in Indian music. But I feel that it cannot be completely excluded from Indian music or for that matter from any art or a group of arts, at least in the sense that harmony is used by philosophers (e.g. pre-established harmony of Leibnitz). *Gītaṁ vādya ca nṛtyaṁ ca trayaṁ saṅgītamucyate* (गीतं वाद्य च नृत्यं च त्रयं संगीतमुच्यते) (*SR*), i.e. vocal music, or instrumental music or dance or a combination of these or any two of these, is called music. In fact, we have seen that *Viṣṇudharmottara Purāṇa* includes painting also in this group. So I feel that in some sense, the principle of harmony is operative in all arts. Melody can be usefully employed only where sound is employed. In the staging of a drama, a harmonious combination of *vibhāvas*, *vyabhicārī bhāvas*, *anubhāva*s and also *vādya, gāna,* etc. and even the lighting arrangement are made use of. But all this is speculative and use of the Western concept of harmony might not be appropriated in the case of Indian music.

Once a friend of mine while discussing with me the nature of music said that music was a configuration of sound. I disagreed with him and said "it was a configuration of sound and silence." Although my reaction was spontaneous there was an important truth in my statement. Unless sound had the background of silence, or the opposite of sound, sound would not be heard at all. I think this is true of *laya* also. *Laya* attempts to measure a cross-section of time. But for measuring this cross-section, we require some background. I find that time supplies this background also. We have seen that Time has two aspects, the occurrent and the continuant. If the time had only the continuant aspect, we would not get the movement at all. The continuant time acts as the (background) dial of a clock and the occurrent aspect moves on it like the hand of a clock. It is the occurrent time which gives us the sensibility of temporal movement. But every movement withers away in the continuent aspect and is reduced to nothingness. The background continuent on the other hand behaves like the store of "nothingness." It is like the sea of silence and gives us the concept of *pralaya* or *abhāva*. In fact, when we look at the world as a system of *multitudes* and look at each object in a distributive manner, we find that the background of each object is nothingness. This is what Buddha would call *śūnya*. The Nyāya philosophers also have toed this idea by resorting to a similar technique in the form of *anuyogī* and *pratiyogī*. Each particular object requires some *ādhāra*. *Viraha* or *abhāva* supplies this *ādhāra* or substratum. That is why each finite knowable object is supposed to be the *pratiyogī* of *abhāva* and *abhāva* is taken to be the *anuyogī* of that object which is related to *abhāva* with *anuyogī-pratiyogī* relation. Thus, in Indian thought whether it is of Sāṁkhya, Vedānta, Buddhism or Jainism, *pralaya* has a great significance. An object stands only on the background of *pralaya* and withers away in *pralaya* itself. In music also, each note comes to the fore and again withers away. Appearance of something and its withering away forms a harmonious whole. I think this is at the background of all arts. This harmony or *laya* in fact, is the ultimate parameter of arts, and includes in it all parameters like *alaṁkāra, rīti, vakratā, aucitya, rasa* and *dhvani* and also indescribability. Bharata in his *Nāṭyaśāstra* talks of eight *rasas*.

अष्टौ नाट्ये रसाः स्मृताः ।

aṣṭau nāṭye rasāḥ smṛtāḥ ।[4]

Perhaps, Abhinavagupta added the ninth *rasa* to it, the *śānta rasa*. One can now see the contrast between eight *rasas* of *nāṭya* and the *śānta rasa*. These eight *rasas* give us a glimpse of occurrents. *Śānta rasa* is like the continuant background without any action or an attempted action. Śrī Jñāneśvara put emphasis on *śānta rasa*. Unfortunately, study in this direction is yet to be attempted. I wish someone does it.

---

4. *NŚ* 6.16 and 6.17.

Appendix 1

About Classical Scholars

Daṇḍin : He gives such an exhaustive treatment of *guṇa*s and *alaṁkāra*s that it is not possible to identify him with any particular school. From the statements in the *Avantī Sundarī Kathā*, he appears to have belonged to the Deccan or to some part south of the Narmadā. Daṇḍin's examples stand out for their originality and except in a few cases he does not borrow his examples from others.

Udbhaṭa : He exercised a profound influence over the *Alaṁkāra Śāstra.* He is quoted with respect by his successors, even when they differ from him. He is the foremost representative of the Alaṁkāra school and his name is associated with several doctrines in the *Alaṁkāra Śāstra.* The *Kumārasambhava* of Udbhaṭa seems to resemble the famous *mahākāvya* of Kālīdāsa with respect to phrases and ideas and even incidents. Udbhaṭa flourished between CE 750 and 850.

Vāmana : He flourished before CE 850 (according to the *Locana*).

Rudraṭa : Very little is known about him. He seems to have been a Kashmirian as his name suggests. He was also called Śatānanda. He was a student of the *Sāmaveda*. He does not mention any author by name in his work. He gives more figures than what Bhāmaha, Daṇḍin and Udbhaṭa give and his treatment is more precise and scientific. He is somewhat later than these writers. He flourished around CE 825-850.

Ānandavardhana : He attained fame as a poet in the region of Avantivarman of Kashmir. The period of his literary activity is between CE 860-890.

Kuntaka : Kuntaka means a small spear and can be compared to the beak of a parrot. The *Vakroktijīvita* is a work of great value and deserves to be rescued from the oblivion into which it has fallen. The work shows originality, great literary acumen and is full of ideas. He believes that it is the poet's own genius that is the source of good poetry.

Mahimabhaṭṭa : He was a Kashmirian as the name indicates. He was very critical of the *dhvani* theory.

Rājaśekhara : He gives far more information regarding his personal history than most Sanskrit poets do. His ancestors seem to have come from Maharashtra. It is clear that he was the *guru* of king Mahendrapāla. He knew many languages and was very fond of Prakrit.

Bhoja : He was one of the illustrious kings of ancient and medieval India. He was a great patron of literature and of poets. He was a builder of temples and a literary man with great achievements. Bhoja is credited with having composed 84 works on almost all sciences of medieval India.

Kṣemendra : He was a Kashmiri writer who wrote on various subjects. He was the son of Prakasendra and grandson of Sindhu and belonged to a rich family.

Ruyyaka : From the *Śrīkaṇṭhacarita* of Makha it appears that Ruyyaka was the teacher of Makha.

Hemacandra : He can be regarded as the brightest amongst the Jain writers. Various aspects of his life are given by the

Kumāra- pālapratibodha of Somaprabha, the *Prabhākaracarita* of Prabhacandra and the *Prabandhakośa* of Rājaśekhara. He was born at Dhandhuka of Modh Bania/parents named *chacha* and *pahini*. Hemacandra's original name was "Cangadeo." His *guru* was Devacandra.

Śobhākar Mitra : He is the author of *Alaṁkāra Ratnākara*.

Viśvanātha : Except for a few bits of information from his own works little is known about his life. He belonged to a brāhmaṇa family that had distinguished itself by learning. His father was Candraśekhara who was a poet and a scholar. He appears to have been an inhabitant of Orissa. He seems to have held some important office at the court of a king, probably of Kaliṅga.

Appaya Dīkṣita : He was a versatile and prolific writer who is credited with authoring over one hundred works. He was a Tamil brāhmaṇa and a Śaivite.

Jagannātha : He is independent in his views and boldly criticizes esteemed ancient writers. But his criticism nevertheless displays correct judgement. He was a Tailaṅga brāhmaṇa. He was the son of Perubhaṭṭa who was also his *guru*. It appears that the title of *paṇḍita-rāja* was conferred upon Jagannātha by Emperor Shah Jahan. *Bhāminī Vilāsa* states that he passed his youth under the Delhi emperor. The literary activity of Jagannātha lies between CE 1620 and 1655. He is the last great writer on Sanskrit poetics.

Appendix 2

Vāmana's Philosophy of Poetry

VĀMANA is one of the very early writers on the philosophy of poetry. He seems to have lived after Bharata and Bhāmaha, but was definitely earlier than Abhinavagupta, Ānandavardhana and Mammaṭa.[1] Though some of the recent writers try to bring him under the influence of *rasa* theory, on account of his aphorism, *dīptarasatvam kāntiḥ,* he seems to be far away from such an influence. Tradition regards him as an advocate of *rīti* theory and makes him a follower of Bhāmaha so far as his views on *alaṁkāra* are concerned. But such a view also is based on certain superficial consideration of words like *guṇa, rīti* and *alaṁkāra* which appear in his writing as also in the writing of Bhāmaha. I think that these words have a different significance for Vāmana.

First, we should contrast his views with those of his predecessors. Bhāmaha described poetry (or literature) as a whole consisting of words and meanings: *śabdārthau sahitau kāvyam* (शब्दार्थौ सहितौ काव्यम्). Bhāmaha himself seems to be aware of the limitations of this definition. So he adds that mere composition of words should not be sufficient for poetry. It should also be beautified or made attractive with figures of speech. "A composition," he writes, "is like the face of a woman who may be herself beautiful but who does not become

1. His date is immaterial for the present purpose.

attractive without ornaments." "Figures of speech" are embellishments of literature. Though Vāmana also gives explanation of "these embellishments of literature" in his work, he does not seem to agree with Bhāmaha in describing poetry in these terms. According to him, Bhāmaha's description of poetry is inaccurate. Poetry is not a whole, composed of words and meanings. It is a whole where *guṇa*s (qualities) and *alaṁkāra* (beauty) also enter as components. It is only by secondary usage that one speaks of literature or poetry as made of words and meanings alone. Vāmana is aware that if the value or beauty factor is omitted from the definition of poetry, certain rules of grammar and logic will also come under the definition of poetry or literature.

Vāmana was aware of the two dimensions of literature: (1) the stuff of which it is made, and (2) the value or the beauty for which it is made. Literature, however, is not the only art which has these two dimensions. It is a common characteristic which literature shares with other arts. Almost every art ought to be studied in these two dimensions. We may take, for instance, the case of sculpture. When one observes and appreciates a statue as a piece of art the appreciation can be expressed as beautiful (or ugly). But the statue is also made out of some material (like stone). In a training school for sculpture if someone is to be trained in the art of making a statue it should not be irrelevent to consider such questions as: (1) what should be the kind of stone used for making such a statue? and (2) What should be the necessary proportion between one limb and the other? All such questions become relevant when we are concerned with the making of a statue. But a statue will not become a piece of art unless the statue also "becomes" beautiful "somehow." The crux of the problem is that the study of this element, "beautiful," cannot be neglected in any philosophy of art or poetry. It is this principle of beauty which is clearly emphasized by Vāmana in his first *sūtra* or aphorism in his work *Kāvyālaṁkārasūtravṛttiḥ*.[2] The value of his theory lies in co-ordinating this principle with the other dimensions of art. He writes, *kāvyam grāhyam alaṁkārāt;* a poetry becomes acceptable as poetry on account of *alaṁkāra*.[3] It should not be irrelevant to emphasise that the word *alaṁkāra* does not mean here a "figure of speech" like simile or metaphor. The word *alaṁkāra* as used in the philosophy of poetry is rather ambiguous; it is used in two different senses. In common usage it stands for "figure of speech." And this common usage makes men turn a deaf ear to the fact that unlike Bhāmaha, Vāmana does not use it here for "figure of speech." In his second *sūtra* Vāmana clearly clarifies his use of the word *alaṁkāra*, *saundaryam alaṁkāraḥ*.

That the word *alaṁkāra* used in the first and second aphorisms does not denote the "figure of speech" becomes clear from the third one. There again he uses the word *alaṁkāra;* but now it signifies the traditional meaning. It is a means for the attainment of Beauty. He uses the pronouns "sa" for denoting *alaṁkāra* which is identical with beauty.[4] Thus, the two uses of the word *alaṁkāra* are obvious in one aphorism. The sense in which it is synonymous with beauty indicates the end. Vāmana writes: this beauty can be attained through avoiding poetic faults and through the introduction of *guṇa*s and "figures of speech."[5] The figure of speech is not an essential characteristic of poetry; nevertheless it adds to the beauty of

2. *Kāvyālaṁkāra* (I.1.6).
3. *na kāntam api nirbhūṣaṇam vibhāti vanitānanam* (न कान्तम् अपि निर्भूषणं विभाति वनिताननम्). (Ibid., I.1.3).
4. *KASV*, III.1.4.
5. *kāvyaśabdo'yama guṇālaṁkāra sanskṛtayoḥ śabdārthayoḥ vartate* (काव्य शब्दोऽयम गुणालकांर संस्कृतियोः शब्दार्थयोः वर्तते). *Kavipriyavṛtti* on (*KASVI* 1.1).

poetry. The *guṇa*s, on the other hand, are essential characteristics of poetry because it is in and through them that the beauty in poetry becomes manifest. Vāmana clearly writes that *guṇa*s are absolutely necessary; for, without them the beauty in poetry cannot emerge. On the other hand, though "figure of speech" adds to the beauty, there can be a beautiful poetry without a figure of speech.[6] Therefore, whereas in the philosophy of poetry a discussion of beauty and quality becomes necessary, a discussion about figures of speech is not necessary. Vāmana writes: just as a beautiful lady looks beautiful even if she is without ornaments so also pure poetry becomes agreeable to the appreciators.

It ought to be clearly understood that for Vāmana, poetry or literature is a kind of a whole made up of parts. The two parts of this whole again are wholes in their own way, viz. a (sub) whole made up of words and a (sub) whole made up of meanings. The whole thus formed out of these two, so to say, is the body of the poetry. Just as a substance or a thing has got qualities so also the two wholes have got *guṇa*s like *ojas, prasāda, mādhurya,* etc. (Perhaps for the sake of brevity Vāmana gives identical names to qualities of words and meanings.) Thus though the poetry seems to be formed out of the two wholes, the whole of words and the whole of meanings, a more critical analysis will reveal that it is composed of four parts, (1) words, (2) the qualities of the words, (3) the meanings, and (4) the qualities of meanings. When a whole is formed out of these four parts, it becomes a poetic whole and poetic beauty or value emerges out of it as its effect, quality or fifth part.

---

6. It may be noted that he uses *alaṁkāra* in the sense of beauty. See (Ibid., I.1.2).

As stated earlier, Vāmana clearly distinguished the two dimensions of poetry, (1) the constitutive, and (2) the value. If a person is to be trained in composing poetry and if he is to be taught the different elements that make poetry, then certainly not the value but the composition aspect will have to be emphasized. I have made a reference to this point earlier. But let me substantiate my point in greater detail. An illustration will make my point clear.

We grow flower plants because we are interested in beautiful flowers. But it is not the beauty that we plant. We have to plant a seed or a seedling and when we plant it we have to know what soil and climatic conditions are required for its growth; we should also like to know the quantity of water that will be required for watering and things like this. When the plant shapes properly it flowers and results in splendour. So also is the case with poetry. If the general conditions of "poetry making" are to be taught one cannot start with beauty. One must be acquainted with the "seeds" or "seedlings," the "soil," "water" and "manure" for poetry. The seed or seedling, water or manure consists of words. A person will have to be "trained" in making a whole of words or words and meanings. The meanings, so to say, would depend on words or sounds, and the beauty of the poetry would depend on these both. The beauty factor in poetry will, thus, depend on word-factors. Being aware of this fact, while emphasizing the element of value in poetry, Vāmana equally emphasized the positive or structural aspect of poetry, and named it as *rīti*. He says that poetry becomes poetry on account of beauty and still asserts that *rīti* is the "soul" of poetry — it is that without which the poetic substratum (composition) would not come into existence.[7] It is very clear from Vāmana's

7. *KASV*, I.1.1.

writing that he regards the *guṇas*, which emerge from patterns of sounds and patterns of meanings, as the cause of the value element, beauty. He defines *guṇas* as the causes of poetic beauty. He does not define them as the cause of poetry. The cause of poetry ought to be distinguished from the cause of the beauty of poetry. These *guṇas* are the effects of the two sub-wholes which lead to a poetic composition.[8] Thus both the *guṇas* and the poetic composition are the effects of the sub-wholes of sound and meaning, though one of them is a quality and the other the substance. This poetic composition and the *guṇas* give rise to poetic beauty. Thus, the poetic beauty has two causes: (1) the poetry itself, and (2) the poetic *guṇas*. This reminds one of the *samavāyī*, and *asamavāyī* causes of the Nyāya system. In order to understand this particular tenet in Vāmana's philosophy of poetry it is necessary to say more about the theory of causation as presented by Nyāya logic.

According to this theory something that is an effect is jointly caused by (1) *samavāyī* cause and (2) *asamavāyī* cause which itself is of the nature of effect. Let us take an instance of a cloth or *paṭa*. Cloth or *paṭa* has two causes amongst others. The thread is supposed to be one such cause of a piece of cloth. But if thread alone were to be there, a piece of cloth would not be made. The conjunction of threads must also enter as another cause in the making of cloth. The threads are supposed to be the material or *samavāyī* cause and the

---

8. This is clear from Vāmana's *sūtra* III.1.3. and his own commentary on it. There Vāmana clearly points out that it is the *guṇas* (poetic qualities) which necessarily produce poetic beauty. His own commentary on the *sūtra*, *pūrve nityāḥ* (सूत्र, पूर्वे नित्याः), III.1.3, makes the point still clearer. He writes: *pūrve guṇāḥ, nityāḥ; tairvinā kāvyaśobhānupapatteḥ* (पूर्वे गुणाः, नित्याः; तैर्विना काव्यशोभानुपपत्तेः). Also see III.1.1 and III.1.2.

conjunction of threads the *asamavāyī* cause. Now, according to the theory put forward by Vāmana, sound-patterns and meaning-patterns which make a poetic whole are the causes of the poetic whole, in the same way as thread is the cause of a cloth or as two halves of the pot are causes of a pot. The combination or conjunction of threads cannot be the material cause because (according to Indian logic) it is a quality, and quality cannot be a material cause. It can either be an effect, e.g. the colour of the cloth is the effect of cloth, or it can be an *asamavāyī* cause, e.g. the colour of the threads is the cause of the colour of the cloth. On the other hand, a substance alone can be a material cause whether of a quality or of a substance. From this it is clear that the sound qualities and the meaning qualities of Vāmana cannot be the material cause of a poetic whole though the sound and meaning patterns are. They cannot also be the *samavāyī* or material cause of the poetic beauty. Just as the cloth itself is the *samavāyī* cause of the colour of the cloth, so also the poetic composition is the *samavāyī* cause of the poetic beauty. But just as the colour of the threads is the *asamavāyī* cause of the colour of the cloth so also the poetic qualities of the sound and meaning are the *asamavāyī* cause of the poetic beauty.

Since a poetic whole, for Vāmana, is a *real* entity, the parts of which it is made are also real entities. The qualities of a sound and meaning exist only in these parts. Therefore, these parts are also entities. Thus, in the world of poetry sounds should be regarded as substance. Otherwise, there would be a danger of a quality inhering a quality. Though it may be doubted as to whether sound is a substance or a quality, as Indian logicians do, no study of poetry can be made unless a status of substance is given to sounds. Sound or *śabda* is the basis or substratum of any literary piece. Again, in the context of poetics the word *artha* which is another part of the poetic whole, is to be understood in the sense of meaning and not in the sense of object. But meaning is a kind of knowledge and this again is a quality of the self (*ātman*) according to Naiyāyikas. So the poetic whole is likely to be thought as made of qualities, pure and simple. But as has been stated above, in the context of poetics both the sounds and meanings jointly and separately should be understood as a substance and not as qualities. Otherwise, the study of poetics would become impossible or would lead to the violation of the rule of logic, namely qualities cannot inhere qualities. There will be again another difficulty. If these are the qualities then the beauty, poetic beauty, cannot arise; for it would require some substratum. Hence, though poetic whole cannot be regarded as a substance in the ordinary sense of the term, it will be desirable to regard it as a substance — a whole made up of parts and exibibiting the nature of effects. As has been pointed out sounds and their meanings would be the material cause of such a poetic whole. From this point of view, I feel that though Vāmana has used the terminology of Indian logic he must have accepted like the Sāṁkhyas and grammar philosophers that sound was a kind of substance. Similarly he must have accepted meaning also as a substance in a way the grammarians accept it as a cause or effect of sound. Though in the context of poetics, the words and meanings have to be considered separately still the meanings do not have existence, separate and independent from sounds. In the ordinary usage meaning cannot be regarded as things. Sound also is their substratum. So a poetic whole is made up of parts some of which are perceptible while the others are unmanifest or *avyakta*. The poetic whole, therefore, is to be regarded as an unusual, peculiar kind of entity. Since a poetic whole is an extraordinary kind of thing: beauty, the final part of this whole also cannot be regarded as "quality" in the ordinary sense of the term. Beauty, therefore, cannot be regarded as a quality like yellow or green. It can be felt but it cannot be perceived. Its causes can be known but it cannot be described. It is, therefore, to be regarded as a second order quality. I feel it is this kind of thinking which was in the mind of Vāmana when he wrote aphorisms III.1.26, III.1.27 and III.1.28. At the end of the chapter on *śabdaguṇa*, Vāmana, asks for the proof of the existence of the *guṇa*s of sound and in the last three aphorisms he gives that proof.[9] These qualities, he writes, are "not non-existing like the son of a barren woman, nor illusory like shell-silver. That they exist can be inferred from the fact that they are felt." I feel that the argument of Vāmana can be extended to the qualities of meaning and also to the poetic value or beauty.

It has already been pointed out that though a poetic whole comprises of sound, meanings, qualities of sound and meaning and beauty as parts, still all these depend upon sound alone for their existence. Neither meanings nor beauty can have an independent existence apart from the substratum which, in this case, is sound. The poetic whole is like a twin engine jet plane, where one engine is dependent on the other for its being put into action and control. The engines, however, act simultaneously and independently and pass out the jet gases which eventually mix up and form one long tail. To an outside observer, it is not the plane alone, but the plane along with the gaseous tail which is the object. However, if the plane is to be controlled, it will have to be controlled by controlling the engine which has a control switch. Similarly, in the case of the poetic whole if any refinement or *saṁskāra* is to be made, it will have to be done on sound or *śadba* alone. For, sound alone

---

9. Vide commentary on ibid., III.1.2, *yuvateriva rūpameva kāvyam āsvādate śabdaguṇam tadapyatīva* (युवतेरिव रूपमेव काव्यमास्वादते शब्दगुणम् तदप्यतीव).

is the vehicle of meaning, which in itself is without form and cannot be physically felt. Thus sound gains primary importance in any theory of poetics. This, however, requires an arrangement of sound or words which can be of different varieties; each arrangement, for example, may represent its own peculiarity of *viśeṣa*. It is this very special arrangement or peculiarity of arrangements which is called *rīti* by Vāmana. According to him this arrangement or *rīti* is of three kinds. But whether it is of three kinds or of less or more is a matter of details and not a matter of principle. The "peculiarity" of arrangement in composition is identical with what Vāmana calls *guṇa*s. This is clear from his aphorism, I.2.8. It is because of this that a discussion of *rīti* (or style) and *guṇa*s becomes significant in a thesis on poetics. Having all this in his mind he must have written the aphorism I.2.6. The arrangement of composition (*padaracanā*) is the body of poetry and its peculiarity (*viśiṣṭattva*) the style. This again could be analysed in terms of *guṇa*s. Thus the aphorism I.2.6. should not be studied in isolation but ought to be studied with I.1.1. and I.1.2. If the relation of the aphorism I.2.6. with I.1.1 and I.1.2. is not taken into consideration, the whole thesis of Vāmana will be misunderstood as he has been generally misunderstood now. It goes without saying that Vāmana's being dubbed as a philosopher of style or of figure of speech is due to such misunderstanding. But as a matter of fact, he is neither an advocate of style for its own sake, nor of figure of speech or *guṇa* for its own sake. He is not just the advocate of figure of speech alone. He does, in fact, talk about them. But that is because there is no direct way of creating poetic beauty. *Guṇa* and *rīti* (and *alaṁkāra*, i.e. figure of speech) are for him only the causes which progressively lead to poetic beauty. To dub Vāmana as a fanatic advocate of *rīti, alaṁkāra, rasa* or *guṇa* is to do injustice to this great philosopher of poetry.

Appendix 3

A Further Note On 'Parā'

IT should not be forgotten that language is for communication. Sound is used merely as an instrument for the operation of communication. But other signs also could be used for communication. Some of those who talk of types of language think that *parā* is also a sound language and take its birth in the lower-navel region of individuals, i.e. in *mulādhāra cakra*. This would really strengthen a wrong belief that "these different" languages are "sound-based" languages only and arise in different regions of the body. This would be a misnomer and make the "languages" private and mystical. Perhaps the correct explanation is that *parā* language is a common "in built" language for all humans, that it has nothing to do with *sounds*, that it is not private, and is *basic* (that is, it belongs to *mulādhāra*) to all humans and is the primary mode of communication. This would, in fact, remove the mist gathered around this fourfold scheme of languges. It should be wrong to superimpose the differentiating characteristics of *vaikharī* as common characteristic on the other types of languges. But I should leave the matter here only for the consideration of experts.

Appendix 4

अथ मानकथनम्

इष्टिका च शिला दारुरयरुकीलादयो प्यमी ।
वास्तुकर्मणि चान्यत्र वस्तुसंज्ञमुदीरितम् ॥

तदस्तु मानयेच्छिल्पी मानदण्डेन सर्वतः ।
तस्मान्मानं शिल्पिवर्गैरवश्यं ज्ञेयमीरितम् ॥

मानज्ञानविहीनैस्तु कर्म कर्तुं न शक्यते ।
कृतश्च कर्म वैफल्यं भजते नात्र संशयः ॥

तन्मानं बहुधा प्रोक्तं तज्ज्ञेयं सूक्ष्मचक्षुषा ।
स्वर्गे लोके मानमादौ गुरुणा संप्रकीर्तितम् ॥

विविधं तश्च मघवा प्रोक्तवान्सुरसंसदि ।
दैवेन नन्दिना तश्च बहुधाविष्कृतं पुरा ॥

तदेव विविध प्रोक्तं नारदेन महर्षिणा ।
मानमेवं बहुविधं कथितं पूर्वसूरिभिः ॥

देवमानुषभूपालप्रासादेषु गृहेषु च ।
मण्टपेषु विमानेषु गोपुरे तोरणे पि च ॥

सोपानेषु प्रतोलीषु वापीकूपादिकेषु च ।
विविधासु च शालासु चन्द्रशालादिकासु च ॥

डोलादिषु गवाक्षेषु खट्वासु प्रतिमासु च ।
उपपीठेषु पीठेषु सिह्मवक्त्रादिकेषु च ॥

अन्येषु शिल्पकार्येषु यन्मानं तश्च योजयेत ।
मानाभावे क्रियादीनां न शोभा न बलादिकम् ॥

द्रव्यनाशाश्चापयशो भवत्येव न संशयः ।
तस्मान्मानं शिल्पिवर्गैरवश्यं ज्ञेयमीरितम् ॥

---

1. *Viśvakarma Vāstuśāstram*, ed., with an introduction by Sri. K. Vasudeva Sastri, Research Pandit, Saraswati Mahal Library, Tanjore, and Major N.B. Gadre, Irrigation & Navigation Commission (retd), Tanjore Saraswati Mahal Series no. 85, Published by Sri. S. Gopalan, Hon. Secy., for the Administrative Committee of the TMSSM Library, Tanjore, 1958.

Bibliography

Aesthetics, Science, Philosophy and Theory of Taste (Vol. I), Ramashraya Shukla (Karunendra), Oriental Publishing House, Kanpur, 1st edn., 1977.

Agnipurāṇam by Shrimanmaharshi Vedavyas Gurumandal Prakashan, Calcutta, 1957.

Analytical Experimental Physics, Michael Ference, Harvey B. Zemon, Regional J. Stephenson, University of Chicago Press, Revised edn. 1956.

Ānandavardhana's *Dhvanyāloka*, by K. Krishnamoorthy, Karnatak University, Dharwar, 1st edn., August, 1974

Arthasaṅgraha, Jauga Bhaskara Pandurang, Javaji Publication, 1927.

Art Experience, M. Hiriyanna, Mysore Kavyalaya Publishers, 1st edn., 1954.

Being and Unity in Western Philosophy, The Verbal Icon — Studies in the Meaning of Poetry, W.K. Wimset Jr., Publisher: University of Kentucky Press, 1st edn., 1958.

Beliefs, Reasons & Reflections, S.S. Barlingay, Indian Philosophical Quarterly Publications, 1st edn., October 1983.

Bhāva Prakāśana, Sharadatanaya, ed. Yadugiri Yatiraja Swami, & K.S. Ramaswami Sastri, Oriental Institute, Baroda, 1968.

Bṛhat-stotra Ratnākaraḥ by Nārāyaṇa Rāma Ācārya, Published by Chaukhamba Orientatia, 1st edn., 1983.

Candralokaḥ, Piyusavarsa Jayadeva, transl. Triloki Nath Dvivedi, Bharatiya Vidya Prakasana, Varanasi, 1st edn., 1992.

Concept of Mind, Gilbert Ryle, Publishers: Hutchinson House, London, Reprint edn., 1955.

Citrasūtra of the Viṣṇudharmottara, C. Sivaramamurti, Kanak Publications, New Delhi, 1978.

Daśarūpakam, Dhanañjaya, Ramasankar Tripathi, Visvavidyalaya Prakasana, Varanasi, 1st edn., 1973.

Dhvanyāloka by Ānandavardhanācārya, Publishers: Maharashtra Rajya Sahitya Sanskriti Mandal, 1983.

Dhvanyāloka, Ānandavardhanācārya, Publishers: Jayakrishna Das Haridas Gupta, Banaras, 1953, ed. Ravishekhar Paṇḍit Badrinath Sarma.

Dhvanyāloka, Ānandavardhanācārya, ed. Mahamahopadhaya Durgaprasad Tukaram, Javaji Publishers, Bombay, 2nd edn., 1911.

Hindī Kāvyādarśa, Ācārya Daṇḍin, transl. Ranvir Sinha, Oriental Book Depot, Delhi, 1958.

History of Sanskrit Poetics, P.V. Kane, Motilal Banarsidass Publication, 4th edn., 1971.

Introduction to Tantra Śāstra, Sir John Woodroffe, Publishers: Ganesh & Co. Madras, 2nd ed., 1952.

Indian Aesthetics & Art Activity, Published by Indian Institute of Advance Study, 1st edn., March 1968.

The Journal of Philosophical Studies by B.D.R. Bhandari, February 1994 and January, April 1989.

Jñānesvarance Kāvyaśāstra, by V.D. Kulkarni, Snehawardhan Publishing House, Pune, 1st edn., 1993.

Kālidāsa's *Kumārasambhava*, ed. M.R. Kale, Publishers: Motilal Banarsidass, Delhi, 7th edn., 1981.

Kāmasūtram, Vatsyayana, Muni Jayakrisnadas Haridas Gupta Publishers, edn., 1986.

Kāśyapaśilpa, transl. R.P. Kulkarni, Maharashtra Rajya Sahitya Sanskriti Mandal, Bombay, 1st edn., March 1987.

Kāvyālaṁkāra, Rudrata Satyadeo Chaudhari, Vasudeo Prakasana, Delhi, 1st edn., 1965.

Kāvyālaṁkāra Sūtravṛtti, Vamana, Gopendratripura Hara Bhupala, Publishers: Paṇḍit Vidyābhūṣana, Paṇḍit Nityabodha Vidyaratna, 3rd edn., 1922.

Kāvyamīmāṁsā of Rājaśekhara, Kamal Abhyankar, Shrividya Prakasana, Pune, 1st edn., 25 November 1992.

Kāvyamālā, 95 Ujjwala Nilamani Shrimad Rūpa Goswami, ed. Paṇḍit Kedarnatha, Publishers: Tukaram Javaji, edn., 1913.

Kāvyaśāstra Pradīpa, Sadashiv Ramacandra Gadgil, Venus Prakasana, Pune, 4th edn., January 1993.

Kāvyānuśāsana, Ācārya Hemacandra, ed. Rasiklal Parikh, Published by Mahavira Jaina Vidyalaya, Bombay, 2nd edn., 1964.

Kāvyamīmāṁsā, Rājaśekhara, transl. Paṇḍit Kedarnatha Sharma, Saraswat Publishers, Bihar Rastrabhasa Parisad, Patna, 1st edn., 1954.

Kalā Aur Saundarya, S.S. Barlingay.

Laya-Tāla-Vicāra, Sharadcander Gokhale, Maharashtra Rajya Sahitya Sanskriti Mandal, Bombay.

"Longinus" on Sublimity, transl. D.A. Russell, Oxford University Press, 1965.

Manasara (On Architecture & Sculpture) Ramacandra Sankar, Walimbe Publishers, Yashwanta Gopal Joshi, Prasad Prakasan, Pune, 1st edn., 12 September 1953.

Meghadūta, Arvind Mangloorkar, Vasant Bapat, Digambar Hatwaline, Publisher: R.J. Deshmukh, 1st edn., 1957.

Nāṭyadarpaṇam, by Ramacandra & Gunacandra, ed. T.C. Upreti, Parimal Publications, Delhi, October 1986.

Nāṭyaśāstra with *Abhinavabhāratī* (B.O.S.).

Nāṭyadarpaṇa, Ramacandra & Gunacandra, ed. G.K. Shrigondekar Published by Oriental Institute, Baroda, 1959.

Nāṭyaśāstram, Bharatamuni, ed. Paṇḍit Kedarnath, Bharatiya Vidya Prakashana, rept. edn., 1983.

Nyāyakośa by Mahamahopadhaya Bhimacarya Jhalalibar, Publishers: The Bhandarkar Oriental Research Institute, Poona, ed. 1928.

Nyāyasiddhāntamañjarī by Janaknātha Bhaṭṭācārya, ed. Paṇḍit Jivanatha Mishra, E.J. Yararus & Co. Medical Hall Press, 1916.

Nyāyaratna, by Manikantha Misra, ed. Paṇḍitrāj V. Subrahmanya Sastri, Government Oriental Manuscripts Library, Madras, 1953.

Parā-Triṁśikā, by Abhinavagupta, The Kashmir Series of Texts & Studies, Research Department, Jammu and Kashmir State edn., 1918.

Philosophical Investigation, Ludwig Wittgenstein, Basil Blackwell, Oxford, 1953.

The Philosophy of Science, ed. P.H. Niddich, Oxford University Press, Rly. House, London, 1968.

Rasagaṅgādhara, Paṇḍitrāj Jagannātha, ed. Giridharasarma Caturvedi, 14 April, 1939.

Rasagaṅgādharan, Paṇḍitraj Jagannātha, transl. Paṇḍit Shri Madanmohan Jha, Chaukhamba Vidyabhavan, Varanasi edn., 1957.

Rasacarcā, Padmakar Dadegaonkar, Publishers, Ramdas Bhatbal, Popular Prakasan, Bombay, 1st edn., 1994.

Rasace Swarūpa, Navabharat; Published in *IPQ,* 1951.

Raṅgaśālā, Narhar Kurundkar, Deshmukh & Co. Publication, Pune, 1st edn., 1994.

Regularity Normativity & Rules of Language and Other Essays in Philosophical Analysis, Rajendra Prasad, Indian Philosophical Quarterly Publications, No. 14, 1st edn., March 1989.

Sāhitya Durpaṇa of Viśvanātha Kavirāja, ed. Kasinatha Panduranga Parab, Published by Tukaram Javaji, Bombay, 1902.

Samarāṅgana Sūtradhāra, Bhoja.

Sanskrit-Tridalam, Keshav Ramrao Joshi, Bharati Prakasan, edn. 1993.

Saṅgītaratnākara, Nihshanka Sharangadeva (Part I), transl. G.H. Taralekar Maharashtra Rajya Sahitya Sanskriti Mandal, Bombay, 1st edn., 1975.

Saṅgītaratnākara, Nihshanka Sharangadeva (Part II), transl. G.H. Taralekar Maharashtra Rajya Sahitya Samskriti Mandal, Bombay, edn. 1980.

Saundaryace Vyākaraṇa, S.S. Barlingay.

Śrī Kāvyālaṁkāra, Shri Bhāmaha by P.S. Subramanyasastri, Wales Press, 1927.

Śṛṅgāra Tilaka, Rudrabhaṭṭa.

Subhāsitaratnabhaṇḍāgāram.

Tantrapaddhati, A study, N.P. Unni. Bharatiya Vidya Prakasana, Delhi, 1st edn., 1987.

Vakrokti, Jivita, A Treatise on Sanskrit Poetics, Ranjanka Kuntaka. ed. Sushil Kumar De, Published by N.C. Paul, Calcutta, 1st edn., 1923, 2nd edn., 1928.

Vāstuśāstra, Vol. I, Hindu Science of Architecture, D.N. Shukla, Vastu Vangmaya Prahasana Shala, Lucknow, 1961.

Vāstuśāstra, Vol. II, Hindu Canons of Iconography & Painting, D.N. Shukla, Vastu Vangmaya Prahasana Shala, Lucknow, May 1958.

Vāstusūtra Upaniṣad, The Essence of Form in Sacred Art, Alice Boner, Sadasiva Rath Sarma, Bettina Baumer, Motilal Banarsidass Publications, 1st edn., 1982, Reprinted, 1986.

Viṣṇudharmottara Purāṇa by Priyabala Shah, Maharaja Sayajirao University, Baroda, 1958.

Index